T0375400

PATHWAY TO UNDERSTANDING THE BIBLE

MAXWELL ADORKOR

Order this book online at www.trafford.com
or email orders@trafford.com

Most Trafford titles are also available at major online book retailers.

© Copyright 2013 MAXWELL ADORKOR.
All rights reserved. No part of this publication may be reproduced, stored in a retrieval system, or transmitted, in any form or by any means, electronic, mechanical, photocopying, recording, or otherwise, without the written prior permission of the author.

Printed in the United States of America.

ISBN: 978-1-4907-0613-9 (sc)
ISBN: 978-1-4907-0612-2 (e)

Trafford rev. 06/25/2013

Trafford PUBLISHING **www.trafford.com**

North America & international
toll-free: 1 888 232 4444 (USA & Canada)
phone: 250 383 6864 ♦ fax: 812 355 4082

CONTENTS

Dedication vii
Acknowledgements ix
Introduction xi

1. Is it difficult to understand the Bible? 1
2. Are we equipped to understand the Bible? 10
3. Where do we begin the search? 16
4. Can the Bible be trusted? 31
5. The Bible under attack 45
6. Who should we trust? 54
7. How many gospel messages do we have? 74
8. Jesus—the true foundation 80
9. Who sent Jesus Christ to earth? 90
10. To whom was Jesus sent? 97
11. How Jesus Christ was raised from birth 105
12. The teachings of Jesus Christ 111
13. Jesus on clean and unclean meats 119
14. Jesus on divorce 130
15. Jesus on tithes and offerings 137
16. Jesus Christ on the passover 142
17. Jesus on the writings of Moses and the Prophets 146
18. Jesus christ on the greatest commandment 171
19. Jesus Christ on the Sabbath 176
20. Jesus Christ on fulfilling the law 183
21. Christ's charge against the Pharisees and teachers of the law 191
22. Jesus Christ was a Jew 194
23. A short history of Man 199
24. A new covenant between God and Israel 255
25. The reasons behind Israel's exiles 257
26. Biblical definition of righteousness 262
27. The loss! 270
28. Why Jesus had to die on man's behalf 276
29. The Kingdom of God restored 279
30. The gospel according to Jesus Christ 287

31. Beginning the journey of preaching the Kingdom of God............. 289
32. Chronological stages in spreading the Kingdom message 293
33. Taking the Gospel to the Gentiles 304
34. Answering the hard questions from Paul 335
35. Paul's letter to the Romans 340

DEDICATION

To my Mother, Grace Adorkor, a virtuous woman, whose price is far above rubies. Your steadfast faith in God through the many trials and challenges of raising six children inspires me to do away with all excuses in life and challenge myself in maximizing the full potential in me. You are the unschooled but educated mother I have ever known. The major lesson I learned from you which is sacrificing your life for the betterment of your children and others has compelled me to do same in writing this book to set others free.

A whole book could not contain what I feel deep inside my heart to tell you. Some words written by other higher minds though seem fitting at this moment to express my love to you for the sacrifices you had to make for your children's survival.

> *"All that I am my mother made me"—John Quincy Addams*
>
> *"A man never sees all that his mother has been to him till it's too late to let her know that he sees it"—William Dean Howells*
>
> *"God could not be everywhere, and therefore He made mothers"—Jewish proverb*
>
> *"There is in all this cold and hollow world no fount of deep, strong, deathless love, save that within a mother's heart"—Felicia Dorothea Browne Hemans*
>
> ***Thank you with all my love.***

And to those who are seeking the truths about God and spirituality with genuine and sincere hearts. It is my hope and prayer that this book will lead you to the right path in knowing the right steps to take yourself instead of forever relying on what others dictate to you and set you free. It saddens my heart to the very core when religion and spirituality is cunningly used by some few to imprison the minds of people instead of being used to reveal a man to himself and thereby manifesting his full potentials in life.

ACKNOWLEDGEMENTS

Thanks to:

My Father, David Adorkor: It is said that humility, integrity and patience are the solid foundation of all the virtues. You have these in abundance and I respect you for that.

Kofi Hammond: For your inspiration and incredible support. Ever since I told you about myself and mission, you've recommended and given me the books to read and the tapes to listen to. You really practice what you preach by proving that money is not everything. I doff my hat for you. I respect you greatly.

Ebenezer Bruce: For more than a decade now, you've taken the place of the brother I never had and sacrificed your life and time on me without complaining or frowning once. I feel guilty calling you a friend. You're simply my big brother.

Mr. & Mrs. Francis Addabor: Francois, I have known you many years and you have been the most straight-up, honest, open and truthful person I've known. Jacqueline, your wife has also been a very good friend. I adore you both. I really do.

Benjamin Doe: For the time spent in teaching me the basics to put me back on track in 2001. No matter where you reach in life, you remain calm, respectful, humble and meek to all. It all started for me when you agreed to teach me back then. Thank you.

Kwame Anane: For being a brother and editor of the manuscript. *Merci.*

Kofi Anane: I appreciate you for always being there for me whenever I needed a helping hand. I cannot thank you enough.

Mavis Dzifa Adorkor: For being the most adorable sister I ever had. I admire the fearless attitude you apply to life. This book was written for young women like you. So far, you are the only one who knows the funny side of me and I can make my dance moves in front of you.

Joyce Sitsofe Adorkor: For giving me a grandson who has become a very good friend and inspiration in the person of Paul Smith Seyram Duncan. And for always seeing to it that I've eaten. You have been such a wonderful niece. I love you.

Christabel Adjei, Godwin Nuhoho Diaba, Evelyn Osei and Millicent Woyo: You guys are some of the nicest and wonderful people I've ever come across.

My Lord and Savior, Jesus Christ, the author and finisher of my faith for choosing me to do this. I feel highly favored and honored. This work is proof that God indeed can choose the foolish and weak things of the world to shame the wise and strong so that no one may boast before Him (1 Cor. 1:26-29).

INTRODUCTION

I'll like to endorse this book with a quote from Elbert Hubbard's book *"Love Life and Work, How to Attain the Highest Happiness for One's Self with the Least Possible Harm to Others."* A paragraph in that book sums up what I'm about to do in this book that you are reading. In what he termed a prayer, he wrote that:

> *"The supreme prayer of my heart is not to be learned, rich, famous, powerful, or 'good,' but simply to be radiant. I desire to radiate health, cheerfulness, calm courage and goodwill. I wish to live without hate, whim, jealousy, envy or fear. I wish to be simple, honest, frank, natural, clean in mind and clean in body, unaffected—ready to say I do not know,' if it be so, and to meet all men on an absolute equality—to face any obstacle and meet every difficulty unabashed and unafraid. I wish others to live their lives too—up to their highest, fullest and best. To that end I pray that I may never meddle, interfere, dictate, give advice that is not wanted, or assist when my services are not needed. If I can help people, I'll do it by giving them a chance to help themselves, and if I can uplift or inspire, let it be by example, inference, and suggestion, rather than by injunction and dictation. That is to say, I desire to be radiant—to radiate life."*

Thanks to the concept of democracy! Each of us is entitled to his own opinions and can therefore say or do whatever pleases him provided he does not infringe on another man's liberty. I'm very much aware of this, so my main purpose for writing this book is not to compel you to change your lifestyle or to impose my decisions on you either, since no individual has the moral right to even try that in our day and age. Even God, the Creator of mankind, does not force us to choose His ways which are meant to serve our own good. Choices have been given to each of us to determine how we want our lives to be led. Plato once wrote that *"Bodily exercise, when compulsory, does no harm to the body;* ***but knowledge which is acquired under compulsion obtains no hold on the mind.****"*

Dr. Wayne W. Dyer once wrote that, *"You cannot learn anything through the efforts of others. The world's greatest teachers can teach you absolutely nothing unless you are willing to apply what they have to offer based on your knowledge.*

Those great teachers only offer you choices on the menu of life. They can make them sound very appealing, and ultimately they may help you to try those items on the menu. They can even write the menu. But the menu can never be the meal."

This agrees with what I once read somewhere accredited to Gautama Buddha that *"Do not believe what you have heard. Do not believe in tradition because it is handed down many generations. Do not believe in anything that has been spoken of many times. Do not believe because the written statements come from some old sage. Do not believe in conjecture. Do not believe in authority or teachers or elders.* ***But after careful observation and analysis, when it agrees with reason and it will benefit one and all, then accept it.****"*

The systems of this age have made it quite possible for us to have easy and faster access to information. For instance, it's much easier to acquire almost all the necessary information one needs on a subject on the internet faster in our days than it used to be some few years back. But the strange thing is that most people do not utilize or put into practice what they learn from these collections of information. This reminds me of a quote in the book of Ezekiel that:

> *My people come to you,* ***as they usually do****, and sit before you, to listen to your words,* ***but they do not put them into practice****. With their mouths they express devotion, but their hearts are greedy for unjust gain. 32 Indeed, to them you are nothing more than one who sings love songs with a beautiful voice and plays an instrument well,* ***for they hear your words but do not put them into practice.*** *(Ezek. 33:31-32)*

I'm well informed that no matter how hard I try, this book is not going to change the entire world or even the Church, since most people only love to express their devotion to the Word of God with their lips but are not that interested in putting them into practice. There are those who will tell you pointblank that they are not going to obey even the voice of God when it is presented to them like what happened in the days of Jeremiah. When God realized that their evil practices would result into destroying themselves and making them an object of curse and reproach among all nations on earth, He sent Jeremiah to warn them of the consequences of their ways. But listen to what they said in response:

> *Then all the men* ***who knew*** *that their wives were burning incense to other gods,* ***along with all the women who were present—a large assembly****—and all the people living in Lower and Upper Egypt, said to Jeremiah, 16* ***"We will not listen to the message you have spoken to us in the name of the LORD!*** *17* ***We will***

> ***certainly do everything we said we would:*** *We will burn incense to the Queen of Heaven and will pour out drink offerings to her just as we and our fathers, our kings and our officials did in the towns of Judah and in the streets of Jerusalem. (Jer. 44:15-17)*

Now, although I know the majority of the populace would not adhere to what I'm about to deliver in this book regarding the underlying foundation of the message contained in the Bible, I also know that there is always a remnant who are usually in the minority searching for the truth and would go through fire to obtain it. I hope you are one of those by the mere fact that you are currently reading this book. Remain with me as we journey along through the Bible. *"Some books are copper, some are silver, and a few are gold: but the Bible alone is like a book all made up of bank notes"—John Newton (1725-1807).* I humbly invite you to "*hear my words, you wise men; listen to me, you men of learning. 3* ***For the ear tests words as the tongue tastes food.*** *4* ***Let us discern for ourselves what is right; let us learn together what is good.*** *(Job 34:2-4)*

THE CULTURE OF BLAMING OTHERS

It seems we now live in a society of fault-finders, complainers, blamers and whiners always talking about why there are myriads of problems on earth but none claiming responsibility for creating them. Like Jack Canfield puts it, *"Most of us have been conditioned to blame something outside of ourselves for the parts of our life we don't like."* Today, we do have individuals and institutions whose job it is to tell us about problems as well as the causal agents of such problems encountered on earth. But at the end of the day, what they do is to merely point an accusing finger at someone else or another institution as being responsible for a problem, excluding themselves.

It is not uncommon to hear children blaming their parents for being responsible for their failures in life. Employees blame their employers for their non-performance at various workplaces. Citizens of nations accuse their leaders for not being creative, innovative and effective enough in coming out with adequate policies and regulations backed with unbiased implementation to bring about improvements in their lives. Those on the African continent in particular accuse their leaders of being corrupt but forget the fact that these so-called corrupt leaders came from their own homes and are only doing what they would do if they were in their shoes.

Unions like the Security Council, AU, ECOWAS, UN, The Arab League, and NATO, occasionally point accusing fingers at each other for being responsible for the failures of each other. You have a so-called superpower like the United States watch its defense system penetrated so much that almost three thousand of its citizens could be killed in a day by hijackers and then accuse Saddam Hussein and Osama bin Laden as being responsible. I thought the US had powerful institutions like the F.B.I., the C.I.A. and the Ministry of Defense. One wonders if they were on strike that fateful day.

This concept of always blaming others did not originate with us and has grown so much that in Africa especially, even when there are mosquitoes in people's rooms at night, someone has to be blamed for it, and that excludes the occupant of the room. So in a situation like that, the government has to take the heat, and blamed for not constructing good drainage systems resulting in stagnant water bodies in the cities and towns which serve as breeding grounds for mosquitoes.

When a very able-bodied young man who refuses to put his hands to the plough is unable to earn enough money and develops a lean purse in the process, demons are blamed for punching holes in his pockets. There are times that even when a pastor who should know better is unable to keep his sexual desires in check and is unable to keep his own zip up resulting in fornication or adultery, the fault is squarely laid on the shoulders of "someone" like the devil to take full responsibility, and the pastor is exempted from wrongdoing himself because they claim he is also a descendant of Adam.

TAKING RESPONSIBILITY AND BEING PART OF THE SOLUTION

> ***Religion that God our Father accepts as pure and faultless is this**: to look after orphans and widows in their distress and to keep oneself from being polluted by the world. (James 1:27)*

I have also identified some things that I would refer to as problems bothering mankind. I have seen several of them, and just like everyone else, I used to feel frustrated as well until it dawned on me to choose and tackle one of these problems bothering us. So unlike most people, instead of repeatedly blaming, whining, complaining and pointing accusing fingers at others for what is going wrong around us, I have rather chosen the path of selecting one of these areas to address. This is because I'm always passionate about hanging around solution-oriented people. What a Kingdom-minded person does is to concentrate on fixing problems rather than wasting his energy telling people how those problems were created and who caused them. The path I have chosen is the one that is very dear to my heart; that is, locating the exact message contained in the Bible. Andrew Bonar wrote: *"I looked for the church and found it in the world. I looked for the world and found it in the church."*

> ***Each one should use whatever gift he has received to serve others,*** *faithfully administering God's grace in its various forms. 11* ***If anyone speaks, he should do it as one speaking the very words of God. If anyone serves, he should do it with the strength God provides, so that in all things God may be praised through Jesus Christ.*** *To Him be the glory and the power forever and ever. Amen. (1 Pet. 4:10-11)*

I have often wondered why is it that if I should give a Biology textbook, for instance, to hundred persons in hundred different countries and ask a question pertaining to something contained in it, they would most likely give me the same answer. But if a Bible is given to a hundred different pastors even in one country and a question is asked about a subject in it, they are most likely to give me different answers or interpretations to the same question. That has always baffled me and I know I'm not the only one in this boat. And when asked "Why is that so?" some teachers of the Bible would often quote *1 Corinthians 2:4* as an excuse that the Bible can *only* be spiritually discerned. That should take us to the question of whether God would intentionally make the Bible difficult to understand or not.

C. H. Spurgeon once wrote that: *"An unwatchful church will soon become an unholy church . . . The main cure of a church comes by strengthening its inner life. When we live near to Jesus, when we drink from the fountain-head of eternal truth and purity, when we become personally true and pure, then our watchfulness is under God, our Safeguard; heresy, false doctrine, and unclean profession are kept far away.* ***Sleeping guards invite the enemy. He who leaves his door unlocked asks the thief to enter. Watchfulness is always profitable, and slothfulness is always dangerous."***

THE BIRTH OF THIS BOOK

I have discovered that there has always been one simple message spread across the pages of this precious book called the Bible that I would be surprised even if there were just two denominations in the world. Most of Christians' theology concludes that the Church has replaced the Israelites as God's people. As a result, they mostly associate the Jews with the content of the Old Testament Scriptures and only use them as references in their studies and teachings. The impression then created is the notion that The New

Testament belongs to Christians whereas the Old is meant for the Jews. *It is my humble but deepest desire to correct this erroneous misconception with this book.* This I feel is my way of serving this generation by contributing to the restoration of God's knowledge on earth to the Gentile believers especially.

In my few years of studying the Bible, I have come to agree with Mr. David H. Stern when He wrote in the introduction of the Complete Jewish Bible that ***"The greatest schism in the world is the separation between the Church and the Jewish people."*** He went further to state that, *"In translating the Jewish New Testament I had had a strong and directed desire to show everyone, Jews and Christians alike,* ***that the New Testament is a thoroughly Jewish book."*** Under the unity of the entire Bible, He pointed out that *"There is no need to collect the first three-quarters of the Bible into the 'Old Testament' and the last quarter into the 'New.'* ***Rather, the Bible is presented as a seamless whole, a unified Word of God, a complete Jewish Bible for all humanity*** *. . . Indeed, the New Testament completes the Tanakh (The Old Testament); so that the New Testament without the Old is as impossible as the second floor of a house without the first, and the Old without the New as unfinished as a house without a roof."*

I have found reading the Bible the most thrilling and fascinating experience to ever happen to me that I have come to appreciate what Patrick Henry said that, *"The Bible is worth all the other books which have ever been printed."* The more I stick to the Bible, the more I'm marveled at the depth of wisdom / mysteries hidden in it for those of us living today especially.

In two sentences, I have learned that the Bible is mainly about the establishment of the Kingdom of God in any environment and how the occupants of that environment (in our case, the people of this earth i.e. both Jews and Gentiles / believers and nonbelievers) are to repent of their ways which always seem right in their own eyes and be transformed in their thinking to wholeheartedly tune their lives to fall in line with the statutes, laws and principles of God which are written down in the pages of the Bible. The result of this acceptance of tuning into the principles of God is then expected to be manifested in the kind of life they live afterwards to the glory of God and for the peoples' own good.

J. C. Ryle once wrote ***"I do not set up myself to be better than other people****, and if anyone asks, 'What are you, that you write this way?' I answer, 'I am a very poor creature indeed.' But I say that I cannot read the Bible without desiring to see many believers more spiritual, more holy, more single-eyed, more heavenly minded, more whole-hearted than they (presently) are.* ***I want to see among believers more of a pilgrim spirit, a more decided separation from the world, a conversation more evidently in heaven, a closer walk with God, and therefore I have written as I have."***

If we truly believe the words of the Bible to be inspired by a Higher Power, then it is incumbent on all of us to seek to fully understand and practice its principles ourselves and then going a step further to teach it to the next generations. Failure to do this would buttress the thought once shared by Billy Melvin who once wrote that: *"My concern is the measure of infiltration by the world into the church. We have been influenced far more than we would like to admit. This infiltration has dulled our effectiveness, blurred our vision, and caused us to adopt worldly standards of success."*

A. W. Tozer also once wrote that: *"We have learned to live with unholiness and have come to look upon it as the natural and expected thing."* Philip Doddridge also wrote, and I agree with him, that *"Let us remember, that whilst we are in this world, we sojourn in a strange land, and are at a distance from our home; and, therefore, do not let us be inordinately affected with anything in it."*

THE CHOICE

Life is about the choices we make. I have chosen to fully devote the last three years of my life to dig deeper into the Bible to locate the exact message that was intended for us by its Author and then to bring it to the open to make its reading, studying and understanding a delight for everyone especially the young men and women of this age. I have been so passionate with this search that, although I had to completely quit my full time job to face several challenges to finish this, it now feels like just yesterday.

I strongly believe that by the time you complete reading, you would have gotten a firm foundation on which angle to now study and understand the Bible without the aid of a Concordance, a Bible Commentary or a teacher. You will get to know who wrote the Bible, how it was written, to whom it was intended, its purpose, how it was preserved, the research that went into proving its contents before writing them down, a short history of Israel and *the true source of Christianity.*

The next thing is that people especially the youth will now feel proud to own and carry Bibles around without feeling ashamed. This would enable them to study it themselves to discover all the powerful principles being discovered by most of the motivational speakers that guarantee true success today. You would also discover the solutions to the problems being encountered on earth today. This is your best shot on the one true non-denominational pathway to understanding the Bible.

MY HEART'S DESIRE

It is my desire and prayer that everyone alive will own a Bible no matter the color of their skin, race or religious background. I believe deep down within my soul that the first thing to buy for a child should be a Bible and not a toy. Your child will surely grow up to read and understand it later.

I'll like to remind you that, although there are several things you will learn from the pages of this book, it is only meant to lead you into falling in love with the Bible like what happened to me. It is meant to serve or assist you as a route or path to direct you into understanding the Bible clearly. That is where the title *"Pathway to Understanding the Bible"* comes from. It is a path to aid you in your studies.

Once you are enlightened to this path, I'll suggest that even if you cannot afford to buy a copy of this book for a friend or a loved one, you pass this very one to them to help them learn what you know. Only tell them in advance to take good care of it and return it in the condition they took it from you. Don't be selfish and keep this knowledge to yourself. Study the Bible and seek to understand the principles found in its pages. After that, apply them to any field of endeavor you find yourself to extend the Kingdom of God on earth.

The only tool you will need aside your Bible is your ability to read. So plunge in and be prepared to learn many wonderful new truths! Make sure you pray for understanding before starting and approach this study with an open mind. God be with you. I love you.

> *"The first and most important book we are to study is the Bible . . . . When we study a book of the Bible we are seeking to be controlled by the intent of the Author; we are determined to hear what He is saying, not what we want Him to say. We want life-transforming truth, not just good feelings. We are willing to pay the price of barren day after barren day until the meaning is clear. This process revolutionizes our lives."—Richard J. Foster*

Chapter One

IS IT DIFFICULT TO UNDERSTAND THE BIBLE?

Ever since I was a kid, I have heard it said time and again that the Bible is difficult to understand and most of its teachers often quote *1 Corinthians 2:14* to support their stance that it can *only* be spiritually discerned. I do appreciate the works of most of these men who have searched into the Bible and written some marvelous books that have paved the way for us to also have the desire and the motivation to delve more into the scriptures ourselves in these last days. I hold such men in high regard and honor for their work; I doff my hat for them. But at the same time it is written *"We accept man's testimony,* ***but God's testimony is greater because it is the testimony of God****, which He has given about His Son." (1 John 5:9)*

So, with all due respect and apology, if we have been told all our lives that because it is spiritually discerned, the Bible is difficult to understand and that until it is interpreted to us by someone else, we wouldn't be able to grasp its full meaning but God's Word says otherwise, then we should be bold and courageous enough to declare openly like John that "*we accept man's testimony,* ***but God's testimony is greater."*** We do accept their testimonies because they are good. But the testimony from God is far greater and superior to what they tell us. I learned from Dr. Myles Munroe that, doing something good does not necessarily mean one is doing the right thing.

> *"When the consensus of scholarship says one thing and the Word of God another, the consensus of scholarship can plumb go to hell for all I care."—Billy Sunday a.k.a William A. Sunday (1862-1935)*

Paul wrote in the book of Ephesians about *"the administration of this mystery,* ***which for ages past was kept hidden in God****, who created all things" (Eph. 3:9)*. This may sound like God intentionally chose to keep His ways a mystery to be hidden from His children forever. But it will interest you to know that when God gave His prophesies to Daniel for instance in the days of old, He did not intend them to be hidden forever. Read carefully what was said in one of such lines:

> *He replied, "Go your way, Daniel, because* ***the words are closed up and sealed until the time of the end****. 10 Many will be purified, made spotless and refined,* ***but*** *the wicked will continue to be wicked. None of the wicked will understand****, but those who are wise will understand."*** *Daniel 12:9-10)*

Jesus asked, *"Which of you, if his son asks for bread, will give him a stone? 10 Or if he asks for a fish, will give him a snake? 11 If you, then,* ***though you are evil****, know how to give good gifts to your children,* ***how much more will your Father in heaven*** *give good gifts to those who ask Him?!" (Matt. 7:9-11).* God never intended His Word to remain a mystery and kept hidden from His children for ever. The question is, "Why would He do that if He loves us so much that He could even sacrifice His only Son to die on our behalf?" What does He stand to gain by keeping His Word a secret from the children He loves so much? Does that make sense? He promises us on several instances that *"****whatever is hidden is meant to be disclosed****, and whatever is concealed is meant to be brought out into the open" (Mark 4:22):*

> *For* ***there is nothing hidden that will not be disclosed****, and nothing concealed that will not be known or brought out into the open. 18* ***Therefore consider carefully how you listen****. Whoever has will be given more; whoever does not have, even what he thinks he has will be taken from him." (Luke 8:17-18)*

It was Jesus Christ who said the above statement and to prove Himself right that He does not lie, He made sure He explained everything to His disciples who were always prepared and available to understand the morals He was teaching through His parables. That was what differentiated His disciples from the Pharisees and the crowd who only heard Him teach in parables without taking the required steps further to carefully consider how they listened. After each sermon in parables, His disciples went to ask Him in private to interpret everything He had said.

One gains understanding and becomes wise in the process when he is able to apply the knowledge or information at his disposal to overcome the daily issues of life. Even with the crowd, Jesus did not only speak in parables but He always "***spoke the word to them, as much as they could understand***."

> ***With many similar parables Jesus spoke the word to them, as much as they could understand.*** *34 He did not say anything to them without using a parable.* ***But when He was alone with His own disciples, He explained everything.*** *(Mark 4:33-34)*

The truth is that in past generations and now, God chooses to speak to His children in various ways through His Words but the majority refuses to listen to what the few who are always in the minority adhere to. For instance, when God said the wicked would continue to be wicked because they would not understand what Daniel was saying in those days, He still said many would at the same time be purified, made spotless and refined because of their wisdom which leads them to understand what they heard. Read those two verses again.

> *He replied, "Go your way, Daniel, because the words are closed up and sealed until the time of the end. 10* ***Many will be purified, made spotless and refined, but the wicked will continue to be wicked.*** *None of the wicked will understand,* ***but those who are wise will understand."*** *(Daniel 12:9-10)*

The same thing happened in the days of Jesus Christ when He walked the face of this earth, breathed the very same air that you and I breathe and felt the heat of the sun just like everyone else today. He spoke in parables to the crowd but He made sure He explained everything to His disciples whenever they were alone. Even with that, they could still not fully grasp everything He taught to the extent that when it was time for Him to ascend into heaven, He had to open their understanding to fully comprehend the Scriptures all over again *(Luke 24:44-49)*. And this has continued to our day and age. Jesus praised the Father for revealing this to His children:

> *At that time Jesus, full of joy through the Holy Spirit, said, "I praise you Father, LORD of heaven and earth,* ***because you have hidden these things from the wise and learned and revealed them to little children.*** *Yes, Father, for this was your good pleasure." (Luke 10:21)*

PROVE ALL THINGS

No matter how safe a thing is concealed in the Bible in particular, there is always the element of revelation if the searcher will continue to seek and knock till the door is opened for him. Questions are bound to be answered if and only if the questioner does not relent in wanting that answer so badly. *"It is impossible to mentally or socially enslave a Bible-reading people. The principles of the Bible are the groundwork of human freedom"—Horace Greeley (1811-1872).* Jesus said:

> *Ask and it will be given to you;* ***seek and you will find****; knock and the door will be opened to you. 8 For everyone who asks receives;* ***he who seeks finds****; and to him who knocks, the door will be opened. (Matt. 7:7-8)*

Although the Bible remains a mysterious Book to many, our Lord Jesus Christ, who died on our behalf that we might have life and whose testimony is greater than men, has promised us that if we will seek to understand it, seek to find the one true message contained in it and never relent in doing so until we get hold of what we are asking and seeking, the door will be opened for us. Wow! John the apostle also wrote that: *"This is the confidence we have in approaching God:* ***that if we ask anything according to His will, He hears us.*** *15 And if we know that He hears us—****whatever we ask—we know that we have what we asked of Him****" (1 John 5:14-15).* God loves and hears us and for that matter will not conceal His word from us if we want to know it. We have to do the seeking first to reach the finding stage.

> *It is the glory of God to conceal a matter, to search out a matter is the glory of kings. (Prov. 25:2)*

After calling the Israelites from Egypt, God said through Moses to tell them that *"Now* ***if you obey me fully and keep my covenant, then out of all nations you will be my treasured possession. Although the whole earth is mine,*** *6* ***you will be for me a kingdom of priests and a holy nation****. These are the words you are to speak to the Israelites" (Exod. 19:5-6).* Later when it was time to call the Gentiles to inherit the covenant promised to Abraham that he was to become the "father of many nations," God again said through Peter that, *"But you* (Gentile believers) *are a chosen people, a royal priesthood, a holy nation,* ***a people belonging to God****, that you may declare the praises of Him who called you out of darkness into His wonderful light. 10* ***Once you were not a people, but now you are the people of God****; once you had not received mercy, but now you have received mercy." (1 Pet. 2:9-10)*

If Gentile believers are today a people belonging to God though they did not qualify for that in the past, like Israel, then we are kings and queens in the assembly of the godly, and it is our collective responsibility to search out every matter that has been concealed by the Almighty King. Searching out these truths will bring out our glory as well.

PAYING THE PRICE

Brian Tracy once said, *"Decide upon your major definite purpose in life and then organize all your activities around it."* There is always something to do to lead you to the truth. You don't just sit with your hands folded waiting for the answers to drop like manner from heaven on your lap. You've got to dig to find gold. It was Napoleon Hill who once said that *"There is nothing like something for nothing."* If you want something badly, you should be prepared to pay the price to attain it. There's nothing precious taken on a silver platter. Understanding makes life simple. But it takes time, discipline, perseverance, passion and other traits to gain understanding into a particular subject. Solomon said, ***"Although it costs you all you have, get understanding."*** Be willing to pay any price for understanding.

> *To the Jews who had believed Him, Jesus said,* ***"If you hold to my teaching, you are really my disciples.*** *32* ***Then you will know the truth****, and the truth will set you free." (John 8:31-32)*

Something is got to give way if we are truly interested in finding the solutions to the numerous problems we face. Christians love to quote the immediate verse above at the least provocation to assure ourselves that we are free in Christ because we feel we know the truth. But if you were to carefully study what Jesus said and did not say in those two verses, you would realize that He actually said one would know the truth and be free in the process if and only if he holds to *His* (Christ's) teaching. Therefore, if one assumes that Christ's teaching or message is outdated and is no longer relevant to our internet and globalization age and yet claims to be a Christian mixing the teachings he received with that of the systems of this world, he would simply be deceiving himself. Holding to His teaching is the price.

For instance, if you claim to be a Christian and yet have a message distinct from what Christ preached and left with the disciples to build upon, then you are just a cranking cymbal *"for no-one can lay any foundation other than the one already laid,* ***which is Jesus Christ****" (1 Cor. 2:11).* John adds that ***"Anyone who runs ahead and does not continue in the teaching of Christ does not have God****: whoever continues in the teaching has both the Father and the Son. 10* ***If anyone comes to you and does not bring this teaching, do not take him into your house or welcome him.*** *11* ***Anyone who welcomes him shares in his wicked work****" (2 John 9-11).* The teaching of Jesus Christ is the only true and reliable foundation that has to be built upon if one truly claims to be a Christian. The whole of this book is built on this principle.

THE WISE AND DISCERNING WILL UNDERSTAND

> *Who is wise? He will realize these things. Who is discerning? He will understand them. The ways of the LORD are right; the righteous walk in them, but the rebellious stumble in them. (Hosea 14:9)*

The ways of God are right and will forever remain so. Those who choose to live by the principles contained in them are called righteous and walk blamelessly in them. But the rebellious who refuse to live by these same principles of God stumble and are ruined for choosing a different path. The ways of God remain unchanged since the days of Adam and Eve because it is written *"He who is the Glory of Israel does not lie or change His mind;* ***for He is not a man, that He should change His mind."*** *(1 Sam. 15:29)* God has not changed His mind from what He had in mind when He created Adam to rule the earth.

> *Go to this people and say, "You will be ever hearing* ***but never understanding****; you will be* ***ever seeing but never perceiving.****" 27 For this people's heart has become calloused;* ***they hardly hear with their ears, and they have closed their eyes. Otherwise they might see with their eyes, hear with their ears, understand with their hearts and turn, and I would heal them.*** *(Acts 28:26-27)*

You see, even as these "hidden" prophesies were given in the past, the people could have understood them if they had listened well enough with their ears and opened their eyes. There is a thin line between hearing and listening. The truth of the Bible became hidden to its intended recipients because they refused to adhere to its requirements and regulations. The fault was then with the people, and not God and His Word. In order to remedy this anomaly, read how God decided to do it:

> *"This is the covenant that I will make with the house of Israel* ***after that time,"*** *declares the LORD. "****I will put my law in their minds and write it on their hearts****. I will be their God, and they will be my people. 34 No longer will a man teach his neighbor, or a man his brother, saying, 'Know the LORD,'* ***because they will all know me, from the least of them to the greatest,****" declares the LORD. (Jer. 31:33-34)*

In past generations, a prophet appears on the scene and continuously warns the people to live their lives according to the principles of God. In our days too, we have pastors in front of pulpits and through other communication networks telling their congregants to know God by following His principles in the Scriptures. But what we need to take note of is the fact that the Word of God has been in existence long before even our great grandparents were born. Yet most of us refuse to even listen to these words let alone study them on our own. We only hear but don't listen to understand.

But a time is coming when no-one will need a pastor, a brother, or a neighbor to remind him or her to live according to these same principles contained in the pages of the Bible. The same principles that people refuse to live by today are, in later times, going to make enough sense to the occupants of this earth and we will all choose to live by them because God is going to make it so. *"For the earth will be filled with the knowledge of the glory of the LORD, as the waters cover the sea" (Hab. 2:14).*

> *"If we abide by the principles taught in the Bible, our country will go on prospering and to prosper; but if we and our posterity neglect its instructions and authority, no man can tell how sudden a catastrophe may overwhelm us and bury all our glory in profound obscurity."— Daniel Webster (1782-1852)*

Different interpretations arise from the writings of Paul that there are times one would wish he should have toned down a bit on the content of some of his letters for every Tom, Dick and Harry to clearly understand. But incidentally, he did not consider any of his writings difficult to understand. He once wrote to the Corinthian Church that ***"For we do not write to you anything you cannot read or understand****. And I hope that, 14 as you have understood us in part,* ***you will come to understand fully*** *that you can boast of us just as we will boast of you in the day of the LORD" (2 Cor. 1:13-14).*

Although Paul himself considered his writings plain and not difficult to understand, his fellow soldier in the faith had a warning to give to us who read his writings today. And as a fellow Christian in the faith, my little and humble appeal to you is that each time you read anything that was penned down by Paul, I'll plead with you with all due respect to heed to this warning from Peter, a loving disciple of Christ who was called to preach the gospel to the Jews just as Paul was sent to the Gentiles. Peter wrote:

> *Bear in mind that our LORD'S patience means salvation, just as our dear brother Paul also wrote to you* ***with the wisdom that God gave him****. 16* ***He writes the same way in ALL HIS LETTERS, speaking in them of these matters. HIS LETTERS CONTAIN SOME THINGS THAT ARE HARD TO UNDERSTAND,***

WHICH IGNORANT AND UNSTABLE PEOPLE DISTORT, AS THEY DO THE OTHER SCRIPTURES TO THEIR OWN DESTRUCTION." *(2 Peter 3:15-16)*

To really appreciate Peter's warning, we need to understand the full meaning of the word *"distort"* in those verses. It is defined as *to change the shape, appearance or sound of something so that it is strange or not clear;* ***to twist or change facts, ideas etc so that they are no longer correct or true.*** Now, in relation to Peter's warning, you would realize that one does not necessarily have to be a bad person to distort the words of Paul and *"the other Scriptures"* of the Bible. His deep knowledge base on the mysteries hidden in the Scriptures from past ages (Eph. 3:9) made his letters difficult to understand, that the ignorant and unstable twist or change them unknowingly, with the excuse of interpreting them, and this results in changing the whole meaning and truth that they were meant to communicate.

For instance, after the resurrection of the LORD Jesus Christ from the dead and His disciples' marvel at what they had experienced in those days, Christ Jesus said to them, *"How foolish you are,* ***and how slow of heart to believe all that the prophets have spoken!*** *26 Did not the Christ have to suffer these things and then enter His glory?" 27* ***And beginning with Moses and all the Prophets, He explained to them what was said in all the Scriptures concerning Himself*** *(Luke 24:25-27).* That is to say that if they had read, understood and believed what the prophets had said in the Scriptures before Christ's arrival, they would have understood what was happening right before their eyes without being taught. The same thing is happening today. The future is hidden in the past.

Everything Jesus, Paul or any of the other apostles taught was clearly stipulated in the Scriptures but they remained hidden mysteries until they were discovered and taught by them to the masses. The Holy Scriptures of the Bible contain all that pertains to what constitutes the truth of God. Its message has been here with us since the days of Moses at least. Upon all the efforts by various kingdoms to suppress the distribution of the Bible to individuals, it has been with us for ages. A number of martyrs have sacrificed their blood to make this possible, though. The Bible always tops the Bestseller list.

YES, THE BIBLE CAN BE UNDERSTOOD

With the above Scriptural verses, I conclude by categorically stating that the Bible is not difficult to understand. It is *"the ignorant and unstable"* who distort its message for their own selfish reasons leading to their destruction. And even if the Bible is difficult to understand, it is only difficult and *not* impossible to be understood. There's nothing impossible with God and seeking to understand the Scriptures of the Bible is one of the possibilities. It can be done. *"If you hear a voice within you saying 'I am not a painter,' then, by all means, paint . . . and that voice will be silenced"*—Vincent van Gogh.

I read somewhere that: *"When you are inspired by some great purpose, some extraordinary project, all your thoughts break their bounds; your mind transcends limitations, your consciousness expands in every direction, and you find yourself in a new, great and wonderful world. Dormant forces, faculties and talents become alive, and you discover yourself to be a greater person by far than you ever dreamt yourself to be."* A Chinese proverb goes: *"A journey of a thousand miles begins with a step."* It may be a long and arduous road. But Leighton Ford once wrote that *"There is no detour to holiness. Jesus Christ came to the resurrection through the cross, not around it."* Let's roll.

Chapter Two

ARE WE EQUIPPED TO UNDERSTAND THE BIBLE?

> *I always thank God for you because of His grace given you in Christ Jesus. 5* ***For in Him you have been enriched in every way—in all your speaking and in all your knowledge****—6 because our testimony about Christ was confirmed in you. 7* ***Therefore you do not lack any spiritual gift as you eagerly wait for our LORD Jesus Christ to be revealed.*** *8* ***He will keep you strong to the end, so that you will be blameless on the day of our LORD Jesus Christ.*** *9 God, who has called you into fellowship with His Son Jesus Christ our LORD, is faithful. (1 Cor. 1:4-9).*

If you happen to be one of those Christians who spend majority of their prayer time binding the devil and demons, asking for power to lead a righteous and blameless life on this very earth, Paul once wrote to his students that "***you do not lack any spiritual gift as you eagerly wait for our LORD Jesus Christ to be revealed.***" He continued by saying that Christ Himself will keep you strong to the end, so that you would be found blameless on the day of the LORD. To stamp his authority on what he was saying, he concluded by saying that God is faithful, meaning there was no lie in what he was writing. How about that? Believing and tapping into that is the key.

> ***Already, you have all you want! Already you have become rich! You have become kings****—and that without us! How I wish that you really had become kings so that we might be kings with you! (1 Cor. 4:8)*

Indeed, with the Word of God in and with us, we already have all we want and we become rich in the process. And please bear in mind that, riches in this verse does not only cover the subject of material wealth but all the areas of *"faith, goodness, knowledge, self-control, perseverance, godliness, brotherly kindness, and love. 8* ***For if we possess these qualities in increasing measure, they will keep us from being ineffective and unproductive in our knowledge of our LORD Jesus Christ"*** *(2 Pet. 1:5-8).* Monetary riches is only a subset of what is being talked about here.

> *"I prayed for Faith, and thought that some day Faith would come down and strike me like lightning. But Faith did not seem to come. One day I read in the tenth chapter of Romans, 'Now Faith cometh by hearing, and hearing by the Word of God.' I had closed my Bible, and prayed for Faith. I now opened my Bible, and began to study, and Faith has been growing ever since."—Dwight L. Moody (1837-1899)*

Paul told the Ephesians: *"Now I commit you to God and to* ***the word of His grace, which can build you up and give you an inheritance among all those who are sanctified"*** *(Acts 20:32).* The apostles knew back then that commitment to the study of the Scriptures and living by its principles was able to build one up and give him or her inheritance among the greats. The reason is because the Scriptures serve as blueprints for us to study and know how people like Abraham and Joseph walked with God for us to follow in their footsteps ***"for everything that was written in the past was written to teach us, so that through endurance and the encouragement of the Scriptures we might have hope"*** *(Rom. 15:4).* Peter adds some flavor to this whole truth in his second letter. He wrote that:

> ***His divine power has given us everything we need for life and godliness through our knowledge of Him who called us by His own glory and goodness.*** *4* ***Through these He has given us His very great and precious promises, so that through them you may participate in the divine nature and escape the corruption in the world caused by evil desires . . .*** *8 For if you possess these qualities in increasing measure, they will keep you from being ineffective and unproductive in your knowledge of our LORD Jesus Christ. (2 Pet. 1:3-4, 8)*

The understanding of some verses in the Bible can replace years of time and energy wasted in binding and loosing demons for being responsible for one's predicament caused by ignorance. It feels great to know that there are qualities to possess in the Bible that *when possessed in increasing measure* may enable us participate in the *"divine nature"* of God and will also keep us from being *"ineffective and unproductive"* in the knowledge of our LORD Jesus Christ. So, to be effective and productive then, we have to search these *"great and precious promises"* in the Scriptures ourselves and apply them. Remember, *"We accept man's testimony,* ***but God's testimony is greater because it is the testimony of God,*** *which He has given about His Son" (1 John 5:9).*

Let's read verse four of the above Scripture again. It says that *"Through these He has given us His very great and precious promises,* ***so that through them you may participate in the divine nature and escape the corruption in the world caused by evil desires."*** So we can actually participate in the divine nature of God and Jesus Christ, and through that escape the corruption in this world caused by evil desires if we would dare to learn how that is achieved. That means divinity in God's nature can be attained right here on earth without even stepping foot in heaven.

Knowing some truths can be frightening at times but we should believe God's Word rather than that of men. That is why Peter calls it, *"His very great and precious promises."* Paul wrote: *"You are all sons of God through faith in Christ Jesus, 27 for all of you who were baptized into Christ have clothed yourselves with Christ" (Gal. 3:26-27).* Just as one is born a child and later grows into manhood, we are also expected to mature into Christ after we are born again.

"Your attitude should be the same as that of Christ Jesus . . . *14 Do everything without complaining or arguing, 15* ***so that you may become blameless and pure children of God without fault in a crooked and depraved generation, in which you shine like stars in the universe*** *16 as you hold out the word of life—in order that I may boast on the day of Christ that I did not run or labor for nothing" (Phil. 2:5, 14-16).* Jesus said His purpose for coming was for us to *"have life and have it to the full" (John 10:10).* The seed of God is planted in us but it is our duty to discover and maximize that potential until we mature and have the same attitude as that of Jesus Christ.

WE ARE SONS OF GOD ON EARTH

There is a verse in the book of Psalms which marvels me anytime I read it. It says: *"I said,* ***'You are "gods";*** *you are all sons of the Most High.' 7* ***But you will die like mere men; you will fall like every other ruler"*** *(Psalm 82:6-7).* Prior to that in verse 5 is written: *"They know nothing, they understand nothing. They walk about in darkness; all the foundations of the earth are shaken."* Isn't it sad to learn that all the foundations of the earth are shaken because you and I walk about in darkness simply because we know and understand nothing which has resulted in rendering us powerless to die like every other men though we were created originally as the sons of God?

We need to discover what the very few have discovered and doing exploits with. The DNA of God is given to us to do whatever we will do to pursue His Kingdom on earth. *What can the righteous do if the foundation be destroyed?* Our failure to discover who we are results in the destruction of the foundations.

In Paul's prayer for the Church in Ephesus, he wrote that *"I pray that out of His glorious riches He may strengthen you with power through His Spirit in your inner being, 17 so that Christ may dwell in your hearts through faith. And I pray that you, being rooted and established in love, 18 may have power, together with all the saints, to grasp how wide and long and high and deep is the love of Christ, 19 and to know this love that surpasses knowledge—**that you may be filled to the measure of all the fullness of God**" (Eph. 3:16-19).* If you are not afraid to hear it, then the purpose of your calling is to grow in your knowledge to "*the measure of **all the fullness of God***" here on earth because *"now we are children of God" (1 John 3:2).* And the good news is that the path is already provided in the Holy Scriptures.

THE SCRIPTURES AS TOOLS FOR MAXIMIZING OUR POTENTIALS

> *But as for you, continue in what you have learned and have become convinced of, because you know those from whom you learned it, 15 and how from infancy you have known the holy Scriptures, **which are able to make you wise for salvation through faith in Christ Jesus**. 16 All Scripture is God-breathed and is useful for teaching, rebuking, correcting and training in righteousness, 17 **so that the man of God may be thoroughly equipped for every good work.** (2 Tim. 3:14-17)*

Please note very carefully that at the time Paul wrote this letter to Timothy, the Holy Scriptures referred to what we now call the Old Testament. Paul was praising Timothy for knowing the Holy Scriptures since he was a kid and reminding him of how they were able to make him wise. He urged him to continue in what he had learnt from them and become convinced of. He then proceeded to remind him of what the Scriptures do when it is learnt. It teaches, rebukes, corrects and trains in righteousness so that the man doing the learning may grow to become thoroughly equipped for every good work in all areas of life. What a promise! Understanding the Bible is one of the *good works* and if we want to understand it, then we just have to go into the Scriptures because one of the things it does is to teach us.

> *See, I have taught you decrees and laws as the LORD my God commanded me, so that you may follow them in the land you are entering to take possession of it. 6 Observe them carefully,* ***for this will show your wisdom and understanding to the nations, who will hear about all these decrees and say, "surely this great nation is a wise and understanding people."*** *7 What other nation is so great as to have their gods near them the way the LORD our God is near us whenever we pray to Him? 8* ***and what other nation is so great as to have such righteous decrees and laws as this body of laws I am setting before you today?*** *(Deut. 4:5-8)*

It is how well you walk blamelessly with the Scriptures that will determine how wise and understanding you are in the affairs of this world. It's not how much good grammar or the number of vocabularies you have at your sleeves. Moses and Paul have said the same thing and Jesus Christ also said that *"the Scriptures cannot be broken" (John 10:35).* We already have all that we need in the Scriptures. All the attempts to try and convince us today that one needs to reach into some outer realm of some spiritual atmosphere before understanding the Bible and the things of God are mainly done to divert our attention from the Scriptures. The Bible reigns supreme when it comes to tracing the source of God's truth.

> *"The Bible, then, has an essential place in the life of a Christian. For the revelation of God leads to worship, the warnings of God to repentance, the promises of God to faith, the commands of God to obedience and the truth of God to witness. It is no exaggeration to say that without Scripture a Christian life is impossible."—John R. W. Stott*

Paul, under the inspiration of the Spirit of God wrote: *"For I have not hesitated to proclaim to you* ***the whole will of God****" (Acts 20:27).* If he did indeed proclaim *"the whole will of God"* in the Scriptures, then we only need to emulate Daniel and strive to understand by *"the books"* written by him. Paul was so convinced of the fact that the gospel he preached could establish us that he wrote: *"Now to Him who is able to establish you* ***by my gospel*** *and the proclamation of Jesus Christ, according to the revelation of the mystery hidden for long ages past, 26* ***but now revealed and made known through the prophetic writings*** *by the command of the eternal God,* ***so that***

all nations might believe and obey Him*—27 to the only wise God be glory for ever through Jesus Christ! Amen" (Rom. 16:25-27).*

He wrote to the Galatians that *"I want you to know, brothers, that the gospel I preached is not something that man made up. I did not receive it from any man, nor was I taught it; rather, I received it by revelation from Jesus Christ" (Gal. 1:11-12).* He went further to write that *"But when God, who set me apart from birth and called me by His grace, was pleased 16 to reveal His Son in me so that I might preach Him among the Gentiles, I did not consult any man, 17 nor did I go up to Jerusalem to see those who were apostles before I was, but I went immediately into Arabia and later returned to Damascus" (Gal. 1:15-17).* He then concluded by saying that: ***"I assure you before God that what I am writing to you is no lie****" (Gal. 1:20).*

So, does that mean that Jesus Christ took Paul to Arabia and taught him all that he preached in a literal classroom like what we have today in the form of attending a school? Of course not! Paul just told us in the book of Romans how it was revealed to him. He said he got the gospel through *"the revelation of the mystery hidden for long ages past,* ***but revealed and made known through the prophetic writings by the command of the eternal God****."* He spent enormous amount of time studying the Scriptures.

To *reveal is to show or bring something to the open that previously could not be seen or known.* The idea is that, it was already in existence but nobody had made the discovery of it yet. For instance, the possibility of flying an airplane was already in existence for ages until it was *"revealed"* to the Wright brothers. This implies that whatever Paul preached was hidden for ages in the prophetic writings of the Scriptures but had not yet been revealed to anyone. The same way, we can also follow the footsteps of people like Paul to search into the Scriptures and fully understand the message it puts across today.

> *"The Bible is not an end in itself, but a means to bring men to an intimate and satisfying knowledge of God, that they may enter into Him, that they may delight in His presence, may taste and know the inner sweetness of the very God Himself in the core and centre of their hearts."—A. W. Tozer (1897-1963)*

Chapter Three

WHERE DO WE BEGIN THE SEARCH?

We need to be reminded of the promise of Jesus Christ when He said, *"Ask and it will be given to you;* ***seek and you will find;*** *knock and the door will be opened to you. 8 For everyone who asks receives;* ***he who seeks finds;*** *and to him who knocks, the door will be opened. 9 Which of you, if his son asks for bread, will give him a stone? 10 Or if he asks for a fish, will give him a snake? 11 If you, then, though you are evil, know how to give good gifts to your children, how much more will your Father in heaven give good gifts to those who ask Him!"* (Matt. 7:7-11). This should encourage us to seek out with every inch of our abilities until we get the answers to our questions.

STICK TO THE PATH OF UNDERSTANDING

Jesus once said, *"Come to me, all you who are weary and burdened, and I will give you rest" (Matt. 11:28).* Solomon wrote: *"Listen, my son, and be wise, and* ***keep your heart on the right path"*** *(Prov. 23:19).* He also wrote that "***Stern discipline awaits him who leaves the path;*** *he who hates correction will die" (Prov. 15:10).* Again, he wrote that "***A man who strays from the path of understanding comes to rest in the company of the dead***" *(Prov. 21:16).* What then, is the path established by God in the Scriptures that we need not to stray from? If there is a path like that in the Bible, then when it is found, we need to be able to humble ourselves as children of the Creator and follow that path for the rest of our lives.

David prayed, *"Show me your ways, O LORD,* ***teach me your paths;*** *5 guide me in your truth and teach me, for you are God my Savior, and my hope is in you all day long" (Psalm 25:4-5).* God does have a path that leads to Him. But how do we find that path? Has He provided us with a map to that effect?

> *"To see in the Bible nothing more than a collection of ordinary human contributions to religious literature would be, in the judgment of those who know it best and prize it most, to fail to see in it that which is its highest and most noble characteristic, namely, a message of God to the human soul—a message of highest moral and spiritual value not to the people of past ages only but to all generations of men in all ages."—Wilbur F. Tillett*

It is written: "***The teaching of the wise is a fountain of life****, turning a man from the snares of death" (Prov. 13:14).* If this is true, then we can follow the teachings of the wise from the Scriptures to lead us to our destination of finding this path.

> *This is what the LORD says: "Stand at the crossroads and look;* ***ask for the ancient paths, ask where the good way is, and walk in it, and you will find rest for your souls.*** *But you said,* ***'We will not walk in it.'*** *17 I appointed watchmen over you and said, 'Listen to the sound of the trumpet!'* ***But you said, 'We will not listen."*** *(Jer. 6:16-17)*

Isn't it wonderful to know that the good path is actually not in the future but hidden with the ancients in the past? The times of the patriarchs, Jesus and the apostles are now ancient to those of us living today. Two thousand years are a very long period indeed. The modern trend today, especially in Ghana, is to hear of programs organized to have an encounter with God or seek the face of the LORD, and other issue like that. It's like the ability to know the path that leads to God is hidden somewhere in the future and has to be revealed by the anointing or power from another man with supernatural capabilities who can only be in a position to hear from God and later communicate it to the people. But the only true path has been specifically laid down in the Scriptures from ages past. You and I only need to search for it.

TAKING A CUE FROM PREVIOUS GENERATIONS

Ask the former generations and find out what their fathers learned, 9 ***for we were born only yesterday and know nothing****, and our days on earth are only but a shadow. 10* ***Will they not instruct you and tell you? Will they not bring forth words from their understanding?*** *(Job. 8:8-10)*

Paul, the apostle wrote to the Romans and asked, *"What advantage, then, is there in being a Jew, or what value is there in circumcision? Much in every way!* ***First of all, they have been entrusted with the very words of God"*** *(Rom. 3:1-2).* ***"The LORD made His ways known to Moses, His deeds to the people of Israel"*** *(Psalm 103:7).* If finding the good path that leads to God lies in asking the former generations, then we have been assured by Paul in the above verses that the Jews have done a great job by preserving what their fathers learned from their dealings with God. In other words, he has recommended the library to visit for our research.

> *O my people, hear my teaching; listen to the words of my mouth. 2 I will open my mouth in parables,* ***I will utter hidden things, things from of old—3 what we have heard and known, what our fathers have told us. 4 We will not hide them from their children; we will tell the next generation the praiseworthy deeds of the LORD, His power, and the wonders He has done. 5 He decreed statutes for Jacob and established the law in Israel, which He commanded our forefathers to teach their children, 6 so that the next generation would know them, even the children yet to be born, and they in turn would tell their children. 7 Then they would put their trust in God and would not forget His deeds but would keep His commands. 8 They would not be like their forefathers—a stubborn and rebellious generation, whose hearts were not loyal to God, whose spirits were not faithful to Him.*** *(Psalm 78:1-8)*

You see, the purposes of the written word of Scriptures is for those of us living today to study to know the path laid down by the Father Himself for us to walk blamelessly in. It's our collective duty and responsibility to study them, walk in them and teach them to our children who will also follow after us. In studying and knowing the likes and dislikes of God and what makes for a good living, we would then be in a better position to avoid the mistakes our forefathers made in walking with the LORD.

All that is required to enable us walk uprightly on earth have been provided in the Scriptures. Solomon wrote ***"A man's own folly ruins his life,*** *yet his heart rages against the LORD" (Prov. 19:3).* It is a man's own ignorance that prevents him from knowing this path, yet he will keep blaming forces outside himself for being responsible.

> *For I do not want you to be ignorant of the fact, brothers, that our forefathers were all under the cloud and that they all passed through the sea. 2 They were all baptized into Moses in the cloud and in the sea. 3 They all ate the same spiritual food 4 and drank*

> *the same spiritual drink; for they drank from the spiritual rock that accompanied them, and that rock was Christ. 5 Nevertheless, God was not pleased with most of them; their bodies were scattered over the desert. 6* ***Now these things occurred as examples to keep us from setting our hearts on evil things as they did****. 7 Do not be idolaters, as some of them were; as it is written: "The people sat down to eat and drink and got up to indulge in pagan revelry." 8* ***We should not commit sexual immorality, as some of them did****—and in one day twenty-three thousand of them died. 9* ***We should not test the LORD, as some of them did****—and were killed by snakes. 10* ***And do not grumble, as some of them did****—and were killed by the destroying angel.*
>
> *11* ***These things happened to them as examples and were written down as warnings for us, on whom the fulfillment of the ages has come****. 12 So, if you think you are standing firm, be careful that you don't fall! (1 Cor. 10:1-12)*

This is coming from none other than the man who had his revelations directly from Christ Jesus and has encouraged us to use what we hear from him as the pattern of sound teaching (2 Tim. 1:13). He once said, *"But when God, who set me apart from birth and called me by His grace, was pleased to reveal His Son in me so that I might preach Him among the Gentiles,* ***I did not consult any man, nor did I go up to Jerusalem to see those who were apostles before I was****" (Gal. 1:15-17).* Now, if there was another way from the examples written down to serve as warnings to us, and also serve as the pathway to God, then Paul surely would have been the right person to reveal this to us. This is because his revelations were directly received from Jesus Christ.

With similar connotation, he wrote to the Romans: ***"For everything that was written in the past was written to teach us, so that through endurance and the encouragement of the Scriptures, we might have hope"*** *(Rom. 15:4).* David wrote that ***"He has revealed His word to Jacob. His laws and decrees to Israel.*** *20* ***He has done this for no other nation; they do not know His laws****" (Psalm 147:19-20).* If we really want to know the path that leads to God, then we need to turn our attention to the Scriptures of the Bible. This is because it reveals God's word to the people of Israel, and God has not done that with any other nation on earth.

> *"This Book has the power not only to inform—but to reform and to transform lives . . . It is supernatural in origin, eternal in duration, divine in authorship, infallible in authority, inexhaustible in meaning, universal in readership, unique in revelation, personal in application and powerful in effect . . . Come to it with awe; read it with reverence, frequently, slowly, prayerfully."—The Gideon's International (Preface to the Bible)*

USING DANIEL AS A PATTERN

As to how to learn from the examples in the Scriptures, let's use the story of Daniel when he and his three friends were called to serve the king of Babylon to illustrate this. But before I make my point, I want us to know who Daniel was before he was even considered to serve in the king's palace. He met the criteria as *a young man from a royal family, handsome and without any physical defect,* ***showing aptitude for every kind of learning, well informed, quick to understand and qualified to serve in the king's palace*** *(Dan. 1:3-5).*

Among Daniel and his friends after the interview, *"The king talked with them, and he found none equal to Daniel, Hananiah, Mishael and Azariah; so they entered the king's service. 20* ***In every matter of wisdom and understanding about which the king questioned them, he found them ten times better than all the magicians and enchanters in his whole kingdom****" (Dan. 1:19-20).* These were Jewish youths exiled in another country but were found to be ten times wiser in all fields of knowledge as compared to the Babylonians.

After revealing a mystery to the king in a dream concerning what was going to happen in the future, *"the king placed Daniel in a high position and lavished many gifts on him. He made him ruler over the entire province of Babylon* ***and placed him in charge of all its wise men.****" (Dan. 2:48)*

It came about that the king died and was succeeded by his son. This king also saw some writing on a wall by a mysterious hand when he was holding a banquet for his officials but could not understand its interpretations just as his astrologers, diviners and enchanters. Although the reward for interpreting the writing on the wall was to be placed in the third position in the kingdom, no-one could do that. The queen at the time came to the king's rescue:

> *The queen, hearing the voices of the king and his nobles, came into the banquet hall. "O king, live forever!" she said. "Don't be alarmed!*

> *Don't look so pale! 11* ***There is a man in your kingdom who has the spirit of the holy gods in him. In the time of your father he was found to have insight and intelligence and wisdom like that of the gods.*** *King Nebuchadnezzar your father—your father the king, I say—appointed him chief of the magicians, enchanters, astrologers and diviners. 12* ***This man Daniel, whom the king called Belteshazzar, was found to have a keen mind and knowledge and understanding, and also the ability to interpret dreams, explain riddles and solve difficult problems.*** *Call for Daniel, and he will tell you what the writing means." (Dan. 5:10-12)*

This was the testimony the queen of the land gave concerning the potential, capabilities and knowledge base of Daniel. The man was so wise that even God, when He was looking for someone to compare with in regards to one possessing wisdom and understanding, asked the king of Tyre ***"Are you wiser than Daniel? Is no secret hidden from you?"*** *(Ezek. 28:3).* If a man could be this wise, then we should try and find out the source of his wisdom and understanding so that we can also tap into it. We should hear it from the horse's own mouth.

> *"In the first year of Darius son of Xerxes (a Mede by descent), who was made ruler over the Babylonian kingdom—2 in the first year of his reign,* ***I, Daniel, understood from the Scriptures, according to the word of the LORD given to Jeremiah the prophet,*** *that the desolation of Jerusalem would last seventy years." (Dan. 9:1-2)*

This was a man well versed in knowledge, wisdom and understanding. From the above verses, we are told he got this wisdom from studying the Scriptures. In the King James Version of the Bible, the word, *"Scriptures"* in the N.I.V is rendered *"Books."* Remember there are thirty-nine Books that make up the Old Testament. He read one of those books and knew in advance what was going to happen in the future. We can also study the Scriptures to know what lies ahead in the future.

He did the same thing to know that eating just fruits and vegetables alone could make one healthier than those who ate all manner of "food items" and wine in the king's palace. Is there a part of the Old Testament that reveals which book he read to know that too? Did he know the secrets of the original food for man? He got that from reading the book of Genesis. It is written:

> *Then God said,* ***"I give you every seed-bearing plant on the face of the whole earth and every tree that has fruit with seed in it. They will be yours for food.*** *30 And to all the beasts of the earth*

> *and all the birds of the air and all the creatures that move on the ground—everything that has the breath of life in it—I give every green plant for food."* ***And it was so.*** *(Gen. 1:29-30)*

At the creation of man, *"every seed-bearing plant"* was given to serve as his food. But what happened? How come that all manner of creatures were permitted to be eaten? Did God made a mistake regarding the food intake of humans and later rectified it? Can we tell what happened?

We can deduce that from the answer Jesus gave when some Pharisees came to ask him, *"Why did Moses command that a man give his wife a certificate of divorce and send her away?" (Matt. 19:7).* They were compelled to ask this question because Jesus had taught them on the subject of marriage and asked the question *"Haven't you read that* ***at the beginning*** *the Creator 'made them male and female', and said, 'For this reason a man will leave his father and mother and be united to his wife, and the two will become one flesh'? 6 So they are no longer two, but one.* ***Therefore what God has joined together, let man not separate****" (Matt. 19:4-6).*

Moses' teachings on marriage to them was to last for all time because David said he learned from long ago that the statutes of God were established to last forever. Jesus' teaching on the subject of marriage seemed to be contradictory to that of Moses. When Jesus was answering their question, which was logical as of then, He said, ***"Moses permitted you*** *to divorce your wives* ***because your hearts were hard. But it was not this way from the beginning****. 9 I tell you that anyone who divorces his wife, except for marital unfaithfulness, and marries another woman commits adultery" (Matt. 19:8-9).*

Jesus explained to them that the reason Moses permitted divorce in the Old Testament was because of the hardness of their hearts and not because the law itself was bad or faulty. After making that point clear to them, He went a step further to take them back to the original design of marriage as God ordained it from the beginning. There was only one thing that could warrant divorce which He said was "*marital unfaithfulness.*"

Now, if He explained the reason why divorce was permitted in Moses' day even though it was not so from the beginning, isn't it obvious He would take us back to the original food man was told to eat and give us the reason why some manner of "creatures" were permitted to be eaten by these same people who were permitted to divorce their spouses because of the hardness of their hearts when it was not so from the beginning? Could it be that they were permitted to eat some creatures too because of the hardness of their hearts?

> *Daniel then said to the guard whom the chief official had appointed over Daniel, Hananiah, Mishael and Azariah, 12 "Please test your*

> *servants for ten days:* ***Give us nothing but vegetables to eat and water to drink.*** *13* ***Then compare our appearance with that of the young men who eat the royal food, and treat your servants in accordance with what you see."*** *14 So he agreed to this and tested them for ten days. 15* ***At the end of the ten days they looked healthier and better nourished than any of the young men who ate the royal food.*** *16 So the guard took away their choice food and the wine they were to drink* ***and gave them vegetables instead.*** *(Dan 1:11-16)*

I don't know much about mechanics but I do know that a car meant to run on petrol does not do well on diesel. It might move around a bit but the engine will surely come to ruin if the tank is not emptied and filled with its required fuel. Notice very carefully that it was not Daniel alone who refused the royal food but his three Hebrew friends as well. When the guard compared their appearance with the rest of the people, he continued serving them vegetables. Were these four keeping some secrets regarding what is to be eaten as food? And what happened to their minds in the process after sticking to just eating the vegetables and drinking water?

> ***To these four young men God gave knowledge and understanding of all kinds of literature and learning.*** *And Daniel could understand visions and dreams of all kinds. 18 At the end of the time set by the king to bring them in, the chief official presented them to Nebuchadnezzar. 19* ***The king talked with them, and he found none equal to Daniel, Hananiah, Mishael and Azariah; so they entered the king's service.*** *20 In every matter of wisdom and understanding about which the king questioned them,* ***he found them ten times better than all the magicians and enchanters in his whole kingdom.*** *(Dan. 1:17-20)*

This was not a mere coincidence on the part of these four that they were all ten times better than those in the king's service at the time. Were they having the same IQ and reading the same books? They were running on the human fuel that made their minds function at its highest peak. They were applying principles that were alien to the rest of the Babylonians. In the end, God gave them the knowledge and understanding of all kinds of literature and learning. It is men like these who have left us with examples on how and where to go for the path that leads to God.

In a nutshell, we have seen from the Scriptures that the place or the source to go in search of the understanding of the Scriptures is actually with the former generations and not in the mouth of any special being with a different DNA today.

> *"When you shall see a soul which, having left all, cleaves unto the Word with every thought and desire, lives only for the Word, rules itself according to the Word and becomes fruitful by the Word—which is able to say with St. Paul, 'for me to live is Christ and to die is gain'—then you may have assurance that this soul is a bride wedded to the Word."—Bernard of Clairvaux (1091-1153)*

LESSONS FROM OUR FATHERS

If we have found the starting point of what we are looking for, then we can also proceed to find out the end of the tunnel. Solomon wrote: *"Train a child in the way he should go, and when he is old he will not turn from it" (Prov. 22:6).* Remember he told us earlier *to be wise and keep our hearts on the right path,* and that *stern discipline awaits him who leaves the path; he who hates correction will die (Prov. 23:19, 15:10).* We have also leant that the Scriptures are serving as examples for us to emulate. Since this is the case, we can go through the Bible to see what our fathers have said concerning the path. What training have they left for the children so that no matter how grown we become we should not turn from?

THE STARTING POINT

> *The fear of the LORD is the beginning of wisdom; all who follow His precepts have good understanding. To Him belongs eternal praise. (Psalm 111:10)*

Solomon taught us to *"Get wisdom, get understanding; do not forget my words or swerve from them. 6 Do not forsake wisdom, and she will protect you; love her, and she will watch over you. 7* ***Wisdom is supreme; therefore get wisdom. Though it cost all you have, get understanding****. 8 Esteem her and she will exalt you; embrace her, and she will honor you. 9 She will set a garland of grace on your head and present you with a crown of splendor" (Prov. 4:5-9).*

It is extremely important that we know the sort of wisdom that Solomon is referring to in these verses as there are several philosophies being paraded as wisdom on earth. Common sense should tell us that what he is talking about is far removed from what we know to exist in the systems of this world. For instance, Jesus told us to turn the other cheek when slapped in the face and give food and drinks to our enemies when they are hungry and thirsty. This was basically a teaching on forgiveness. But the system of this world will call us dumb, stupid and cowards if any of that is done to someone who wrongs us.

Paul wrote "We *do, however, speak a message of wisdom* ***among the mature, but not the wisdom of this age, who are coming to nothing.*** *7* ***No, we speak of God's secret wisdom, a wisdom that has been hidden and that God destined for our glory before time began.*** *8 None of the rulers of this age understood it, for if they had, they would not have crucified the LORD of glory" (1 Cor. 2:6-8).* We need only the wisdom of God to lead us to this path.

If the fear of the LORD is the beginning of God's wisdom, then we need to again ask our fathers how to tap into it because we are told this wisdom is supreme to all else and that though it costs us all we have, we should get understanding in addition to it.

WHERE CAN WE FIND WISDOM AND UNDERSTANDING?

> ***"But where can wisdom be found? Where does understanding dwell?*** *13 Man does not comprehend its worth; it cannot be found in the land of the living. 14 The deep says, 'It is not in me': the sea says, 'It is not with me.' 15 It cannot be bought with the finest gold, nor can its price be weighed in silver. 16 It cannot be bought with the gold of Ophir, with precious onyx or sapphires. 17 Neither gold nor crystal can compare with it, nor can it be had for jewels of gold. 18 Coral and jasper are not worthy of mention; the price of wisdom is beyond rubies. 19 The topaz of Cush cannot compare with it, it cannot be bought with pure gold. (Job 28:12-19)*

If it is true that wisdom cannot be found in the land of the living and man does not understand its worth, and if it cannot be bought with no amount of money or the precious minerals of this earth either, then where does it reside? ***"Where then does wisdom come from? Where does understanding dwell?*** *It is hidden from the eyes of every living thing, concealed even from the birds of the air. 22 Destruction and Death say, 'Only a rumor of it has reached our ears' (Job 28:20-22).*

> ***God understands the way to it, and He alone knows where it dwells,*** *24 for He views the ends of the earth and sees everything under the heavens. 25 When He established the force of the wind and measured out the waters, 26 when He made a decree for the rain and a path for the thunderstorm, 27 then He looked at wisdom and appraised it; He confirmed it and tested it. 28* ***And He said to man,***

'THE FEAR OF THE LORD—THAT IS WISDOM, AND TO SHUN EVIL IS UNDERSTANDING.' *(Job 28:23-28)*

Who, then, is the man that fears the LORD? He will instruct him in the way chosen for him. 13 He will spend his days in prosperity, and his descendants will inherit the land. 14 ***The LORD confides in those who fear Him; He makes His covenant known to them*** *(Psalm 25:12-14)*. This was confirmed in Job at one time when he said to his friends who had come to comfort him that *"I will teach you about the power of God;* ***the ways of the Almighty I will not conceal****" (Job 27:11)*. To be classified as wise is to fear the LORD, and to have understanding is to shun evil based on that fear or reverence for the LORD.

> *"The Word of God is in the Bible like the soul is in the body."—Peter Taylor Forsyth*

Solomon wrote: *"The path of life leads upward for the wise to keep him from going down to the grave" (Prov. 15:24)*. There has been a path since the days of our forefathers. With the help of God and the Scriptures which He gave us to serve as a guide, we will find this path. There is no other way apart from the Scriptures.

It is written "*To man belong the plans of the heart, but from the LORD comes the reply of the tongue" (Prov. 16:1)*. Again, it is written that *"There is no wisdom, no insight, no plan that can succeed against the LORD. 31 The horse is made ready for the day of battle, but victory rests with the LORD" (Prov. 21:30-31)*. We are again reminded by David that *"Know that the LORD is God. It is He who made us, and we are His; we are His people, the sheep of His pasture" (Psalm 100:3). To God belong wisdom and power; counsel and understanding are His (Job 12:13)*. God's own path is the best and true path to follow. There is no other.

GOD'S WORD IS THE FOUNDATION FOR PURITY

How can a young man keep his way pure? ***By living according to your word****. 10 I seek you with all my heart; do not let me stray from your commands. 11* ***I have bidden your word in my heart that I might not sin against you.*** *(Psalm 119:9-11)*

Several years after hiding the words of God in his heart that he might not sin against Him, let's hear David's testimony about the fruits he later reaped for doing so. He wrote in *Psalm 119:97-106* as follows:

> *Oh, how I love your law! I meditate on it all day long. 98* ***Your commands make me wiser than my enemies,*** *for they are ever with me. 99* ***I have more insight than all my teachers, for I meditate on your statutes.*** *100* ***I have more understanding than the elders, for I obey your precepts.*** *101 I have kept my feet from every evil path so that I might obey your word* (Remember that to have understanding is to shun evil). *102 I have not departed from your laws, for you yourself have taught me. 103 How sweet are your words to my taste, sweeter than honey to my mouth! 104* ***I gain understanding from your precepts; therefore I hate every wrong path****. 105* ***Your word is a lamp to my feet and a light for my path****. 106 I have taken an oath and confirm it, that I will follow your righteous laws.*

For planting that seed, he definitely had to reap its fruits because it is written "*Do not be deceived: God cannot be mocked.* ***A man reaps what he sows.*** *8 The one who sows to please his sinful nature, from that nature will reap destruction; the one who sows to please the Spirit, from the Spirit will reap eternal life" (Gal. 6:7-8).*

Notice carefully that David linked sticking to God's law to being directly taught by God Himself in *verse 102*. So, if we also want to be taught by God Himself today and we have been told to ask the former generations on how to do that, then it is quite obvious to know where David our forefather would tell us to turn our attention to.

THE FEAR OF THE LORD DEFINED

Let's now ask our forefathers to again teach us what really constitutes the fear of the LORD as there are several interpretations being given as its meaning today. David was so full of wisdom that they said he possessed the spirit of an angel *(2 Sam. 14:17, 20)*. He taught these things to his son Solomon and he also became the wisest man who ever lived and made gold to be like dust on the streets of Jerusalem. The testimonies of these two should be enough to teach us what we need to know about the fear of the LORD.

> *Come, my children, listen to me;* ***I will teach you the fear of the LORD****. 12 Whoever of you loves life and desire to see many*

> *good days, 13* ***keep your tongue from evil and your lips from speaking lies.*** *14* ***Turn from evil and do good; seek peace and pursue it.*** *15 The eyes of the LORD are on the righteous and His ears are attentive to their cry; 16 the face of the LORD is against those who do evil, to cut off the memory of them from the earth.*

We are being told by one of our forefathers that the fear of the LORD begins with keeping our tongues from evil and keeping our lips from speaking lies. It doesn't end there but we should take it a step further and completely turn from evil and start doing good. We should seek peace at all times and pursue it till our dying days. And the immediate effects of doing these are that we will see many good days, the eyes of the LORD will be on us 24/7, and His ears will be attentive to our prayers.

> ***The fear of the LORD is the beginning of wisdom, and knowledge of the Holy One is understanding.*** *11* ***For through me your days will be many, and years will be added to your life.*** *12* ***If you are wise, your wisdom will reward you;*** *if you are a mocker, you alone will suffer." (Prov. 9:10-12)*

Completely avoiding the way of sin is the beginning (or the foundation blocks to be laid to start building the structure) of wisdom. Having this knowledge at your disposal is the first step to possessing wisdom and to really know God is understanding. It is written: "***He who conceals his sins does not prosper, but whoever confesses AND RENOUNCES THEM finds mercy***" *(Prov. 28:13).* Notice that he equates knowledge of the Holy One to understanding. Job also taught us earlier that shunning evil is understanding. Then we can conclude that completely avoiding the evil ways of this world constitutes understanding the ways of God. It is again written that *"The fear of the LORD adds length to life, but the years of the wicked are cut short" (Prov. 10:27).*

TO FEAR THE LORD IS TO LIVE UPRIGHTLY

> *He whose walk is upright fears the LORD, but he whose ways are devious despises Him." Prov. 14:2)*

To *"despise," is to dislike and have no respect for someone or something.* So, all the excuses you have been giving since you became a Christian and still continuing in your evil ways claiming you are a descendant of Adam are simply your way of advertising your disrespect for the Almighty God. You revere Him by living an upright and pure life. The vulture has no business to do in the barber's shop. It is only a dog that returns to its vomit.

> *He who fears the LORD has a secure fortress, and for his children it will be a refuge. 27* ***The fear of the LORD is a fountain of life, turning a man from the snares of death.*** *(Prov. 14:26-27)*

Most Christians have wrongly interpreted the fear of the LORD to mean being afraid or scared of Him. This fear is about reverence. It's about respect for a loving Father. It's about simply taking God's word as what it is by obeying it. You don't begin to challenge Him with the knowledge of this world which is coming to nothing. For instance, if He tells you *not to have sexual relations with your father's wife who may or may not be your real mother (Lev. 18:8)*, you don't go around arguing and giving reasons why it is normal with you. God says the reason why He doesn't want you to do that is because it is going to dishonor your own father.

> ***The fear of the LORD teaches a man wisdom****, and humility comes before honor. (Prov. 15:33)*

You see, the mere fact that you can desist from sinning will set you on the path of attaining wisdom. Understanding the reasons why it is not right to sin is the starting point. When you grow in the knowledge of God and know the effects of sin on the human race, then you will be in a position to stay away from it completely. It doesn't take binding and losing the devil and demons to stop sinning. It takes the understanding of its negative effects and consequences on the sinner and those around him at large on the face of this earth.

WHO GAINS FROM OUR RIGHTEOUS OR EVIL ACTS?

> *"If you sin, how does that affect Him (God)? If your sins are many, what does that do to Him (God)? 7 If you are righteous, what do you give to Him (God), or what does He (God) receive from your hand? 8* ***Your wickedness affects only a man like yourself, and your righteousness only the sons of men."*** *(Job 35:6-8)*

Most people have been taught to believe that they are doing God a favor by living a righteous and sinless life. They seem to picture God as some stern looking hard-faced papa who sits on a throne with some long white robe wearing white long beard in heaven who frowns His face whenever His children commit sins and is happy when they do something righteous.

But the truth is that God will continue to be who He is forever and ever, no matter what and how we choose to live our lives. Even if all of us die and leave this earth empty, God will still remain who He is. Nothing can change God.

> *"Just as those at sea, who have been carried away from the direction of the harbor they are making for, regain the right course by the clear sign of some beacon or mountain peak, so the Scripture guides those adrift on the sea of life back to the harbor of God's will."—Gregory of Nyssa (C. 335-394)*

Until it dawns on your spirit to know and understand that your righteousness and/or sinful nature only affects your well-being and your fellow human being on this earth, you would not fully grasp the foundation of wisdom which starts from understanding the effects of sinning and thereby staying away from it. Shun your evil ways, stop sinning and live an upright and sinless life. That is the beginning of wisdom.

> *"The fear of the LORD leads to life:* ***then one rests content, untouched by trouble."*** *(Prov. 19:23)*

The words of the Scripture which are our examples and warnings lead to life when followed to the letter. *Elijah was a man just like us. He prayed earnestly that it would not rain, and it did not rain on the land for three and a half years. Again he prayed, and the heavens gave rain, and the earth produced its crops (James 5:17-18).* The same way, Adam and Methuselah were people just like us but they each lived for more than nine hundred years and above. If only we would want to study what our forefathers left for us, we would go far beyond where they stopped.

> *Blessed is the man who always fears the LORD, but he who hardens his heart falls into trouble. (Prov. 28:14)*

Well, this is what our forefathers have said. This is what the Scriptures teach. It now behooves on us to accept and follow what they taught as the Word of the Most High God or not. Or we can decide to scheme and distort the word of the Scriptures to suit what we want our itchy ears to hear. The ball is now in our courts. We can either take it or leave it; period.

CHAPTER FOUR

CAN THE BIBLE BE TRUSTED?

To answer this question well as to whether the Bible can be trusted or not has to do with first of all knowing whose words are contained in it and then accepting it as the final say regarding what is called truth. *"Can you fathom the mysteries of God? Can you probe the limits of the Almighty? 8 They are higher than the heavens—what can you do? They are deeper than the depths of the grave—what can you know? 9 Their measure is longer than the earth and wider than the sea" (Job 11:7-9). "Can anyone teach knowledge to God, since He judges even the highest?" (Job 21:22)*

> *"The Bible demands commentary because of its importance and character. It contains the sacred Scriptures of Judaism and Christianity and the primal literature of our culture; its significance for religion and culture calls for perennial work to interpret its texts in every generation. The books collected in the Bible were written in three different languages, in a succession of cultures, across centuries of time. To understand them, we need to call upon all the resources which the new knowledge available in our time can provide about their thought."—James L. Mays (Harper Bible Commentary, 1988)*

GOD'S PLANS REMAIN THE SAME THROUGH ALL GENERATIONS

> ***The plans of the LORD stand firm forever, the purposes of His heart through all generations*** *(Psalm 33:11).*

Peter reminds us that there are things in Paul's letters *"that are hard to understand, which ignorant and unstable people distort, as they do the other Scriptures, to their own destruction" (2 Pet. 3:16)*. It's sad to say that what some teachers of the Bible do by trying to interpret its message is to rather end up leaving it distorted. Even Jesus Christ, before and after His death and resurrection from the dead, didn't need anything outside what our forefathers had left behind, which is the Scriptures, to serve as examples to teach His disciples.

Coming across two of his disciples who failed to understand what was happening in their time, Jesus did not call down any Spirit from outer space to make things clearer for them to comprehend what was going on. But "***beginning with Moses and all the Prophets, He explained to them what was said in all the Scriptures concerning Himself***" *(Luke 24:27)*. And later when He came in the midst of His disciples, *He said to them, "This is what I told you while I was still with you: everything must be fulfilled that is written about me in the Law of Moses, the Prophets and the Psalms." 45* ***Then He opened their minds so they could understand the Scriptures*** *(Luke 24:44-45)*. If Jesus did not go around or ahead of the Scriptures to teach His message, who are we to think we can make a move like that? Have we grown more spiritual, powerful and knowledgeable than Christ, Paul and the rest of the apostles?

> *And the words of the LORD are flawless, like silver refined in a furnace of clay, purified seven times. (Psalm 12:6)*

To say that something is flawless simply means it is perfect. And a perfect thing is anything that is having everything that is necessary; complete and without faults or weaknesses. Some synonyms that come to mind for the word flawless are: complete, whole, entire, finished, unbroken, thorough, mature, ripe and absolute. Now, the Scripture says the words of the LORD are flawless. It then uses a figure of speech to say that it has been purified seven times which simply means it has been tried, tested and proven to be absolutely true. This should not surprise any of us because if it wasn't capable of doing so, Paul wouldn't tell Timothy that the Scriptures were able to make him *wise and thoroughly equipped for every good work*. Jesus Himself testified that the Scriptures cannot be broken.

> *As for God, His way is perfect; the word of the LORD is flawless. He is a shield for all who take refuge in Him. (Psalm 18:30)*

It is written, "*In the beginning was the Word, and the Word was with God,* ***and the Word was God.*** *2 He was with God in the beginning" (John 1:1-2)*. It says "the Word was God." Peter also wrote that *"Above all,* ***you must understand that no prophesy of Scripture came about by the prophet's own interpretation.*** *21* ***For prophesy never had its origin in the will of man, but men spoke from God as they were carried along by the Holy***

Spirit" *(2 Pet. 1:20-21)*. If this is true, which it is, then the Words of God and God Himself are ONE and the same. This makes the Word perfect and becomes a shield of refuge for whoever trusts in it.

POSITIVE EFFECTS OF LIVING BY THE WORD

> *The law of the LORD is perfect,* ***reviving the soul****. The statutes of the LORD are trustworthy,* ***making wise the simple****. 8 The precepts of the LORD are right,* ***giving joy to the heart****. The commands of the LORD are radiant,* ***giving light to the eyes****. 9 The fear of the LORD is pure,* ***enduring forever. The ordinances of the LORD are sure and altogether righteous****. 10 They are more precious than gold, than much pure gold; they are sweeter than honey, than honey from the comb. 11 By them is your servant warned;* ***in keeping them there is great reward.*** *(Psalm 19:7-11)*

The word *"revive"* is defined *as to become, or to make somebody or something become, conscious or healthy and strong again*. It is the word of God that revives your soul. A *statute is defined as "a law that is passed by a parliament, council, etc. and formally written down."* Since we've now been told by one of our forefathers that *"prophesy never had its origin in the will of man, but men spoke from God as they were carried along by the Holy Spirit,"* then the statutes of the LORD simply refers to the Words of God which have been written down for us to study and apply in our lives. David assures us that these words are trustworthy, and that we can count on them to make us wise. We already know what it means to fear the LORD which is the beginning of wisdom. If we trust His words, we'll practise them and that will lead us to wisdom.

Another word for precept is a principle and it implies a rule about how to behave or what to think. The LORD has His precepts written down for us which are distinct from the systems of this world. Living by His precepts, He says, is the right thing to do which gives joy to the heart of man. David applied these principles in his life and said at a point ***"I gain understanding from your precepts****; therefore I hate every wrong path. Your word is a lamp to my feet and a light for my path" (Psalm 119:104-105)*.

The fear of the LORD equals attaining the wisdom of God. Since this wisdom hasn't got expiry dates written on it, it remains pure at all times and endures forever. We do hear of best-sellers every now and then but most of them soon fade out from the system because the supposed "success principles" they teach become obsolete, outdated and in the long run gets relegated to the background for another one to take over, and the same cycle is repeated over and over again.

But the Bible has remained the all-time Best-seller. It is not just the Bible that is selling but the wisdom contained in its pages. You don't judge a book by its cover but its content *"For the word of the LORD is right and true; He is faithful in all He does. 5 The LORD loves righteousness and justice; the earth is full of His unfailing love (Psalm 33:4-5). "England has two books: the Bible and Shakespeare. England made Shakespeare, but the Bible made England"—Victor Hugo (1802-1885).*

THE LORD'S PRECEPTS ARE TRUSTWORTHY

> *Great are the works of the LORD; they are pondered by all who delight in them. 3 Glorious and majestic are His deeds, and His righteousness endures forever . . . 7 The works of His hands are faithful and just;* ***all His precepts are trustworthy.*** *8* ***They are steadfast forever and ever****, done in faithfulness and uprightness. 9 He provided redemption for His people;* ***He ordained His covenant for ever****—holy and awesome is His Name. (Psalm 111:2-9)*

The word *"forever"* is often used to say that a particular situation or state will always exist. It is written that ***"He who is the Glory of Israel does not lie or change His mind; for He is not a man, that He should change His mind"*** *(1 Sam. 15:29).* It is again written that ***"Remember this, fix it in mind, take it to heart****, you rebels. 9 Remember the former things, those of long ago; I am God, and there is no other; I am God, and there is none like me. 10* ***I make known the end from the beginning, from ancient times, what is still to come. I say: My purpose will stand, and I will do all that I please"*** *(Isaiah 46:8-10).* Now, if we claim to trust in the Word of God, do we doubt Him when He says His precepts and covenant were meant to last forever? Because the LORD does not change His mind, His words remain the same forever. The children of your great grandchildren will come and meet the Word of God still unchanged. Think about that.

Where are your forefathers now? And the prophets, do they live forever? 6 But did not my words and my decrees, which I commanded my servants the prophets, overtake your forefathers? (Zech. 1:5-6). Generations may come and go but the words of the LORD remain intact. Every word in the Scriptures including those that sound "silly" to the modern world, like *"an eye for an eye,"* were all meant to serve our own good. Solomon wrote *"Evil men do not understand justice,* ***but those who seek the LORD understand it fully****" (Prov. 28:5).* I'll give God's own reasons and purposes for each of the laws, decrees, statutes, commands and precepts in my subsequent books if it's the LORD'S will.

> ***Your word, O LORD, is eternal; it stands firm in the heavens.*** *90* ***Your faithfulness continues through all generations;*** *you established the earth, and it endures. 91 If your law had not been my delight, I would have perished in my affliction. 93* ***I will never forget your precepts, for by them you have preserved my life.*** *(Psalm 119:89-93)*

There you have it again! The Word of God is eternal and stands firm in the heavens. For a testimony about the wisdom of David as to whether he is worthy to be taken seriously at his word, it was said about him that *"My lord has wisdom like that of an angel of the LORD—**he knows everything that happens in the land**" (2 Sam. 14:20).* The man who knew everything that happened in the land says that had it not been his delight in the law of the LORD, he would have perished earlier in those days. And it was the precepts of the LORD that preserved his life. How was that possible? Well, as regards his health, for instance, he chose only what the Scriptures prescribed for him to eat and not to eat. He chose never to pay evil for his good towards others even though his life was in constant danger, simply because the Scriptures said so. He confessed his sins and completely renounced them when he was confronted with them. He made this his habit that he once said the Word of God had become a lamp to his feet.

THE SECRET TO DAVID'S GREATNESS

> *"Oh, how I love your law! I meditate on it all day long. 98 Your commands make me wiser than my enemies, for they are ever with me. 99 I have more insight than all my teachers, for I meditate on your statutes. 100* ***I have more understanding than the elders, for I obey your precepts.*** *101 I have kept my feet from every evil path so that I might obey your word. 102 I have not departed from your laws, for you yourself have taught me. 103 How sweet are your words to my taste, sweeter than honey to my mouth! 104 I gain understanding from your precepts; therefore I hate every wrong path. 105* ***Your word is a lamp to my feet and a light for my path.*** *106* ***I have taken an oath and confirmed it that I will follow your righteous laws."*** *(Psalm 119:98-106)*

The secrets to the greatness of David are all hidden in those verses that we just read. There were things he did to be qualified to have the Savior of the world come through his lineage. It didn't get to him by chance. The commands of the LORD made him wiser than the rest. He had more insight than all his teachers because he meditated on the statutes of the LORD. He had more understanding than the elders because he obeyed the precepts of the LORD.

> *Righteous are you, O LORD, and your laws are right. 138* ***The statutes you have laid down are righteous; they are fully trustworthy****. 139 My zeal wears me out, for my enemies ignore your words. 140* ***Your promises have been thoroughly tested, and your servant loves them****. 141 Though I am lowly and despised, I do not forget your precepts. 142* ***Your righteousness is everlasting and your law is true****. 143 Trouble and distress have come upon me, but your commands are my delight. 144* ***Your statutes are forever right****; give me understanding that I may live. (Psalm 119:137-144)*

Humanly speaking, I just can't find the most fitting words to express how privileged I am to be taught by the father of Solomon. *To say that something is right is to do something morally good or acceptable; what is correct according to law or a person's duty*. The LORD calls His words right and fully trustworthy. Like me, David felt pain in his heart because the majority of the people who are expected to receive and implement the principles of God for their own good have rather chosen to follow fables, totally ignoring the way of the Lord. The promises in the Bible were thoroughly tested by our forefathers before passing them to the next generations. The LORD'S statutes are to last forever.

GOD'S STATUTES ESTABLISHED TO LAST FOREVER

> *Those who devise wicked schemes are near, but they are far from your law. 151 Yet you are near, O LORD,* ***and all your commands are true****. 152* ***Long ago I learned from your statutes that you established them to last forever.*** *(Psalm 119:150-152)*

If something is true, it is usually connected with facts rather than things that have been invented or concocted. The commands of the LORD are simply true, period. And the earthly great grandfather of our LORD Jesus Christ says *he learned from long ago that the statutes of the LORD were established to last forever.* It is written: ***"But the plans of the LORD stand firm for ever, the purposes of His heart through all generations"*** *(Psalm 33:11)*. If it is true that God established His statutes to last forever, and He does not change His mind, then, are we excluded from eternity? The

Scriptures can never be broken. Jesus said until heaven and earth disappears, not a single jot will disappear from God's word. Can you be courageous enough for once and accept this as the very Words of God? The answer lies with you.

> ***All your words are true; all your righteous laws are eternal.*** *(Psalm 119:160)*

Contrary to what you have heard all this while, all of God's laws are righteous and are there to serve each and every generation that will appear on earth. Changing the commands and laws of God would be like changing God Himself. He is timeless and ageless. He will forever remain the same God with the same principles governing the universe.

> *Seven times a day I praise you for your righteous laws. 165* ***Great peace have they who love your law, and nothing can make them stumble.*** *166 I wait for your salvation, O LORD, and I follow your commands. 167 I obey your statutes for I love them greatly. (Psalm 119:164-167)*

Some of these things sound unbelievable at times that a man will actually pray seven times a day just in praise of the laws of God in the Scriptures. But I can assure you that when you also become enlightened into these things, you would do more than that. For instance, I see the solutions to all the problems on our planet in the Scriptures. But unfortunately the world has turned deaf ears to them. And the people who are supposed to teach it have resolved to explaining or interpreting it instead of first understanding it and passing on the teaching. "*Though it costs you all you have, get understanding.*"

GOD AND HIS WORD ARE THE SAME

> *I will bow down towards your holy temple and will praise your name for your love and your faithfulness,* ***for you have exalted above all things your Name and your Word.*** *(Psalm 138:2)*

"*In the beginning was the Word and the Word was God.*" God and His Word are the same so if you choose to ignore His Word, it is simply God you have ignored. Practically speaking, if I want to disrespect any of my parents, there wouldn't be a better and simpler way to do that than to just ignore what they ask me to do. It's as simple as that. So if you refuse to live by the Words of Scripture contained in the Bible, it is simply the LORD God you are ignoring because He has exalted His Name, which equals His Word above everything else.

> ***He has revealed His Word to Jacob, His laws and decrees to Israel.*** *20* ***He has done this for no other nation; they do not know His laws.*** *(Psalm 147:19-20)*

Jacob is the same as Israel in the Bible. God Almighty says He has revealed His Word to Jacob and His laws and decrees to Israel. In order not to create any confusion in the future He stressed on the fact that He has not revealed His Words, laws and decrees to any other nation on earth. There is no other nation that has the Word of God as the people of Israel. For instance, the teachings and principles of Plato, Karl Max and Stalin did not originate from Israel, and therefore cannot be taken to replace those of the LORD God. Paul confirmed this when he wrote to the Romans that: *"What advantage, then, is there in being a Jew, Much in every way!* ***First of all, they have been entrusted with the very words of God"*** *(Rom. 3:1-2).*

PARENTS' FIRST RESPONSIBILITY: TEACHING THE WORD TO THEIR WARDS

> *My son, keep your father's commands and do not forsake your mother's teaching. 21 Bind them upon your heart forever; fasten them around your neck. 22 When you walk, they will guide you; when you sleep, they will watch over you; when you awake, they will speak to you. 23* ***For these commands are a lamp*** *[speaking his father's language],* ***this teaching is a light, and the corrections of discipline are the way to life****, 24 keeping you from the immoral woman, from the smooth tongue of the wayward wife. (Prov. 6:20-24)*

I have read about, heard and seen some parents forcing unhealthy things down the throats of their children all in the name of advising them and insisting the children should abide by whatever they teach them based on the above Scriptural verses. But they forget the fact that what they are told to teach their children is the Word of God and not just any teachings that come from the wisdom of this world. It is written: *"Only be careful, and watch yourselves closely so that you do not forget the things your eyes have seen or let them slip from your heart as long as you live.* ***Teach them to your children and to their children after them****"* (Deut. 4:9).

"So the Bible is to help us learn how to live in the kingdom of God here and now. It teaches us how to morph. It is indispensable for this task. I have never known someone leading a spiritually-transformed life who had not been deeply saturated in Scripture."—John Ortberg

So it is the Word of God that parents are commanded to teach their children. The children on the other hand are told to bind these teachings on their necks as symbols. The Word of the LORD deals with all the youthful issues of life. The Word is a lamp to the feet of any youth who chooses the path of the LORD. Adhering to the Word and leading a disciplined life on earth is the sure way to life.

KEEPING GOD'S COMMANDS TO LIVE SECURELY

> ***Keep my commands and you will live; guard my teachings as the apple of your eye.*** *3 Bind them on your fingers; write them on the tablet of your heart. 4 Say to wisdom, "You are my sister" and call understanding your kinsman; 5* ***they will keep you from the adulteress, from the wayward wife with her seductive words.*** *(Prov. 7:2-5)*

This is a promise from God that we will live the abundant life if we keep His commands. Paul wrote to the Corinthians that ***"Now the body is not made up of one part but of many.*** *If the foot should say, 'Because I am not a hand, I do not belong to the body,' it would not for that reason cease to be part of the body. 16 And if the ear should say, 'Because I am not an eye, I do not belong to the body,' it would not for that reason cease to be part of the body. If the whole body were an eye, where would the sense of hearing be? If the whole body were an ear, where would the sense of smell be? 18* ***But in fact, God has arranged the parts in the body, every one of them, just as He wanted them to be*** *(1 Cor. 12:14-18).*

It is true that no part of the body is more important than the other, yet you will agree with me that the eye is one part of the body that receives quite a great deal of attention from everyone living because of how delicate it is among the parts. This is often done consciously or unconsciously. God is saying that just as we protect our eyes from any harm that might come in contact with it, we should guard His teachings as the apple of our eyes. The heart is often used in the Bible and other writings to represent the centre or the very core of man, the controlling centre of every decision that springs out of man. And we are told to write these teachings on the tablet of our hearts.

> *To you, O men, I call out; I raise my voice to all mankind. 5 You who are simple, gain prudence; you who are foolish, gain understanding. 6 Listen, for I have worthy things to say; I open my lips to speak what is right. 7 My mouth speaks what is true, for my lips detest wickedness. 8* ***All the words of my mouth are just; none of them is crooked or perverse.*** *9* ***To the discerning all of them are right; they are faultless to those who have knowledge.*** *10 Choose my instruction instead of silver, knowledge rather than choice gold, for wisdom is more precious than rubies, and nothing you desire can compare with it . . . 13* ***To fear the LORD is to hate evil;*** *I hate pride and arrogance, evil behavior and perverse speech . . . 15 By me kings reign and rulers make laws that are just; 16 by me princes govern, and all nobles who rule on earth . . . 18 With me are riches and honor, enduring wealth and prosperity. (Prov. 8:4-18)*

As you mature in the knowledge of God and grow into the full knowledge of Christ, you would learn that truly having Christ Jesus dwelling in your inner being grants you the grace and power to possess this wisdom that Solomon is writing about in these verses. In fact, he was actually talking about Jesus Christ when under the inspiration of the Spirit of God, he was mentioning this wisdom.

> *The LORD works out everything for His own ends—even the wicked for a day of disaster. (Prov. 16:4)*

Solomon wrote in the Book of Ecclesiastes that *"I know that everything God does will endure forever, nothing can be added to it and nothing taken from it.* ***God does it so that men will revere Him****. Whatever is has already been, and what will be has been before; and God will call the past to account" (Prov. 3:14-15).* Indeed, there is nothing new under the sun. The Word of the LORD stands firm forever and ever. It will never be done away with. No matter how sophisticated the systems of this world get, the Word of God will remain the same.

> *"The Scriptures come first. If you are in doubt upon any subject, you must, first of all, consult the Bible about it, and see whether there is any law there to direct you. Until you have found and obeyed God's will as it is there revealed, you must not ask nor expect a separate, direct, personal revelation. A great many fatal mistakes are made in the matter of guidance by the overlooking of this simple rule."— Hannah Whitall Smith (1832-1911)*

LESSONS FROM THE APOSTLES

The greater part of what I have said so far concerning whether the Bible can be trusted or not came from the Old Testament. Most of the modern-day Christians have been brain-washed to accept the teaching that the Old Testament has been done away with and nailed to a certain cross when Jesus died for our sins. So, for giving such people the benefit of the doubt, let me quote some few things from the New Testament as well for you to know how much research work was carried out for these Words to be written down. And do not forget the fact that the apostles of Christ Jesus also constitute our forefathers, and we need to be careful to study their stories and search out for the results they've left behind for us to emulate.

> *That which was from the beginning,* ***which we have heard, which we have seen with our eyes, which we have looked at and our hands have touched—this we proclaim concerning the Word of life****. 2 The life appeared; we have seen it and testify to it, and we proclaim to you the eternal life, which was with the Father and has appeared to us. 3* ***We proclaim to you what we have seen and heard, so that you also may have fellowship with us****. And our fellowship is with the Father and with His Son, Jesus Christ. 4 We write this to make our joy complete. (1 John 1-4)*

This is what came out from the pen of John that they did not receive these things written from any obscure corners of the earth; rather they were there, saw and heard everything with their own eyes and ears. And it was the same gospel they learned from the LORD that they proclaimed as the gospel of Christ. The message they received was not altered in any way to meet the demands of the day for it to be accepted by the secular world. They didn't compromise on the foundational truths they received from their Master. They did not adjust the gospel of Christ to make it marketable and "attractive" to the world. They didn't borrow ideas from the world and branded them "Christian" to make them sell to win crowds.

> *Many have undertaken to draw up an account of the things that have been fulfilled among us, 2 just as they were handed down to us* ***by those who from the first were eye-witnesses*** *and servants of the word. 3 Therefore,* ***since I myself have carefully investigated everything from the beginning, it seemed good to me also to write an orderly account for you, most excellent Theophilus,*** *4* ***so that you may know the certainty of the things you have been taught.*** *(Luke 1:1-4)*

Although Luke was not a direct disciple of Jesus Christ, he received his information from those who *"were eye-witnesses and servants of the Word."* The Word in that passage refers to Jesus Christ because it is written: *"In the beginning was the Word, and the Word was with God,* ***and the Word was God*** *. . . 14* ***The Word became flesh and made His dwelling among us.*** *We have seen His glory,* ***the glory of the One and only, who came from the Father,*** *full of grace and truth" (John 1:1-2, 14).* Being the wise man that he was, Luke only chose to write an orderly account of his version after he had carried out thorough investigations into every inch for the recipients (i.e. you and me) to know the certainty of what he had been taught. The Bible was not written by amateurs.

> *The Spirit gives life; the flesh counts for nothing.* ***The words I have spoken to you are spirit and they are life.*** *(John 6:63)*

Words are actually spirits. Take, for instance, a child who has heard all his life how ugly, timid and stupid he looks by his parents. The majority of such children grows up lacking in confidence, zeal and is always shy and finds it difficult to mingle with the rest of the society. In the same way, a child who has heard all his life how smart, intelligent and handsome he looks normally comes out best in his field of endeavor. The story is told of a sixty year old marriage which broke up because the wife said to the husband that he resembled his father in terms of his anger. Jesus also says that His Words give life. This means if we implement His teachings, we will be in a position to deal with all the hard questions of life.

> *For I did not speak of my own accord, but the Father who sent me commanded me what to say and how to say it, 50* ***I know that His command leads to eternal life****. So whatever I say is just what the Father has told me to say. (John 12:49-50)*

The LORD has said in the Psalms that *"I will not violate my covenant or alter what my lips have uttered" (Psalm 89:34).* It is also written about God, *"He who is the Glory of Israel does not lie or change His mind; for He is not a man that He should change His mind" (1 Sam. 15:29).* Now, if Jesus says that He was sent by the Father, then it simply means that He could not say anything that was contrary to what the Father had said earlier in the Scriptures prior to His coming to earth because the Father does not lie or change His mind. Jesus Himself said: *"I tell you the truth, no servant is greater than his master,* ***nor is a messenger greater than the one who sent him****" (John 13:16).* Jesus Christ had [has and will forever have] the Word of God. He Himself is the Word and therefore cannot alter Himself.

> *"Every Christian ought to be a Bible Reader. It is the One Habit, which, if done in the right spirit, more than any other one habit, will make a Christian what he ought to be in every way."—Halley's Bible Handbook, 1965*

WE MUST NOT ADD TO OR SUBTRACT FROM THE SCRIPTURES

We have been equipped very much with the words in the Bible so much so that we have been commanded not to add or subtract from it. Even Jesus Christ who *"is the image of the invisible God, the firstborn over all creation" (Col. 1:15)* did not add to or subtract from what had been written. When John the Baptist tried to prevent Him from being baptized by him (John), Jesus replied, *"Let it be so now;* ***it is proper for us to do this to fulfill all righteousness.****" Then John consented (Matt. 3:15).* Although He could have easily done what the devil was asking of Him, Jesus replied each of his requests by saying that ***"It is written."*** That means that He could not go beyond what was already written in the Scriptures. In the same way, we have no right in adding to or subtracting from the Word of God. This should not be hard to take.

Zophar, the friend of Job asked, *"Can you fathom the mysteries of God? Can you probe the limits of the Almighty? 8 They are higher than the heavens—what can you do? They are deeper than the depths of the grave—what can you know? 9 Their measure is longer than the earth and wider than the sea" (Job 11:7-9).* Now, you who are claiming equality into the stature of Christ Jesus and trying to add to or subtract from what is already written—are you really sure of what you are saying, teaching and doing? What can you do and what can you know? Can you understand the mysteries of God more than God Himself? Humble yourself, friend.

> *Every word of God is flawless; He is a shield to those who take refuge in Him. 6 Do not add to His words, or He will rebuke you and prove you a liar. (Prov. 30:5-6)*

Jesus once said, *"For there is nothing hidden that will not be disclosed, and nothing concealed that will not be known or brought out into the open" (Luke 8:17).* The Word of God has been with man for not less than four thousand years now and it still makes sense when applied to our lives. How old are you that you want to teach the omnipotent, omnipresent and omniscient

God? Has it come to that level where you think you can actually teach God something He doesn't know? Wait till you are at least a hundred years old. *"For God will bring every deed into judgment, including every hidden thing, whether good or evil" (Eccl. 12:14).*

> *The Teacher searched to find just the right words,* ***and what He wrote was upright and true.*** *11* ***The words of the wise are like goads, their collected sayings like firmly embedded-nails given by One Shepherd.*** *12* ***Be warned, my son, of anything in addition to them.*** *Of making many books there is no end, and much study wearies the body." (Eccl. 12:10-12)*

You see, the collected materials in the Scriptures are like firmly-embedded nails delivered from One Shepherd—God—through various wise men in the past ages to those of us living today. Because these writings are true and upright, we have been warned from adding anything further to or subtracting from them. At the later part of verse twelve, it seems Solomon was pleading with us to stick to the Bible because he knew there would be other books published in every generation. He was, in a sense, saying that adding other materials to the Word of God would only weary our minds. I have done some little reading myself and I can assure you that the Bible reigns supreme to any other book I've ever read.

> *I warn everyone who hears the words of the prophecy of this book: If anyone adds anything to them, God will add to him the plagues described in this book. 19 And if anyone takes words away from this book of prophecy, God will take away from him his share in the tree of life and in the holy city, which are described in this book. (Rev. 22:18-19)*

Friends in the assembly of the Most High God, you can bet your life on the Bible, and there is no need to either add or take anything from it. The words in it are life to those who find them. The Scriptures are there *"for attaining wisdom and discretion; for understanding words of insight; 3 for acquiring a disciplined and prudent life, doing what is right and just and fair; 4 for giving prudence to the simple, knowledge and discretion to the young—5 let the wise listen (or study) and add to their learning, and let the discerning get guidance—6 for understanding proverbs and parables, the sayings and riddles of the wise" (Prov. 1:2-6).* The Scriptures are 100% trustworthy.

Chapter Five

THE BIBLE UNDER ATTACK

"*Bible reading is an education in itself." (Lord Tennyson Alfred, 1809-1892)* The paths mostly chosen by people pertaining to the choices or philosophies they apply in approaching life remind me of a quote that reads: *"The greatest hazard in life is to risk nothing. The person who risks nothing does nothing and has nothing. You may avoid suffering and sorrow, but you simply cannot learn, feel, change, grow, live or love chained by your certitudes. You'll be a slave. Only the person who risks is free."*

Personally, I wouldn't begrudge a person for applying this approach to life as I have been a risk taker myself. I have made some decisions in life which mostly seem unwise to friends and family. But the question is "Must you risk everything in life without personally taking the initiative and time to investigate yourself what you are getting yourself into?" It is true some things are better left unsaid but some risks, when taken, can be very expensive. With all the several warnings given by God through the prophets, Jesus and later His apostles about the distortion of His Word in later days, must we just risk it and blindly hope that God will protect us from the distorted versions that are being taught in place of the Word of God just because someone claims he has been anointed to interpret the Bible?

In the introduction of his book *"Liar's Paradise,"* Mr. Graham Edmonds wrote that:

> *"Deception is endemic in our corporate society and everyone who works within a company (large or small) has to decide at some point, whether a life of lying is for them. For some it comes naturally, even unconsciously (as they lie to themselves),* ***while for others it's a game that has to be learned, but whichever way you look at it, there's a choice to be made . . .*** *Evil characters in movies are always the most watchable and it's the same in real life, we can't help it . . .* ***good equals boring while evil equals excitement. We're drawn to people who offer a little danger and we like***

> ***to take risks. It's dull being good all the time so why not spice up life with a little mischief?...*** *On the face of it lying works in most areas of businesses so* ***if your aim is to make as much money as possible then it's a profitable policy, but the question is 'Can you live with it?'***
>
> *"Before we answer this and get too moral and self-righteous, it's worth taking time to think what sort of a world it would be if everyone told the truth and there were no lies. There would be no crime and what would we watch on TV? ...*
>
> *"Normal business couldn't function, and whichever society exists would be a heartless one,* ***with no doubt, massive unemployment****. There would be no end to the tedium of it.* ***Life would be boring as no doubt we would all clam up, being crippled by the endless criticism that complete honesty brings. We need lies for the world to function and to smooth the interaction between us. LIES ARE THE LUBRICANT THAT DAMPENS THE FRICTION THAT TOTAL HONESTY BRINGS."*** (Emphasis mine)

In this same book, Mr. Graham Edmonds said that the ultimate degree of deceit is to tell *"a lie so large it must be true because no one would dare to say it if it wasn't."* This, he said, was a 'trick' inherited from the Nazis and their propagandist Dr. Joseph Goebbels who said: ***"If you tell a lie big enough and keep repeating it, people will eventually come to believe it."*** I must admit that just reading the introduction of this book alone by my learned colleague has been an eye opener for me and I'm very grateful and privileged to have had the opportunity to read it.

> *"Every type of destruction that human philosophy, human science, human reason, human art, human cunning, human force, and human brutality could bring to bear against a book has been brought to bear against this Book, and yet the Bible stands absolutely unshaken today. At times, almost all the wise and great of the earth have been pitted against the Bible, and only an obscure few for it. Yet it has stood."—Reuben Archer Torrey (1856-1928)*

The collection of writings that we know as the Bible, or the Holy Scriptures, was recorded over a period of more than 1,600 years. The earliest part of this collection was written by Moses; the last, by a disciple of Jesus Christ called John about a hundred years after His birth. Efforts to silence the Scriptures have a long history extending from well before our Common Era, through the middle Ages, and down to modern times. An early record of such efforts dates back to the time of God's prophet Jeremiah, who lived over 600 years before the birth of Jesus Christ.

THE START OF FIGHTING AGAINST THE BIBLE

Jeremiah was once directed by God to write in a scroll a message condemning the sinful inhabitants of ancient Judah, and warning them that their capital city, Jerusalem, would be destroyed unless they changed their ways. His secretary, Baruch, read the message aloud in public in Jerusalem's temple. He read it a second time in the hearing of Judah's princes, who took the scroll to king Jehoiakim. *As the king listened to God's words, he did not like what he heard. So he cut the scroll into pieces and burned it (Jer. 36:1-23).*

> *After the king burned the scroll containing the words that Baruch had written at Jeremiah's dictation, the word of the LORD came to Jeremiah: 28 "Take another scroll and write on it all the words that were on the first scroll, which Jehoiakim king of Judah burned up." (Jer. 36:27-28)*

Some years later, exactly as God's word through Jeremiah had foretold, Jerusalem was destroyed and many of its rulers were slain, and its inhabitants were taken into exile in Babylon. The messages that the scroll conveyed—and a record of the circumstances surrounding the attack made upon it—have survived until our day in the book of Jeremiah.

King Jehoiakim was not the only person in pre-Christian times who attempted to burn God's Word. Following the breakup of the Greek Empire, Israel came under the influence of the Seleucid dynasty. The Seleucid king Antiochus Epiphanes, who ruled from 175 to 164 B.C.E., wanted to unite his empire in Greek or Hellenistic culture. To that end, he attempted to force Greek ways, customs and religion on the Jews in those days.

About 168 B.C.E., Antiochus Epiphanes plundered God's temple in Jerusalem. On top of the altar, he built another in honour of the Greek god Zeus. He also banned the observance of the Sabbath and prevented the Jews from circumcising their sons on the eighth day according to the custom of God. The penalty for non-compliance was death.

An element of that religious purgation was Antiochus' attempt to destroy all scrolls of the Law. Although he pursued his campaign throughout Israel, he failed to destroy all copies of the Hebrew Scriptures available at the time. Some carefully-concealed scrolls may well have escaped the flames inside

Israel, and copies of the Holy Scriptures were known to have been preserved by colonies of Jews living elsewhere.

Another prominent ruler who tried to destroy the Scriptures was the Roman Emperor Diocletian. In 303 C.E., he promulgated a series of increasingly harsh edicts against Christians. This resulted in what some historians have termed "The Great Persecution." His first edict ordered the burning of copies of the Scriptures and the demolition of Christian meeting places.

Harry Y. Gamble, professor of religious studies at the University of Virginia, wrote: *"Diocletian took it for granted that every Christian community, wherever it might be, had a collection of books and knew that those books were essential to its viability."* Church historian Eusebius of Caesarea, Palestine, who lived during that period, reported: *"We saw with our eyes the houses of prayer cast down to their foundations from top to bottom, and the inspired and sacred Scriptures committed to the flames in the midst of the market-places."*

Three months after Diocletian's edict, the mayor of the North African city which later became known as Constantine, is said to have ordered the Christians to hand over all their "writings of the law" and "copies of scripture." Accounts of the same period tell of Christians who preferred to be tortured and killed rather than to hand over copies of the Bible to be destroyed.

The shared intent of Jehoiakim, Antiochus, and Diocletian was to wipe out God's Word. Yet the Bible has survived all attempts to destroy it. Various rulers have also continued in this practice since the rules afore mentioned. Most of them claimed that Bible burning were not attempts to destroy the Bible. Rather, they were simply trying to keep the Bible out of the hands of the common people. But why would they want to do that? And to what heights did they go in their efforts to suppress Bible reading among people? And who are the common people anyways?

It is written about Christ that *"He came and preached peace to you who were far away and peace to those who were near. 18 For through Him we both have access to the Father by one Spirit. 19 Consequently, you are no longer foreigners and aliens, but fellow citizens with God's people and members of God's household, 20 built on the foundation of the apostles and prophets, with Christ Jesus Himself as the chief cornerstone . . . 22 And in Him you too are being built together to become a dwelling in which God lives by His Spirit." (Eph. 2:17-22)* There are no common people in Christ.

THE MAIN REASON BEHIND PREVENTING BIBLE READING

The main reason why all these rulers have thought of destroying the Bible is the fact that they believe, like Mr. Graham pointed out, that ***"We need lies for the world to function and to smooth the interaction between us. Lies are the lubricant that dampens the friction that total honesty brings."*** To them, good equals boring while evil equals excitement and the latter is good for business while the former is not. They believe it is dull being good all the time and so lies must be used to spice life up with a little mischief here and there. The contents of the Bible repeatedly point an accusing finger straight at them for the processes they use to keep the rest of mankind in subjection to their hypocritical lies intended to make profits at the expense of the lives of living souls created in the image and likeness of God.

For instance, some years back, the United States of America used to have the Ten Commandments pasted on the wall of law courts and other public places like schools. They were also kept in major centres in their cities where people could read them at will. That is no longer the case. Most people especially Christians have been convinced to think that it's because of the Name of God and the mention of Sabbath that made them take that decision. But it is actually the last five of the commandments that necessitated that call. The last half of the Ten Commandments read:

> *You shall not murder. 14 You shall not commit adultery. 15 You shall not steal. 16 You shall not give false testimony against your neighbour. 17 You shall not covet your neighbour's house. You shall not covet your neighbour's wife, or his manservant or maidservant, his ox or donkey, or anything that belongs to your neighbour. (Exod.20:14-17)*

Those in high places think total honesty and righteousness make the world a boring place to live in, which in turn make it unsuitable for the smooth running of businesses to aid the maximisation of profits, and therefore have to lubricate the truths of God with lies, murder, stealing, adultery, covetousness and giving false testimonies against each other.

For instance, how do you expect the pharmaceutical industries to be in business if the youth of today decide to wait till marriage before they engage in any form of sexual contact? That alone would reduce the number of various sexually transmitted diseases like gonorrhoea, syphilis, candidiasis and AIDS. And how do you expect the billion-dollar industries to market their goods and services when the citizens of a nation are told not to covet their neighbour's properties and possessions? One has to covet to make an impulse buy. Preaching the abolition of the Ten Commandments from the law courts in the name of freedom of religion indirectly makes it okay to steal, murder, covet, sleep with the wife of your friend but just make sure you don't end up being caught and that's good for business.

Now, isn't it obvious to know why some *"Christians"* too are bent on seeing to the removal of the statutes, commands, decrees and laws which the LORD established to last forever from being observed today? A pastor can now look straight into one's eye and tell blatant lies in the name of God. For something to be changed means that it is wrong, deformed or outdated. Is it okay for a Christian to steal, murder, commit adultery, give false testimony or covet anything that belongs to his or her neighbour? Jesus was right when He said, *"You have a fine way of setting aside the commands of God in order to observe (or market) your own traditions" (Mark 7:9).*

Some of the traditions or ideas of the elders today include the belief that: ***"We need lies for the world to function and to smooth the interaction between us. Lies are the lubricant that dampens the friction that total honesty brings."*** Like modern-day journalism, it seems truth does not sell. It's often bad news items that do. Has it occurred to you to ask why the various media houses spend most of their major bulletins on the bad things that are happening in the world? That is how the media game is played. They create panic in the hearts and minds of people to feel that the world is coming to an end, and in the end, most of them are filled with fear and confusion and turn to crave for knowing what will happen next.

The world is filled with good people as well. There are those who live their entire lives thinking about how to make this world a better place for others especially the poor to live in. There are those who know they cannot change the entire world yet spend time concentrating on how to better the lives of those in their little communities. As a man thinks in his heart, so is he. If you think the world is only dark and is controlled by the devil, that's what you will see for the rest of your life.

To some of us, *"God is the King of all the earth . . . He reigns over the nations." (Psalm 47:7-8) "The heavens are yours, and yours also the earth; You founded the world and all that is in it" (Psalm 89:11-12).* No matter how bleak and dark the world seems to you, if you can declare with Joshua that *"As for me and my household, we will serve the LORD," (Josh. 24:15)* God will repeat what He said to Noah, Abraham, Isaac and Jacob to you that *"I will make you into a great nation and I will bless you; I will make your name great, and you will be a blessing" (Gen. 12:2).*

The Bible reveals exactly how the systems of the world operate and therefore those in high places would not want us have access to its full details. Why won't China, for instance, allow its citizens to own Bibles? It is because if its citizens read the Bible, they would know that God did not create a man to be ruled by another man through systems like communism.

The circulation of the Bible is even more impressive in the light of the numerous attempts that have been made throughout the world to suppress it. The 19th century theologian Albert Barnes once wrote: *"No book has excited so much opposition as this; but it has survived every attack which power, talent, and eloquence have ever made on it."* He continued, *"But no army ever survived so many battles as the Bible, no ancient bulwark has endured so many sieges, and stood so firm amid the thunders of war and the ravages of time; and no rock has been swept by so many currents, and has still stood unmoved."*

> *"The Bible—banned, burned, beloved—is more widely read, more frequently attacked than any other book in history. Generations of intellectuals have attempted to discredit it; dictators of every age have outlawed it and executed those who read it. Yet soldiers carry it into battle, believing it more powerful than their weapons. Fragments of it smuggled into solitary prison cells have transformed ruthless killers into gentle saints."—Charles. W. Colson*

During the periods of colonisation in Africa, the European nations came to rule and made slaves out of our ancestors in their own backyards. They later found that process tedious and decided to offer us freedom in the form of independence. This even made ruling our lands easier for them. This is because it offered them the opportunity to just lend monies to us through their various agencies. In the end, they decide for us how that money is to be used to maximise their return on investment. They become the masters while we remain slaves. Solomon wrote, *"The borrower is servant to the lender."* To give you a fair idea of how this is done through their agents in every nation, let's read these few paragraphs from Bill Hughes' book *"The Enemy Unmasked:"*

> *"It is necessary to understand that the Federal Reserve Bank is not owned by the United States government, as many believe.* ***The central bank, the Federal Reserve Bank, is a private bank, owned by some of the richest and most powerful people in the world. This bank has nothing to do with the U.S. government other than the connection, which allows the operation described below.*** *The private Federal Reserve Bank has a total, government-enforced monopoly in money. Before we had the central bank, each individual bank competed with other banks; the customers, the consumers, got the best deal, not anymore.*
>
> ***"We all know that today the United States government borrows money and operates under astronomical debt. Why***

> ***is this so?*** *Common sense dictates that a policy of such enormous debt will sooner or later destroy the organisation that practises it, because the interest on its debt must increase beyond its income, making payoff impossible.*
>
> *"Now to our scenario. Roughly, here is how the operation proceeds. Suppose the United States government wants to borrow a billion dollars. The government issues a bond for this amount, much as a water company does when it wants to raise money for a new pipeline or a new dam. The government delivers this bond of the billion dollars to the Federal Reserve Bank. The Federal Reserve Bank takes the bond and writes an order to the Department of Printing and Engraving to print the billion dollars' worth of bills. After about two weeks or so, when the bills are printed, the Department of Printing and Engraving ships the bills to the Federal Reserve Bank, which then writes a cheque for about two thousand dollars to pay for printing the billion dollars' worth of bills. The Federal Reserve Bank then take the billion dollars and lends the billion dollars to the United States government, and the people of the country pay interest at an exorbitant rate each year on this money, which came out of nothing. The owners of the Federal Reserve Bank put up nothing for this money.*
>
> ***"We see, therefore, that when the United States government goes into debt one dollar, a dollar plus the interest goes into the pockets of the owners of the Federal Reserve Bank.*** *This is the largest, the most colossal theft ever perpetrated in the history of mankind, and it is so slick, so subtle, and so obfuscated by propaganda from the news media that the victims are not even aware of what is happening.*
>
> *"The Constitution of the United States gives to Congress the power to coin. If Congress coined its own money as the Constitution directs, it would not have to pay the hundreds of billions of dollars of interest that it now pays each year to the bankers for the national debt, for money that came out of nothing. Money coined by Congress would be debt-free.* ***All the central banks in other countries operate the way the Federal Reserve does.****"* (Emphasis mine).

If this is done right before the eyes of the thousands of *"prophets"* who hear from God in a country like the U.S., how much more those of us on the African continent? Does God approve of this system to be used on His children or has it escaped His notice? How can someone heal another of blindness but cannot read unless assisted by a pair of glasses? How can one heal such diseases like AIDS, cancer, Alzheimer and Leukaemia but die of mosquito bites? Doesn't God care about banking and financing? I've read the Bible, and I know He does.

In the same way, instead of fighting battles to destroy the Holy Scriptures of the Bible, these forces working behind the scenes have joined hands with some "Church" groups and are gradually belittling the words of God through the medium of trying to interpret the Bible. And some of them have succeeded in preaching a complete message that is absolutely different from what we have in the Bible. It is absolutely true that: *"If you tell a lie big enough and keep repeating it, people will eventually come to believe it."*

Chapter Six

WHO SHOULD WE TRUST?

There are several denominations today calling for our attention and almost each one of them has a message that is distinct from the rest and yet calls it the truth of God. It seems the Church cannot agree on one message that the first century Church had under Christ. There seems to be nothing called absolute truth in our society again that we can all accept and pursue. Political parties have different definitions of truth. Religious groups have their own. Media houses also have theirs as most cover the same events but with different interpretations. Just who has the truth? If we want to know the truth about the exact message in the Holy Scriptures, who should we trust to tell us nothing but the truth?

"The Bible is the one Book to which any thoughtful man may go with any honest question of life or destiny and find the answer of God by honest searching."—John Ruskin (1819-1900)

SHOULD WE TRUST THE "MAN OF GOD"?

I used to think that once a verse is quoted from the Bible to support a statement, that settles it that the truth of God is being told. But I later learnt that when the devil came to tempt the LORD Jesus he didn't quote from any other book but the same Scriptures we have today. If conspiracy theories are not only reserved for the secular world but to the church as well, then, completely relying on the "man of God" simply because he quotes from the Bible can be dangerous at times.

The issue of salvation cannot be left to someone else to do on our behalf. Paul has told us that: ***"Everything that was written in the past was written to teach us****, so that through endurance and the encouragement of the Scriptures, we might have hope." (Rom. 15:4)* We can therefore search into the past to see how the "men of God" tried to project into the future regarding what is to be expected of those living in our midst today.

There are several places in the Bible where God tells us to listen to the voice of His servants the prophets, who we often hear a lot about since days of old. But there are several places in the same Bible that He prompts and warns us to make sure that some proper research work is carried out before seriously listening to these same prophets. We can now read just two of such chapters from the Scriptures:

> *If anyone does not listen to my words that the prophet speaks in my name, I myself will call him to account. 20* ***But a prophet who presumes to speak in my name anything I have not commanded him to say, or a prophet who speaks in the name of other gods, must be put to death.*** *21* ***You may say to yourselves, "How can we know when a message has not been spoken by the LORD?"*** *22* ***IF WHAT A PROPHET PROCLAIMS IN THE NAME OF THE LORD DOES NOT TAKE PLACE OR COME TRUE, THAT IS A MESSAGE THE LORD HAS NOT SPOKEN. THAT PROPHET HAS SPOKEN PRESUMPTUOUSLY. Do not be afraid of him*** *(Deut. 18:19-22)*

To *"presume" is to behave in a way that shows a lack of respect by doing something that you have no right to do.* It is written that *"Surely the Sovereign LORD does nothing without revealing His plan to His servants the prophets" (Amos 3:7).* It is also written *"Do not steal.* ***Do not lie. Do not deceive one another. Do not swear falsely by my Name and so profane the name of your God.*** *I am the LORD" (Lev. 19:11-12).*

For a prophet whose word is supposed to be taken as the very oracle of God to speak something presumptuously will simply imply God is telling a lie. He represents God and serves as His mouthpiece on earth. It is written ***"He who is the Glory of Israel does not lie*** *or change His mind; for He is not a man, that He should change His mind" (1 Sam. 15:29).* God asks *"I am the LORD, the God of all mankind. Is anything too hard for me?" (Jer. 32:27).* There's nothing too difficult for God to do to make Him lie.

The words of a true prophet are taken to be that of the LORD Himself so for a prophet to say something presumptuous is simply an attempt to make God out to be a liar and someone who changes His mind like any ordinary man does. That prophet is profaning the Name of God. The latter part of the command says *"Do not be afraid of him."* He is to die for telling such a lie. How do I know that?

> *"But a prophet who presumes to speak in my name anything I have not commanded him to say, or a prophet who speaks in the name of other gods, must be put to death" (Deut. 18:20).*

Personally, I believe this law is one of the reasons why they don't want us to live by the principles in the Old Testament to enable them say blatant lies and whatever comes to their minds without substantiating them with facts and most importantly, results.

> *"An honest man with an open Bible and a pad and pencil is sure to find out what is wrong with him very quickly."—A. W. Tozer (1897-1963)*

LESSONS FROM PAST PROPHETS

Let's now back-date into history to the time of Jeremiah to see the records of what the prophets of the day did concerning their responsibilities and duties. If the prophets who are required to represent God can completely turn their backs to what is expected of them and follow after their own manufactured ways of teaching the word even in the temple of God, then we need to open our eyes and ears into the Scriptures very well and do some proper studies ourselves.

> *Concerning the prophets: My heart is broken within me; all my bones tremble. I am like a drunken man, like a man overcome by wine, because of the LORD and His words.*
> *10 The land is full of adulterers; because of the curse the land lies parched and the pastures in the desert are withered.* ***The prophets follow an evil course and use their power unjustly.***
> ***11 Both prophet and priest are godless; EVEN IN MY TEMPLE I FIND THEIR WICKEDNESS,"*** *declares the LORD.*
> *12 "Therefore their path will become slippery; they will be banished to darkness and there they will fall. I will bring disaster on them in the year they are punished," declares the LORD.*
> *13 "Among the prophets of Samaria I saw this repulsive thing:* ***They prophesied by Baal and led My people Israel astray****.*
> *14 And among the prophets of Jerusalem I have seen something horrible:* ***They commit adultery and live a lie. They strengthen the hands of evildoers, so that no-one turns from his wickedness. They are all like Sodom to me;*** *the people of Jerusalem are like Gomorrah."*
> *15 Therefore, this is what the LORD Almighty says concerning the prophets: "I will make them eat bitter*

> *food and drink poisoned water,* ***because from the prophets of Jerusalem ungodliness has spread throughout the land."*** *16 This is what the LORD Almighty says:* ***"Do not listen to what the prophets are prophesying to you; they fill you with false hopes. They speak visions from their own minds, not from the mouth of the LORD.*** *17 They keep saying to those who despise me, 'The LORD says: You will have peace.' And to all who follow the stubbornness of their hearts they say, 'No harm will come to you.' 18* ***But which of them has stood in the council of the LORD to see or to hear His Word? Who has listened and heard His Word?***
>
> *20 The anger of the LORD will not turn back until He fully accomplishes the purposes of His heart. In days to come you will understand it clearly. 21* ***I did not send these prophets, yet they have run with their message; I did not speak to them, yet they have prophesied.*** *22* ***But if they had stood in my council, they would have proclaimed my words to My people and would have turned them from their evil ways and from their evil deeds.*** *23 "Am I only a God nearby," declares the LORD, "and not a God far away?" (Jer. 23:8-23)*

You see, a prophet's duty among other things is to proclaim the Word of God to the people till they turned from their evil ways. A true prophet of God is required to weaken the hands of evildoers and make them turn from their wickedness. If evildoers or sinners feel comfortable in the presence of a prophet, then both the prophet and the sinner are like Sodom and Gomorrah in the sight of God.

> *"Can anyone hide in secret places so that I cannot see him?" declares the LORD. "Do not I fill heaven and earth?" declares the LORD. 25* ***I have heard what the prophets say who prophesy lies in my name. They say, 'I had a dream! I had a dream!'*** *26* ***How long will this continue in the hearts of these lying prophets, who prophesy the delusions of their own minds?*** *27 They think the dreams they tell one another will make my people forget my name, just as their fathers forgot my name through Baal worship. (Jer. 23:24-27)*

God says: *"When a prophet of the LORD is among you, I reveal myself to him in visions, I speak to him in dreams" (Num. 12:6).* But what is mostly the message of these visions and dreams? The Big Papa upstairs replies through Jeremiah that, ***"From early times*** *the prophets who preceded you and me have prophesied war, disaster and plague against many countries and great kingdoms. 9* ***But the prophet who prophesies peace will be recognised as one truly***

sent by the LORD, only if his prediction comes true" *(Jer. 28:8-9).* I feel like making no comment but I cannot go on without saying a word about this.

God reveals Himself to His prophets through visions and speaks to them through dreams. They are two different things. He then tells us that the purpose for which prophesies are given is to tell the people about the advent of wars, disasters and plagues. It didn't end there. But the only time that prophecy is to be used to deliver a peaceful message and thus be taken as the Word of God is only if the prediction took place. For instance, the angel who spoke to Zechariah and Mary delivered a message of peace and his prediction took place.

How about the predictions on TV these days? Even while standing in front of a congregation, they claim, *"I have a dream, I have a dream."* I leave that to your own perusal and assessment. We accept the testimony of men, but the testimony of God is greater and superior.

> *"Let the prophet who has a dream tell his dream,* ***but let the one who has my word speak it faithfully****. For what has straw to do with grain?" declares the LORD. 29 "Is not my word like fire," declares the LORD, "and like a hammer that breaks a rock in pieces? 30* ***"Therefore,"*** *declares the LORD,* ***"I am against the prophets who steal from one another words supposedly from me.*** *31 Yes," declares the LORD,* ***"I am against the prophets who wag their own tongues and yet declare, 'The LORD declares.'*** *32 Indeed, I am against those who prophesy false dreams," declares the LORD.* ***"They tell them and lead my people astray with their reckless lies, yet I did not send or appoint them. They do not benefit these people in the least,*** *declares the LORD. (Jer. 23:28-32)*

In summation, we have seen that:

1. It is possible for a prophet to follow an evil course and use his power unjustly.
2. Both a prophet and a priest (pastor?) can lead a godless life even in the temple of God.
3. It is also possible for a prophet to prophesy by a different spirit apart from the Spirit of God, and in the process, lead the people astray.
4. It is also possible that a prophet will commit adultery in the form of sleeping with another man's wife or serve other gods.
5. It is again possible for him to live a life of lies by encouraging sinning in the land instead of preventing it.

6. The worst of all is the fact that it is possible for ungodliness to spread throughout the land due to the negligence and selfish interests of the prophets in the land.
7. It is again possible for a prophet to fill you with false hopes by speaking from his own mind visions that are not from God, and in the process, God could sternly warn us not to listen to them. It is possible for God to personally say *"I did not send these prophets, yet they have run with their message; I did not speak to them, yet they have prophesied."* It is actually possible for a prophet to wag his own tongue and later declare, 'The LORD declares.'

"God has not left us in the dark to wonder and guess. He has clearly revealed His five purposes for our lives through the Bible. It is our Owner's Manual, explaining why we are alive, how life works, what to avoid, and what to expect in the future . . . . To discover your purpose in life you must turn to God's Word, not the world's wisdom."—Rick Warren

This is coming from the Old Testament but we shouldn't forget what Paul told us that ***"These things happened to them as examples and were written down as warnings for us, on whom the fulfilment of the ages has come.*** *12 So, if you think you are standing firm, be careful that you don't fall (1 Cor. 10:11-12)!* If it is possible for a prophet or a pastor to lead you astray, then it should be your top-most priority to keep yourself up to speed when it comes to the Scriptures.

> *But the people have not returned to Him who struck them, nor have they sought the LORD Almighty. 14 So the LORD will cut off from Israel both head and tail, both palm branch and reed in a single day; 15 the elders and prominent men are the head,* ***the prophets who teach lies are the tail.*** *16* ***Those who guide this people mislead them, and those who are guided are led astray.*** *17 Therefore the LORD will take no pleasure in the young men, nor will He pity the fatherless and widows,* ***for everyone is ungodly and wicked, every mouth speaks vileness.*** *(Isa. 9:13-17)*

In his first letter to Timothy, Paul wrote that *"The Spirit clearly says that in later times some will abandon the faith and follow deceiving spirits* ***and things taught by demons****. 2 Such teachings come through hypocritical liars, whose consciences have been seared as with a hot iron. 3 They forbid people to marry and order them to abstain from certain foods, which were created to be* *received with thanksgiving by those who believe and who know the truth" (I Tim. 4:1-3).*

It can easily be deduced from the above verses that most of us do not see demons with our naked eyes. But the Scriptures say that some will abandon the truth of God and follow *things taught by demons* and deceiving spirits. How is that achieved? They invade the churches with their hypocrisies and quote the Bible to cover their diabolical intents to deceive the unsuspecting masses who think quoting from the Bible makes one a "man of God." Even Jesus warned us in advance and said: *"Watch out for false prophets. They come to you in sheep's clothing,* ***but inwardly they are ferocious wolves****" (Matt. 7:15).*

PERSONAL RESPONSIBILITY OF STUDYING THE SCRIPTURES

It is pretty obvious to learn from these verses that one is not required to blindly follow the dictates of what someone says merely because the person claims to be a prophet, a pastor or a representative of an organisation. If Jesus had not known the Scriptures in advance, the devil could have told Him that he (the devil) was a prophet or "a man of God" as he quoted from the same Scriptures that Jesus knew. Being a student of the Holy Scriptures is an individual responsibility which cannot, and should not, be left to someone else. With this, I'm always thankful and grateful to God and my parents for giving me the opportunity to be able to, at least, read and write. It is written in the Scriptures:

> *These commandments that I give you today are to be upon your hearts. 7* ***Impress them on your children****. Talk about them when you sit at home and when you walk along the road, when you lie down and when you get up. 8 Tie them as symbols on your hands and bind them on your foreheads. 9 Write them on the door-frames of your houses and on your gates. (Deuteronomy 6:6-9)*

The time for us to know the Scriptures is not when we have grown in years with our minds seared with the *"wisdom of this world,"* but the right and the appropriate time is actually when we are still young with nothing written on the screens of our minds. It is therefore the responsibility of parents to see to it that their wards who they love so dearly are introduced to the Scriptures at the early stages of their lives. If our children are left to be taught and influenced by their friends, teachers at school and the internet alone, they are exposed to all kinds of information at such early stages of their lives which leave them vulnerable and confused as to whose advice to heed to later.

> *Listen, my son, to your father's instruction and do not forsake your mother's teaching. 9 They will be a garland to grace your head and a chain to adorn your neck. (Prov. 1:8-9)*

It is because the LORD had commanded parents earlier in the book of Deuteronomy to impress His word upon their children to live according to the teachings of the Scriptures that He is now telling the children in turn to listen to the instructions and teachings of their parents in the book of Proverbs. The teachings and instructions being referred to are the commandments, statutes, precepts, decrees and laws of God in the Scriptures.

> *Honour your father and your mother, so that you may live long in the land the LORD your God is giving you. (Exod. 20:12)*

There are uncountable number of people who have shipwrecked their lives through honouring their parents by heeding to the advice they took from them. The honour that is being referred to in the above Scripture is the one that is reserved for the LORD Himself. It is His Word which if parents teach their children and they also adhere to without turning to the left or to the right that the length of their lives will be prolonged.

> *My son, **if you accept my words and store up my commands** (that you are taught by your parents) **within you**, 2 turning your ear to wisdom and applying your heart to understanding, 3 and if you call out for insight and cry aloud for understanding, 4 and if you look for it as for silver and search for it as for hidden treasure, 5 **then you will understand the fear of the LORD and find the knowledge of God**. 6 **For the LORD gives wisdom, and from His mouth comes understanding. (Prov. 2:1-6)***

There's always a choice to make after hearing the word of God. Your parents are obligated to teach you the teachings of the Scriptures and you also have your part to play by choosing to either live by those principles or not. Merely memorising the Scriptures in your head will not do you any good until you act upon them. Jesus Christ once said: "*Anyone who breaks one of the least of these commandments and teaches others to do the same will be called least in the kingdom of heaven, **but whoever practises and teaches these commands will be called great in the kingdom of heaven." (Matt. 5:19)***

> *See, I have taught you decrees and laws as the LORD my God commanded me, so that you may follow them in the land you are entering to take possession of it. 6 **Observe them carefully, for this***

> ***will show your wisdom and understanding to the nations, who will hear about all these decrees and say, "Surely this great nation is a wise and understanding people. (Duet. 4:5-6)***

It is only after you have accepted the words of God, and practised living by them that you become wise. Your wisdom reflects in what you do with your life. *"If you accept my words and store up my commands within you . . . then you will understand the fear of the LORD* ***and find the knowledge of God.*** *6* ***For the LORD gives wisdom****, and from His mouth comes understanding" (Prov. 2:1-6).* Prof. Jesus Christ again said: *"Therefore, everyone who hears* ***these words of mine,*** *(not that of anyone including your pastor and parents)* ***and puts them into practice is like a wise man who built his house on the rock.*** *25 The rain came down, the streams rose, and the winds blew and beat against that house; yet it did not fall,* ***because it had its foundation on the rock.*** *(Matt. 7:24-25)*

> *See, I am setting before you* ***today*** *a blessing and a curse—27* ***the blessing if you obey the commands of the LORD your God*** *that I am giving you today; 28* ***the curse if you disobey the commands of the LORD your God and turn from the way I command you today by following other gods,*** *which you have not known. (Duet. 11:26-28)*

As you sow, so shall you reap. God does not love or hate anyone more than the other. His principles are there in the open for everyone to choose to live by or reject. His blessing and prosperity follow those who practise those ways He has established to last forever. On the flip side, curses are bound to follow the rest of mankind who reject His ways. The choice is yours.

> *"The Bible should be taught so early and so thoroughly that it sinks straight to the bottom of the mind where everything that comes along can settle on it."—Northrop Frye (1912-1991)*

SHOULD WE JUST TRUST IN MEN?

It is difficult to read the minds of those around us. You never can tell what motivates people to do what they do on daily basis. Well-known public figures around the world portray themselves in ways that are totally different from what they truly are in their closets. Most R & B and Pop stars seem to preach the best sermons on love in most of their famous songs but can hardly stay in a relationship for a year. Most of them preach against violence yet die from these same things they preach against. The same thing applies to most of the best-selling authors around the world. The youth, who are mostly ignorant about what truly makes one successful and famous in life, are usually misled to blindly copy the "masks" worn by these artists mainly for the sake of marketing themselves.

So, should we trust in men at all in what they preach and portray? And if we are to do that, who should we rely on to tell us the absolute truths of life? If we want to know the truth, who should we turn to? Should we rely on journalists who work for media houses and mostly seek to determine the thinking pattern of society? Once again, we need to remind ourselves with what Paul said that ***"Everything that was written in the past was written to teach us."*** In that case, we can travel into the past to see what happened in the ages gone by to learn what lies in store for us in trusting our fellow man to teach us the unadulterated word of God. This should give us a fair idea of how we need to live our lives today.

John Swinton, former Chief of Staff of the New York Times, who was considered to be the dean of his profession, made a most revealing statement in 1953. At a New York Press Club dinner, he declared:

> *"There is no such thing, at this date of the world's history, in America, as an independent press. You know it, and I know it. There is not one of you who dares to write your honest opinions, and if you did, you know beforehand that it would never appear in print. I am paid weekly for keeping my honest opinion out of the paper I am connected with. Others of you are paid similar salaries for similar things,* ***and any of you who would be so foolish as to write honest opinions would be out on the streets looking for another job****. If I allowed my honest opinions to appear in one issue of my newspaper, before twenty-four hours my occupation would be gone.* ***The business of the journalist is to destroy the truth; to lie outright; to pervert; to vilify; to fawn at the feet of mammon, and to sell his country and his race for his daily bread. You know it and I know it, and what folly is this toasting an independent press? We are the tools and vassals of rich men behind the scenes. We are the jumping jacks; they pull the strings and we dance. Our talents, our possibilities and our lives are all the property of other men. We are intellectual prostitutes.****—Multiple contributors, A U.S. Police Action: Operation Vampire Killer, The American Citizens and Laumen Association, pp. 18, 19. (culled from Bill Hughes' book, "The Enemy Unmasked")*

That was in 1953. But has this phenomenon changed? You are entitled to your own opinions, and I do respect them. Personally, I have watched some journalists like Barnaby Phillips, Rageh Omar and Anas Aremeyaw Anas, who have risked their lives by going to some of the remotest parts of the world just to put a smile on the face of one simple peasant farmer or cover the story on human trafficking and slavery. They surely wouldn't do that if it were only for the money. I have also seen the bad and the ugly as well. If that is how a former Chief of Staff describes his profession, can it be relied upon for answers to our questions in life? Some time back in history, God said through the mouth of Jeremiah that:

> *Beware of your friends; do not trust your brothers. For every brother is a deceiver, and every friend a slanderer. 5 Friend deceives friend, and no-one speaks the truth. They have taught their tongues to lie; they weary themselves with sinning. 6* ***You live in the midst of deception****; in their deceit they refuse to acknowledge Me," declares the LORD . . . 8* ***Their tongue is a deadly arrow; it speaks with deceit. With his mouth each speaks cordially to his neighbour, but in his heart he sets a trap for him.*** *(Jer. 9:4-8)*

It is written about Jesus in the book of John that *"Now while He was in Jerusalem at the Passover Feast, many people saw the miraculous signs He was doing and believed in His Name. 24* ***But Jesus would not entrust Himself to them, for He knew all men.*** *25* ***He did not need man's testimony about man, for He knew what was in a man"*** *(John 2:23-25).* This too was written down as an example for us to emulate so as to prevent us from doing things that would make us laugh at the wrong side of our mouths. I have had some wonderful friends without whom I would not be writing this literary piece. I also know the speed of trust but God's Word supersedes all else.

> *"No Greater Moral Change ever passed over a nation than passed over England in the latter part of the reign of Queen Elizabeth. England became the people of a Book, and That Book Was The Bible. It was Read by Every Class of People. And the Effect was Amazing. The Whole Moral Tone of the Nation was Changed."—John Richard Green (1837-1883)*

HOW ABOUT TRUSTING THE JUDGMENT OF THE OLD?

How about the aged? Does wisdom or truth reside only with the man with grey hair? Should we just listen to someone simply because he or she is old and advanced in years? There is a saying in my area that literally translates, "*The aged is never wrong.*" Let's try and answer that with a verse in the Scriptures through the mouth of Elihu, one of Job's friends who were with him during his illness.

> *I am young in years, and you are old; that is why I was fearful, not daring to tell you what I know. 7* ***I thought, 'Age should speak; and advanced years should teach wisdom.'*** *8* ***But it is the spirit in man, the breath of the Almighty that gives him understanding.*** *9* ***It is not only the old who are wise, not only the aged who understand what is right.*** *(Job 32:6-9)*

This man under the inspiration of God says it is the spirit in man that gives him understanding. So, what does the Scriptures say about trusting in man? We can now go a step further to study a few things the LORD says regarding trusting in men to tell us His truths at all times.

> *This is what the LORD says:* ***"Cursed is the one who trusts in man, who depends on flesh for his strength and whose heart turns away from the LORD****. 6 He will be like a bush in the wastelands;* ***he will not see prosperity when it comes****. He will dwell in the parched places of the desert, in a salt land where no-one lives. (Jer. 17:5-6)*

One of the flaws I've noticed about why the secular world finds it difficult to accept the Word of God, and thus renders it ineffective and unproductive in their lives is how it is presented to them. Some of the pastors today only seem to have stored the Scriptures in their heads and quote them at will in the faces of people but fail to explain how relevant the Word is to their personal lives. They seem to know all that God has said about every subject but fail to tell people the purposes for which God established them. But the truth is that God explains why He said everything in the Scriptures.

LIVE BY THE WORD OF GOD FOR YOUR OWN GOOD

Religion makes people think that God needs our help to make Him who He is. Like I said earlier, all that is written in the Scriptures is only meant for our own good. I'm always surprised to see how the major religions on earth strive to fight and kill each other in the name of fighting for God. Jesus didn't leave His disciples with tanks and ammunitions to be taken to the ends of the earth to win souls for God. God is love and until you can love your fellow human being, no matter his colour or the race or the religion he belongs to, you don't know anything about God, talk less of fighting for Him.

> *Do you think this is just? You say, 'I shall be cleared by God.' 3* ***Yet you ask Him, 'What profit is it to me, AND WHAT DO I GAIN BY NOT SINNING?'*** *4 I would like to reply you and to your friends with you . . . 6 If you sin, how does that affect Him? If your sins are many, what does that do to Him? 7 If you are righteous, what do you give to Him or what does He receive from your hand? 8* ***Your wickedness affects only a man like yourself, and your righteousness only the sons of men.*** *(Job 35:2-8)*

Choosing either to lead a righteous life or not does not add to or subtract from God. It is extremely important that you understand that God does not need our worship or praise to make Him who He is. If that were the case, He would have made it compulsory for us to live according to His principles. But He leaves us with choices to always choose between living by His Word or not. You and I will sooner or later disappear from the face of this earth. But the Almighty will exist forever, our righteousness or unrighteousness notwithstanding. It is for our own good if we choose to obey the teachings of the Scriptures. There was a time in history that all sinned, and fell short of the glory of God. But even at that juncture, God did not collapse and die because there was no-one truly worshipping Him. It is not our worship that makes or unmakes Him.

> *And now, O Israel, what does the LORD your God ask of you but to fear the LORD your God, to walk in all His ways, to love Him, to serve the LORD your God with all your heart and with all your soul, 13 and to observe the LORD'S commands and decrees that I am giving you today* ***FOR YOUR OWN GOOD****? (Duet. 10:12-13)*

God has provided the answers to every question that we could ever ask in His Word. For example, when I was a young lad, I used to wonder about where all the major rivers and streams flow to without flooding the earth. I found the answer in the book of Ecclesiastes where it says: *All streams flow into the sea, yet the sea is never full.* ***To the place the streams come from, there they return again*** *(Eccl. 1:7).* I found the answer there.

"Has it ever struck you that the vast majority of the will of God for your life has already been revealed in the Bible? That is a crucial thing to grasp."—Paul E. Little (1928-1975)

The same thing applies to the answers on the biblical keys to prosperity, health and peaceful co-existence with one another. Unlike the deceptions being preached by the wolves in sheep skin that the only keys to wealth is by paying tithes and offerings, the true keys to financial independence is taught by the wisest and the richest man who ever lived before Jesus Christ in the book of Proverbs. It will interest you to know that high on his list on the route to prosperity are not fasting, prayer, tithing and offerings, as we have it taught today. Below is one of his teachings on the way to prosperity.

> *Go to the ant, you sluggard;* ***consider its ways and be wise!*** *7 It has no commander, no overseer or ruler, 8 yet* ***it stores its provisions in summer and gathers its food at harvest.*** *(Prov. 6:7-8)*

You would be in a better position to understand this verse if you've read any of Aesop's works. Creatures are often used in his fables to represent human behaviours. Just as the ant stores up its provisions and gathers its food at harvest though it has no leader, the lazy youth is being reminded by Solomon to do away with the excuses of not having anyone to help him to make use of his potentials and capabilities in order to make a living for himself because a time is coming when he would reap whatever he planted in his youthful days. A man reaps what he sows.

> *How long will you lie there, you sluggard? When will you get up from your sleep? 10* ***A little sleep, a little slumber, a little folding of the hands to rest****—11* ***and poverty will come on you like a bandit and scarcity like an armed man*** *(Prov. 9-11).*

The word *"sluggard"* is defined *as a slow, lazy person*. Can you identify with people like that? They are often experts at procrastinating, and will not put their brains, which are part of God's creation, to work. Mostly, they want to see themselves walking on the waves of the sea like Jesus did before knowing that God is with them. Instead of staying with a book of Scripture, like the Proverbs of Solomon, to study the path to true prosperity, you will find them even from Monday to Friday praying non-stop for hours, fasting and binding the devil and his demons in order to get rich.

Yet, majority of the richest men in both history and today who make just about three percent of the world's population but actually rule the world from behind the scenes do not pass through that means of binding even mosquitoes before making their billions. China is a communist nation but it is likely to overtake the U.S. in terms of trade and industry soon. They didn't achieve that feet by binding the devil in Jesus' Name. Did they?

I know this will sound outrageous and controversial to you that there is not a single soul in the whole of the Bible who solely prospered financially through tithes and offerings or binding of the devil. It's not categorically stated anywhere in the Scriptures. They all achieved their wealth through the proper application of the principles of God in the Scriptures and hard work in their various fields of endeavours.

In Paul's first letter to the Thessalonians, he wrote: *"Make it your ambition to lead a quite life,* ***to mind your own business and to work with your hands just as we told you,*** *12* ***so that your daily life may win the respect of outsiders and so that you will not be dependent on anybody"*** *(1 Thess. 4:11-12).* Applying the principle of leadership by example, he practised what he preached as he added: *"For you yourselves know how* ***you ought to follow our example. We were not idle when we were with you, nor did we eat anyone's food without paying for it. On the contrary, we worked night and day, labouring and toiling so that we would not be a burden to any of you"*** *(2 Thess. 3:7-8).*

Paul hated laziness so much that he specifically commanded his students to keep away from anyone who is idle and does not live according to what he taught them. I thought Paul would be proud of someone who is idle or lazy but spends most of his time at church premises from Monday to Friday binding demons to be rich. Read the full line to make your own judgment and conclusion:

> *In the name of the LORD Jesus Christ,* ***we command you,*** *brothers, to* ***keep away from every brother who is idle and does not live according to the teaching you have received from us.*** *7 For you yourselves know how you ought to follow our example.* ***We were not idle when we were with you,*** *8* ***nor did we eat anyone's food without paying for it. On the contrary, we worked night and day, labouring and toiling so that we would not be a burden to any of you.*** *9 We did this, not because we do not have a right to such help,* ***but in order to make ourselves a model for you to follow.*** *10* ***For even when we were with you, we gave you this rule: "IF A MAN WILL NOT WORK, HE SHALL NOT EAT."*** *11* ***We hear that some among you are idle.*** *They are not busy; they are busybodies. 12* ***Such people we command and urge***

> ***in the LORD Jesus Christ TO SETTLE DOWN AND EARN THE BREAD THEY EAT.*** *13 And as for you, brothers, never tire of doing what is right." (2 Thess. 3:6-13)*

These verses are written there in the pages of the New Testament. I can't go into details as that would divert the purpose of this book. The basic truth is that it takes wisdom to prosper and maintain prosperity. It is written: ***"Of what use is money in the hand of a fool, since he has no desire to get wisdom"*** *(Prov. 16:17)?* To prosper actually starts from the mind. It is written: *"Train a child in the way he should go, and when he is old he will not turn from it" (Prov. 22:6). "He who walks with the wise grows wise, but a companion of fools suffers harm" (Prov. 13:20). "Plans fail for lack of counsel, but with many advisers they succeed" (Prov. 15:22).*

The vultures are always gathered at where the carcass is. If you want to be wealthy, you need to first of all hang around such people, listen and practise what they teach you. Wealthy people mostly do not care much about who is in power. They know and apply the laws of wealth creation in their daily lives. And they don't hang around losers who only seek to find fault in everything that goes on around them. Winners are always busy accessing the opportunities in what you term problems and difficulties. Until recently in Ghana, people only saw how filthy our cities had become and were whining as usual. But the owner of Zoom Lion (a sanitary company) saw an opportunity in that filth and now employs thousands of workers all over the country and beyond the shores of Ghana clearing the filth.

Lazy hands make a man poor, but diligent hands bring wealth. *(Prov. 10:4)*

Henry J. Kaiser once said that *"Problems are only opportunities in work clothes."* Rosalynn Carter also said *"You have to have confidence in your ability, and then be tough enough to follow through."* Knowing everything about a particular problem and praying about it without doing anything in terms of finding a solution to it does not make anyone prosperous. If it were, religious folks would be the richest people on earth. But you and I know the facts. Even if you win the lotteries, you still wouldn't know how to manage the money and would sooner or later lose it all. Solomon wrote: ***"He who works his land will have abundant food, but the one who chases fantasies will have his fill of poverty"*** *(Prov. 28:19).*

> *"What I began to see was that the Bible is not essentially, as I had always more or less supposed, a book of ethical principles, or moral exhortations, of cautionary tales about exemplary people, of uplifting thoughts—in fact, not really a religious book at all . . . I saw it instead as a great, tattered compendium of writings, the underlying and unifying purpose of all of which is to show how God works through the Jacobs and Jabboks of history to make Himself known to the world and to draw the world back to Himself."—Frederick Buechner*

Now, back to why God entreats us that *"cursed is the man who puts his trust in man."* God wouldn't tell you not to put your trust in another man without revealing the reasons why He said so. Before I proceed to do this, I want to introduce you to some basic rules as well as the keys to reading and understanding the Words of the Bible. God said through Isaiah that:

> *And these also stagger from wine and reel from beer: Priests and prophets stagger from beer and are befuddled with wine; they reel from beer, they stagger when seeing visions, they stumble when rendering decisions. 8 All the tables are covered with vomit and there is not a spot without filth. 9* ***"Who is it he is trying to teach? To whom is he explaining his message? To children weaned from their milk, to those just taken from the breast? For it is: Do and do, do and do, rule on rule, rule on rule; a little here, a little there."*** *(Isaiah 28:7-10)*

Paul also wrote to Timothy that: "In the presence of God and of Christ Jesus, who will judge the living and the dead, and in view of His appearing and His kingdom, ***I give you this charge****: 2* ***Preach the Word; be prepared in season and out of season;*** *correct, rebuke and encourage—with great patience and careful instruction" (I Tim. 4:1-2).*

The basic requirement of a pastor, a prophet or anyone who teaches the Word of God is for him to bear in mind that he is not teaching children who have just been taken from the breast or children weaned from their milk. The Word of God represents the ultimate source of wisdom that is found under the sun. So whoever claims to be a teacher of it has to be fully prepared for it indeed. That is why Paul told Timothy to *"be prepared in season and out of season."* Whatever you teach will be questioned, and you must be adequately prepared in season and out of season to have the answers on your finger tips. A champion must always be available to defend his title.

You can achieve this by knowing that the answers to our questions, which represent the true wisdom of God, are not found on just one page at a given time in the Scriptures but are actually scattered all over its pages. So God is saying through the mouth of Isaiah that when it comes to searching for the truths of His Word, we can achieve that by searching through the Bible ***"Rule on rule, rule on rule, a little here, a little there."***

Now, in order to understand God's own reason for saying that one must not put his or her trust in his fellow human being in teaching him the truths of His Word, we can use the principle of "*a little here and a little there*" to arrive at His purposes for saying that. We can follow Paul and search into the Scriptures which are meant to serve as examples for us. That should take us to another place in the Bible where God said:

> *The godly have been swept from the land; not one upright man remains. All men lie in wait to shed blood; each hunts his brother with a net. 3* ***Both hands are skilled in doing evil; the ruler demands gifts, the judge accepts bribes, the powerful dictates what they desire—they all conspire together.*** *4 The best of them is like a brier,* ***the most upright worse than a thorn hedge.*** *The day of your watchmen has come, the day God visits you. Now is the time of their confusion. 5* ***Do not trust a neighbour; put no confidence in a friend. Even with her who lies in your embrace be careful of your words.*** *6* ***For a son dishonours his father, a daughter rises up against her mother, a daughter-in-law against her mother-in-law—a man's enemies are the members of his own household*** *(Micah 7:2-6).*

This was a case in history and was written down to teach us. It doesn't mean that all your brothers are bad, and that everyone should be seen with a suspicious eye. Paul wrote to Timothy and to all of us to mark this that: "*There will be terrible times in the last days. 2 People will be lovers of themselves, lovers of money, boastful, proud, abusive, disobedient to their parents, ungrateful, unholy, 3 without love, unforgiving, slanderous, without self-control, brutal, not lovers of the good, 4 treacherous, rash, conceited, lovers of pleasure rather than lovers of God—5* ***having a form of godliness but denying its power. Have nothing to do with them****" (2 Tim. 3:1-5).* These are some of the basic reasons why God is saying you simply can't trust man in these days, including the pastors, to teach you on the statutes and precepts of God. You never know what motivates him to preach to you.

> *Oh, that my head were a spring of water and my eyes a fountain of tears! I would weep day and night for the slain of my people. 2 Oh, that I had in the desert a lodging place for travellers, so that*

> *I might leave my people and go away from them:* ***for they are all adulterers, a crowd of unfaithful people.*** *3 They make ready their tongue like a bow, to shoot lies;* ***it is not by truth that they triumph in the land. They go from one sin to another;*** *they do not acknowledge me, declares the LORD. 4* ***Beware of your friends; do not trust your brothers. For every brother is a deceiver, and every friend a slanderer.*** *5* ***Friend deceives friend, and no-one speaks the truth. They have taught their tongues to lie; they weary themselves with sinning.*** *6* ***You live in the midst of deception:*** *in their deceit they refuse to acknowledge me," declares the LORD (Jer. 9:1-6)*

We've already established the fact that obeying the instructions of the LORD serves our own good, and does not change who God is in the least. We normally tend to trust in people based on what we see with our eyes and hear with our ears which mostly prove to be wrong in the long run. But "*the LORD does not look at the things man looks at. Man looks at the outward appearance, but the LORD looks at the heart" (1 Sam. 16:6-7).* Just take a deep breath, meditate on these quotes, and then juxtapose them with what is happening in our societies today to prove what was written thousands of years back by God.

The next question to ask ourselves is: what's in the heart of a man that his fellow men fail to see but God sees? Going *"there a little"* will take us to the book of Jeremiah where God said "***The heart is deceitful above all things and beyond cure. Who can understand it?*** *(Jer. 17:9).*

I count it a blessing to have experienced things firsthand in my personal life to prove the veracity of these things. Some of us have learned the hard way to judge people around us not by their claims that they have good intentions towards us but by the effects of their actions and inactions on our lives. What does it matter if a friend intended good things and had only our good interests at heart but the effects of their actions or inactions lead to ruin and confusion in our lives at the end of the day?

You can now see that one does not need to just quote verses like these and start proclaiming them in the ears of others that one must not put his trust in man, without clearly explaining why. Jesus once said "***If you love me, you will obey what I command*** *. . . 21 Whoever has my commands and obeys them,* ***he is the one who loves me*** *. . . 23* ***If anyone loves me, he will obey my teachings****. He who does not love me will not obey my teaching. 24 These words you hear are not my own; they belong to the Father who sent me" (John 14:15, 21, 23-24).*

He once told the Jews who had believed in Him that: *"****If you hold to my teaching****, you are really my disciples. 32 Then you will know the truth, and* *the truth will set you free" (John 8:31-32).* Almost all denominations quote these two verses to support their beliefs. But we've learnt earlier that it is only those who hold to and practise His teaching who will be set free and not just those who quote them. That should also take us to the question of the exact message He brought from heaven to earth.

Having the teachings or the commands of Jesus Christ is one thing and actually obeying them or putting them into practice is another. After hearing the message of the Kingdom of God, one is expected to decode his memory so to speak of all the junk information he had earlier been exposed to since birth. He then stays at the feet of God through adequate study of the Bible to renew his mind. This renewal of the mind too does not need to take years or even months to complete. It can be done in a day, depending on how long it takes to understand a particular subject.

> *Do not conform any longer to the pattern of this world,* ***but be transformed by the renewing of your mind. Then you will be able to test and approve what God's will is****—His good, pleasing and perfect will. (Rom. 12:2)*

Assume that I had been ignorant of the demands of the Scriptures prior to my conversion to Christianity, and I used to disrespect my parents, fornicate, steal, covet what belongs to others, slander and kill to survive, which is a pattern of this world. The day my mind is renewed is the day I would be exposed to the truth and fully understand why I should no longer engage myself in those activities again. That would reveal the good, pleasing and perfect will of God to me.

I don't need to bind demons to respect my parents. It's simply a matter of understanding, which reflects in the choices I make to either respect the commands of God or not. To *renew* is simply to begin something again after a pause or an interruption. The purpose for which you are created is revealed to you and that necessitates the leaving behind of all the evil ways you used to live in. You then become a *renewed* person after a pause.

> *"So great is my veneration for the Bible that the earlier my children begin to read it, the more confident will be my hope that they will prove useful citizens to their country, and respectable members of society."—John Quincy Adams (1767-1848)*

Chapter Seven

HOW MANY GOSPEL MESSAGES DO WE HAVE?

Addressing those in authority who teach the gospel in his first letter to the Corinthian Church, Paul wrote: *"Even though you have ten thousand guardians in Christ,* ***you do not have many fathers, for in Christ Jesus I became your father through the gospel.*** *16* ***Therefore, I urge you to imitate me.****" (1 Cor. 4:15-16).* We can only accept Paul as our father through the gospel and imitate him in the process when we know the message entrusted to him by God through Christ Jesus. He wrote that *"Men ought to regard us as servants of Christ and as those entrusted with the secret things of God." (1 Cor. 4:1)*

As Gentile believers in the faith, we need to know who the LORD Jesus appointed to deliver the gospel to us. This is because it wouldn't be hard or difficult for us to accept his testimony if we know the man chosen to do that. Indeed, if we truly respect the Scriptures and take them as the very words of God, then we should take it seriously who was sent to preach the gospel of the kingdom of God to us.

PAUL: THE APOSTLE TO THE GENTILES

After Paul was struck with blindness and Ananias was called to go and pray over him to restore his sight, the mandate on Paul's life was revealed to us by God.

> *But the LORD said to Ananias, "Go!* ***This man*** *(Paul)* ***is my chosen instrument to carry my name before the Gentiles and their kings*** *and before the people of Israel." (Acts 9:15)*

Because he was the chosen vessel to carry the gospel to the Gentiles and their kings, Paul had much insight into the Scriptures concerning how the Gentiles were to be integrated into the family of God that even the apostles who had been with Jesus in person were finding some things hard to understand. There were times he had to rebuke Peter when he felt he was going off the track in pursuing the Lord's duties. Peter himself admitted that because of the wisdom given to Paul, his letters were difficult to understand and warned the ignorant from distorting them to their own destruction. Things that remained a mystery from ages past were easily revealed to Paul the apostle by revelation from the Lord *(Eph. 3:9)*.

He wrote about himself that *"I want you to know, brothers, that the gospel I preached is not something that man made up. 12 I did not receive it from any man, nor was I taught it; rather,* ***I received it by revelation from Jesus Christ****" (Gal. 1:11-12)*. Everything Paul preached from day one was revealed to him by Jesus Christ through revelations into the Scriptures. It must be established here that since he was chosen or appointed to accomplish a mission for Christ, he could at most be like his Master. He couldn't preach anything that was different from that of his Master and contradict what Jesus taught.

> *"Everything in the Christian Faith goes back ultimately to the story of Jesus recorded in the little books we call the Gospels. As all true Christian morality is based on the ethics of Jesus, so all sound Christian doctrines must be built on the person and work of Christ, as they are presented to us in the Gospels."—A. M. Hunter*

THE TEACHINGS OF JESUS CHRIST IS THE FOUNDATION

It is written about Jesus Christ that: To the Jews who had believed Him, *Jesus said, "****If you hold to my teaching, you are really my disciples****. 32 Then you will know the truth, and the truth will set you free" (John 8:31-32)*. Paul also taught us that ***"For no-one can lay any foundation other than the one already laid, which is Jesus Christ."*** *(1 Cor. 3:11)* So, if there cannot be any other gospel apart from the gospel of Christ, Paul and the rest of the apostles, then in our day too, there shouldn't be any other gospel apart from that of Jesus Christ. It is written that: *"A student is not above his teacher,* ***but everyone who is fully trained will be like his teacher.****" (Luke 6:40) "I tell you the truth,* ***no servant is greater than his master, nor is a messenger greater than the one who sent him****" (John 13:16)*.

THE MYSTERY OF GOD REVEALED THROUGH THE GOSPEL

> *Surely you have heard about the administration of God's grace that was given to me for you, 3* ***that is, the mystery made known to me by revelation****, as I have already written briefly. 4 In reading this, then, you will be able to understand my insight into the mystery of Christ, 5 which was not made known to men in other generations as it has now been revealed by the Spirit to God's holy apostles and prophets. 6* ***This mystery is that through the gospel the Gentiles are heirs together with Israel, members together of one body and sharers together in the promise in Christ Jesus.*** *(Eph. 3:2-6)*

In these short verses of the Bible, we can clearly see the mystery Paul was talking about. He says that through the gospel, the Gentiles are heirs together of one body and sharers together in the promise. We will later cover what promise he was referring to. But for now we should know that the Gentile believers in the faith share the same promise with Israel *("the firstborn son")* or Jacob and we are of one body. The examples that were written down by the forefathers apply to all of us from the Gentile nations who have come to know the God of the patriarchs through the gospel.

> *Make every effort to keep the unity of the Spirit through the bond of peace. 4* ***There is one body and one Spirit—just as you were called to one hope when you were called****—5* ***one LORD, one faith, one baptism;*** *6* ***One God and Father of all****, who is over all and through all and in all. (Eph. 4:3-6)*

The God of Adam, Noah, Abraham, Isaac, Jacob, Joseph, Moses, David, Isaiah, Jeremiah, Ezekiel, Esther, Hosea, Joel, Amos, Obadiah, Jonah, Micah, Nahum, Habakkuk, Zephaniah, Haggai, Zechariah, Malachi, John the Baptist, Peter and Paul is not different from the God preached to the Gentiles. And He does not change but remains the same for ever. It is the same hope that the Jew has that the Gentile is also hoping to attain. We all belong to the same God and Father. We have one faith and baptism as that of the Israelites. We cannot do anything that is separated from the Israelites. We all have and use the same textbook—the Holy Bible. Paul said that the advantage of being a Jew is the fact that: *"First of all* ***they have been entrusted with the very words of God****" (Rom. 3:1).* For a Gentile believer to have access to the Word of God he has to go to the original source—the Jews—to obtain it.

For there is no difference between Jew and Gentile—the same LORD is LORD of all and richly blesses all who call on Him, *13 for, "Everyone who calls on the Name of the LORD will be saved" (Rom. 10:12-13).*

THE KINGDOM MESSAGE REMAINS THE SAME FOREVER

In Paul's second letter to the Corinthians, he wrote: *"For if someone comes to you and preaches a Jesus other than the Jesus we preached, or if you receive a different spirit from the one you received, or a different gospel from the one you accepted, you put up with it easily enough" (2 Cor. 11:4).* He actually knew what he taught, and admonished his listeners never to let go off what they had heard. Preaching the gospel of Jesus does not only mean trying to market His Name around the world for people to know how famous He is. But its true meaning is to practise the teachings He brought to man. Jesus said, *"Everyone who hears these words of mine* ***and does not put them into practice*** *is like* ***a foolish man*** *who built his house on sand" (Matt. 7:26).*

> ***But even if we or an angel from heaven should preach a gospel other than the one we preached to you, let him be eternally condemned!*** *9 As we have already said, so now I say again: If anybody is preaching to you a gospel other than what you accepted, let him be eternally condemned! (Gal. 1:8-9).*

Paul knew there were false apostles masquerading as brothers in the faith. So he advised his students not to just associate with any of them with the hope that they would be safe. He didn't leave his students with the message that they should allow the weeds to grow with the seeds until God comes to do His own weeding. He once wrote: *"Join with others in following my example, brothers,* ***and take note of those who live according to the pattern we gave you****" (Phil. 3:17). So then,* ***just as you received Christ Jesus as LORD, continue to live in Him,*** *7* ***rooted and built up in Him, strengthened in the faith as you were taught, and overflowing with thankfulness*** *(Col. 2:6-7).* ***Test everything. Hold on to the good*** *(1 Thess. 5:21).* Each of us is entitled to identify the one and only gospel of Christ and get rooted and built in it, just as we were taught from the beginning.

> ***Let the Word of Christ dwell in you richly as you teach and admonish one another with all wisdom,*** *and as you sing psalms, hymns and spiritual songs with gratitude in your hearts to God. 17 And whatever you do, whether in word or deed, do it all in the*

> *Name of the LORD Jesus, giving thanks to God the Father through Him. (Col. 3:16-17)*

Paul's teaching was based on the teaching of the LORD Jesus Christ. There was nothing added or taken from it. ***"If anyone teaches false doctrines and does not agree to the sound instruction of our LORD Jesus Christ and to godly teaching,** 4 **he is conceited and understands nothing**. He has an unhealthy interest in controversies and quarrels about words that result in envy, strife, malicious talk, evil suspicions 5 and constant friction between men of corrupt mind, who have been robbed of the truth and who think that godliness is a means to financial gain (1 Tim. 6:3-5).* Did you get that? Paul says that if anyone teaches something that does not agree with the teachings of Christ, that person understands nothing. That includes Paul because he himself was a student of Jesus Christ.

> *And of this gospel I was appointed a herald and an apostle and a teacher . . . 13 **What you have heard from me, keep as the pattern of sound teaching**, with faith and love in Christ Jesus (2 Tim. 11-13).*

ENTRUSTING WHAT WE'VE HEARD TO THE NEXT GENERATIONS

In his second letter to Timothy, he wrote: *"And the things you have heard me say in the presence of many witnesses **entrust to reliable men who will also be qualified to teach others**" (2 Tim. 2:2).* With a similar tone, he wrote: ***"We must pay more careful attention, therefore, to what we have heard, so that we do not drift away"** (Heb. 2:1).* We'll soon get to know the message Jesus preached and later entrusted to people, like Paul, to preach to us. The same message preached from the very beginning was to remain intact for all generations. We are not to "*drift away*" from what we have heard from the beginning. Please keep this in mind as it is one of the keys to understanding the Bible.

> *We have come to share in Christ **if we hold firmly till the end the confidence we had at first.** (Heb. 3:14)*

We cannot preach any other gospel today apart from what the Disciples of Christ taught us. Paul was the man appointed to teach us. And he taught nothing apart from the gospel of Christ. It is written that *Jesus Christ and the Father are one*. They have the same Words. Whoever teaches anything below or beyond this and calls it a revelation from God is only a dreamer. Once again, *"A student is not above his teacher, but everyone who is fully trained will be like his teacher" (Luke 6:40). "I tell you the truth, no servant is greater than his master, nor is a messenger greater than the one who sent him" (John 13:16).*

> *"The Bible is the supreme source document of Christianity but it is not the private property of Christians. It has a power and pertinence for people of every kind and in every age. It speaks about God but it also speaks from God and concerns itself with the struggles, tragedies, aspirations and destinies of humanity itself. This has given it a contemporary relevance across the centuries and enabled it to be a light on the journey of life for all humankind."—Roy Williamson*

Chapter Eight

JESUS—THE TRUE FOUNDATION

It is obvious a house is not built from the roof but from the ground. Since we have been reliably informed that we cannot preach or teach any other gospel apart from that of Jesus Christ, it is incumbent on us to locate this gospel of Christ first which is the foundation and then proceed on building the structure on top of it. Before we trace the teachings of Jesus Christ, it will be appropriate for us to know a bit about who He is, whose message He taught and the people He was sent to. Allowing the Bible to reveal these to us gradually introduces the truths of the Scriptures to us in bits.

I must warn you though that there are several things you will find hard to believe as you read along but they are there in your Bible all this while. I encourage you to take heart and humble yourself to the Bible, and not what men have taught us to believe in place of the plain words of God. Remember, we accept the testimony of man, but the testimony of God is far greater and supreme.

> *"Thanks be to the gospel, by means of which we also, who did not see Christ when He came into this world, seem to be with Him when we read His deeds."—St. Ambrose (C. 339-397)*

WHO IS JESUS CHRIST?

The purpose of this book is to trace the basic message of the Bible to you so as to enable you gain the basic line or route upon which to study your Bible and, in the process, make its reading and studying fascinating anytime you pick it. It is my desire to avoid all controversies in matters relating to doctrines taught by others. *We have already learnt that we are supposed to learn and teach nothing apart from the gospel of Christ.* So, whether we like it or not and if only we claim to be Christians, then we have no choice than to heed to this advice and stick to His message. *There is no other gospel apart from His.*

I am not going to argue here over whether Jesus Christ is God or whether He is one of the members of a three-in-one God or whether He is the Son of God. That would divert our attention from the main purpose of this book. Because of that, I have decided to just put down a few things that the disciples who lived with Him for at least three years wrote concerning Him. As we read along, His personality will be clearly revealed to us.

> *In the beginning was* ***the Word, and the Word was with God, and the Word was God****. 2 He was with God in the beginning. 3* ***Through Him all things were made****; without Him nothing was made that has been made. 4 In Him was life, and that life was the light of men. 5 The light shines in the darkness, but the darkness has not understood it . . . 10* ***He was in the world, and though the world was made through Him, the world did not recognise Him.*** *11* ***He came to that which was His own, but His own did not receive Him****. 12 Yet to all who received Him, to those who believed in His Name, He gave the right to become children of God—13 children born not of natural descent, nor of human decision or a husband's will, but born of God. 14* ***The Word became flesh and made His dwelling among us****. We have seen His glory, the glory of the One and Only, who came from the Father, full of grace and truth . . . 18* ***No-one has ever seen God, but God the One and Only, who is at the Father's side, has made Him known.*** *(John 1:1-18)*

From the above verses, we know that there was a certain beginning; whether it is six thousand years ago or some billions of years ago—that is not our concern here. We are being told from these verses that there was a certain beginning when there was a Being called the Word who was ***with*** God. We are also told that everything was made ***through*** this Being. Along the line, this Being became flesh and made His dwelling among His own people on earth but the world failed to receive Him. At the same time, there were some who were able to believe in His message and received Him. To such people, He gave them the right to become the children of God.

We have been told from these verses that *"no-one has ever seen God,* ***but God the One and only, who is at the Father's side, has made Him known.****"* Please read carefully. It says, *"In the beginning was the Word, and the Word was* ***with God****, and the Word was God."* Then, we also have *"God the One and only, who is at the Father's side has made Him (God) known."*

Take note that the Scriptures did not say all things were made *by Him*. Rather, it says, ***"through Him all things were made."*** That is to say, for instance, that if I deliver a message from my father in France to my brothers in Ghana my father would have communicated *"through"* me. I would not take full credit for whatever was agreed upon by my father and brothers. The same way, if a president of a particular nation gets things done *through* his ministers, he still gets the credits for everything though he did not touch anything with his hands. I'm now communicating to you *through* this book. The book is the medium but the style of writing and the ideas are mine so to speak.

It is written about the LORD Jesus Christ that:

> ***He is the image of the invisible God, the firstborn over all creation.*** *16 For by Him all things were created: things in heaven and on earth, visible and invisible, whether thrones or powers or rulers or authorities; all things were created by Him. 17 He is before all things, and in Him all things hold together. 18 And He is the head of the body, the church; He is the beginning and* ***the firstborn from among the dead, so that in everything He might have the supremacy.*** *19* ***For God was pleased to have all his fullness dwell in Him, and through Him to reconcile to Himself all things, whether things on earth or things in heaven****, by making peace through His blood, shed on the cross." (Col. 1:15-20)*

We read that ***"For God was pleased to have all His fullness dwell in Him*** *(Jesus Christ),* ***and through Him*** *to reconcile to Himself (God the Father) all things."* Paul wrote that our *"attitude should be the same as that of Christ 6 Who,* ***being in the very nature of God****, did not consider equality with God something to be grasped, 7 but made Himself nothing, taking the very nature of a servant. Being made in human likeness 8 and being found in appearance as a man, He humbled Himself and became obedient to death—even death on a cross! 9* ***Therefore God exalted Him to the highest place and gave Him the Name that is above every name****, 10 that at the name of Jesus every knee should bow, in heaven and on earth and under the earth, 11 and every tongue confess that Jesus Christ is LORD,* ***to the glory of God the Father****" (Phil. 2:5-11).*

In Paul's first letter to the Corinthians, he wrote: *"We know that an idol is nothing at all in the world and that* ***there is no God but One****. 5 For even if there are so-called gods, whether in heaven or on earth (as indeed there are many "gods" and many "lords"), 6* ***yet for us there is but One God, the Father, from whom all things came and for whom we live****; and there is but One LORD, Jesus Christ,* ***through whom all things came and through whom we live****" (1 Cor. 8:4-6).* It is written: *"Hear O Israel: The LORD our God, the LORD is One" (Deut. 6:4).* Whether the word translated LORD here is a compound word or not, the Scriptures say that Word is One; period! *"For us, there is but One God, the Father."*

All things, both seen and unseen came *"from"* God, the Father, and we all live for Him. Yet, everything came *"through"* our LORD Jesus Christ because God the Father was pleased to have all His fullness dwell in Christ and in the process exalted Him to the highest place and gave Him the Name that is above every other name including mine. It is written:

> *But Christ has indeed been raised from the dead, the first fruits of those who have fallen asleep. 21 For since death came through a man, the resurrection of the dead comes also through a man. 22 For as in Adam all die, so in Christ all will be made alive. 23 But each in his own turn: Christ, the first fruits; then, when He comes, those who belong to Him. 24* ***Then the end will come, when He*** *(Jesus Christ)* ***hands over the kingdom to God the Father after He has destroyed all dominion, authority and power. 25 For He must reign until He has put all His enemies under His feet.*** *The last enemy to be destroyed is death. 27 For He "has put everything under His feet."* ***Now when it says that "everything" has been put under Him, it is clear that this does not include God Himself, who put everything under Christ.*** *28 When He has done this,* ***then the Son Himself will be made subject to Him who put everything under Him, so that God*** *(the Father)* ***may be all in all.*** *(1 Cor. 15:20-28)*

These verses are self-explanatory and it's important to know that I didn't write them. You don't need anyone to delve into any spiritual field to explain this to you. It says that a time is coming in the future called the end when Jesus Christ will hand over the kingdom to God the Father after He has reigned and destroyed all dominion, power and authority. Whether this is going to happen tomorrow or the next thousand years, I do not know.

All that we are told is that it is going to happen. At that future time too, the Son Himself (Jesus Christ) will be made subject to God who put everything under Him so that God the Father may be all in all. To teach anything different from this means you are saying you understand the Scriptures more than Paul did. You surely can understand the Scriptures more than me but it would take you a while to do that with Paul's knowledge about understanding the mysteries and revelations of God. Yes, Jesus said we would do more than He did but I'm yet to see someone walk on the face of even a lake in one village.

> *And we know that in all things God works for the good of those who love Him, who have been called according to His purpose. 29* ***For those God foreknew He also predestined to be conformed to the likeness of His Son, that He might be the firstborn among***

> ***many brothers***. *30 And those He predestined, He also called; those He called, He also justified; those He justified, He also glorified. (Rom. 8:28-30)*

THE FIRSTBORN AMONG MANY BROTHERS

Note that it says those God predestined and foreknew were to be conformed to the likeness of His Son so that the LORD Jesus Christ might be *"the firstborn among many brothers [and sisters]"*. It is written that: *"In the LORD, woman is not independent of man, nor is man independent of woman" (1 Cor. 11:11)*. Do not doubt this. One of Jesus' assignments was to give people the right to become children of God if they believe and receive Him. *(John 1:12-13)*. John wrote *"Dear friends, **now we are children of God**, and what we will be has not yet been made known. **But we know that when He appears, we shall be like Him**, for we shall see Him as He is. 3 Everyone who has this hope in him purifies himself, **just as He is pure**" (1 John 3:2-3)*. Jesus is not the brother of God but His firstborn Son. Therefore if we are now children of God, then Jesus is our Big Brother because He is the firstborn Son of God.

> *No-one who is **born of God** will continue to sin, because God's seed remains in Him; he cannot go on sinning, **because he has been born of God**. 10 **This is how we know who the children of God are and who the children of the devil are:** Anyone who does not do what is right is not a child of God; nor is anyone who does not love his brother. (1 John 3:9-10)*

You see that although what we will be is yet to be made known when Christ appears, yet at the very moment that we are here on earth, we are the sons of God if we repent and practise the teachings of Christ. The criteria for identifying who the children of God are have even been given. Doing the right things at all times and loving our fellow men as ourselves are the two given in these verses. And it is actually possible to live a righteous life as well. It is written: *"Whoever claims to live in Him must walk as Jesus did" (1 John 2:6)*. We are saved to walk as Jesus did on earth and not to wait for some flight to take us into space before living the righteous life of our Big Brother Jesus Christ in a different realm.

> *"When our minds find inner agreement with the truth expressed in the passages, we embrace the mind of Christ as our own, for these great Scriptural truths are the very things Jesus believed. These truths constitute the faith, hope and love in which He lived. And as they become ours, His mind becomes our mind. Then we become true co-labourers with God, as brothers, sisters and friends of Jesus in the present and coming Kingdom of God. We can then know and understand in its fullness the guidance God gives to His children."— Dallas Willard*

It is by the grace of God the Father and Jesus Christ my LORD and Saviour that I have lips and the fingers to say and type these things. Jesus Christ is my LORD and personal Saviour. I make all my prayer requests through Him and live according to His teachings by asking everything in His Name to the Father. He has been given the Name that is above every other name and at the mention of His Name, every knee including my very own must bow both in heaven and in earth. But that excludes the knees of God the Father who delegated that authority to Him.

Much as it sounds strange in our ears because it has been taught this way for centuries, God the Father is not God to us alone but to Jesus Christ as well. In several places of the Bible, we read verses like: *"May the God who gives endurance and encouragement give you a spirit of unity among yourselves as you follow Christ Jesus, 6 so that with one heart and mouth you may glorify* ***the God and Father of our LORD Jesus Christ"*** *(Rom. 15:5-6).*

That came from the pen of none other than Paul, the apostle who was taught by Christ Jesus Himself when he was praying for his students to remain united. He knew that after that was achieved, they would glorify the God and Father of our LORD Jesus Christ. With a similar tone, he wrote to the Corinthian church that: *"Praise be to* ***the God and Father of our LORD Jesus Christ, the Father of compassion and the God of all comfort*** *. . ." (2 Cor. 3-4).* Again, he wrote: *"**the God and Father of the LORD Jesus,** who is to be praised for ever, knows that I am not lying (2 Cor. 11:31).*

> ***Praise be to THE GOD AND FATHER OF OUR LORD JESUS CHRIST,*** *who has blessed us in the heavenly realms with every spiritual blessings in Christ. 4 For He chose us in Him before the creation of the world to be holy and blameless in His sight. In love 5 He predestined us to be adopted as His sons through Jesus Christ, in accordance with His pleasure and will—6 to the praise of His glorious grace, which He has freely given us in the One He loves. (Eph. 1:3-6)*

Later in these verses, Paul was to make a bold statement when He said he was asking *"the God of our LORD Jesus Christ, the glorious Father"* to give his students the Spirit of wisdom and revelation to enable them to know Him better. I think Paul would have been accused of blasphemy by the modern-day Pharisees if he had been around to say that our God is God to Jesus Christ too. But read this:

> *I keep asking . . . that 17* ***the God of our LORD Jesus Christ, the glorious Father****, may give you the Spirit of wisdom and revelation, so that you may know Him (the Father) better. I pray also that the eyes of your heart may be enlightened in order that you may know the hope to which He has called you, the riches of His glorious inheritance in the saints, 19 and His incomparably great power for us who believe. That power is like the working of His mighty strength, 20 which He (God) exerted in Christ when He (God) raised Him (Christ) from the dead and seated Him (Christ) at His (God's) right hand in the heavenly realms, 21 far above all rule and authority, power and dominion, and every title that can be given, not only in the present age but also in the one to come. 22* ***And God placed all things under His feet and appointed Him to be head over everything for the church, which is His body, the fullness of Him who fills everything in every way.*** *(Eph. 1:15-23)*

It is very true that Jesus Christ runs the show in everything that happens in the affairs of both man and the spiritual realms. There is no denying this fact but it is equally true that He was appointed by God the Father to have this position. Very soon, we will get to learn from the Scriptures that Jesus taught the same things, and they are in your Bible. Paul wrote to Timothy: *"Now to the King eternal, immortal, invisible,* ***THE ONLY GOD****, be honour and glory forever and ever. Amen." (1 Tim. 1:17)*

> ***For there is One God and One mediator between God and men, the man Christ Jesus****, 6 who gave Himself as a ransom for all men—the testimony given in its proper time. 7 And for this purpose I was appointed a herald and an apostle—****I am telling the truth, I am not lying****—and a teacher of the true faith to the Gentiles. (1 Tim. 2:5-7)*

You should know by now that there is nowhere Paul or any of the apostles categorically stated that the God in the Bible is a group of personalities all in one, equal in authority and power. I don't know about you. But I do believe in the words of the Bible the exact way it is, and I believe people like Paul when they say things to teach us. Like I said earlier,

I say it again that whether the Hebrew text translated God in a particular passage was compound or plural, Paul said *"there is One God."* The Scriptures say *"Hear O Israel: The LORD our God,* ***the LORD is One*** *(Deut. 6:4).* The God of the patriarchs was, and still is one and the same.

> ***In the sight of God, who gives life to everything,*** *AND of Christ Jesus, who while testifying before Pontius Pilate made the good confession, I charge you 14 to keep this command without spot or blame until the appearing of our LORD Jesus Christ, 15 which God will bring about in His own time—GOD, THE BLESSED AND ONLY RULER, THE KING OF kings AND LORD OF lords, WHO ALONE IS IMMORTAL AND WHO LIVES IN UNAPPROACHABLE LIGHT, WHOM NO-ONE HAS SEEN OR CAN SEE. To Him be honour and might forever. Amen. (1 Tim. 6:13-16)*

When Philip found Nathaniel after meeting Jesus Christ himself, he told him: *"We have found the One Moses wrote about in the Law, and about whom the prophets also wrote—Jesus of Nazareth, the Son of Joseph" (John 1:45).* We can just go through the Old Testament to look for all that have been said about Jesus there and compare them to what is being taught today about Him. The only claim the so-called interpreters of the Bible have is when they say they've had revelations into these things. But mostly, their revelations are brushed aside by another one from another "man of God" and the cycle continues. Paul's revelations remain relevant throughout all generations till date.

JESUS' OWN WORDS ABOUT HIMSELF

> *The One who comes from above is above all; the one who is from the earth belongs to the earth, and speaks as one from the earth. The One who comes from heaven is above all. 32 He testifies to what He has seen and heard, but no-one accepts His testimony. 33 The man who has accepted it has certified that God is truthful. 34* ***For the One whom God has sent speaks the words of God,*** *for God gives the Spirit without limit. 35* ***The Father loves the Son and has placed everything in His hands."*** *(John 3:31-35)*

Jesus Christ was sent by God the Father from heaven to accomplish a mission on His behalf. Yet He qualifies to be called God as well because He was in the very nature of God. Answering the Jews who were questioning Him about His claim of being the Son of the Father, He asked: *"If He called them "gods", to whom the word of God came—and the Scripture cannot be broken—36* ***what about the One whom the Father set apart as His very own and sent into the world?*** *Why then do you accuse me of blasphemy because I said, 'I am God's Son' (John 10:35-36)?* So if we are called sons of God today, how much more does Christ who is the very firstborn (Son) and image of God deserves to be called God when He actually came down from heaven!

> *"It takes time to grow into Jesus the Vine; do not expect to abide in Him unless you will give Him that time. It is not enough to read God's Word, or meditations as here offered . . . Therefore, my brother who wants to learn to abide in Jesus, take time each day, before you read, while you read, and after you read, to put yourself into living contact with the living Jesus, to yield yourself distinctly and consciously to His blessed influence, so will you give Him the opportunity of taking hold of you, of drawing you up and keeping you safe in His almighty life."—Andrew Murray (1828-1917)*

In Jesus' own words He prayed thus: *"Father, the time has come. Glorify your Son, that your Son may glorify you. 2* ***For you granted Him authority over all people that He might give eternal life to all those you have given Him****. 3 Now THIS IS ETERNAL LIFE:* ***that they may know you, THE ONLY TRUE GOD, AND JESUS CHRIST, whom You have sent.*** *4 I have brought You glory on earth by completing the work You gave me to do. 5 And now, Father, glorify me in Your presence with the glory I had with You before the world began" (John 17:1-5).*

Did you notice that Jesus said that to know "*the only true God and Jesus Christ"* is eternal life? All these are written in the pages of the Bible. Jesus Himself said that "*for the Father is greater than I" (John 14:28).* It is so adorable trying to give Jesus fans with regard to how great He is. But the truth is that Jesus too, like God, does not need our fans to make Him who He is. Jesus didn't brag about His position and has not asked us to do that for Him. Talking about His attitude, Paul said that: *"Being in very nature God,* ***did not consider equality with God something to be grasped, 7 but made Himself nothing, taking the very nature of a servant, being made in human likeness.*** *8 And being found in appearance as a man, He humbled Himself and became obedient to death—****even death on a cross****" (Phil. 2:6-8).*

Jesus said, *"Whoever has my commands and obeys them,* ***he is the one who loves me.*** *He who loves me will be loved by my Father, and I too will love him and show myself to him" (John 14:21).* It is not the making of noise on top of our voices about what Jesus can do or not that shows our love for Him. You don't force the Name of Christ down the throats of unbelievers in your locality to show how much you love Him. Obeying His commands and teachings are what you should be doing. I hope I have briefly given you a fair idea of who Christ Jesus is and we can continue from here. That should be our first brick laid on the land.

Chapter Nine

WHO SENT JESUS CHRIST TO EARTH?

"Hold fast to the Bible as the sheet-anchor of your liberties; write its precepts in your hearts and practise them in your lives. To the influence of this book we are indebted for all the progress made in true civilisation, and to this we must look as our guide in the future."—Ulysses S. Grant (1822-1885)

In order not to confuse you, I have chosen not to quote from parts of the Bible that would require further interpretations by another man with some super DNA into spiritual matters before making you understand. The practice of some *"super-apostles"* normally is to quote a phrase or a verse in the Bible and tell you it doesn't mean what it says. They then go back and pick either the Hebraic or the Greek words used in interpreting those verses and at the end of the day, what you have is their own versions of the Bible, which results in the distortion of the Scriptures. If that continues unchecked, then very soon, I believe we will soon have Bibles that will suit the opinion of each individual. Bible versions like the KJV and the NIV are enough to help us understand the basic truths at least in the Bible.

In avoiding such an attempt and answer the question of who sent our LORD Jesus Christ, I have limited the answers wholly to what the LORD Jesus said of Himself concerning who sent Him and what His assignment on earth was. Jesus was not mute, deaf or dumb and on more than one occasions He told us who sent Him. It will be appropriate to hear it from the horse's own mouth:

JESUS SAID WHAT THE FATHER TOLD HIM TO SAY

> ***For I did not speak of my own accord, but the Father who sent me commanded me what to say and how to say it.*** *50 I know that His command leads to eternal life.* ***So whatever I say is just what the Father has told me to say.*** *(John 12:49-50)*

The God and Father of us all including our LORD and Saviour Jesus Christ, created everything both seen and unseen in heaven and on earth "*through*" our LORD Jesus Christ. Everything has been placed under the supervision of Christ Jesus. But remember we read earlier that *"Then the end will come, when He hands over the kingdom to God the Father after He has destroyed all dominion, authority and power. 25 For He must reign until He has put all His enemies under His feet." (1 Cor. 15:24-25)*

Jesus Christ is now reigning and He is obviously going to reign for a very long time in addition. He is my LORD and Saviour and I am proud of that. But a time is coming in future when He will hand over the kingdom to God the Father after He has completed His mission. Paul wrote: *"For He (God) has put everything under His (Jesus') feet.* ***Now when it says that "everything" has been put under Him, it is clear that this does not include God Himself, who put everything under Christ.*** *28* ***When He has done this, then the Son Himself will be made subject to Him who put everything under Him, so that God may be all in all****" (1 Cor. 15:27-28).*

In describing the nature of God, Paul said that He is "*the blessed and only Ruler, the King of kings and Lord of lords,* ***who alone is immortal and who lives in unapproachable light, whom no-one has seen or can see****" (1 Tim. 6:15-16).* Note that Paul said no-one has seen God and no-one can see Him. But let's read this: *"Dear friend, do not imitate what is evil but what is good.* ***Anyone who does what is good is from God. Anyone who does what is evil has not seen God"*** *(3 John 11). The world and its desires pass away,* ***but the man who does the will of God lives forever*** *(1 John 2:17).* If this is said about us, what do you expect to be said about Jesus Christ who has been with the Father from the beginning?

> *"The only proper response to this world which Jesus brings with Him from eternity is simply to do it. Jesus has spoken: His is the Word, ours is the obedience. Only in the doing of it does the Word of Jesus attain its honour, might, and power among us."—Dietrich Bonhoeffer (1905-1945)*

Now, because He was on a mission He had to say and do exactly what He was appointed, commissioned and directed to do. We are told that Jesus is the mediator of a covenant that is superior to that of Moses and is founded on better promises *(Heb. 8:6)*. To *mediate is to try to end a disagreement between two or more people or groups by talking to them and trying to find things that everyone can agree on*. A mediator then is a person or an organisation that tries to get agreement between people or groups who disagree with each other.

> *Hear, O heavens! Listen, O earth! For the LORD has spoken: "I have reared children and brought them up,* ***but they have rebelled against me.*** *3 The ox knows his master, the donkey his owner's manger, but Israel does not know, my people do not understand." 4 Ah, sinful nation, a people loaded with guilt, a brood of evildoers, children given to corruption!* ***They have forsaken the LORD; they have spurned the Holy One of Israel and turned their back on Him.*** *(Isa. 1:2-4)*

The two parties or groups that Jesus is mediating between are God and the human race. On the part of God, Jesus had to say exactly what He was told to say and do in order not to overstep His boundary, because He was sent to represent a party in negotiating a deal between them. He could not speak on His own accord. He was even commanded on how to say everything He said by God the Father. But He had compassion on the human race and called His disciples friends at times because they had lost touch with what was in store for them.

> *The One who comes from above is above all; the one who is from the earth belongs to the earth, and speaks as one from the earth. The One who comes from heaven is above all. 32 He testifies to what He has seen and heard, but no-one accepts His testimony. 33 The man who has accepted it has certified that God is truthful. 34* ***For the One whom God has sent speaks the words of God, for God gives the Spirit without limit****. 35* ***The Father loves the Son and has placed everything in His hands*** *(John 3:31-35).*

With the exception of God the Father, Jesus Christ our LORD is above every power, dominion and authority. This is because He represents the very image of God, and the Father has given the Spirit without limit to Him and He speaks the very words of God the Father. This is why He could tell His disciples, at one time, that once they had seen Him, they had seen the Father also. Two cannot walk except they agree. For Him to be at the very right hand side of God, then they must think alike. It's impossible to see the

Father in person. But Jesus would tell you precisely what the Father would tell you at every moment in time.

> *Jesus gave them this answer: "**I tell you the truth, the Son can do nothing by Himself; He can do only what He sees His Father doing, because whatever the Father does the Son also does.** 20 For the Father loves the Son **and shows Him all He does.** Yes, to your amazement He will show Him even greater things than these . . . 22 Moreover, the Father judges no-one, but has entrusted all judgment to the Son, **that all may honour the Son just as they honour the Father**. He who does not honour the Son does not honour the Father. 24 "**I tell you the truth, whoever hears my word and believes Him who sent me has eternal life and will not be condemned; he has crossed over from death to life** (John 5:19-24).*

Jesus Himself said He cannot do anything by Himself, and that He can only do what He sees His Father do. No-one has seen the Father except Jesus Christ because He came from Him and has His words. The teachings of Jesus therefore must be taken as that of the Father. In that case, the honour and praises due the Father can be appropriated by the Son as well. He again said at the latter part that whoever hears His word and believes in the One who sent Him has eternal life and has crossed over from death to life. I believe the words of Jesus.

> ***By myself I can do nothing; I judge only as I hear**, and my judgment is just, **for I seek not to please myself but Him who sent me.** (John 5:30)*

I often hear those in the secular world expressing love for their favourite artistes that even if they cough and recorded it on a CD, they would buy it because of their love for them. I also choose to take Jesus by His own words no matter how it sounds to my ears. Jesus would never brag! With all the power, dominion and authority He possessed, and still possesses, He still said that He could do nothing by Himself. I'm not surprised though because even when He healed the sick, He warned those around not to tell anyone including those healed. The Bible says He was tested in every way like us. I keep wondering how could He still manage His humility in spite of popular acclamation, especially by ladies, to be made a King between age 30 and 33. He was and is simply an amazingly humble LORD and Saviour!

> ***For I have come down from heaven not to do my will but to do the will of Him who sent me.** 39 And this is the will of Him*

> *who sent me, that I shall lose none of all that He has given me, but raise them up at the last day. 40 For my Father's will is that everyone who looks to the Son and believes in Him shall have eternal life, and I will raise him up at the last day. (John 6:38-40)*

Jesus did not hide or shy away from the fact that He was sent by the Father to the human race. In the above verses that we just read, He gives us the will of the Father when He sent Him. That will is still there now—that anyone who looks to Jesus Christ and accepts His teachings shall have eternal life because those words of Jesus come from the Father Himself.

> *Then Jesus, still teaching in the temple courts, cried out, "Yes you know me, and you know where I am from.* ***I am not here on my own, but He who sent me is true. You do not know Him,*** *29* ***but I know Him because I am from Him and He sent me."*** *(John 7:28-29)*

It is written that: *"With many similar parables Jesus spoke the word to them, as much as they could understand. 34 He did not say anything to them without using a parable. But when He was alone with His own disciples, He explained everything" (Mark 4:33-34).* If what we just read above is also one of His parables, then it is obvious this is one of the *"as much as they could understand"* because it is so plain and straight to the point. He has made it so plain that even a kindergarten child should be able to grasp its meaning.

> *"Who are you?" they asked. "Just what I have been claiming all along," Jesus replied. "I have much to say in judgment of you.* ***But He who sent me is reliable, and what I have heard from Him I tell the world.****" 27 They did not understand that He was telling them about His Father. 28 So Jesus said, "When you have lifted up the Son of Man, then you will know that I am the One I claim to be,* ***and that I do nothing on my own but speak just what the Father has taught me. The One who sent me is with me; He has not left me alone, for I always do what pleases Him.****" (John 8:25-29)*

There isn't even a single place in the entire Bible where Jesus Christ compared Himself to God the Father as being equal with Him in position, power and authority. In fact He actually said at one place that ***"the Father is greater than I"*** *(John 14:28).* And I'm glad that was not written in an incomprehensible language to warrant any interpretations and/or misinterpretations. It is written that: *"For this reason a man will leave his father and mother and be united to his wife, and the two will become one flesh"*

(Eph. 5:31). It is equally true that though they are one flesh, the man is still the head. Jesus said, *"I and the Father are One" (John 10:30).* That is very true but God the Father is still the Head. Paul wrote: *"Now I want you to realise that the head of every man is Christ, and the head of the woman is man,* ***and the head of Christ is God*** *(1 Cor. 11:3).*

> *Jesus said to them, "If God were your Father, you would love me, for I came from God and now am here.* ***I have not come on my own; but He sent me****" (John 8:42)*

Our LORD and Saviour is never ashamed to admit that He was sent by God the Father to the human race. He did not come on His own accord and He has not failed to admit that to us in these verses we have read so far. He took the work of God so seriously that at one time He said, *"As long as it is day,* ***we must do the work of Him who sent me****. Night is coming, when no-one can work" (John 9:4).* That is Jesus on true business ethics for you! There were days He was in the temple at dawn teaching. The woman allegedly caught in adultery was brought to Him in the temple at dawn *(John 8:2-4).*

> *"Father, the time has come. Glorify your Son, that your Son may glorify you. 2* ***For you*** *(God)* ***granted*** *Him (Jesus)* ***authority over all*** *people that He might give eternal life to all those you have given Him. 3* ***Now this is eternal life: that they may know you, The Only True God, and Jesus Christ, whom you have sent.*** *4 I have brought you glory on earth* ***by completing the work you gave me to do****. 5 And now, Father, glorify me in your presence with the glory I had with you before the world began." (John 17:1-5)*

I will defeat the purpose for which this book is being written now if I want to give the actual relationship between God the Father and the LORD Jesus Christ as I would have to start from the book of Genesis down to the last page of Revelations. But for now, let's just accept Jesus' own words that He was sent from heaven to do God the Father's work. He has also informed us that although everything was created *"through"* Him, yet God the Father is greater than He is. I don't know about you but I believe Jesus on whatever He says.

> *Jesus said, "Do not hold on to me, for I have not yet returned to the Father. Go instead to my brothers and tell them,* ***'I am returning to my Father and your Father,*** **TO MY GOD AND YOUR GOD."** *(John 20:17)*

Jesus prayed that we may know *"the only true God."* Now, after His resurrection He told this woman that He was going to His God who is our

God as well. If Jesus Himself calls God the Father His God, then what is the big deal that it is never mentioned to us today? It's like a taboo to say that in public, yet Jesus said it Himself. *To the Jews who had believed Him, Jesus said, "**If you hold to my teaching, you are really my disciples**. 32 Then you will know the truth, and the truth will set you free" (John 8:31-32).* There's nothing fascinating as studying to understand the Scriptures yourself.

> *"Men of Israel, listen to this: Jesus of Nazareth was a man **accredited by God to you** by miracles, **wonders and signs which God did among you through Him**, as you yourselves know. 23 **This man was handed over to you by God's set purpose and fore-knowledge;** and you, with the help of wicked men, put Him to death by nailing Him to the cross. 24 **But God raised Him from the dead, freeing Him from the agony of death**, because it was impossible for death to keep its hold on Him." (Acts 2:22-24)*

Each time I hear this part of the Bible read in the churches and on television networks by most preachers today, I hear the congregants chanting and feeling elated when it gets to where it says *"because it was impossible for death to keep its hold on Him."* One begins to wonder if the purpose of attending church services these days is to go there to chant as supporters for Jesus Christ. Peter spent at least three years with the LORD and is also adding some things to who sent Jesus Christ on His mission. First, we know from him that Jesus was given accreditation by God the Father to do all He did. To give *accreditation* to someone or an institution is to officially approve something or somebody as being of an accepted quality or standard. This has to be done by somebody or an organisation that is *higher in rank* than the one being accredited. Jesus was given His accreditation by God the Father.

So we are told by Peter that Jesus was accredited to perform miracles, signs and wonders. We also know from the above that it was actually God the Father who was doing these things "*through*" Him. Everything that happened before, during and after His resurrection we are told happened because of God's set purpose and fore-knowledge. And it was God who raised Him from the dead. I hope we have added another brick to the foundation.

> *"Christ is the focus of the entire Bible, and you need to study it to know what He is like. Too often we study the Bible for the sake of theological arguments or to answer questions. Those things are important, but the main point of Bible study is to know more about Christ so that you can be like Him."—John MacArthur*

Chapter Ten

TO WHOM WAS JESUS SENT?

As I said earlier, clearly understanding Jesus Himself, the message He brought from heaven, His mode of communication, who sent Him to whom, and at what time, will make it easier for even a toddler to understand the Scriptures. Even though Christ was sent to redeem the human race, He had a set time to reach out to all of them. It is no fluke that He chose only twelve out of the thousands that followed Him. It took Him three years to impart what He knew to them and even asked them at a point to wait to be filled with the Holy Spirit before they began their assignment of taking the gospel to the whole world.

CHRIST'S MODE OF COMMUNICATION

I believe we now know where Christ came from and who sent Him. We must also know His mode of communication as that will help us know whether to take His words literally or not as there was nothing He said to the crowd and the Pharisees without using parables. It was only His disciples who had the opportunity to hear Him interpret His own parables to them. It is written: *"O my people, hear my teaching; listen to the words of my mouth. 2* ***I will open my mouth in parables, I will utter hidden things, things from of old****—3 what we have heard and known, what our fathers have told us" (Psalm 78:1-3).* Since He came from the Father and had the very words of His Father, He chose to speak in parables just like His Father.

> *Jesus spoke all these things to the crowd in parables;* ***He did not say anything to them without using a parable****. 35 So was fulfilled what was spoken through the prophet: "I will open my mouth in parables, I will utter things hidden since the creation of the world." (Matt. 13:34-35)*

This implies that the prophecy in the Psalms was meant for Jesus. Before His coming to the earth, Jesus was to utter hidden things from of old. He was to utter what the fathers had heard, known and told the children. But He was supposed to say all that in parables. Even Jesus stuck to the Scriptures.

This is one of the major keys to understand the Scriptures, especially the New Testament. It says that Jesus did not say anything to the crowd without using a parable. ***A parable is a short story that teaches a moral or spiritual lesson.*** Because of this, you cannot read a verse like *"I have given you authority to trample on snakes and scorpions and to overcome all the power of the enemy; nothing will harm you" (Luke 10:19)* and set off on a trampling spree to kill real snakes and scorpions with your bare feet. Even the One who said that did not do that in reality. *He taught them many things by parables and, in His teaching, said . . . (Mark 4:2).*

> *With many similar parables Jesus spoke the word to them,* ***as much as they could understand. He did not say anything to them without using a parable. But when He was alone with His own disciples, He explained everything*** *(Mark 4:33-34).*

One would argue that it is not his fault if he does not understand the parables of Jesus Christ then. But you should also know that He only spoke "*as much as they could understand.*" That is, if they had paid much attention to what He taught, they would have understood everything He said although they were taught in parables. If they had gone a step further after hearing Him speak in parables and asking Him questions pertaining to what He meant, they would have had a different story to tell. It didn't end there though. Anytime He was alone with His own disciples, after speaking a parable to the crowd, He would take time to explain everything in details for them to learn and understand the moral or the spiritual lessons He meant to impart to His listeners.

> *"It is one thing to be told that the Bible has authority because it is divinely inspired, and another thing to feel one's heart leap out and grasp its truth."—Leslie D. Weatherhead (1893-1976)*

As an example of this, let's read a parable Jesus told the crowd in the presence of His own disciples and later see what transpired. Those who had the time to ask for the meanings to His parables had their needs met by understanding the lesson He was teaching through the parables.

> ***Then He told them many things in parables,*** *saying: "A farmer went out to sow his seed. 4 As he was scattering the seed, some fell along the path, and the birds came and ate it up. 5 Some fell on rocky places, where it did not have much soil. It sprang up quickly, because the soil was shallow. 6 But when the sun came up, the plants were scorched, and they withered because they had no root. 7 Other seeds fell among thorns, which grew up and choked the plants. 8 Still other seeds fell on good soil, where it produced a crop—a hundred, sixty or thirty times what was sown. 9 He who has ears, let him hear." (Matt. 13:3-9)*

Immediately after this particular parable was taught, it remained as such to both the disciples and the crowd until one group made the effort to start asking questions regarding what had been taught: "*The disciples came to Him and asked, '**Why do you speak to the people in parables**?' 11 He replied, 'The knowledge of the secrets of the kingdom of heaven has been given to you, but not to them . . . 13 This is why I speak to them in parables: Though seeing, they do not see; though hearing, they do not hear or understand.'" (Matt. 13:10-13).*

Even though Christ Jesus was speaking to them in parables, they could have *"seen"* what they were not *"seeing"* and *"heard"* what they were not *"hearing"* if they had paid attention to His words. Solomon wrote: *"Even a child is known by his actions, by whether his conduct is pure and right. Ears that hear and eyes that see—the LORD has made them both" (Prov. 20:11-12).* In all fields of endeavour, it is those who are willing to go the extra mile that always get the results they seek. One man looks and sees a rock. Another man sees the same thing and sees a diamond covered in dirt. There is a line in one of Don Williams' songs that says: *"If you want to find gold, go digging in the mountain."*

In our day too, people are looking but are not seeing anything. They keep hearing and watching things happen right before their eyes but do not understand them. Do you know the sort of peaceful atmosphere we could all enjoy if we would practise the *"funny idea"* of staying single and abstaining from sex until marriage alone? You keep *"seeing"* but do not *"see"* and keep *"hearing"* but do not *"hear"* anything because you have not been trained in the things of God.

Can you imagine what would happen to the nation that would actually implement the law *"Thou shall not lie?"* I mean a nation where even lying to your own kids is a crime punishable by law! *As a man thinks in his heart, so is he.* We have been brain-washed to accept that these things are impossible, and it has become our reality but that is not true. It can actually be altered.

"Because God does not speak to us every day from the heavens, and there are only the Scriptures alone, in which He has willed that His truth shall be published and made known unto even the end, they can be fully certified to the faithful by no other warrant than this: that we hold it to be decreed and concluded that they came down from heaven, as though we heard God speaking from His own mouth."— John Calvin (1509-1564)

After telling them the reasons why the crowd had to be taught in parables, Jesus went further to narrate the meaning of the parable in plain language that every Tom, Dick and Harry could understand. No-one has any authority then to further interpret what the LORD had interpreted Himself. That would mean claiming to be more insightful than He is which is impossible. Jesus said we would do more than He did if only we believed. But He also said: *"A student is not above his teacher, but everyone who is fully trained will be like his teacher."* Between Jesus and you—who is the teacher and who is the student? Don't forget that it is purely by His grace that you are even chosen from among the lot to preach His word. Do not be arrogant! I just laugh at those who claim to be more powerful than He is today.

> ***Listen then to what the parable of the sower means***: *19 When anyone hears the message about the kingdom and does not understand it, the evil one comes and snatches away what was sown in his heart.* ***This is the seed that was sown along the path [The meaning]****. 20 The one who received the seed that fell on rocky places is the man who hears the word and at once receives it with joy. 21 But since he has no root, he lasts only a short time. When trouble or persecution comes because of the word, he quickly falls away [****the meaning****]. 22 The one who received the seed that fell among the thorns is the man who hears the word, but the worries of this life and the deceitfulness of wealth choke it, making it unfruitful [****the meaning****]. 23 But the one who received the seed that fell on good soil is the man who hears the word and understands it [****the meaning****]. He produces a crop, yielding a hundred, sixty or thirty times what was sown." (Matt. 13:18-23)*

I don't know the magnitude of your IQ but I don't think you need other revelations into the mind of God to understand this after it has been explained by no other teacher but Jesus Christ of all teachers. At this stage, you can simply either take it or leave it. *"You will be ever hearing but never understanding; you will be ever seeing but never perceiving. For this people's heart has become calloused; they hardly hear with their ears, and they have closed their eyes. Otherwise they might see with their eyes, hear with their ears, understand with their hearts and turn, and I would heal them" (Matt. 13:14-15).*

Another example will do. Before His death on the cross, Jesus told one of the criminals who were crucified with Him that: ***"today you will be with me in paradise"*** *(Luke 23:42-43)* after the criminal had told Him to remember him in His kingdom. There are those who take this literally and conclude that whoever dies in the faith goes straight into heaven after death because of what Jesus said.

The first thing to remember is the fact that ***"He did not say anything to them without using a parable. But when He was alone with His own disciples, He explained everything"*** *(Mark 4:33-34).* Secondly, we know Jesus did not go straight to heaven after His death until after three days at least. Yet He told the criminal that He would be with Him in paradise the same day that they were both hanging on the trees. After His resurrection and being seen by Mary at the tomb, Jesus said, *"Do not hold on to me,* ***for I have not yet returned to the Father. Go instead to my brothers and tell them 'I am returning to my Father and your Father,*** *to my God and to your God" (John 20:17).* That was after spending three days and nights in the tomb.

After His resurrection from the grave Jesus told Mary to inform His brothers that He was then returning to His Father. If this is the case, should we take what He told the criminal literally? You can answer that for yourself. *"But Christ has indeed been raised from the dead,* ***the first fruits of those who have fallen asleep.*** *21 For since death came through a man, the resurrection of the dead comes also through a man. 22 For as in Adam all die, so in Christ all will be made alive. 23 But each in his own turn:* ***Christ, the first fruits; then, when He comes, those who belong to Him****" (1 Cor. 15:20-23).*

JESUS CAME FIRST TO SAVE THE LOST TRIBE OF ISRAEL

Now, back to the people Jesus was sent to. Meeting Zacchaeus, who was a tax collector, Jesus said to him, *"Today salvation has come to this house, because this man, too, is a son of Abraham. 10* ***For the Son of Man came to seek and to save what was lost****" (Luke 19:9-10).* What was lost that Christ came to seek and save? Isaiah gives us the answer.

> *Hear, O heavens! Listen, O earth! For the LORD has spoken: "I* ***reared children and brought them up, but they have rebelled against me.*** *3 The ox knows his master, the donkey his owner's manger, but Israel does not know, my people do not understand." 4 Ah, sinful nation, a people loaded with guilt, a brood of evildoers,*

> *children given to corruption!* ***They have forsaken the LORD; they have spurned the Holy One of Israel and turned their backs on Him*** *(Isaiah 1:2-4).*

When God called the children of Israel out of Egypt, He intended for them to be His *"treasured possession."* He told them: *"Now if you obey me fully and keep my covenant, then out of all nations you will be my treasured possession.* ***Although the whole earth is mine,*** *6* ***you will be for me a kingdom of priests and a holy nation****" (Exod. 19:5-6).* The Israelites could not deliver on their part of the deal, and went off the course. Instead of becoming a kingdom of priests and a holy nation, this is what God later said about them:

> *"As it is written "There is no-one righteous, not even one; there is no-one who understands, no-one who seeks God. 12* ***All have turned away, they have together become worthless; there is no-one who does good, not even one****." 13 "Their throats are open graves; their tongues practise deceit." "The poison of vipers is on their lips." 14 Their mouths are full of cursing and bitterness." 15 "Their feet are swift to shed blood; 16 ruin and misery mark their ways, 17 and the way of peace they do not know." 18 "There is no fear of God before their eyes" (Rom. 3:10-18).*

Please be reminded of the fact that although these verses were coming from the New Testament, they were actually quoted from the Old Testament by Paul to teach the Gentiles on the subject of salvation. That was how the Israelites became lost. And since God does not change His mind on His work-in-progress, He sent Jesus Christ to seek and to save them back. The whole world including the people on earth belongs to God but He said, *"Israel is my firstborn son" (Exod. 4:23)* of nations just like Adam was His firstborn son as a man. A house is built from the ground, starting with the foundation. You can have your own blueprint but still the house has to start from somewhere. The children of Israel were chosen as the firstborn son to serve as the foundation of the house that was being built to increase and cover the whole earth.

> *Then Jesus asked, "What is the kingdom of God like? What shall I compare it to? 19* ***It is like a mustard seed, which a man took and planted in his garden. It grew and became a tree, and the birds of the air perched in its branches****" (Luke 13:18-19).*

When God decided to create men to rule and take dominion over the earth, He created Adam and Eve like the mustard seed knowing very well that they would grow to become a tree which would cover the face of the earth. When that generation was lost, He went and entered into a covenant with Noah. After him came Abraham, which later extended to cover his children. These children also lost the mark and were alienated from God, their Father.

> *"The only way we can discern the true from the false is to know the Shepherd's voice—God's Word. One of the primary reasons we need to be in a disciplined study of the Scriptures is so we can saturate ourselves in the truth. When we know the truth and we are presented with that which is false, we will instinctively recognise it. Measuring philosophies or theologies or opinions or sermons or books or doctrines or counsel by the Word of God is like exposing the crookedness of a stick by placing a straight stick beside it"—Anne Graham Lotz.*

So when it was time for Jesus to seek and save what was lost, He had to start from the already laid-down foundation, which started with Abraham and his children. First, He had to go to His own to start from scratch again. ***"He came to that which was His own**, but His own did not receive Him. 12 Yet to all who received Him, to those who believed in His Name, He gave the right to become children of God—13 children born not of natural descent, nor of human decision or a husband's will, but born of God." (John 1:11-13).*

> *Jesus left that place and went to the vicinity of Tyre. He entered a house and did not want anyone to know it; yet He could not keep His presence secret. 25 In fact, as soon as she heard about Him, a woman whose little daughter was possessed by an evil spirit came and fell at His feet. 26 **The woman was a Greek, born in Syrian Phoenicia**. She begged Jesus to drive the demon out of her daughter. 27 **"First let the children eat all they want,"** He told her, **"for it is not right to take the children's bread and toss it to their dogs."** 28 **"Yes LORD,"** she replied, "**but even the dogs under the table eat the children's crumbs**." 29 Then He told her, "For such a reply, you may go; the demon has left your daughter." 30 She went home and found her child lying on the bed, and the demon gone (Mark 7:24-30).*

Notice the scenario carefully. Here was Jesus on the scene with so much power that the people had never seen or experienced before, and was healing all kinds of diseases and driving out evil spirits from those who believed. He never gave any objection to anyone apart from this woman who asked Him for a favour to heal her daughter. But with this woman, He objected to granting her request. Why? The woman was from Greece (a Gentile) and therefore was not part of the *"firstborn son"* who was lost. Jesus had to find a way to say something to this woman without offending her in the process.

Remember that He spoke to the crowd in parables as much as they could understand. He told her to *"First let the children eat all they want,* ***for it is not right to take the children's bread and toss it to their dogs.****"* Since this was a parable, we should know who the children, the bread and the dogs represent. The children are those of the firstborn son who was lost—that is, the children of Israel. The bread represents the blessings reserved for the children, which, in that case, was the healing or the deliverance being sought by this woman from Greece to have her daughter healed, and the dogs are the people outside the canopy of God's umbrella—the uncircumcised Gentiles who were not part of Israel at the time.

> *"Men turn this way and that in their search for new sources of comfort and inspiration, but the enduring truths are to be found in the Word of God"—Elizabeth, The Queen Mother (1900-2002).*

Jesus came to save the human race but He went for the Jews first. Later, He trained and taught His disciples. And when they had fully matured into His teaching, they were empowered to take the message to the whole world. Peter was with Jesus for a period of three years. When Cornelius sent men to him to preach the gospel to him and his entire family he declined by saying ***"You are well aware that it is against our law for a Jew to associate with a Gentile or visit him****. But God has shown me that I should not call any man impure or unclean" (Acts 10:28).* Why must he wait till Jesus had gone to heaven to realise that? That was because there was a time in God's own timetable to reach out to the Gentile believers. His ministry was concentrated mainly on His own that was lost from the beginning. Another brick has been laid, I believe.

Chapter Eleven

HOW JESUS CHRIST WAS RAISED FROM BIRTH

Now that we know who sent Him, His mode of communication and those He was sent to, we can now proceed to His early life on earth to see if we can see the path He chose until He was fully grown to accomplish His purpose for us all. We will start with His parents.

GOD CHOOSES THE RIGHTEOUS IN EVERY GENERATION TO WORK WITH

> *This is how the birth of Jesus Christ came about: His mother Mary was pledged to be married to Joseph, but before they came together, she was found to be with child through the Holy Spirit. 19* ***Because Joseph her husband was a righteous man*** *and did not want to expose her to public disgrace, he had in mind to divorce her quietly. (Matt. 1:18-19)*

In God's dealings with man in every generation, He always looks out for a man who is dedicated to His course and works through him. Long before the laws and commandments were given, God said about Noah that ***"Noah was a righteous man, blameless among the people of his time, and he walked with God"*** *(Gen. 6:9).* About Abraham too, He said *"Abraham obeyed me and kept my requirements, my commands, my decrees and my laws" (Gen. 26:5).*

The same way, when He needed someone to be the earthly father of our LORD Jesus Christ, He had to choose someone who was righteous and walked blamelessly in His ways. Joseph was chosen because he was righteous in God's sight. God did the same thing with the parents of John the Baptist.

> *In the time of Herod king of Judea there was a priest named Zechariah, who belonged to the priestly division of Abijah; his wife Elizabeth was also a descendant of Aaron. 6* ***Both of them were upright in the sight of God, observing all the LORD'S commandments and regulations blamelessly*** *(Luke 1:5-6).*

One common denominator of all these people was that they all chose to walk blamelessly and righteously before God in His commandments. They did not become righteous because the LORD had chosen and given them their various assignments but it was rather their way of life long before they were chosen. Solomon wrote: *"Gray hair is a crown of splendour;* ***it is attained by a righteous life****" (Prov. 16:31).* Righteousness attracts blessings and other favours from both God and men. After quitting my job to write this book, I had several job offers on the grounds of integrity, not on grounds of certificates or qualifications, but I had to let them go.

Isaiah wrote "***The fruit of righteousness will be peace; the effect of righteousness will be quietness and confidence forever****" (Isa. 32:17).* Is there any correlation between living a righteous life and being used by God to fulfil His purposes on earth? A look into the lives of various personalities in the Bible proves that there is. The Biblical definition of righteousness will be given in a later chapter.

JESUS HAD THE WORD OF GOD IMPRESSED UPON HIM FROM BIRTH

Because Jesus was going to live with flesh and blood as His parents, He had to come in contact with those who had the ability to teach Him the requirements of God from His childhood because it is written: *"These commandments that I give you today are to be upon your hearts. 7* ***Impress them on your children****. Talk about them when you sit at home and when you walk along the road, when you lie down and when you get up. 8 Tie them as symbols on your hands and bind them on your foreheads. 9 Write them on the door-frames of your houses and on your gates" (Deut. 6:6-9).*

Because they knew the laid-down precepts and statutes of God regarding the raising up of a child, Jesus' parents did all that was needed to be done for a new-born child in raising Him from a godly home. Before His birth, a prophecy was given to His mother Mary that: *"He will be great and will be called the Son of the Most High. The LORD God will give Him the throne of His father David, 33 and He will reign over the house of Jacob forever; His kingdom will never end" (Luke 1:32-33).*

Definitely, the parents of the One to reign over the house of Jacob forever must be in a position to teach Him from infancy the ways of God before He even grew up to further it Himself. *"Train up a child in the way he should go and when he is old he will not depart from it" (Pro. 22:5).* This is why God had to choose a family that was righteous, blameless and capable of training the future King of Israel. They had to know everything in advance to be able to impart them to their child.

> *On the eighth day, when it was time to circumcise Him, He was named Jesus, the Name the angel had given Him before He had been conceived. 22 When the time of their purification according to the Law of Moses had been completed, Joseph and Mary took Him to Jerusalem to present Him to the LORD 23 (as it is written in the Law of the LORD, "Every firstborn male is to be consecrated to the LORD), 24 and to offer a sacrifice in keeping with what is said in the Law of the LORD: "a pair of doves or two young pigeons." (Luke 2:21-24)*

This was done in obedience to what is written: *"Consecrate to me every firstborn male. The first offspring of every womb among the Israelites belong to me, whether man or animal" (Exod. 13:2). "When Joseph and Mary had done everything required by the Law of the LORD, they returned to Galilee to their own town of Nazareth. 40* ***And the child grew and became strong; He was filled with wisdom, and the grace of God was upon Him"*** *(Luke 2:39-40). "And Jesus grew in wisdom and stature, and in favour with God and men" (Luke 2:52).* At such tender age, Jesus was being taught the laws and commandments of God the Father to get His mind saturated with them at the very early stages of His life.

"Instruct a wise man and he will be wiser still; teach a righteous man and he will add to his learning" (Prov. 9:9). Jesus may have been born the Son of God and have the genes of a very wise man. But as parents, they were under the obligation to take responsibility of their child and teach Him till He knew everything pertaining to righteousness because the survival of His throne was going to depend on that. *"Every year His parents went to Jerusalem for the Feast of the Passover. 42 When He was twelve years old, they went up to the Feast,* ***according to the custom"*** *(Luke 2:41-42).* After the Feast, He was nowhere to be found. It took three days to find Him, and guess where He was found.

> *After three days* ***they found Him in the temple courts, sitting among the teachers, listening to them and asking questions.***

> *47 Everyone who heard Him was amazed at His understanding and His answers (Luke 2:46-47).*

It is written: ***"For the lips of a priest ought to preserve knowledge, and from his mouth men should seek instruction—because he is the messenger of the LORD Almighty"*** *(Mal. 2:7).* Although He was the High Priest, He still had to stay with the teachers and learn these things from them to keep Himself abreast with the systems of man. Wise or not, He still had to learn from those who preceded Him. Ezra was a typical example of this, *"For Ezra had devoted himself to the study and observance of the Law of the LORD, and to teaching its decrees and laws in Israel" (Ezra 7:10).* He became very learned in matters concerning the commands and decrees of the LORD for Israel.

Jesus took that path at a very early stage of His life and in the process turned out to become the Highest Priest of all. *"For lack of guidance a nation falls,* ***but many advisers make victory sure"*** *(Prov. 11:14).* ***"He who walks with the wise grows wise,*** *but a companion of fools suffers harm" (Prov. 13:20).* ***"It is not good to have zeal without knowledge,*** *nor to be hasty and miss the way" (Prov. 19:2).* There are those who claim to be so spiritual that they will never read any other material from the secular world. But how can you win a brother to the faith if you do not understand his way of thinking or what motivates him in life? No matter where you reach in life, you still have to continually learn.

Jesus became so learned and wise that even those who wanted to trap Him and have Him killed could not hide their admiration for His knowledge and integrity. This is one of their testimonies about Him. *"Teacher," they said,* ***"we know you are a man of integrity and that you teach the way of God in accordance with the truth. You aren't swayed by men, because you pay no attention to who they are"*** *(Matt. 22:16).* How about that for a testimony from your enemies who are bent on seeing you dead? Powerful stuff indeed!

Jesus was so zealous for the path already laid down that when John the Baptist was reluctant to baptise Him, He replied that *"Let it be so now;* ***it is proper for us to do this to fulfil all righteousness"*** *(Matt. 3:15).* He took time to prepare well for His ministry that even at one time when His mother asked Him to perform a miracle at a wedding feast, He replied, *"My time has not yet come" (John 2:4).* He did not spend His youthful days partying with girls. There was one time that His disciples were surprised to see Him alone talking to a woman *(John 4:27).* He was thirty when He began His ministry *(Luke 3:23)* but did not use His age as an excuse to flex His muscles around.

On account of His adequate preparations before taking up the mantle, His teaching was different from what the people had ever experienced. "*The people were amazed at His teaching,* ***because He taught them as One who had authority, not as the teachers of the law"*** *(Mark 1:22).* He meant business and knew what He was talking about at every point in time because He had spent enough time in preparing for what He taught.

JESUS' DUTY AND SCHEDULE

He revealed one of His purposes for coming to earth when He said, *"Let us go somewhere else—to the nearby villages—****so that I can preach there also. That is why I have come."*** *39 So He travelled throughout Galilee, preaching in their synagogues and driving out demons (Mark 1:38-39).* His duty was to take the gospel to those who needed it. So whenever He entered into a village, He went into their synagogues especially on the Sabbath to teach. On the day of His arrest, He asked, *"Am I leading a rebellion that you have come out with swords and clubs to capture me? 49* ***Every day I was with you, teaching in the temple courts****, and you did not arrest me. But the Scriptures must be fulfilled" (Mark 14:48-50).*

> ***Each day Jesus was teaching at the temple****, and each evening He went out to spend the night on the hill called the Mount of Olives, 38* ***and all the people came early in the morning to hear Him at the temple*** *(Luke 21:37-38).*

When He was in Jerusalem for any of the Feasts His aim was to teach at the temple during the early hours of the day and spend the rest of the evening on the Mount of Olives. Like we just read, people came to listen to Him preach at the temple courts. But when He was outside Jerusalem, He went and taught in their synagogues. "*Coming to His home town,* ***He began teaching the people in their synagogue****, and they were amazed" (Matt. 13:54).* "*When the Sabbath came, He began to teach in the synagogue, and many who heard Him were amazed" (Mark 6:2).* At one time, He began teaching in the temple courts at dawn when a woman caught in adultery was brought to Him *(John 8:2).*

> *"The Word of God is true because God Himself will make it true in us. You have much to learn, much to overcome, and much to surrender to see that power. But this will come about if you will approach your Bible study, determined that God's Word has omnipotent power to work out every blessing it promises."—Andrew Murray (1828-1917)*

Jesus did not build a church building that was separated from the Jewish synagogues or the temple where He taught. He only came to re-establish the message of the Kingdom of God which had been lost to the people while the Jews who did not believe in Him called His way a sect. He taught with much understanding and insight into the Word of God. The identifying mark to know who has been sent from God was clearly stated in the Scriptures that Jesus could not deviate from it.

One of the standards written in the Scriptures to spot a man who claims to represent God is that: ***"To the law and to the testimony! If they do not speak according to this word, they have no light of dawn"*** *(Isaiah 8:20).* Had Jesus not taught according to the Scriptures, it would not have taken the Pharisees that long to kill Him since He had become a thorn in their flesh. The difference between them was that He taught the truth of God with authority and even drove out demons from people and set them free. Another brick is added, I believe.

Chapter Twelve

THE TEACHINGS OF JESUS CHRIST

This should take us to the teaching of Christ Jesus. There are dozens of views on what He actually taught when He came to earth. There are those who come out each time with "new revelations" into what actually constitutes the message He preached. This has been done over the years that the true message of Christ is quietly losing its ground. Instead of taking His message about the Kingdom of God as it is, people have been taught to always wait for periodic new revelations like music albums from their "stars" before they can understand the Scriptures.

In order not to follow suit, and come out with a different gospel of my own and claim it was revealed to me in a dream or a vision, I have chosen to concentrate on the answers Jesus gave whenever He was asked a question regarding the Words of God. Paul said, *"By the grace God has given me, I laid a foundation as an expert builder, and someone else is building on it. But each one should be careful how he builds. 11* ***For no-one can lay any foundation other than the one already laid****, which is Jesus Christ" (1 Cor. 3:10-11).* Therefore, any teaching that is contrary to that of Jesus Christ is questionable.

To avoid all arguments and the controversies surrounding this topic, we should all show some restraint and humble ourselves to what the Master has taught us to emulate. If we claim to love and respect Jesus Christ so much, then it should not be that hard for us to accept and believe what He left with us. If He says something that seems to contradict what Paul or any of the other apostles have taught us, we should again submit ourselves to His authority and delve deeper into the Scriptures until we are clear in our minds. Personally, I am yet to find a single contradiction in the Bible from Genesis to Revelations.

CHRIST'S FORMULAR FOR DEALING WITH THE DEVIL

We will start with how Jesus Christ dealt with temptations as Paul told us that He was tempted in every way just like us but was able to live a sin-free life on this very earth. *"Because He Himself suffered when He was tempted, He is able to help those who are being tempted" (Heb. 2:18).* We will start with His encounter with the devil. His responses and dealings with life's issues in His day clearly reveal what He came to teach us.

Solomon taught us to *"Train up a child in the way he should go, and when he is old he will not turn from it" (Prov. 22:6).* Jesus was taught by His parents, and made sure He walked with the wise to increase His knowledge base. David asked the question *"How can a young man keep his way pure?* It is *"By living according to your word" (Psalm 119:9).* Jesus was in His very early thirties when He was tempted by the devil. So, as a young man by then, He was leaving us, the youth especially, with an example on how to deal with the devil.

Very soon we will get to know that Jesus was a very good student of the Scriptures. Daniel said he understood by books. David was one of the wisest men in the Scriptures. He gave some clues as to how he also acquired his level of wisdom. He wrote: *"Your commands make me wiser than my enemies, for they are ever with me. 99 I have more insight than all my teachers, for I meditate on your statutes. 100 I have more understanding than the elders, for I obey your precepts . . . 105 Your word is a lamp to my feet and a light for my path" (Psalm 119:98-105).* That tells us that the man was a voracious reader of the Scriptures that it became his lamp to guide him in the affairs of life. If I was asked to give you a piece of advice, I would tell you to start devouring books.

Solomon again wrote that *"**The heart of the discerning acquires knowledge; the ears of the wise seek it out**" (Prov. 18:15).* Aside His divinity, Jesus had done good service to His knowledge into the Scriptures to be able to handle all the circumstances of life. When it was time for Him to be tempted by the devil to do things that were contrary to the teachings of the statutes of God, He knew exactly what to say and do in each of those moments.

> *Jesus, full of the Holy Spirit, returned from the Jordan and was led by the Spirit in the desert, 2 where for forty days He was tempted by the devil. He ate nothing during those days, and at the end of them He was hungry. 3 The devil said to Him, "If you are the Son of God, tell this stone to become bread." 4 **Jesus answered, "It is written: 'Man does not live on bread alone."** 5 The devil led Him to a high place and showed Him in an instant all the kingdoms of the*

> *world. 6 And he said to Him, "I will give you all their authority and splendour, for it has been given to me, and I can give it to anyone I want to. 7 So if you worship me, it will all be yours." 8* ***Jesus answered, "It is written: 'Worship the LORD your God and serve Him only.'"*** *9 The devil led Him to Jerusalem and had Him stand on the highest point of the temple. "If you are the Son of God," he said, "throw yourself down from here. 10 For it is written: 'He will command His angels concerning you to guard you carefully; 11 they will lift you up in their hands, so that you will not strike your foot against a stone.'" 12* ***Jesus answered, "It says: 'Do not put the LORD your God to the test'"*** *(Luke 4:1-12).*

Whoever the devil was or is, he made some serious blunders when he went to tempt the LORD Jesus Christ. It is obvious he had read parts of the Scriptures but had failed to read all of it and didn't even understand those parts he read and in the process went on to distort them in front of Jesus, thereby embarrassing himself. He had not read and understood the part that said, *"Listen to the words of my mouth.* ***I will open my mouth in parables,*** *I will utter hidden things, things from of old" (Psalm 78:1-2).* Neither did he read the part that said: *"I spoke to the prophets, gave them many visions* ***and told parables through them****" (Hosea 12:10).* The devil did not realise that he was merely quoting to Christ parables without really understanding their moral teachings.

> *Who is it he is trying to teach? To whom is he explaining his message? To children weaned from their milk, to those just taken from the breast?*

Just like his disciples of today, the devil assumed that making a statement that is contrary to the statutes of God and later quoting a phrase or a verse from the Bible to support it should make it inspired, and taken as the word of God. In that case, his listeners would be compared to children weaned from their milk or those just taken from the breast. *"We do, however, speak a message of wisdom among the mature, but not the wisdom of this age or of the rulers of this age, who are coming to nothing" (1 Cor. 2:6).* But the surprising aspect is that most people are caught in their web simply because they refuse to study the Scriptures for themselves. My personal desire is to see the end of this practice.

One must not think that everyone is daft when it comes to the Bible and just quote things from it without substantiating them, thinking his listeners would not do any background check on what is being communicated. Paul was delighted with the Bereans because *"they were of more noble character than the Thessalonians,* ***for they received the message with great eagerness and examined the Scriptures every day to see if what Paul said was true****" (Acts 17:11).*

You are not teaching some group of children or some bunch of ignorant folks when you are quoting from the Scriptures. There are those who have done their personal research well like Jesus and those who, after hearing you speak, will go into the Bible to search if what you said was true. So never take your listeners or readers for granted. You may be embarrassed like the devil was embarrassed in the presence of Jesus.

> *For it is: Do and do, do and do, rule on rule, rule on rule; a little here, a little there. (Isaiah 28:10)*

The LORD said He will open His mouth in parables through David. Now we are getting to know that because the one teaching His word should not think he is teaching children weaned from milk or those just taken from the breast, His word is actually, *"Do and do, do and do,* ***rule on rule, rule on rule; a little here, a little there.****"* One must therefore go in search of all the *"little here and there"* in the Bible before arriving at any conclusions. ***"For the lips of a priest ought to preserve knowledge, and from his mouth men should seek instruction—because he is the messenger of the LORD Almighty****" (Mal. 2:7).*

For instance, you can't read a verses like *"Bring the whole tithe into the storehouse, that there may be food in my house.* ***Test me in this and see if I will not throw open the floodgates of heaven and pour out so much blessing that you will not have room enough for it," (Mal 3:20)*** and just spend the rest of your life paying tithes without paying attention to the work of your hands and idly expecting to be blessed financially. This is because it is also written: *"Lazy hands make a man poor, but diligent hands bring wealth" (Prov. 10:4). "He who works his land will have abundant food, but the one who chases fantasies will have his fill of poverty" (Prov. 28:19).* ***"For even when we were with you, we gave you this rule: "If a man will not work, he shall not eat"*** *(2 Thess. 3:10).* The one who gives the best tithe offerings every month will become the poorest in the land if he refuses to work with his mind and hands.

Being a youth in His early thirties, Jesus had stored the word of Scriptures just like David in His heart that He might not sin against God. *"For we do not have a high priest who is unable to sympathise with our weaknesses, but we have one who has been tempted in every way, just as we—****yet was without sin****" (Heb. 4:15).* The word of God was a lamp to His feet and a light for His path. The only Constitution He knew and practiced was that of God the Father and nothing else.

So when the devil challenged Him to change a stone to a loaf of bread, there was no need for Him to pay any attention to him because the Constitution He knew simply said in *Deuteronomy 8:3* that, *"Man does not live on bread alone."* Note that Jesus was *"full of the Holy Spirit"* when He met the devil. Yet He didn't go about displaying how powerful He was to the devil by babbling in other languages but simply stayed calm, obeying the commands of God. The devil was disarmed and had to try something else. Jesus could not use hunger as an excuse to break any of God's commands. I don't know if it has something to do with our age. I relate very well to the words of Christ. I just turned thirty-five today. But this book was actually completed two years back. And He lived for thirty-three years on earth.

> *"If you find something that speaks to your condition, becomes authoritative, then roll it over and over in the mind. Rolling it over in the mind, it will become an atmosphere, then an attitude, then an act. When Jesus was pressed by temptation in the wilderness He answered in the words of Scripture. These words had become a part of Him, and in the crisis they naturally passed from the stage of assimilation and atmosphere to that of attitude and act."—E. Stanley Jones (1884-1972)*

Beaten hands down, he tried to persuade Jesus with worldly possessions, telling Him to just bow and worship him in return for the authority and splendour of the kingdoms. He didn't realise that Jesus had read verses like ***"A faithful man will be richly blessed, but one eager to get rich will not go unpunished,"*** *(Prov. 28:20)* ***"Do not wear yourself out to get rich; have the wisdom to show restraint,"*** *(Prov. 23:4) and* ***"Dishonest money dwindles away, but he who gathers money little by little makes it grow."*** *(Prov. 13:11)* Jesus was later to teach the seeking of the kingdom of God and its righteousness first and all other things to be added in addition.

Jesus knew all these from the Scriptures before meeting satan the devil. You don't wait till you are tempted before trying to figure out what to do. You must be prepared at all times. When Joseph realised he could not stand Potiphar's wife, he didn't pray in tongues but rather trusted in his heels and resorted to running. That was his way of defeating the devil. *"Flee fornication"* was to be written later.

It is written: *"Pay attention and listen to the sayings of the wise; apply your heart to what I teach,* ***for it is pleasing when you keep them in your heart and have all of them ready on your lips****" (Prov. 22:17-18).* Because He had armed Himself by applying and keeping all the teachings and sayings of the wise in His heart, Jesus simply quoted *Deuteronomy 6:13* to the devil, which says that: *"Fear the LORD your God, serve Him only and take your oaths in His Name."* Brother Lucifer, the devil had to try something else again because he was defeated again.

He again displayed his ignorance in misunderstanding another line of the Scriptures and literally asked Jesus to throw Himself down from the highest point of the temple. Jesus is the Word of God. He said those things in the Scriptures and knew their full meanings. Realising the devil was ignorant in the Scriptures, He again quoted *Deuteronomy 6:16* to him that: *"Do not test the LORD your God as you did at Massah."*

YOU MUST WALK AS JESUS DID

> ***We know that we have come to know Him*** *(God)* ***if we obey His*** *(God's)* ***commands.*** *4* ***The man who says, "I know Him*** *(God),"* ***but does not do what He*** *(God)* ***commands is a liar, and the truth is not in him.*** *5 But if anyone obeys His word, God's love is truly made complete in him.* ***This is how we know we are in Him*** *(God): 6* ***Whoever claims to live in Him*** *(God)* ***must walk as Jesus did.*** *(1 John 2:3-6)*

There are several ways and means taught by some preachers today regarding how to deal with the devil and demons. The true children of God are told to walk as Jesus did. So how did Jesus deal with the devil? Did He bind or loose him? Or did He call down thunder and brimstone to strike his forehead because He (Jesus Christ) Himself was "*full of the Holy Spirit*" when He had this encounter with him? I keep wondering if they read the same Bible I read.

WRONG USE OF THE KEYS FOR BINDING AND LOOSING

Which part of the Bible says that the Scriptural verse *"I will give you the keys of the kingdom of heaven; whatever you bind on earth will be bound in heaven, and whatever you loose on earth will be loosed in heaven" (Matt. 16:19)* is reserved only for binding and loosing the devil and demons? It says *"whatever."* If we could decide to show true love to other human beings who do not belong to our families, church, faith, race or country and choose to forgive each other for all the wrongs done against us, it shall be bound in heaven and true brotherliness would be in existence. If we decide never to tell lies again and tell only the truth (and nothing else but the truth) to our fellow human beings, not taking advantage of their lack of insight into the Scriptures, that too shall be bound in heaven.

THE HABIT OF MAKING THE DEVIL APPEAR BIGGER THAN GOD

> *In the very same way, these dreamers pollute their own bodies, reject authority and slander celestial beings. 9 But **even the archangel Michael**, when he was disputing with the devil about the body of Moses, did not dare to bring a slanderous accusation against him, but said, "The LORD rebuke you!" 10 **Yet these men speak abusively against whatever they do not understand; and what things they do understand by instinct, like unreasoning animals—these are the very things that destroy them.** (Jude 8-10)*

The same Bible, which says *"our struggle is not against flesh and blood, but against the rulers, against the authorities, against the powers of this dark world and against the spiritual forces of evil in the heavenly realms" (Eph. 6:12)*, also says that *"**If you make the Most High your dwelling**—even the LORD, who is my refuge—10 **then no harm will befall you, no disaster will come near your tent.** 11 **For He will command His angels concerning you to guard you in all your ways**; 12 they will lift you up in their hands, so that you will not strike your foot against a stone" (Psalm 91:9-12). "**The angel of the LORD encamps around those who fear Him, and He delivers them**" (Psalm 34:7).* What, do you believe that the powers of this dark world and the spiritual forces of evil in the heavenly realms are more powerful than the Most High God?

> *Submit yourselves, then, to God. Resist the devil, and he will flee from you. 8 **Come near to God and He will come near to you.** (James 4:7-8).*

The religious folks in Christendom who represent the Pharisees today among the Gentile believers always want to show their spiritual muscles by trying to physically resist the devil through any means to be noticed. Ignorantly, their members also follow suit because that is what is taught by their leaders. If the blind lead the blind, both of them will fall into a ditch.

James first said we should submit ourselves to God. Then he said we should resist the devil and he will flee from us. This is the part they love and you will see them physically trying to resist the devil through binding and loosing him with their physical strength through prayer mostly. But James did not end it there. He finished by saying that we should come near to God and He will come near to us. Now, my question is when the chicks run to take cover under the wings of the mother hen, does the eagle which scoops down take the mother and the chicks away? Can the devil take someone away from God's hands? Your responsibility is to get near to God and He will take care of the rest.

"The best evidence of the Bible being the Word of God, is to be found between its covers. It proves itself"—Charles Hodge (1797-1878).

If I'm reliably informed that God will come near to me if I come near to Him, then what is my worry trying to bind and loose some brother Lucifer who will be around for at least the next one thousand years even when I'm gone from the face of the earth? Our responsibility is to *"**make the Most High our dwelling**—even the LORD, who is our refuge—10 **then no harm will befall us, no disaster will come near our tent, for He will command His angels concerning us to guard us in all our ways.**"* I don't know about you but I prefer this to the former of fighting a monster you and I cannot kill. The battle to destroy the devil is the LORD'S, not yours.

Chapter Thirteen

JESUS ON CLEAN AND UNCLEAN MEATS

Like I said earlier, I am going to simply use Jesus' responses and dealings with others in His day to answer the controversies surrounding His teachings today. The Word of God taught abstinence from some groups of creatures for the Jews. But others are saying Christ came to make such creatures clean, once the one eating them prays to sanctify them. We are told to walk as Christ walked if we are in Him, and no-one can lay any other foundation apart from the one already laid, which is Jesus Christ. We can only copy Him and not what someone says. An encounter with the Pharisees on this subject should explain this to us once and for all.

> *The Pharisees and some of the teachers of the law who had come from Jerusalem gathered round Jesus and 2* ***saw some of His disciples eating food with hands that were "unclean", that is, unwashed****. 3 (The Pharisees and all the Jews do not eat unless they give their hands a ceremonial washing,* ***holding to the tradition of the elders****. 4 When they come from the market-place they do not eat unless they wash.* ***And they observe many other traditions, such as the washing of cups, pitchers and kettles.)***
>
> *5 So the Pharisees and teachers of the law asked Jesus, "****Why don't your disciples live according to the tradition of the elders*** *instead of eating their food with 'unclean' hands?" 6 He replied, "Isaiah was right when he prophesied about you hypocrites, as it is written: "'These people honour me with their lips, but their hearts are far from me. 7* ***They worship me in vain; their teachings are but rules taught by men****.'*
>
> *8* ***You have let go of the commands of God and are holding on to the traditions of men****." 9 And He said to them: "****You have a fine way of setting aside the commands of God in order to***

> ***observe your own traditions!*** *10* ***For Moses said,*** *'Honour your father and your mother,' and 'Anyone who curses his father or mother must be put to death.' 11* ***But you say that*** *if a man says to his father or mother: 'Whatever help you might otherwise have received from me is Corban' (that is, a gift devoted to God), 12 then you no longer let him do anything for his father or mother. 13* ***Thus you nullify the word of God by your tradition that you have handed down. And you do many things like that.***"
>
> *14 Again Jesus called the crowd to him and said, "Listen to me, everyone, and understand this. 15* ***Nothing outside a man can make him 'unclean' by going into him. Rather, it is what comes out of a man that makes him 'unclean'*** *. . ."*
>
> *17 After he had left the crowd and entered the house,* ***his disciples asked Him about this parable.*** *18 "Are you so dull?" He asked. "Don't you see that nothing that enters a man from the outside can make him 'unclean'? 19 For it doesn't go into his heart but into his stomach, and then out of his body." (In saying this, Jesus declared all food items "clean".)*
>
> *20 He went on: "What comes out of a man is what makes him 'unclean'. 21 For from within, out of men's hearts, come evil thoughts, sexual immorality, theft, murder, adultery, 22 greed, malice, deceit, lewdness, envy, slander, arrogance and folly. 23 All these evils come from inside and make a man 'unclean'." (Mark 7:1-23).*

My dear brothers in the faith, my only plea with you as we study these few verses is that we can all be bold enough to respect the teachings of Jesus and for once take Him at His own words. So, let's have a step by step account of what actually transpired between Him and these Pharisees and teachers of the law in this case and see what they were actually discussing to know what was being taught.

We were not told the exact location that Jesus was teaching. But as He did, some Pharisees and teachers of the law who had come from Jerusalem gathered around Him and *saw some of His disciples eating without first washing their hands*. They were surprised to see that, because their own traditions taught that after returning from a place like the market, one must wash his hands before eating. This had become the norm at the time that almost all the Jews were observing it. These traditions were inherited from their fathers and there were many of such practices like washing of cups, pitchers and kettles. These traditions were nowhere written in the book of the Law of Moses or the Prophets.

Being a rabbi who taught in the synagogues and the temple courts, they expected Jesus to know these traditions and observe them as well. So when they saw His disciples doing what they thought was wrong, they asked Him, ***"Why don't your disciples live according to the tradition of the elders*** *instead of eating their food with 'unclean' hands?" (Verse 5)* Please notice very carefully the question asked. *It was about why His disciples were not observing the tradition of the elders.* The question asked did not even have anything whatsoever to do with the dietary commands or laws of God in the Scriptures.

In replying, Jesus called them hypocrites for introducing traditions that seemed religious but were actually intended to set aside the statutes of God in order to replace them with theirs. It is written about Jesus that: *"He is the image of the invisible God, the firstborn over all creation. 16* ***For by Him all things were created: things in heaven and on earth, visible and invisible,*** *whether thrones or powers or rulers or authorities,* ***all things were created by Him and for Him****. 17 He is before all things, and in Him all things hold together" (Col. 1:15-17).* It is also written: *"Do not add to what I command you and do not subtract from it, but keep the commands of the LORD your God that I give you" (Deut. 4:2).*

If there was something to be added to or subtracted from the word of God, Jesus would have known better and done so, since all things were created through Him. It wouldn't be the responsibility of either the Pharisees or the teachers of the law to teach Him that. Knowing their hearts, Jesus quoted from Isaiah and said, *"These people honour me with their lips, but their hearts are far from me. They worship me in vain;* ***their teachings are but rules taught by men."*** They wanted to impose the traditions they inherited from their fathers on Jesus and His disciples. This was the battle Paul had to fight with them in his time when they wanted the Gentile believers to be circumcised at all cost and have them observe their own Sabbaths and legalistic observances, which were not in the original laws of God.

> *"Explain the Scriptures by the Scriptures."—Clement of Alexandria (C. 150-215)*

Because He didn't want us to misinterpret His words and read our own meanings into how they had been worshipping the LORD in vain, Jesus gave His own reasons why He said that.

First He said, ***"You have let go of the commands of God and are holding on to traditions of men."*** How did they let go of the commands of God? He continued, ***"You have a fine way of setting aside the commands of God in order to observe your own traditions!"*** Knowing how cunning and scheming people can be, He decided to list some of the commands of God that had been set aside and replaced with the traditions of men. He then went on to quote two verses from the Scriptures which they had set aside. In quoting those Scriptures in this context, He was emphasising the fact that they were still in force and not annulled but they were making the people believe so.

He continued, *"For Moses said, 'Honour your father and your mother,' (Exod. 20:12) and 'Anyone who curses his father or mother must be put to death' (Lev. 20:9)* ***But you say*** . . . In the name of religion, the Pharisees and teachers of the law had succeeded in replacing the commands of God with their own traditions. They made nonsense of the word of God and sought to replace them with their own. It is interesting to know that, of all the commands in the Old Testament, Jesus would mention the one on children and their respect towards their parents.

God commands in the Old Testament, which is useful for correcting, rebuking, teaching and making us wise that anyone who curses his father or mother must be put to death. Jesus called them hypocrites and, in effect, worshipping God in vain for setting aside a command like that and replacing it with something else. How about that for a shocker? If you think Jesus was just some Jewish young man with smiles and always giggling around like some teenager who has found a new lover, then you better think again. It takes guts to exercise authority. He never tolerated any nonsense in His path. He went beating people when they turned the temple of God into a market place. Jesus does not tolerate disrespect towards one's parents.

> *"The four gospels are essential to our understanding of who Jesus was and what He taught and did, and therefore they are fundamental to our understanding of Christianity . . . . Put out of your mind the Sunday School image of a smiling Jesus carrying a lamb on His shoulders through a summer meadow. Imagine instead a kindly but forthright person surrounded by an angry mob in a narrow Near Eastern back street, telling them that they've had their religion wrong for centuries and that He alone has got it right . . . ."—Derek Williams*

In the process of succeeding in this act of setting aside the commands of God, they were nullifying the Word of God with their own traditions which they had inherited from their ancestors. And they had many of such traditions in place of the true Word of God. Unfortunately, these traditions have continued to our day. You have experts in oratory who have triumphed in making the Word of God in the Scriptures of no effect through their teachings. But just as Jesus stood up to them and leaving us an example, some of us are ready to do same by teaching the plain and simple Word of God.

Now, instead of answering their question of why His disciples did not wash their hands before eating in accordance with the traditions of the elders, He didn't mince words by calling them hypocrites, and reminded them that their worship of God was in vain. It was then that He called the crowd and addressed them with this parable that: *"Nothing outside a man can make him 'unclean' by going into him. Rather, it is what comes out of a man that makes him 'unclean'."* We know this was a parable because after they had gone home His disciples came to ask of the meaning of this parable *(Verse 17).*

Explaining this, He asked His disciples who were all Jews at the time that: *"Don't you see that nothing that enters a man from outside can make him 'unclean'? For it doesn't go into his heart but into his stomach, and then out of his body."*

We have learned that Jesus was raised in a Jewish environment. He came to His own who were all Jews as well. He was sent to the lost sheep of Israel. Earlier, He had rebuked the Pharisees and insulted them for setting aside the commands of God and holding to their own traditions. So what does the same commands they had set aside say concerning what is to be eaten or not? The question even didn't have anything to do with food. It was about the washing of hands before eating, which wasn't in the original statutes of God. He was addressing Jews. And a Jew knows what constitutes food and what doesn't. Although a pig, for instance, is a delicacy to others in other nations, it is not regarded as food to a Jew.

Paul wrote to the Ephesians: *"But among you there must not be even **a hint of** sexual immorality, **or of any kind of impurity**, or of greed, **because these are improper for God's holy people**. 4 Nor should there be obscenity, foolish talk or coarse joking, which are out of place, but rather thanksgiving. 5 For of this you can be sure: **No immoral, impure or greedy person**—such a man is an idolater—**has any inheritance in the kingdom of Christ and of God**. 6 Let no-one deceive you with empty words, **for because of such things God's wrath comes on those who are disobedient**. 7 Therefore, do not be partners with them" (Eph. 5:3-7).*

Jesus was in effect saying that washing one's hands before eating had nothing to do with living a righteous life. A normal food item like what Daniel and his friends ate will just do its normal work in the systems and the rest come out as faeces. They had already set aside the commands of God and observing their own traditions instead rendering their worship of God in vain. So why were they even bothering themselves with washing their hands before eating, which was not even stipulated in the commands of God? That teaching was just some cover up strategy to keep the people in darkness.

The washing of hands before eating does not stop anyone from having evil thoughts, involving oneself in sexual immorality, theft, murder, adultery, greed, malice, deceit, lewdness, envy, slander, arrogance, and folly. What has washing of hands got to do with abstaining from the vices mentioned, anyway? It doesn't make any sense; let alone worth considering. After being a student under the tutelage of Christ Himself for at least a period of three years, Peter said he had never eaten anything impure in his lifetime. Who do you trust, Jesus or the others?

PAUL ON CLEAN AND UNCLEAN MEATS

We can now hear Paul's reaction and reply to these traditions of the elders. He wrote to the Colossians that:

> *Since* ***you died with Christ to the basic principles of this world****, why, as though you still belonged to it, do you submit to its rules? 21 "Do not handle! Do not taste! Do not touch!"? 22* ***These are all destined to perish with use, because they are based on human commands and teachings****. 23* ***Such regulations indeed have an appearance of wisdom, with their self-imposed worship, their false humility and their harsh treatment of the body, but they lack any value in restraining sensual indulgence.*** *(Col. 2:20-23)*

These were the things he was mostly referring to when you hear him condemning the observance of the law. But unfortunately, people turn to misunderstand these things to mean the statutes and precepts of God. There was no way Paul could say that God's commands and teachings have an appearance of wisdom in them. That would have meant he was wiser than God. I would have personally accused him of blasphemy. He didn't say that. The teachings he was referring to were based on human commands and teachings. There is nothing like *"Do not taste"* in the Law.

"As I spent time chewing over the endless assurances and promises to be found in the Bible, so my faith in the living God grew stronger and held me safe in His hands. God's Word to us, especially His Word spoken by His Spirit through the Bible, is the very ingredient that feeds our faith. If we feed our souls regularly on God's Word, several times each day, we should become robust spiritually just as we feed on ordinary food several times each day and become robust physically. Nothing is more important than hearing and obeying the Word of God."—David Watson

GIVEN GREENLIGHT TO EAT ALL MANNER OF CREATURES?

Now, back to *verse 19* where the translators said that Christ declared all food items *"clean"* by what He said. If the subject matter under discussion had nothing to do with the actual food but rather on the washing of hands before eating, how could they make a claim like that? If you choose to eat snakes, scorpions, rats, cockroaches, bed bugs, caterpillars, frogs, pork, bats, apes, baboons, a dog, which returns to its vomit and the rest, that is your own tradition and not something you can associate with Jesus Christ. He affirmed the fact that a child who curses his father or mother should be dealt with according to what the Scriptures say. How much more the eating of creatures with "poisons" in their systems? Do not add to His teachings because you are forbidden to do so.

> *Do not add to what I command you and do not subtract from it, but keep the commands of the LORD your God that I give you (Deut. 4:2).*

There are others too who misunderstand the content of a letter Paul wrote to Timothy to mean that all "food items" are now clean to be eaten. My only plea to such people is to take time to patiently read the Bible in context for themselves and not just base their understanding on some few verses of it read to them by others. I believe that to spend a whole day on even a verse, read and reread it until it is completely understood is better than some few minutes on a chapter without getting anything. Like I have done so far, let's carefully read what Paul was talking about.

> *The Spirit clearly says that* ***in later times some will abandon the faith and follow deceiving spirits and things taught by***

> ***demons.*** *2* ***Such teachings come through hypocritical liars,*** *whose consciences have been seared as with a hot iron. 3* ***They forbid people to marry and order them to abstain from certain foods, which God created to be received with thanksgiving by those who believe and who know the truth.*** *4* ***For everything God created is good, and nothing is to be rejected if it is received with thanksgiving,*** *5 because it is consecrated by the word of God and prayer. (1 Tim. 4:1-5)*

I don't know how you read those verses but I'll humbly ask you to go back and read it again but this time very slowly. Paul was telling Timothy that a time was coming that some would abandon the faith or the gospel of Christ and start teaching things they received or learned from demons. He made him aware that such people were liars. Now, to alert him on how to identify such people when he met them, he went on to list their teachings or doctrines for him.

Two marks that distinguished them were that: *"They forbid people to marry* ***and order them to abstain from certain foods."*** The first thing to note here is that God has given a detailed list of what constitutes food and what does not and we've learnt He does not change His mind. The second aspect is the fact that God has never in any part of the Bible forbidden men from marrying. This demonic institution was teaching and *"ordering them to abstain from certain foods,* ***which God created to be received with thanksgiving by those who believe and know the truth."*** And remember that the Word of God in the Scriptures is what constitutes truth and nothing else.

There are those who believe and know the truths about what constitutes food and what does not. To such people, *"everything God created (to be eaten as food) is good, and nothing (that is created to be eaten as food by the Creator) is to be rejected if it is received with thanksgiving,* ***because it is consecrated by the Word of God*** *(on foods) and prayer.* Those foods have already been consecrated by God Himself because it is He who has ordered us to receive them with thanksgiving. Sticking to what He has said proves that you know the truth.

KEEP IT TO YOURSELF

One cannot talk about food in the Scriptures without treating Romans 14. I'm not a fan of those who read just verses in the Bible and start arguing about things. So I'll suggest you read the whole book of Romans before centring on this chapter.

Accept him whose faith is weak, without passing judgment on disputable matters. 2 One man's faith allows him to eat everything, but another man, whose faith is weak, eats only vegetables. 3 The man who eats everything must not look down on him who does not, and the man who does not eat everything must not condemn the man who does, for God has accepted him . . . 6 He who eats meat, eats to the LORD, for he gives thanks to God; and he who abstains, does so to the LORD and gives thanks to God. 7 For none of us lives to himself alone and none of us dies to himself alone. 8 If we live, we live to the LORD; and if we die we die to the LORD.

13 Therefore let us stop passing judgment on one another. Instead, make up your mind not to put any stumbling-block or obstacle in your brother's way. 14 As one who is in the LORD Jesus, I am fully convinced that no food is unclean in itself. But if anyone regards something as unclean, then for him it is unclean. 15 If your brother is distressed because of what you eat, you are no longer acting in love. Do not by your eating destroy your brother for whom Christ died. 16 Do not allow what you consider good to be spoken of as evil. 17 For the kingdom of God is not a matter of eating and drinking, but of righteousness, peace and joy in the Holy Spirit, 18 because anyone who serves Christ in this way is pleasing to God and approved by men.

19 Let us therefore make every effort to do what leads to peace and to mutual edification. 20 Do not destroy the work of God for the sake of food. All food is clean, but it is wrong for a man to eat anything that causes someone else to stumble. 21 It is better not to eat meat or drink wine or to do anything else that will cause your brother to fall.

22 So whatever you believe about these things keep between yourself and God (Rom. 14:1-22).

It is of immense importance that we carefully and patiently read these verses before jumping into any conclusions. For example, Paul calls the faith of the one who eats only vegetables weak. Does that mean vegetarians are weak in faith? Of cause not. That would have meant he was breaking his instruction of not condemning others for what they believed about these things. Daniel and his three friends ate only vegetables but were ten times wiser than everyone in Babylon. Were they weak in faith?

Verses 3 and 6 give us the gist or the topic under discussion. One man eats everything and the other who abstains limits what he eats to only vegetables. He was teaching them on how to peacefully co-exist under the same roof without looking down on each other's beliefs.

You would recall that *the circumcised believers criticised Peter for going into the house of uncircumcised men and eating with them (Acts 11:2-3).* That was because up until Peter's vision, the brothers were still with the belief that it was against their law for a Jew to associate with a Gentile or visit him (Acts 10:28). This subject brought so much argument and debate that even Peter who first had the revelation to take the gospel to the Gentiles was at times led astray.

> *Before certain men came from James,* ***he*** *(Peter)* ***used to eat with the Gentiles****. But when they arrived,* ***he began to draw back and separate himself from the Gentiles*** *because he was afraid of those who belonged to the circumcision group. 13 The other Jews joined him in his hypocrisy, so that by their hypocrisy even Barnabas was led astray (Gal. 2:12-13).*

At the time of writing Romans 14, this subject had grown that it became judgmental for people to be judged according to their choice of food. This became a stumbling block to others and was preventing them from coming to Christ or staying after they had been saved. To rectify this, Paul called on the brothers to compromise on each other's personal beliefs and concentrate on the bigger picture with this remark: ***"If your brother is distressed because of what you eat, you are no longer acting in love. Do not by your eating destroy your brother for whom Christ died****. 16 Do not allow what you consider good to be spoken of as evil. 17 For the kingdom of God is not a matter of eating and drinking, but of righteousness, peace and joy in the Holy Spirit."*

For me, there's nothing of strict doctrine in those remarks. Paul is simply saying that if I enjoy eating apples or grapes but meets or visits a brother who is distressed for what I consider good and decides to stop following Christ, then I'm no longer acting in love. The reason he said is because the most important things to strive for in the Kingdom of God is righteousness, peace and joy in the Holy Spirit and not about what to eat and what not to eat. There are some who read these verses and conclude that there would not be eating in the Kingdom of God.

> *Let us therefore make every effort to do what leads to peace and to mutual edification. 20 Do not destroy the work of God for the sake of food. All food is clean, but it is wrong for a man to eat anything that causes someone else to stumble. 21 It is better not to eat meat or drink wine or to do anything else that will cause your brother to fall.*

Anything mutual has to do with actions that affect two or more people equally. And edification also has to do with the improvement of somebody's mind or character. Paul is saying that when we gather as a group of believers, we should make every effort to do only things that would contribute to the mutual edification of each other and not prevent them from improving their minds and characters through the Word of God for the sake of food.

So what should we do about our beliefs on such subjects?

> *One man considers one day more sacred than another; another man considers every day alike. Each one should be fully convinced in his own mind. 6 . . . He who eats meat, eats to the LORD, for he gives thanks to God; and he who abstains, does so to the LORD and gives thanks to God (Rom. 14:5-6).*

All of us come from different backgrounds before salvation through Christ. Someone from China might still consider eating frogs and snakes as his delicacy. Even though the thought of a frog meat on a plate might make me throw up, that does not give me the right to look down on that person for whom Christ died. For the life of this brother, righteousness, peace and joy in the Holy Spirit in the Kingdom of God, Paul is saying I shouldn't condemn him by starting to quote God's Word directly into his face to force him to stop eating those creatures. I might lose him completely.

Paul's recommendation is to teach this man until "*Each one should be fully convinced in his own mind*" about what is good to be eaten as food according to God's own standards. As to whether those creatures are hygienic for our health or not, Paul says *"If we live, we live to the LORD; and if we die, we die to the LORD. So, whether we live or die, we belong to the LORD" (Rom. 14:8). So whatever you believe about these things keep between yourself and God (Rom. 14:22).*

> *"Walking in faith brings you to the Word of God. There you will be healed, cleansed, fed, nurtured, equipped, and matured."—Kay Arthur*

Chapter Fourteen

JESUS ON DIVORCE

"*Whoever claims to live in Him must walk as Jesus did.*" "*If you love me, you will obey what I command*" *(John 14:15).* Jesus' response to questions clearly reveals His teachings to us. We will now take a look at one of such responses on the subject of divorce and see what He taught on that subject, which will translate into His views on the commands of God. *Some Pharisees came and tested Jesus, and this is what ensued between them and Jesus:*

> *"Is it lawful for a man to divorce his wife?" 3 "What did Moses command you?" He replied. 4 They said, "Moses permitted a man to write a certificate of divorce and send her away." 5* ***"It was because your hearts were hard that Moses wrote you this law,"*** *Jesus replied. 6* ***"But at the beginning of creation God 'made them male and female'.*** *7 'For this reason a man will leave his father and mother and be united to his wife, and the two will become one flesh.* ***So they are no longer two, but one****. 9 Therefore, what God has joined together, let man not separate." (Mark 10:2-9)*

Without getting ourselves too spiritual than Jesus Himself in trying to go two thousand years back seeking the Greek or Hebraic words used in translating those verses, let's just humbly assess what happened in these verses. As His custom was, crowds had come to gather around Him in Judea as He began to teach them. Some Pharisees and teachers of the law, wanting to test Him, asked a straight forward question that: *"Is it lawful for a man to divorce his wife?"* The book of Matthew puts it this way: *"Is it lawful for a man to divorce his wife* ***for any and every reason?****" (Matt. 19:3).*

To paraphrase that in our day is to say that they wanted to know if it was lawful in the Scriptures for one to file for a divorce *"for any and every reason"* like ill health, bad breathe, bankruptcy, impotence, one partner's inability to cook good food, untidiness, loss of so-called chemistry between couples, accusations levelled against one partner for no longer being romantic and/

or sexy. Just think of all the excuses given today in the name of democracy, where spouses can actually file for divorce after ten years of marriage with children to look after with the excuse that one partner has a problem with the other. My question is where were you looking when you first met? Were you blindfolded?

It is written: *"Be careful to do what the LORD your God has commanded you; do not turn aside to the right or to the left. 33 Walk in all the way that the LORD your God has commanded you, so that you may live and prosper and prolong your days in the land that you will possess" (Deut. 5:32-33).* These teachers of the law and the Pharisees were supposed to be teaching the statutes of God to the people and not asking question about what they were expected to have answers for. Surprised at their question, because they were expected to know the answer, Jesus asked them in reply with a question: *"What did Moses command you?"* In other words, being teachers of the law, they were supposed to know the answer from the writings of Moses. At one time, He asked Nicodemus *"You are Israel's teacher and do you not understand these things" (John 3:10)?*

Remember they accused Jesus of using the powers of Beelzebub to heal and perform His miracles. The source of their testing was to find Him saying something contrary to what Moses had taught in the Scriptures in order to use as basis for His arrest. Moses had said many things starting from the book of Genesis. But because they wanted to trap Him in His words, they went straight to say that: *"Moses permitted a man to write a certificate of divorce and send her away."* They thought Jesus was going to tread this line and start to downplay the institution of marriage by elaborating on the various grounds on which one can divorce his spouse like accusing one's wife of having drooped breasts after ten years of marriage with three children and consequently filing for a divorce. This was a similar trick played on Him when they asked Him whether it was right to pay taxes to Caesar.

Being a well-equipped student of the Scriptures, Jesus gave them the reason why that law was *added*. He told them: *"It was because your hearts were hard that Moses wrote you this law. But at the beginning of creation God 'made them male and female'.* Being the Greatest Teacher of all, He went to the original purpose of marriage and quoted *Genesis 1:27* and *Genesis 2:24* to give them the original purpose of the institution of marriage. A man and his wife become one flesh after marriage. *"They are no longer two, but one. Therefore what God has joined together, let man not separate."* This is the teaching in the Scriptures on marriage when Christ was on earth. We will soon see if He changed it or not.

> *"So often we have a kind of vague, wistful longing that the promises of Jesus should be true. The only way really to enter into them is to believe them with the clutching intensity of a drowning man."— William Barclay*

His disciples, wanting to have a clearer understanding on this subject, asked Him about it and He again told them: *"Anyone who divorces his wife and marries another woman commits adultery against her. 12 And if she divorces her husband and marries another man, she commits adultery."* Please bear in mind that I am not talking about whether the teachings of Christ are relevant and can be applied to our day. I have confined this book to simply giving you what He taught. But if you care to know from this stage, His teachings would have been the perfect solutions to all the numerous problems on earth. But that is a new topic to be dealt with in an upcoming book.

He made it clear in another place, as He said *"It has been said, 'Anyone who divorces his wife must give her a certificate of divorce. But I tell you that anyone who divorces his wife,* ***except for marital unfaithfulness****, causes her to become an adulteress, and anyone who marries the divorced woman commits adultery" (Matt. 5:31-32).* After this teaching, the disciples together said to Him, *"If this is the situation between a husband and wife, it is better not to marry" (Matt. 19:10).*

Realising it was hard for them to accept the teaching on marriage and divorce at the time, Jesus replied, *"Not everyone can accept this word, but only those to whom it has been given. 12 For some are eunuchs because they were born that way; others were made that way by men; and others have renounced marriage because of the kingdom of heaven.* ***The one who can accept this should accept it****" (Matt. 19:11-12).*

A eunuch is a man who has been castrated, especially one who guarded women in some Asian countries in the past. When His disciples learned the truth about marriage from their Master, they said among themselves that, *"it is better not to marry."* After hearing this coming from His students, Jesus did not lower the mark but only told them, and to us, that *"Not everyone can accept this word . . . The one who can accept this should accept it."* In other words, what He taught on the subject of marriage was to take us to the beginning to reveal to us God's own design of marriage.

MARRIAGE MEANT TO BRING HAPPINESS

Marriage is such a very huge and special institution designed by God to bring happiness to two individuals who leave their families to start their own. It is meant to bring happiness to each other, not pain and agony. God was so concerned about the happiness of a recently married couple that He made it a law in the Old Testament that a man should not be sent on any government duties or even go to war; he should just stay at home making his wife happy for a whole year.

> ***If a man has recently married,*** *he must not be sent to war* ***or have any other duty laid on him.*** *For one year he is to be free to stay at home* ***and bring happiness to the wife he has married.*** *(Deut. 24:5)*

Can you imagine that and try to fathom what could be that important and more urgent than war in a nation? The God of the Old Testament who placed the "yoke of bondage" on people, rates the happiness of a recently married woman higher than the national interest of a country. Contrary to what people think, God respects women just as He respects men in all the Scriptures. The institution of marriage should be clearly understood from God's perspective before drawing any conclusions. Lack of understanding makes people turn to fumble in this.

A WOMAN'S RESPONSIBILITY IN MARRIAGE

> *Wives, submit to your husbands as to the LORD. 23 For the husband is the head of the wife as Christ is the head of the church, His body, of which He is the Saviour. 24* ***Now as the church submits to Christ, so also wives should submit to their husbands in everything.*** *(Eph. 5:22-24)*

God exudes law and order. Because there are two individuals who may have been champions in their own ranks and come from different homes with different backgrounds that come together to enter into this institution of marriage, He made laws to establish peaceful coexistence between them. Two captains cannot ride the same boat. He made the man the head and commands the woman to be submissive to him in everything. The men are always excited when they hear this verse quoted in their hearing. From my own observation, most men have abused this command and turn to mistreat their spouses with this. It is true that wives must submit to the husbands in everything. But it doesn't end there.

THE MAN'S RESPONSIBILITIES IN MARRIAGE

> *Husbands,* ***love your wives, just as Christ loved the church and gave Himself up for her*** *26 to make her holy, cleansing her by the washing with water through the word, 27 and to present her to Himself as a radiant church, without stains or wrinkles or any other blemish, but holy and blameless. 28* ***In this same way, husbands ought to love their wives as their own bodies. He who loves his wife loves himself.*** *29 After all, no-one ever hated his own body,* ***but he feeds and cares for it, just as Christ does the church—*** *30 for we are members of His body. (Eph. 5:25-30)*

Just as the woman is told to submit to her husband as the church is submitted to Christ, the man is also told to love, feed and care for the woman just as Christ does for His church. A man's love should remain with his wife that at any moment in time, there would not be stains, wrinkles or any other blemish found on her. A man's worth should be reflected in his wife's body by the love and care he lavishes on her. Remember that you are in there to make each other happy. Marriage with the man neatly dressed with the wife shabbily kept is incomplete on the part of the man.

HOW MUCH MUST ONE LOVE HIS SPOUSE?

> *This is how we know what love is:* ***Jesus Christ laid down His life for us. And we ought to lay down our lives for our brothers.*** *17 If anyone has material possessions and sees his brother in need but has no pity on him, how can the love of God be in him? 18 Dear children,* ***let us not love with words or tongue but with actions and in truth.*** *(1 John 3:16-18)*

The way to express your love to your wife is to lay down your life for her as Christ did for you. Jesus Christ said, loving our neighbour as ourselves sums up the whole law. Which of your neighbours is closer to you than your own wife? Love must be sincere. One of the wicked things in life is to marry a woman and not love her, leaving her stranded. If you have not trained yourself to love a particular woman to the end of life, please don't marry her in the first place. It would be better for you to remain single. It takes a man with courage to marry and fulfil his responsibilities as a real husband. Marriage is an institution reserved for men and not for "boys."

> *Let no debt remain outstanding,* ***except the continuing debt to love one another****, for he who loves his fellow-man has fulfilled the law. 9 The commandments, "Do not commit adultery," "Do not murder," "Do not steal," "Do not covet," and whatever other commandment there may be, are summed up in this one rule:* ***"Love your neighbour*** *(your wife)* ***as yourself****." 10 Love does no harm to its neighbour (his wife).* ***Therefore love*** *(for your wife)* ***is the fulfilment of the law*** *(Rom. 13:8-10).*

It is always good to know and understand God's own purposes for doing something and not just hold on to traditions of men. After creating the first and only man on earth, *The LORD God said, "**It is not good** for the man to be alone. I will make a helper suitable for him" (Gen. 2:18).* To say that something is good is to say that it is of high quality or an acceptable standard. Other words that come to mind as synonyms are pleasant, favourable, skilful, morally right, and so on. The opposite then applies in saying it is not good.

How did God solve that part of man He realised was not good? *"But for Adam no suitable helper was found" (Gen. 2:20).* God created a woman, *"and He brought her to the man." (Gen. 2:22).* Note that Adam did not ask God for a wife. But it was God who realised it was not good (it was incomplete, unsuitable) for the man to be alone, and created the woman to fill that gap of incompleteness. Adam was busily working in the field and naming the animals when God realised this about him. When that was achieved, the Scriptures say: *"For this reason* (which reason?—the reason that a man grows to a stage in life when it is not good for him to be alone and will need a woman to fill that void) *a man will leave his father and mother and be united to his wife, **and they will become one** (Gen. 2:24).*

Why do they become one and no longer two? The reason is that the man was created to be a complete whole but later he turned out not to be good enough for the purpose. So, when the other "accessory" was introduced by the Manufacturer, they still became one although they were two separate individuals. A car for instance has different and many parts but at the end of the day, it still becomes *"a car."* The woman came to be a helper to the man; not to serve him. In this way, marriage then becomes an institution of helping each other and not baby-sitting each other.

"What is the mark of a Christian? Faith working by love. What is the mark of faith? Unhesitating conviction of the truth of the inspired words, unshaken by any argument either based on the plea of physical necessity or masquerading in the guise of piety. What is the mark of a believer? To hold fast by such conviction in the strength of what Scripture says and dare neither to set it at nought nor to add to it."— Basil of Caesarea (330-379)

Chapter Fifteen

JESUS ON TITHES AND OFFERINGS

Paying tithes and offerings in church is a very important subject that folks in the mainstream fields do not play with. It is written: *"Bring the whole tithe into the storehouse, that there may be food in my house. Test me in this and see if I will not throw open the floodgates of heaven and pour out so much blessing that you will not have room enough for it"* (Mal. 3:10).

If you are one of those who accuse pastors of spending your tithes on their personal issues, one of the purposes for which tithes was introduced was to see to it that there was enough food in the house of God. The priests at the time this law was instituted were not supposed to work but were to spend their entire life studying and teaching the Word of God. The criticisms arise today because some of these pastors today do not even have the time to study the Bible; they just attend some so-called Bible school somewhere and the next thing you know, they are teaching what someone has taught them. Becoming a priest or a pastor is not something you learn in a two-year course of study. It's a lifetime job. ***"For the lips of a priest ought to preserve knowledge, and from his mouth men should seek instruction—because he is the messenger of the LORD Almighty"*** *(Mal. 2:7)*.

What results from this is the fact that, because they don't study the Bible enough, most of them merely resort to teaching what the masses want to hear. One teacher tells us to go to the left on a subject and calls it the new revelation from God. Another teacher also under the same inspiration tells us to go to the right on the same subject and calls it the revelation from God. In the process, some are beginning to lose trust in the word of God because they do not know who to trust. Some only see the church as just some form of business avenues on the part of the pastors and are therefore refusing to pay their tithes. The cycle then continues that if enough tithes are not paid to have enough food in the *"house,"* then a way must be found by the pastors, which results in teaching anything that the masses want to hear.

But if there is enough food in the *"house,"* then they would stick to their Bibles and do proper studies into the word and teach the people the pure and unadulterated Word of God. That is when He says *"I will prevent pests from devouring your crops, and the vines in your fields will not cast their fruit" (Mal. 3:11)* because the pastor's stomach is full and does not worry about fending for himself and therefore has time and energy to feed you the true Word of God on the keys to Biblical prosperity, which when applied, would deliver you from the shackles of poverty. Understanding is the key to tithing.

Your tithing will help your pastor's lips preserve knowledge to enable men seek God's instructions from him because that is his responsibility. Solomon wrote that: *"He who is full loathes honey, but to the hungry even what is bitter tastes sweet" (Prov. 27:7).* That is to say, if pastoring is someone's call or job, which he is satisfied with, because he is adequately compensated financially, then nothing will lure him into going outside his boundary to covet by teaching things that are contrary to the principles of God in the Scriptures.

Tithing then is one of the ways by which God works through individuals to rule the earth. It's a cycle and once you understand it, it becomes a delight to participate in it. God blesses the work of your hands. He then asks you to take a fraction of your income into His house to make sure there is food in there. Food here covers everything that goes into running this house smoothly. Then, once the pastor and the house are full, he is able to loathe or abhor all the pleasures of the world and sticks his nose into the Scriptures the whole of his life for you. He then matures to the point where he would teach you nothing but the unadulterated Word of God.

LIVING FROM PREACHING THE GOSPEL

Once you receive the pure Word of God from the pastor, you receive the knowledge of God from him which when applied makes you wise in the things of God. You are then able to bear enough fruits based on the wisdom acquired and your income increases. This reflects in your tithes again and the pastor is motivated to do more by way of searching deep into the pages of the Scriptures on your behalf. The cycle continues like that.

> *Who serves as a soldier at his own expense? Who plants a vineyard and does not eat of its grapes? Who tends a flock and does not drink of the milk? . . . 13 Don't you know that those who work in the temple get their food from the temple, and those who serve at the altar share in what is offered on the altar? 14* ***In the same way,***

> ***the LORD has commanded that those who preach the gospel should receive their living from the gospel.*** *(1 Cor. 9:7, 13-14)*

This is the purpose of tithes. It is not wrong though, if a pastor who is able to provide for his own means chooses to be in the ministry of God for the love of his fellow man and not demand things in return. Paul said although he had all these privileges, he still chose to work with his own hands so that he would not be a burden to anyone. How about that?

> *If others have this right of support from you, shouldn't we have it all the more?* ***But we did not use this right. On the contrary, we put up with anything rather than hinder the gospel of Christ . . .*** *15* ***But I have not used any of these rights.*** *And I am not writing this in the hope that you will do such things for me. I would rather die than have anyone deprive me of this boast (1 Cor. 9:12-15)*

Paul says he had this right of living from preaching the gospel of Christ but did not use it because he did not want to hinder the growth of the gospel he was preaching. He and Barnabas chose to work for their living. He asked: *"Or is it only I and Barnabas who must work for a living?" (1 Cor. 9:6).* He later wrote: *"For you yourselves know how you ought to follow our example. We were not idle when we were with you, 8 nor did we eat anyone's food without paying for it.* ***On the contrary, we worked night and day, labouring and toiling so that we would not be a burden to any of you. 9 We did this, not because we do not have the right to such help, but in order to make ourselves a model for you to follow.*** *10 For even when we were with you, we gave you this rule: 'If a man will not work, he shall not eat" (2 Thess. 3:7-10).*

Somewhere in 1998, I stopped attending church, not because I didn't like the church I was attending. I had to stop simply because I didn't have the money to put into the collection bowl each time that was due. I couldn't sit and watch people pass me by when it was time to do this. It was embarrassing for me, to say the least. I experienced many of my saddest moments whenever they asked for tithes and offerings and anything that had to do with money because I was jobless then. In the end, I could not attend again and that was it. These were some of the things Paul was preventing in his time in order not to hinder the spread of the gospel. I could have been lost for good, had it not been for the saving grace of God upon my life.

ACCURATE APPLICATION OF GOD'S COMMANDS

Now, back to Jesus' teaching on paying tithes and offerings. He said, *"Woe to you, teachers of the law and Pharisees, you hypocrites! You give a tenth of your spices—mint, dill and cummin.* ***But you have neglected the more important matters of the law—justice, mercy and faithfulness. You should have practised the latter, without neglecting the former****" (Matt. 23:23).*

Simply put, He first rebuked them for paying tithes of everything to the tiniest bit. He said they were doing all that but were neglecting the most important aspects of the law which concerns justice, mercy and faithfulness. Because *Zion will be redeemed with justice, her penitent ones with righteousness (Isa. 1:27)*, He said, *"You should have practised the latter,* ***without neglecting the former."*** In effect, He was saying that the most important aspects of the law were to show justice, mercy and faithfulness to God and man. Because they were not doing these, He called them blind guides leading the blind.

Paying of tithes was in the Old Testament Scriptures before Christ's arrival on earth. He came to teach its full implications and how it should be done as a command from the Most High God. *"Through Him all things* (including the commands) *were made; without Him nothing was made that has been made" (John 1:3).*

Tithe has to be paid with the right attitude. God is not obligated to bless you in any way if you pay your tithes and offerings but neglect the more important aspects of the Word of God, and live in repeated sins. What does a governor think he is doing by paying tithes and offerings when he had embezzled tax-payers' monies for his private expenses? If you cannot show love and care to the woman you've married whom you see each morning, then what are doing paying tithes and offerings? Yes, by all means, pay tithes and offerings. But do not neglect the more important aspects of the law.

John wrote to us that: *"If anyone says, 'I love God,' yet hates his brother, he* (or she) *is a liar. For anyone who does not love his brother* (or sister), *whom he* (or she) *has seen, cannot love God, whom he* (or she) *has not seen. 21 And He has given us this command: Whoever loves God must also love his brother* (or sister). It is your love for God and His ministry that is making you pay tithes and offerings. The same love for God must be extended to reach the people around you who are in dire need in the society. God will not personally descend on earth to feed or clothe an orphan. Be merciful to mankind.

Whichever position you find yourself in, in the society, use it to show how just, merciful and faithful you can be in applying the principles of God which in the long run help everyone. There is more to life than selfishness and greed on the part of people to amass wealth in this age. There is nothing wrong with being wealthy. But wealth must be earned from the sweat of an individual. Don't scheme to get wealthy and insult God with your tithes and offerings. You would only be piling curses on your life.

The right way of interpreting Scripture is to take it as we find it, without any attempt to force it into any particular system."—Richard Cecil (1837-1920)

Chapter Sixteen

JESUS CHRIST ON THE PASSOVER

So much debate has gone into whether Jesus celebrated the Jewish festivals or not. Like we have done so far, we will just hear His responses to questions that pertain to the celebration of some of these festivals to know what He taught on that subject to learn whether He celebrated these festivals or not. There is no need arguing over this. The Scriptures cannot be broken and must speak for itself.

> *On the first day of the Feast of Unleavened Bread, the disciples came to Jesus and asked, "**Where do you want us to make preparations for you to eat the Passover?**" 18 He replied, "Go into the city to a certain man and tell him, 'The Teacher says: My appointed time is near. **I am going to celebrate the Passover with my disciples at your house.**'" 19 **So the disciples did as Jesus had directed them and prepared the Passover** (Matt. 26:17-19).*

> *On the first day of the Feast of Unleavened Bread, when it was customary to sacrifice the Passover lamb, Jesus' disciples asked Him, "**Where do you want us to go and make preparations for you to eat the Passover?**" 13 So He sent two of His disciples, telling them, "Go into the city, and a man carrying a jar of water will meet you. Follow him. 14 Say to the owner of the house he enters, 'The Teacher asks: **Where is my guest room, where I may eat the Passover with my disciples?**' 15 He will show you a large upper room, furnished and ready. Make preparations for us there." 16 **The disciples left, went into the city and found things just as Jesus had told them. So they prepared the Passover.** (Mark 14:12-16)*

It is required of every Jew to observe this command of observing the Passover. Looking at the way the question was framed, we see it was something He had been doing all along. They asked Him: *"Where do you want us to make preparations for you to eat the Passover?"* From Mark's rendition of this, we can see that Christ had already made His own arrangement all along and there was even a certain man in the city who was aware of this. He sent two of His disciples to go ahead in search of this man and to ask him to show them the Teacher's guest room where He could eat the Passover with His disciples. The man concerned was to show them a large upper room, furnished and ready to accommodate at least thirteen individuals.

As the disciples went into the city in search of this *"certain man,"* they found everything just as Jesus had told them. Jesus then celebrated the Passover in this upper room with His disciples. It was when they were at the table, celebrating the last Feast of Unleavened Bread before His death that He introduced what is termed the Lord's Supper, to be done in remembrance of Him till He comes.

Jesus once said that foxes have holes to live in but the Son of Man has nowhere to lay His head. Now, there are those who take this statement to mean that Jesus did not have a place to stay and preach, and that it is evil to be rich, for Jesus was poor. Such preachers should read a line like this:

> *When the two disciples heard Him say this, they followed Jesus. 38 Turning round, Jesus saw them following and asked, "What do you want?" They said, "Rabbi" (which means Teacher), "where are you staying?" 39 "Come," He replied, "and you will see."* ***So they went and saw where He was staying, and spent that day with Him.*** *It was about the tenth hour (John 1:37-39).*

At an early age of thirty, Jesus had a place where He stayed and could accommodate three people at a go. We are not told about Christ's financial records but He surely did not live in poverty. He could afford a guest room of His own which was big enough to accommodate thirteen individuals at a time without the knowledge of any of His disciples. This also does not mean He lived in affluence, because that has not been given to us either. In effect, we now know that Christ celebrated the Jewish festival called Passover.

There was one time that Jesus *"purposely stayed away from Judea because the Jews there were waiting to take His life" (John 7:1).* Due to that, He went around in Galilee. *"However,* ***after His brothers had left for the Feast, He went also****, not publicly, but in secret . . . 14 Not until halfway through the Feast did Jesus go up to the temple courts and begin to teach" (John 7:10, 14).* His life was in danger and they could have killed Him at the least chance they got. But because it was customary for Him to attend this festival, He did.

THE PASSOVER IS A LASTING ORDINANCE FOR ALL GENERATIONS

When God told the children of Israel to start observing the Passover, He told them, *"This is a day you are to commemorate;* ***for the generations to come you shall celebrate it as a festival to the LORD—a lasting ordinance****" (Exod. 12:14).* Now, an *ordinance is "an order or a rule made by a government or somebody in a position of authority."* And to *commemorate is to remind people of an important person or event from the past with a special action or object.*

God commanded the children of Israel to observe the Passover as a lasting ordinance for all generations to always remind them of that miraculous event of rescuing them from the most powerful king on earth at the time.

Unlike the Jews in Jesus' days, this festival was opened to every Gentile who wanted to participate in its observance even as they were not associated with Israel in those days because it is written that: *"An alien (Gentile) living among you who wants to celebrate the LORD'S Passover must do so in accordance with its rules and regulations. You must have the same regulations for the alien and the native-born" (Num. 9:14).*

> *"But you are a chosen people, a royal priesthood, a holy nation, a people belonging to God, that you may declare the praises of Him who called you out of darkness into His wonderful light. 10 Once you were not a people, but now you are the people of God; once you had not received mercy, but now you have received mercy" (1 Pet. 2:9-10).*

The 6th of March every year is a special day in the life of every Ghanaian. This is because that was the day we obtained our independence from the British. Although I wasn't born in those years, I joyfully observe this day because it marks our independence (Passover) from colonisation. I wasn't around to witness what transpired into that but I do believe what my ancestors have established for our generation to follow. The children of Israel also attained their independence (Passover) from colonialism under the Egyptians in the past and were commanded to observe that day as an ordinance every year just as every Ghanaian has been commanded to observe the 6th of March every year since 1957.

Paul taught us that *"through the gospel the Gentiles are heirs together with Israel, members together of one body, and sharers together in the promise in Christ Jesus" (Eph. 3:6).* If Gentiles could participate in the observance of the Passover in the past, then there is nothing wrong for a Gentile believer to participate in its observance now that Paul has revealed the truth to us that "*through the gospel the Gentiles are heirs together with Israel, members together of one body, and sharers together in the promise in Christ Jesus.*" There's therefore nothing wrong with a Christian observing this feast.

> *"The authority of Scripture must be followed in all things, for in it we have the truth as it were in its secret haunts."—John Scotus Erigena (C. 810-877)*

Chapter Seventeen

JESUS ON THE WRITINGS OF MOSES AND THE PROPHETS

So much has been said about Jesus' teaching on the commands, precepts, statutes, decrees, laws and the writings of the other prophets in the Scriptures. Some teachers of the Bible erroneously conclude the teachings of Paul to mean that Christ nailed all statutes, commands, precepts, decrees and the laws in the Old Testament with Him on the cross when He was crucified. They often quote *John 13:34-35* where Jesus said, *"**A new command I give you:** Love one another. As I have loved you, so you must love one another. By this all men will know that you are my disciples, if you love one another"* to teach that it replaces all the statutes of God in the Scriptures.

Again, we will not try to argue over this with our own interpretations or understanding. Neither are we going to search for the Hebraic, Aramaic, nor the Greek words used in the translation of the New Testament. We know we do not serve a God of confusion. We will simply resort to the writings of Jesus to hear His own teachings on the Old Testament Scriptures.

THE PHARISEES SIT IN MOSES' SEAT

> *Then Jesus said to the crowds and to His disciples: "**The teachers of the law and the Pharisees sit in Moses' seat.** 3 **So you must obey them and do everything they tell you. But do not do what they do, for they do not practise what they preach.** 4 They tie up heavy loads and put them on men's shoulders, but they themselves are not willing to lift a finger to move them (Matt. 23:1-4).*

Jesus had just finished answering questions from some teachers of the law and the Pharisees who were always looking out for a way to trap Him in what He said. After one of such sessions, He called both His disciples and the crowds together to tell them that these same teachers and Pharisees who were always on the lookout to trap and arrest Him *sit in Moses' seat,* so they must not only obey them but actually do everything they told them to do. Prior to that, He had had several encounters with them where He called them various names such as brood of vipers, wolves in sheep's skin and blind guides. So, as the Great Teacher that He was, He had to substantiate His reasons for saying what He had said.

Several prophecies preceded Jesus, which are yet to be fulfilled even in our day and in future. It is written: *"And now, O Israel, what does the LORD your God ask of you* ***but*** *to fear the LORD your God,* ***to walk in all His ways,*** *to love Him, to serve the LORD your God with all your heart and with all your soul, 13 and to observe the LORD'S commands and decrees that I am giving you today* ***for your own good****" (Deut. 10:12-13).* For the people to walk in His ways, love Him and to observe all His commands there had to be a group of people who would be around to teach these things to them. We just read somewhere that: ***"the lips of a priest ought to preserve knowledge, and from his mouth men should seek instruction—because he is the messenger of the LORD Almighty****" (Mal. 2:7).*

Since the laws, commands, decrees, statutes and precepts were given through Moses, the Jews made his name synonymous with the words that came through him. That is why Jesus said the teachers of the law and the Pharisees sit in *Moses'* seat. Moses represented God in dealing with the people. So whatever he said came from the seat of God. The Pharisees had been authorised to teach the statutes of God to the citizenry and the people on their part were expected to obey and do whatever they were taught on behalf of *"Moses."* Jesus said, *"You must obey them and do everything they tell you."*

> *"We believe that the Word contained in these books has proceeded from God, and receives its authority from Him alone, and not from human beings. And in that, it is the rule of all truth, containing all that is necessary for the service of God and for our salvation, it is not lawful for anyone, even for angels, to add to it, to take away from it, or to change it."—French Confession of Faith*

If Jesus had ended it there without saying anything further He would have left all of us confused. If they were simply supposed to obey the Pharisees and the teachers of the law just because they sit in Moses' seat, then there was no need for Jesus to have even come to die such a shameful death on the cross and be humiliated like they did to Him. At the very onset of

His ministry, he had had several encounters with them and had been calling them names. So why would He tell the people to obey what the same *"brood of vipers"* taught them?

PRACTISE WHAT YOU PREACH

Listen very carefully to His words as that is the only way you can understand what you read from the Bible at all times. *"But do not do what they do."* The question is: what were the teachers doing that the people were being cautioned not to do? ***"For they do not practise what they preach."*** Isn't that plain and simple? He said somewhere that ***"But everyone who hears these words of mine and does not put them into practice is like a foolish man who built his house on sand"*** *(Matt. 7:26).* In effect, Jesus was telling His disciples and the rest of the people, and down to us, that merely memorising the Scriptures in one's head and quoting them at the least provocation do not amount to anything if one does not practise what he is preaching.

James puts this into perspective when he wrote that: ***"Do not merely listen to the word, and so deceive yourselves. Do what it says.*** *23 Anyone who listens to the word but does not do what it says is like a man who looks at his face in a mirror 24 and, after looking at himself, goes away and immediately forgets what he looks like. 25 But the man who looks intently into the perfect law that gives freedom, and continues to do this,* ***not forgetting what he has heard, but doing it—he will be blessed in what he does"*** *(James 1:22-25).*

The blessing comes based on what you do and not what you hear and preach in the hearing of others. The Pharisees and teachers of the law had the Word of God *(or "Moses")* alright but were not practising it themselves. Unlike our time, the people in Jesus' day were even lucky that Jesus Himself admonished them to obey and observe whatever the Pharisees told them to do. In our time, most of the modern-day Pharisees do not even know what the Bible is all about. They just join the hearsay queue and preach whatever is being said in the market squares. The problem Jesus had with the teachers and was telling his disciples not to copy or emulate was that: *"They tie up heavy loads and put them on men's shoulders,* ***but they themselves are not willing to lift a finger to move them."***

LOVE FOR POSITIONS MORE THAN SERVICE TO GOD

Again, Jesus could not say that about them without providing facts for the people to identify with when He had previously told them in the same breath that *they sit in Moses' seat* and must therefore be obeyed in everything they taught the people. So He started by giving them the reasons why He said that. Please listen very carefully to His words and compare them to our day to see what He would be saying to some people if He were here physically. Jesus started by saying that:

> ***"Everything they do is done for men to see:*** *They make their phylacteries wide and the tassels on their garments long; 6* ***they love the place of honour at banquets and the most important seats in the synagogues;*** *7 they love to be greeted in the market-places* ***and to have men call them 'Rabbi.'*** *(Matt. 23:5-7)*

Jesus was giving examples of some of the things they were doing that the people were not to emulate. He pointed out the fact that they did everything for men to see to be praised. They took the highest seats in the synagogues and loved the place of honour at every banquet they attended. They loved their titles more than what the titles represented. Phylacteries were some small boxes containing scriptural verses worn by them on their foreheads and arms. Jesus said they made these boxes wide to portray that they knew the Scriptures and had them at their finger tips, which wasn't true.

For instance, Jesus said, *"When you give to the needy, do not let your left hand know what your right hand is doing, 4 so that your giving may be in secret" (Matt. 6:3-4)* but the Pharisees of today, especially those in the West travel mostly to some of the remotest parts of the world in Africa and Asia, drill some bore-hole for the people and provide them with some fruit juices and stuffs. That is all good. But the next thing you know is a video coverage showing what was done. This is aired on their TV and radio networks for months advertising how good their church is.

I'm an African and I know what poverty is about. The greater part of my life has been spent in poverty until I got saved by the LORD'S grace. One thing I do know for a fact is that no-one loves to live in poverty. It is very dehumanising to showcase someone on national TV telling the whole world about how poor he is. It is true that a beggar has no choice. But if there is one gift you can present to the poor, I know it is the showing of respect to his privacy even in times of his needs. Let's not take advantage of the poor because they are poor to promote our own selfish interests. ***"Be careful not to do your 'acts of righteousness' before men, to be seen by them.*** *If you do, you will have no reward from your Father in heaven" (Matt. 6:1).*

Do you see someone or an organisation here in Jesus' words as you read? He continued: *"But you are not to be called 'Rabbi', for you have only One Master and* ***you are all brothers.*** *9* ***And do not call anyone on earth 'father', for you have One Father, and He is in heaven.*** *10 Nor are you to be called 'teacher', for you have One Teacher, the Christ. 11 The greatest among you will be your servant. 12 For whoever exalts himself will be humbled, and whoever humbles himself will be exalted" (Matt. 23:8-12).*

Jesus said the reason why a teacher of the law was not supposed to be called *"rabbi"* or a *"teacher"* is the fact that there is only One Teacher, who He was. So the title of *"Teacher"* is reserved for Him alone. He went on to say that all those listening to Him at that time, which included His disciples, were brothers in the faith. At another place he said: *"You are my friends if you do what I command. I no longer call you servants, because a servant does not know his master's business. Instead,* ***I have called you friends, for everything that I learned from my Father I have made known to you****" (John 15:14-15).*

It is written in the Scriptures that: *Jesus called them together and said,* ***"You know that the rulers of the Gentiles lord it over them, and their high officials exercise authority over them.*** *26* ***Not so with you. Instead, whoever wants to become great among you must be your servant,*** *27* ***and whoever wants to be first must be your slave****—28 just as the Son of Man did not come to be served,* ***but to serve****, and to give His life as a ransom for many" (Matt. 20:25-28).*

The systems of doing things on earth are directly opposite to how it is done in the kingdom of God. That is why God kept repeating to the Israelites not to live their lives the way other nations lived. It is the leaders of this sinful world who love to suppress the people of a country by treating them like some caged animals. With them, the leader is supposed to be served by those under him. But in the kingdom of God, it is rather the leader who should become the highest ranking servant among the people. He sacrifices his life to see to it that the right things are done according to the Word of God.

Jesus said they were not to call anyone on earth *'father.'* The reason He gave for that was simple—we all have One Father who is in heaven. Therefore, that Name *'Father,'* is reserved for the God and Father of us all. I'm not going to talk much about this now. But just imagine an employee announcing to everyone that he is the CEO of a company when the real CEO is still in office. Christianity seems to be the only place where subordinates take on their boss's titles upon themselves and brag about it. Why must we even dare to covet no other person's position than God the Father Himself? Jesus continued with this:

> *"Woe to you teachers of the law and Pharisees, you hypocrites! You travel over land and sea to win a single convert,* ***and when he becomes one, you make him twice as much a son of hell as you are****" (Matt. 23:15).*

Through the power of the internet and other communication gadgets in modern times like TV, radio, fax, email, mobile phones, Facebook, twitter, and the rest, it has become very easy to win a convert no matter how far away he or she may be. But the question is after he is converted, what kind of message is fed into his head? Is he won over to be transformed to mature into the stature of Christ which is the purpose of our calling, or is he won over just to warm the bench and increase the number of members for the pastor to be branded as the one pastoring the largest church in town?

FORCING ONES WAY INTO THE KINGDOM OF GOD

Addressing the question of the writings of Moses and the prophets at another time, Jesus said, *"The Law and the prophets were proclaimed until John. Since that time, the good news of the kingdom of God is being preached, and everyone is forcing his way into it. 17 It is easier for heaven and earth to disappear than for the least stroke of a pen to drop out of the Law. 18 Anyone who divorces his wife and marries another woman commits adultery, and the man who marries a divorced woman commits adultery" (Luke 16:16-18).*

Luke 16:16 is one of the verses in the Bible that those who love to do things for men to see like to base their stance on. In the King James Version, it is rendered *"The law and the prophets were until John: since that time the kingdom of God is preached,* ***and every man presseth into it****."* Matthew records this in the KJV: *"And from the days of John the Baptist until now the kingdom of heaven suffereth violence,* ***and the violent take it by force****." The NIV has it: "From the days of John the Baptist until now, the kingdom of heaven has been forcefully advancing,* ***and forceful men lay hold of it****" (Matt. 11:12).*

Because of the words *"forceful men lay hold of it" or "the violent take it by force,"* most of today's Christians have been taught to think they have to be violent in their walk with God, especially in their prayers, to succeed in life. Yet Jesus never used force in driving out any demon. He only spoke the word and they obeyed Him. He was even calmer when He was in the very presence of the devil. It takes knowledge into the Word of God to live the abundant life in the Scriptures, not force or violence. Remember that God did not say His people are destroyed from the power of the devil, but from lack of knowledge. We shouldn't forget the fact that Jesus was speaking in parables when He said those things.

He was rather giving a lecture on how it is easier for heaven and earth to disappear than for *"a stroke of a pen to disappear from the Scriptures."* He once told the crowd that John was the prophesied Elijah to come before Him. He said that: *"among those born of women there has not risen anyone greater than John the Baptist; yet he who is least in the kingdom of heaven is greater than he" (Matt. 11:11).* What Jesus was saying was that the Law and prophets had been proclaimed until John, and He was continuing it with the message of the kingdom of God.

"He who is least in the kingdom of heaven" that Christ was talking about referred to Himself. At the time of saying this, all had sinned and fell short of the glory of God; there was none righteous. Until His death and resurrection to redeem man from his sinful nature, man had become utterly worthless *(Rom. 3:9-18).* It is only after the mustard seed of Christ planted in the soil of this earth began to bear fruit through salvation that man became a living soul again, taking the original nature which was created in the image and likeness of God. We will go into this later in the book.

Whether we understand and accept what He said or not, what prompted that was the earlier statement that it was easier for heaven and earth to disappear than for a stroke of a pen to disappear from the Law. To stress on that, He gave an example of what He was teaching by quoting from the Law one of the commands and making it binding on His listeners. He took them to the original purpose of marriage again to stress that, from God's point of view no-one was required to divorce his wife for any reason except for marital unfaithfulness. Please bear in mind that at that dispensation of teaching these things, when He said someone was guilty of adultery, what He actually meant was that the person was going to face the death penalty.

THE HIDDEN TRUTH ON SEX

The secular world does not see anything wrong with having multiple sexual partners even after marriage. Unfortunately, today's Christian has also been brainwashed to only read religious connotations to the restrictions placed on sex outside marriage. Why do you think God would command that fornicators be killed in the Old Testament if there was nothing serious about it. Always bear in mind that it is the individual who gains or suffers for everything done on earth. The law of reaping whatever you sow holds true in all spheres of life. The truth about sex is hidden in Leviticus 17:10-12 where it is written that:

> *"Any Israelite or any alien living among them who eats any blood—I will set my face against that person who eats blood and will cut him off from his people. 11* ***For the life of a creature is in the blood****, and I have given it to you to make atonement for yourselves on the altar; it is the blood that makes atonement for one's life. 12 Therefore I say to the Israelites, "****None of you may eat blood nor an alien living among you eat blood****" (Lev. 17:10-12).*

Man is a creature and has blood running through his veins. If you are a Christian who believes the Scriptures, and it says *"the life of a creature is in the blood,"* then man is simply what his blood is made of. If you have sex with a person who is suffering from any of the sexually transmitted diseases, you are transferring blood which is the life of the other person into your veins to become like him or her. ***"Do you not know that he who unites himself with a prostitute is one with her in body?*** *For it is said,* ***"The two shall become one flesh.****" (1 Cor. 6:16).* If you doubt this, go straight for a medical test today and see where they start the diagnosis from. Just a drop of your blood sample can tell them all they need to know about your health.

Sex, whether protected or not is the most dangerous but secretly kept tool used by the institutions in high places to make their billions. This should help you understand why Paul said that: *"Flee from sexual immorality.* ***All other sins a man commits are outside his body, but he who sins sexually sins against his own body****" (1 Cor. 6:18).* Your blood, which is your life, is polluted with another person's own the moment there is a sexual encounter. If sexual partner A has STD 1 and sexual partner B has STD 2, you would have your blood, which is your life, to be polluted with STD 1 and STI 2. It's as simple as that. Sex is not only fun and pleasurable. It's a matter of life and death.

I often laugh but feel pity at the same time when people especially the youth of today brag about the number of sexual partners they've been with. Such people are only advertising their ignorance in life. Just the fluid transferred from each other during sex can cause your ruin. I want to reserve the revelations of the Old Testament Scriptures to you in later books. But let me give you a feel of it regarding how God shows His love towards us by giving us some laws in the Old Testament that most Christians no longer consider relevant to our age. God made it a law that:

> *"When a man has an emission of semen (through sex), he must bathe his whole body with water, and he will be unclean till evening. 17 Any clothing or leather that has semen on it must be washed with water, and it will be unclean till evening. 18* ***When a man lies with a woman and there is an emission of semen, both must***

> ***bathe with water, and they will be unclean till evening.****" (Lev. 15:16-18)*

At a glance, this sounds religious and irrelevant to our age. But read that again and try to remember how former president of the United States Bill Clinton was accused of sleeping with Monica Lewinsky. They found traces of his semen in his coat after months of sex. What this means is that it doesn't take being a medical doctor to know that a man's semen does not die easily after ejaculation the same way it does when it enters a woman.

That same semen which bears the life of a creature in it and is likely to be infested or diseased might have samples on the hands of the sexual partners and also touch the mattresses on which the sex act took place. For your own good, safety and protection, and in order not to transmit that diseased samples to others through handshake and even touching food items while eating with others, God says it is better you take a bath immediately after each sexual encounter. Is that a yoke of bondage? I think it's a yoke of freedom to set us free from the dangers of all sexually transmitted diseases.

On the third day of July 2012, the front page of the Daily Graphic reported that, "The DNA Centre at the Korle-Bu Teaching Hospital says it has the facilities to assist the law enforcement agencies in the detection of crime." It went further to state that their "machines could determine the identity of criminals by extracting DNA from saliva, hair, *blood, semen* or ***any other bodily fluid*** left at a crime scene or on the victims by the perpetrators." Think about that. A word to the wise is enough.

> *"No sciences are better attested than the religion of the Bible."—Sir Isaac Newton*

Modern-day Pharisees and teachers of the law are teaching the youth of today that it takes time to grow in the knowledge of God and have one's mind renewed. So if someone is unable to control his sexual desires, for instance, although he is not married, he is encouraged to just continue attending church services and continue to pray for forgiveness because Christ is at the right side of God interceding for him. In this way, he continues to pile polluted blood upon blood and *"any other bodily fluid"* into his veins and die later in the process, because he was not told the truth.

But the truth is that, most of these modern-day Pharisees, teachers of the law and the business institutions are all working for one force, which is there but is unseen with the naked eyes. Their number one weapon is to tread on the ignorance of the masses. Like commercial magicians, they use tricks to fool the audience who pay to watch them being fooled while their eyes are fully open. Prophets, priests and citizens alike take advantage of their fellow human beings for the sake of making profits.

> *The land is full of adulterers; because of the curse the land lies parched and the pastures in the desert are withered.* ***The prophets follow an evil course and use their power unjustly.*** *11* ***Both prophet and priest are godless; EVEN IN MY TEMPLE I FIND THEIR WICKEDNESS,"*** *declares the LORD . . . 14 And among the prophets of Jerusalem I have seen something horrible:* ***They commit adultery and live a lie. They strengthen the hands of evildoers, so that no-one turns from his wickedness. They are all like Sodom to me;*** *the people of Jerusalem are like Gomorrah."15 Therefore, this is what the LORD Almighty says concerning the prophets: "I will make them eat bitter food and drink poisoned water,* ***because from the prophets of Jerusalem ungodliness has spread throughout the land"*** *(Jer. 23:10-11, 14-16).*

Abstinence from fornication and adultery is not to punish anyone but to save us from death. Stop reading only religious meanings into the Bible and use your common sense at times to understand it. God will not die because you and I fornicate. ***You ask Him, 'What profit is it to me, and what do I gain by not sinning?'*** *. . . 6 If you sin, how does that affect Him? If your sins are many, what does that do to Him? 7 If you are righteous, what do you give to Him, or what does He receive from your hand? 8 Your wickedness affects only a man like yourself, and your righteousness only the sons of men (Job 35:3-8).* It is for your own health and longevity that you are being restrained from sex, especially that of adultery.

God's statutes protect you by "*keeping you from the immoral woman, from the smooth tongue of the wayward wife. 25 Do not lust in your heart after her beauty or let her captivate you with her eyes, 26* ***for the prostitute*** *(someone who sleeps with more than one sexual partner)* ***reduces you to a loaf of bread, and the adulteress preys upon your very life****" (Prov. 6:23-26).* Solomon added that: ***"But a man who commits adultery lacks judgment; whoever does so destroys himself"*** *(Prov. 6:32).* You would be caught, disgraced through stoning leading to one's death at the time of Jesus.

Fornication reduces you to a loaf of bread though you are alive and walking. After sex, your blood is contaminated because of the mixture of blood from another partner. It's not fun to have multiple sexual partners. It is a serious business transaction where you trade your very life for an hour's worth of fun in a partner's bosom. Maybe, I'm uncivilised, but I wouldn't do that. Just know what you are receiving into your system anytime you are having sex. That's all that is important. You need to be informed and the rest is your own cup of tea. No amount of prayer and fasting is required for one to stop engaging himself in sexual sins. Access to the right information is the key.

This is why Jesus said whoever divorces his wife and marries another is guilty of committing adultery. Do not be surprised about this for He even said a child who curses his parents should be put to death. That came from the mouth of Jesus and not Moses. He wasn't being harsh on anyone but showing His love for them.

A CORPSE IN THE ASSEMBLY OF THE GODLY

There are so many other things hidden in the Old Testament Scriptures, especially that the modern-day Pharisees will not tell the public because they are working for institutions, which appointed them to do their biddings. One of such dangerous things is to carry a corpse into the church premises. There is absolutely nothing religious about the law barring that from being done. It is sheer display of ignorance to do that.

If you take the dead body of someone who died from anthrax poisoning or Ebola or any of the deadly airborne diseases into the church and open the casket of the dead in the full glare of the people, what you are doing is transferring those airborne diseases or virus to the public. If you think the modern "Pharisees" do not know this, you must be kidding yourself. Some do it out of ignorance though. All that people call rituals of God in the Old Testament are actually life saving principles hidden in the pages of the Bible. I read somewhere that: ***"The greatest disease in the world is ignorance, it has caused more damage than any cancer."*** It is a thousand times true.

> *"The Holy Scriptures given by inspiration of God are of themselves sufficient to the discovery of the truth."—Athanasius (C. 296-373)*

Jesus was teaching about the wisdom hidden in the Scriptures that had been ignored by the people at that time to rather hold on to the traditions of the elders which they had used to replace the true Word of God. The Scriptures were the lamp to David's feet. The best gift I ever had was the Bible. There is so much hidden in it that I feel like I don't even know up to 1% of the truths contained in its pages.

THE PARABLE OF LAZARUS AND THE RICH MAN

I hope you can now understand Jesus. After saying these things about how difficult it is for a stroke of a pen to disappear from the Law of "Moses" and wanting to make it stick into their skulls, He told them a parable that:

> *"There was a rich man who was dressed in purple and fine linen and lived in luxury every day. 20 At his gate was laid a beggar named Lazarus, covered with sores 21 and longing to eat what fell from the rich man's table. Even the dogs came and licked his sores. 22* ***The time came when the beggar died and the angels carried him to Abraham's side****. The rich man also died and was buried. 23 In hell, where he was in torment, he looked up and saw Abraham far away, with Lazarus by his side. 24 So he called to him, 'Father Abraham, have pity on me and send Lazarus to dip the tip of his finger in water and cool my tongue, because I am in agony in this fire.'*
>
> *25 "But Abraham replied, 'Son, remember that in your lifetime you received your good things, while Lazarus received bad things, but now he is comforted here and you are in agony. 26 And besides all this,* ***between us and you a great chasm has been fixed****, so that those who want to go from here to you cannot, nor can anyone cross over from there to us.'*
>
> *27 "He answered, 'Then I beg you, father, send Lazarus to my father's house, 28 for I have five brothers.* ***Let him warn them, so that they will not also come to this place of torment.****' 29 "****Abraham replied, They have Moses and the Prophets; let them listen to them.****' 30 "'No, father Abraham,' he said, '****but if someone from the dead goes to them, they will repent****.' 31 "He said to him, '****If they do not listen to Moses and the Prophets, they will not be convinced even if someone rises from the dead****.'"* (Luke 16:19-31)

The first thing to note to understand this is to remember that it was a parable and could not be taken literally. We know it was a parable because of His audience listening to Him at the time. He had just finished a parable about a shrewd manager in verses one to thirteen. When the Pharisees heard Him, they were sneering at Him in verse fourteen. It was immediately after that when He started to teach about *"Moses and the Prophets"* again. *"He did not say anything to them without using parables" (Matt. 13:34).*

The crust of that teaching was that man should not wait till he or she is dead to seek for an opportunity to come back to life and expect to be given a second chance to obey God. A great chasm has been created between the dead and the living making it impossible for one to communicate with the other. Yet the message, which teaches, rebukes, corrects and is able to make one wise and thoroughly equipped for every good work in the lifetime of every soul, is contained in the books of *"Moses"* and that of the Prophets. In effect, Jesus was saying that, the time to get saved is when one is alive on earth. There is no second chance after one is dead and buried.

> *As a cloud vanishes and is gone, so he who goes down to the grave does not return. 10 He will never come to his house again; his place will know him no more (Job 7:9-10).*

The issue of being in hell fire, wishing to have a drop of water on the tongue was not the subject matter of what the Master was teaching. That would mean the parable had been taken literally without understanding its moral teaching being imparted.

INHERITING ETERNAL LIFE

On another occasion, Jesus had the opportunity to teach on this subject of *"Moses and the Prophets"* when a young but rich Jewish ruler came to ask Him a question about what he must do to inherit eternal life. As usual, we will look into what transpired between the two without reading our own meanings into it before making any conclusions:

> *Now a man came up to Jesus and asked, "Teacher, what good thing must I do to get eternal life?" 17 "Why do you ask me about what is good?" Jesus replied.* ***"There is only One who is good. If you want to enter life, obey the commandments."***
>
> *18 "**Which ones**?" the man enquired. Jesus replied, "Do not murder, do not commit adultery, do not steal, do not give false testimony, 19 honour your father and mother," and "love your neighbour as yourself."*
>
> *20 "All these I have kept," the young man said. "**What do I still lack**?" 21 Jesus answered, "**If you want to be perfect**, go, sell your possessions and give to the poor, and you will have treasure in heaven. Then come, follow me." 22 When the young man heard this, he went away sad, because he had great wealth. (Matt. 19:16-22)*

Jesus had left a place where He taught that little children were not to be hindered from coming to Him because the kingdom of God belonged to them as well, and had gone on to place His hands on them when out of the blue, this young but rich man came to ask Him a question about how to attain eternal life. He asked, *"Teacher, what good thing must I do to get eternal life.*

It is written: *"I gave them my decrees and made known to them my laws, for the man who obeys them will live by them" (Ezek. 20:11).* Before answering his question, Jesus took the time to explain to him that the only Person or Being to be called good is God the Father and not any other human being on earth. He then went on to answer his question based on the above that *"If you want to enter life, obey the commandments."* That was plain and simple. But being a Jew from birth, the young man knew about *"Moses and the Prophets"* as well as the traditions of the elders which had been handed down to them. And even with Moses and the Prophets, he had to be clear on some parts. It is written:

> *This is what the LORD Almighty, the God of Israel, says: Go ahead, add your burnt offerings to your other sacrifices and eat the meat yourselves! 22 For when I brought your forefathers out of Egypt and spoke to them,* ***I did not just give them commands about burnt offerings and sacrifices,*** *23* ***but I gave them this command: Obey me, and I will be your God and you will be my people. Walk in all the ways I command you that it may go well with you.*** *(Jer. 7:21-23)*

You see, the actual commands given to the Israelites when they were chosen as the *"firstborn son"* of God were statements like: *"If you listen carefully to the voice of the LORD your God and do what is right in His eyes, if you pay attention to His commands and keep all His decrees, I will not bring on you any of the diseases I brought on the Egyptians, for I am the LORD, who heals you" (Exod. 15:26).* The commands on burnt offerings and sacrifices were given because of another reason I will touch on in a minute.

PURPOSES OF THE BLOOD SACRIFICES

The purposes of the blood sacrifices were given in the book of Leviticus about blood. It is written: *"Any Israelite or any alien living among them who eats any blood—I will set my face against that person who eats blood and will cut him off from his people. 11 For the life of a creature is in the blood,* ***and I have given it to you to make atonement for yourselves on the altar; it is the blood that makes atonement for one's life.*** *12 Therefore I say to the*

Israelites, "None of you may eat blood nor an alien living among you eat blood" (Lev. 17:10-12).

"The sting of death is sin" (1 Cor. 15:56) and *"the wages of sin is death" (Rom. 6:23).* It is also written that: *"The soul who sins is the one who will die. The son will not share the guilt of the father, nor will the father share the guilt of the son. The righteousness of the righteous man will be credited to him, and the wickedness of the wicked will be charged against him" (Ezek. 18:20).*

Since the wages of sin is death, then any sinful man was dead although he was walking around. God chose to atone for the life of the individual who is to die as his wages for the sins committed by offering the blood of an animal in place of him for the people to always bear in mind that sin leads to death: *"For the life of a creature is in the blood,* ***and I have given it to you to make atonement for yourselves on the altar; it is the blood that makes atonement for one's life."*** Those sacrifices were in a sense symbolic to remind them of the fact that they were killing themselves through their multiple sins. God does not need blood offerings for Himself. *"This is an illustration for the present time, indicating that the gifts and sacrifices being offered were not able to clear the conscience of the worshipper" (Heb. 9:9).* David wrote:

> *I do not rebuke you for your sacrifices or your burnt offerings, which are ever before me. 9* ***I have no need of a bull from your stall or of goats from your pens, 10 for every animal of the forest is mine, and the cattle on a thousand hills.*** *11 I know every bird in the mountains, and the creatures of the field are mine. 12* ***If I were hungry I would not tell you, for the world is mine, and all that is in it. 13 Do I eat the flesh of bulls or drink the blood of goats****? (Psalm 50:8-13)*

If God does not eat the flesh of bulls or drink the blood of goats and yet commanded the Israelites to perform these sacrifices on His altar, then we should strive to know why: "*What, then, was the purpose of the law [of bull and goats sacrifices for atonement of one's life]?* ***It was added because of transgression until the Seed to whom the promise referred had come****" (Gal. 3:19).*

> *The Holy Spirit was showing* ***by this*** *that the way into the Most Holy Place had not yet been disclosed as long as the first tabernacle was still standing. 9* ***This is an illustration for the present time, indicating that the gifts and sacrifices being offered were not able to clear the conscience of the worshipper.*** *10* ***They are only a matter of food and drink and various ceremonial***

> ***washings—external regulations applying until the time of the new order.*** *(Heb. 9:8-10)*

Although this was an illustration to show them that the way to the Most Holy Place had not yet been disclosed, God arranged it in those days that *"The blood of goats and bulls and the ashes of a heifer sprinkled **on those who are ceremonially unclean sanctify them so that they are outwardly clean"** (Heb. 9:13). In fact, the law requires that nearly everything be cleansed with blood, and without the shedding of blood there is no forgiveness" (Heb. 9:22).*

> *When Christ came as High Priest of the good things that are already here, He went through the greater and more perfect tabernacle that is not man-made, that is to say, not a part of this creation. 12* ***He did not enter by means of goats and calves, but He entered the Most Holy Place once for all by His own blood,*** *having obtained eternal redemption . . . . 14 How much more, then, will the blood of Christ, who through the eternal Spirit offered Himself unblemished to God,* ***cleanse our consciences from acts that lead to death,*** *so that we may serve the living God! (Heb. 9:11-14)*

If you read the whole book of Hebrews starting from the very first chapter, you would realise that Paul was actually comparing the ministry of Christ to that of Moses for the Hebrews to have faith in Christ, which was the new covenant. In these verses that we have just read, he was just teaching them the purposes of the *"external regulations"* being applied until the time of the new order in Christ.

The Jews of old were concentrating much on the symbolic things of God more than the purposes for which they were established. For instance, when it was time for the Gentiles to be saved, *"Some of the believers who belonged to the party of the Pharisees stood up and said, 'The Gentiles must be circumcised and required to obey the law of Moses'" (Acts 15:5).* Most of the misunderstanding of Paul's writings stems from peoples' inability to locate how Paul dealt with these issues of what a Gentile is supposed to do and not to do to be saved.

> ***The law*** (which law?—the matter of food and drink and various ceremonial washings—external regulations applying until the time of the new order which were not able to clear the conscience of the worshipper) ***is only a shadow of the good things that are coming—not the realities themselves.*** *For this reason* ***it can never, by the same sacrifices repeated endlessly year after year, make perfect those who draw near to worship*** *. . . 3* ***But those sacrifices*** [now he is calling the law *"those sacrifices"*] ***are***

> ***an annual reminder of sins, 4 because it is impossible for the blood of bulls and goats to take away sins.*** *(Heb. 10:1-3)*

Paul wrote to the Colossians that *"See to it that no-one takes you captive through the hollow and deceptive philosophy,* ***which depends on human tradition*** *and the basic principles of this world rather than on Christ" (Col. 2:8).* This was after some of the believers who belonged to the group of the Pharisees were insisting that the Gentiles would have to be circumcised and forced into observing the Law of Moses. Let's read carefully what Paul taught on that subject.

> *When you were dead in your sins and in the uncircumcision of your sinful nature,* ***God made you alive with Christ. He forgave us all our sins, 14 having cancelled the written code, with its regulations, that was against us and that stood opposed to us; He took it away, nailing it to the cross.*** *(Col. 2:13-14)*

The question to ask is that, at what time was the Gentiles dead in their sins and was in the uncircumcision of their hearts? Peter, after being with Jesus for three years, said to Cornelius, who was a Gentile, and his family that *"You are well aware that it is against our law for a Jew to associate with a Gentile or visit him" (Acts 10:28).* Gentiles, just like the Jews, were all under sin. They *"had turned away and had altogether become worthless: there was no-one who did good, not even one" (Rom. 3:12).* Their sins had resulted into a sting of death upon their lives *(1 Cor. 15:56). "For all have sinned and fall short of the glory of God" (Rom. 3:23),* and *the wages of sin is death (Rom. 6:23).*

The Gentiles up to the time of being saved were not even having the *"matter of food and drink and various ceremonial washings—external regulations applying until the time of the new order"* which was serving as an illustration for the new order. So, until they engaged in the offering of blood to atone for all the sins committed prior to their being saved, they were dead in their sinful nature *"and without the shedding of blood there is no forgiveness" (Heb. 9:22).*

Therefore, the written code and its regulations were that, the Gentile was already dead in his sinful nature and must not even be associated with. But what happened? ***God made you*** *[the Gentile]* ***alive with Christ. He forgave us all our sins, having cancelled the written code, with its regulations that was against us, and that stood opposed to us; He took it away, nailing it to the cross.***

The sins of the Gentile sinner prior to knowing Jesus Christ had not been atoned for with blood. It is this sin that Christ came to forgive him of by cancelling the regulations of death as punishment, taking all of them away and nailing them to the cross. It is not the statutes of God in the Scriptures that were nailed to the cross but the sins which would have received the death penalty. It is written that: *"The soul who sins is the one who will die" (Ezek. 18:20).* The sinner had to die for his sins but Jesus came to atone for him by dying on his behalf [in place of the blood sacrifices from bulls or goats]. The death penalty placed upon the life of the sinner is the written code and its regulation was for him to incur the death penalty or to have his death atoned for with blood which Jesus did on every sinner's behalf for once.

> *Therefore do not let anyone judge you by what you eat or drink, or with regard to a religious festival, a New Moon celebration or a Sabbath day. 17 These [the blood sacrifices] are a shadow of the things that were to come; the reality, however, is found in Christ. 18* ***Do not let anyone who delights in false humility and the worship of angels disqualify you for the prize.*** *(Col. 2:16-18)*

Paul tells us in the book of Galatians that *"Those who want to make a good impression outwardly are trying to compel you to be circumcised. The only reason they do this is to avoid being persecuted for the cross of Christ. 13 Not even those who are circumcised obey the law, yet they want you to be circumcised that they may boast about your flesh" (Gal. 6:12-13).* You see, these people were not preaching the same message Paul preached. They were running the ministry as some sort of a business entity and only cared about avoiding being persecuted. Paul said those people were actually worshipping angels and not God. Later in the book we will get to know how they did this. Remember also that Paul continually warned his students to be wary of false prophets in their midst.

Those were the Pharisees who had found a fine way of setting aside the commands of God in order to observe their own traditions. If they tried enforcing the observance of their own traditions on Jesus Christ, how much more the Gentiles? This should not surprise us. The most important thing is that Christ dealt with them and left us with an example for us to also follow. Now, please read the next few verses very carefully.

> ***Since you died with Christ to the basic principles of this world, why, as though you still belonged to it, do you submit to its rules:*** *21 "Do not handle! Do not taste! Do not touch!" 22 These are all destined to perish with use,* ***because they are based on human commands and teachings.*** *23* ***Such regulations indeed have an appearance of wisdom, with their self-imposed worship****, their false humility and their harsh treatment of*

> *the body, but they lack any value in restraining sensual indulgence. (Col. 2:20-23)*

Jesus said, *"You have let go of the commands of God and are holding on to the traditions of men. You have a fine way of setting aside the commands of God in order to observe your own traditions! . . . 13 Thus you nullify the word of God by your tradition that you have handed down.* ***And you do many things like that****" (Mark 7:8-13).* There were several other things that were being done but were not recorded in the pages of the Bible. But to avoid controversy, we will limit ourselves to what we have in the Bible.

These traditions were different from the commands of God but had the appearance of wisdom in them, anyway. They were human commands and teachings that were being forced down the throats of the Gentile believers. But even with the blood sacrifices, Christ came to settle that for the Gentile on the cross. *Therefore, if anyone is in Christ, he is a new creation: the old has gone, the new has come! (2 Cor. 5:17).*

> *Therefore no-one will be declared righteous by observing the law; rather through the law we become conscious of sin. 21* ***But now a righteousness from God, apart from law, has been made known, to which the Law and the Prophets testify****. 22* ***This righteousness from God comes through faith in Jesus Christ to all who believe. There is no difference****, 23 for all have sinned and fall short of the glory of God, 24 and are justified freely by His grace through the redemption that came by Christ Jesus. (Rom. 3:20-24)*

LIVING THE NEW LIFE

We can now read some few verses further to understand this teaching without much emphasis. *"What shall we say, then? Shall we go on sinning, so that grace may increase? 2 By no means!* ***We died to sin: how can we live in it any longer?*** *3 Or don't you know that all of us who were baptised into Christ Jesus were baptised into His death? 4* ***We were therefore buried with Him through baptism into death in order that, just as Christ was raised from the dead through the glory of the Father, we may live a new life****" (Rom. 6:1-4).*

> *"The Gospel is within you, and you are its evidence; it is preached to you in your own bosom, and everything within you is a proof of the truth of it."—William Law (1686-1761)*

One of the purposes for Christ's coming to earth was to sacrifice Himself on behalf of man to atone for our sins. Why did He have to do that? The sting of death is sin. For all have sinned and fall short of the glory of God. And the wages of sin is death. These are the written codes for us all, and the regulations of death for all of us who sinned were against every sinner. Now, we all died when Christ died on our behalf and took our punishment for us, which was death. Baptism by immersion into water is used as a symbol to represent the death, burial and resurrection of that old sinful body that died.

Christ then resurrected after His death from the grave in glory. When a man is brought out from the water during baptism, it also symbolizes his resurrection from death like Jesus. But this time, his old sinful nature which sinned and died is resurrected in glory. At this time, the man is a new creature taken back to the original image and likeness of God as he was created in the beginning. He does not sin again to die once more "***because anyone who has died has been freed from sin***" *(Rom. 6:7).*

> ***Now if we died with Christ, we believe that we will also live with Him.*** *9 For we know that since Christ was raised from the dead, He cannot die again* ***(just as we cannot allow ourselves to die again through sin)****; death no longer has mastery over Him. 10 The death He died, He died to sin once for all; but the life He lives (representing the life we live after our resurrection from baptism into Christ), He lives to God.*
>
> *11* ***In the same way, count yourselves dead to sin but alive to God in Christ Jesus.*** *12* ***Therefore do not let sin reign in your mortal body so that you obey its evil desires.*** *13 Do not offer the parts of your body to sin, as instruments of wickedness, but rather offer yourselves to God, as those who have been brought from death to life;* ***and offer the parts of your body to Him as instruments of righteousness.*** *14* ***For sin shall not be your master, because you are not under law, but under grace.*** *(Rom. 6:8-14)*

I cannot go into much detail here as that would betray the purpose of this chapter. But all that Paul is trying to teach here is that the system under the old covenant required that after every sin, the sinner had to offer blood in atonement for his sins, which the Jews were trying to impose on the Gentiles. But Christ came to offer Himself once for everyone alive. In effect, the sinful nature, which was prone to sin, died in Christ and was resurrected in glory as a new creation. *In the same way, count yourselves dead to sin but alive to God in Christ Jesus. 12 Therefore do not let sin reign in your mortal body so that you obey its evil desires (Rom. 6:11-12).* Our sinful nature used to be a slave to sin but is now required to become slaves to righteousness. We are no longer under that law of sacrificing blood for our sins again but under the grace of God where sin does not reign in our bodies so that we obey its desires.

> ***You have been set free from sin and have become slaves to righteousness*** *. . . Just as you used to offer the parts of your body in slavery to impurity and to ever-increasing wickedness,* ***so now offer them in slavery to righteousness leading to holiness*** *. . . 21 What benefit did you reap at that time from the things you are now ashamed of? Those things result in death! 22 But now that you have been set free from sin and have become slaves to God, the benefit you reap leads to holiness, and the result is eternal life. 23 For the wages of sin is death, but the gift of God is eternal life in Christ Jesus our LORD. (Rom. 6:18-23)*

It is important to note that the emphasis of Paul's teaching was on what one becomes after salvation. According to the gospel, it is believed that one is set free from sin and becomes a total slave to righteousness. A *slave* is a person who is legally owned by another person and is forced to work for them. In this sense, God owns you after salvation and you become a slave who leads a totally righteous life that qualifies you to become holy, leading to eternal life. But unlike human slave masters, God does not force us to lead this holy life but admonishes us to willingly offer to do that. For instance, if a robot is programmed not to break any law, then the written laws on paper does not matter to it, because it is never going to break anything written therein.

The actual commands for the *"firstborn son"* were meant for each and every living soul. ***"The same law applies to the native-born and to the alien living among you"*** *(Exod. 12:49).*

For I desire mercy, not sacrifice, and acknowledgement of God rather than burnt offerings *(Hosea 6:6).* God is only interested in His children obeying His commands and making righteousness reign in every nation. Listen to this: *"I hate, I despise your religious feasts; I cannot stand your assemblies. 22 Even though you bring me burnt offerings and grain offerings, I will not accept them. Though you bring choice fellowship offerings, I will have no regard for them. 23 Away with the noise of your songs! I will not listen to the music of your harps. 24* ***But let justice roll on like a river, righteousness like a never-failing stream! Did you bring me sacrifices and offerings for forty years in the desert, O house of Israel"*** *(Amos 5:21-25)?*

> *The former regulation is set aside because it was weak and useless 19 (for the law made nothing perfect), and a better hope is introduced, by which we draw near to God . . . 27* ***Unlike the other high priests, He does not need to offer sacrifices day after day, first for His own sins, and then for the sins of the people. He sacrificed for their sins once for all when He offered Himself.*** *(Heb. 7:18-19, 27)*

The purpose for which a man is saved is not just to be numbered among the believers and then tied to some doctrines of the religious folks with a promise of a ticket in hand to be taken to some outside country beyond the stars in future. One is saved to take on the original image and likeness of God which was lost in the Garden of Eden. A saved man does not continue in sin and does not need such blood sacrifices again. You shall know the truth and the truth shall set you free. You need to fully understand this teaching before even accepting to be baptised in the Name of Jesus Christ.

And after knowing the truth, if you go back to your sinful ways, then you should also know what the Scriptures say about your reward. Paul wrote that: ***"If we deliberately keep on sinning after we have received the knowledge of the truth, no sacrifice for sins is left,*** *27 but only a fearful expectation of judgment and of raging fire that will consume the enemies of God" (Heb. 10:26-27).* Christ Jesus came to offer Himself as the perfect sacrifice and died on our behalf to atone for all the sins we had committed, and took us back to our original state.

"***Dear friends, now we are children of God****, and what we will be has not yet been made known. But we know that when He appears, we shall be like Him, for we shall see Him as He is." (1 John 3:2)* The time to become the children of God is not in the future but now that we believe, and are saved by Christ's sacrifice on our behalf. *"We know that we have come to know Him if we obey His commands. 4 The man who says, 'I know Him,' but does not do what He commands is a liar, and the truth is not in him. 5 But if anyone obeys His word, God's love is truly made complete in him. This is how we know we are in Him. 6 Whoever claims to live in Him must walk as Jesus did (1 John 2:3-6)."*

After we have come to know Him and have become His children at this very moment, then we know that ***"No-one who is born of God will continue to sin, because God's seed remains in him; he cannot go on sinning, because he has been born of God.*** *10* ***This is how we know who the children of God are and who the children of the devil are****: Anyone who does not do what is right is not a child of God; nor is anyone who does not love his brother" (1 John 3:9-10).* The blood sacrifices were performed when someone sinned. But after one is born again of God, he cannot go on sinning to partake in the offering of any blood sacrifice anymore. Jesus would have to die again for him. And since that is impossible, he would have to dance to his own tune.

> *"Nobody ever outgrows Scripture; the Book widens and deepens with our years."—Charles Haddon Spurgeon (1834-1892)*

Those sacrifices and offerings of blood were added, because of transgression of the Laws and commands of God. But when one is truly born of God, he simply cannot sin and, in the process, be made to offer any sacrifices again. But the original commands like *"do not steal"* and "*do not commit adultery"* remain forever in every corner of the earth. Not even those in the pornographic industry will feel good when you sleep with their wives. Stealing is prohibited in all countries including Iran and North Korea.

Because it was a relevant question asked by a typical Jewish mind, Jesus went on to state a few of those commands, which were immutable as God Himself is, in every generation that David learnt were established to last forever. *Jesus replied, "'Do not murder', 'do not commit adultery', 'do not steal', 'do not give false testimony', 19 'honour your father and mother,' and 'love your neighbour as yourself'"* in answer to his question. None of these commands had anything to do with offering blood sacrifices on an altar because Jesus wasn't referring to such commands. Even God Himself will stop being God if He should break any of these commands. God will not steal or commit adultery.

Can you imagine Jesus Christ caught in adultery or stealing because He has redeemed us from the curse of the law? The Sanhedrin would have killed Him a long time earlier if He had dared to break even one of these commands. There are several such commands in the Scriptures but since He could not list all of them, Jesus resorted to just the Ten Commandments because they were easy to remember by any Jewish mind. The second reason Jesus started from that angle was that it is written: *"To the law and to the testimony! If they do not speak according to this word, they have no light of dawn" (Isa. 8:20).* The testimony refers to the Ten Commandments. "*When the LORD finished speaking to Moses on Mount Sinai, He gave him* ***the two tablets of the Testimony,*** *the tablets of stone inscribed by the finger of God" (Exod. 31:18).*

Now, if the young man had not been exposed to these commands in advance, He would have simply taken Jesus at His word and gone home to do as He was told without saying a word in protest: *"All these I have kept," the young man said.* ***"What do I still lack?"*** You see, he wanted to know what a man who keeps the whole commands of God from birth like himself could still be lacking. Personally, I thank him for asking such a question because I feel he asked that question for all of us. Occasionally, we should all set aside time to assess ourselves to see if we are truly serving God with our hearts and minds or not. There wasn't a better teacher to answer such a question like the Master Himself, Jesus Christ.

Jesus taught him and all of us that it was possible to lose the mark after doing all that. In the man's situation, it was his riches which had become so dear to him. He made sure he kept all the commands of God but his heart wasn't in it. Such was an example for those who think their righteousness either add to or subtract from God. *"If you are righteous, what do you give to Him, or what does He receive from your hand? 8 Your wickedness affects only a man like yourself, and your righteousness only the sons of men" (Job 35:7-8).* Such people assume that godliness is about just performing rituals like visiting "holy" sites and making vows. No, all these have to be done justly, faithfully and blamelessly in the sight of both God and man.

He had his thinking flawed so Jesus had to teach him on how to understand the Scriptures and truly follow them with his whole spirit, soul and body. Jesus answered, ***"If you want to be perfect****, go, sell your possessions and give to the poor, and you will have treasure in heaven.* ***Then come, follow me."*** He was obeying the commands from infancy, which was good. But if he wanted to be ***"perfect,"*** then he had to go the extra mile by paying a serious attention to what, in his walk with God, hindered his growth. Mark rendered it, *"One thing you lack" (Mark 10:21).* Note that Jesus told him to follow Him after he had sold all his possessions. The disciples had done same and left their families behind to follow Christ. If he had done that, he would have had the opportunity to be around the Teacher at all times to enable him learn the nitty-gritty of the kingdom of God.

This young man had a good foundation by obeying the commands from childhood, but the structure on it was not strong enough, and would have collapsed if there was any serious storm. The Master was giving him the opportunity to straighten things up. But like most of us, He could not take what was offered to him as the solution to his problem. *"When the young man heard this, he went away sad, because he had great wealth."* For the Bible to record that he had great wealth means it was a very difficult task that he was being asked to do by our LORD and Saviour.

The next thing to note here, unlike it is being taught today, is the fact that Jesus did not tell him to stop obeying the commands of God to come and follow Him. Jesus Himself said, *"Do not think that I have come to abolish the Law or the Prophets; I have not come to abolish them but to fulfil them"*

(Matt. 5:17). Once again, you don't need the Hebraic or the Greek word used in this verse to understand what He said. It simply says what it says there.

I'm told that if you want to keep a thing hidden from the black man, write it in a book. Now that we can read, write and find these truths on our own, they now want to tell us that it is only what they conclude to be the interpretations of these writings that are to be accepted and obeyed, without asking questions. But that's a lie! Some of us have chosen to read and understand the Bible on our own. Everyone can do the same. It is not true when someone tells you that the Bible is difficult to understand. Whoever says that is a liar, and wants to keep you in the dark for him to lord it over you.

Personally, I believe this rich young man, like King Solomon, would later come back to his senses and adhere to what he was taught either before or after the death and resurrection of Jesus Christ. If truly he had been well versed in the Scriptures, then he surely might have read about Solomon to reconsider his decisions. He would have reached the point where he would learn from Solomon's mistakes and pursue true righteousness rather than the pleasures of this earth.

Chapter Eighteen

JESUS CHRIST ON THE GREATEST COMMANDMENT

The Bible is mostly written in parables but when you learn the basics, it becomes plain and simple to understand. In one of His encounters with a teacher of the law, we can hear of Jesus' teaching on upholding the statutes of God in the Old Testament (*"Moses and the Prophets")*. Outright show of disrespect to both God and Jesus make some of the modern-day Pharisees refuse to rely on the teachings of God in the Bible, and then go on to twist the words of Paul to fall within their standards. Lies should not be told in the name of Christ to blind the masses who do not read the Scriptures.

> *One of the teachers of the law came and heard them debating. Noticing that Jesus had given them a good answer, he asked Him, "Of all the commandments, which is the most important?" 29 "The most important one," answered Jesus, "is this: 'Hear, O Israel, the LORD our God, The LORD is One. 30 Love the LORD your God with all your heart and with all your soul and with all your mind and with all your strength.' 31 The second is this: **'Love your neighbour as yourself.' There is no commandment greater than these."***
>
> *32 "Well said, teacher," the man replied. "You are right in saying that God is One and there is no other but Him. 33 To love Him with all your heart, with all your understanding and with all your strength, **and to love your neighbour as yourself is more important than all burnt offerings and sacrifices."***
>
> *34 **When Jesus saw that he had answered wisely, He said to him, "You are not far from the kingdom of God."** And from then on no-one dared ask Him any more questions. (Mark 12:28-34)*

Jesus had just finished debating with the Sadducees over *"Moses and the Prophets"* when another teacher of the law came to hear Him answer correctly to a certain question about marriage after the resurrection. We know they were debating over the commandments because in *verse 19* of the same chapter they asked Him, *"Teacher,* ***Moses wrote for us that*** *if a man's brother dies and leaves a wife but no children, the man must marry the widow and have children for his brother."* It was the reply given by Jesus in *verses 24 to 27* that the teacher heard and knew Jesus had given them the right answer. Subsequently, he came over to test Him with a question of his own to give him the most important of all the commandments given through Moses.

In simple but plain language, Jesus quoted from *"Moses,"* where it is written: *"Hear, O Israel: The LORD our God, the LORD is One. Love the LORD your God with all your heart and with all your soul and with all your strength" (Deut. 6:4).* To prove to this teacher that He was well informed about the Scriptures, Jesus went ahead to add the second when He was not even asked. He again quoted from *Leviticus 19:18* where it is written: *"Do not seek revenge or bear a grudge against one of your people,* ***but love your neighbour as yourself.*** *I am the LORD."* After quoting these two, He said, ***"There is no commandment greater than these."*** Why did He say that?

John, like his Master, gives us the reasons why these two are the greatest. He wrote: *"We know that we have come to know Him if we obey His commands. The man who says, "I know Him," but does not do what He commands is a liar, and the truth is not in him.* ***But if anyone obeys His word, God's love is truly made complete in him. This is how we know we are in Him"*** *(1 John 1:3-5).* So, if you want to know whether you obey the LORD with all your heart, mind, soul and strength, just read these verses from John to assess how you are faring. That is the first or the most important of all the commandments. Every other command hangs on loving God and carrying out His commands.

> ***And this is love: that we walk in obedience to His commands.*** *As you have heard from the beginning,* ***His command is that you walk in love.*** *(2 John 6)*

The second most important commandment is this: ***"Anyone who claims to be in the light but hates his brother is still in the darkness.*** *10 Whoever loves his brother lives in the light,* ***and there is nothing in him to make him stumble.*** *11 But whoever hates his brother is in the darkness;* ***and walks around in the darkness; he does not know where he is going, because the darkness has blinded him"*** *(1 John 1:9-11).* Strong words! But why is that so? It is because ***"If anyone says, 'I love God,' yet hates his brother,***

he is a liar*. (Why?)* ***For anyone who does not love his brother, whom he has seen, cannot love God, whom he has not seen****. 21 And He has given us this command:* ***Whoever loves God must also love his brother****" (1 John 4:20-21).*

I don't think you need a Bible Commentary, a Bible Concordance or even a Dictionary to understand what we just read. The Spirit of God says, you don't even know where you are going if you don't love your brother. Just how can you claim to love God whom you've not seen with your own eyes if you cannot love your brother, sister, father, mother, cousin or friend who add up to be your neighbours whom you see with your very eyes on daily basis? You must be a good liar and a fake Jew or Christian!

> *Let no debt remain outstanding,* ***except the continuing debt to love one another, for he who loves his fellow-man has fulfilled the law****. 9 The commandments, "Do not commit adultery," "Do not murder," "Do not steal," "Do not covet,"* ***and whatever other commandment there may be, are summed up in this one rule****:* ***"Love your neighbour as yourself."*** *Love does no harm to its neighbour.* ***Therefore love is the fulfilment of the law.*** *(Rom. 13:8-10)*

If you truly love your neighbour, you would never sleep with his wife, knowing very well that you wouldn't feel too excited if that was done to you. No matter how great you are at forgiving others, you wouldn't take it lightly if someone dear to you is murdered in cold blood. Love will help you take into consideration the toil and hardship people went through to amass their wealth and make it hard for you to steal from them. Contrary to what we have been made to believe, the commandments rather teach us to have genuine and true love toward others even if they are strangers to us. Those commands make us become conscious of sins and thereby restricting us from offending others.

> *"What a book! Great and wide as the world, rooted in the abysmal depths of creation and rising aloft into the blue mysteries of heaven. Sunrise and sunset, promise and fulfilment, birth and death, the whole human drama: everything is in this book. It is the Book of Books, Biblia."—Heinrich Heine (1797-1856)*

JESUS' DEFINITION OF A NEIGHBOUR

Who, then, is a neighbour or a brother that both Jesus and John were talking about in these verses? Is it someone who has the same DNA as mine or has the same colour as myself or belongs to the same race as I, or attends the church I attend? Who exactly is a brother or a neighbour to us? Is it the man who lives next door or the one who shares the same apartment with us? Just who is a neighbour?

Since it is written that *"Whoever claims to live in Him must walk as Jesus did,"* and *"no-one can lay any foundation other than the one already laid, which is Jesus Christ,"* we should go and ask Jesus Christ to tell us who a neighbour or a brother is and, when the answer is given, we will know how to treat such a person. Paul wrote: *"Follow my example, as I follow the example of Christ" (1 Cor. 11:1).*

> ***Now Jesus' mother and brothers came to see Him****, but they were not able to get near Him because of the crowd. 20 Someone told Him, "Your mother and brothers are standing outside, wanting to see you." 21 He replied, "****My mother and brothers are those who hear God's word and put them into practice.****" (Luke 8:19-21)*

It is written that *"The fruit of righteousness will be peace; the effect of righteousness will be quietness and confidence forever" (Isaiah 32:17). "The remnant of Israel will do no wrong; they will speak no lies, nor will deceit be found in their mouths. They will eat and lie down and no-one will make them afraid" (Zeph. 3:13). "Righteousness exalts a nation but sin is a reproach to any people".* No matter how great a nation's army is, once it's moral fabric in society is destroyed, that nation is on the verge of collapsing. You don't need guns to defeat a nation which allows its youth to engage in whatever pleases them.

Any form of unrighteousness should be avoided at all costs. If your own flesh and blood will not see the wisdom in the Word of God and put them into practice, then you have no business tolerating them in their sins. You can only love them as sinners who need to be saved through the preaching of the Word. *"But now I am writing to you that* ***you must not associate with anyone who calls himself a brother but is sexually immoral or greedy, an idolater or a slanderer, a drunkard or a swindler. With such a man do not even eat****" (1 Cor. 5:11).*

Don't you know that a little yeast works through the whole batch of dough? Little drops of water make a mighty ocean. Once the Words of God are neglected in the name of such inferior principles like racism, nepotism, corruption, in favour of party faithful and the like, a nation is on the highway to destruction. This is why Jesus said that it is not those who hear His words or have the same DNA as Himself but those who actually put His words into practice that are His brothers and sisters. Attending the same church does not make us brothers and sisters; putting the Word of God into practice does. Jesus used the parable of the Good Samaritan to teach this principle well.

So, now that we know who our neighbours are and how to love them as ourselves, we can now proceed with the encounter between the teacher of the law and Jesus. After hearing Jesus' answer to his question, he said, "*Well said, Teacher. You are right in saying that God is one and there is no other but Him. To love Him with all your heart, with all your understanding and with all your strength,* ***and to love your neighbour as yourself is more important than all burnt offerings and sacrifices.***" That should tell us that there were some of the teachers of the law and Pharisees who knew the truths of God but were not teaching them in public.

This particular teacher knew that there were things to do which were more important than all the burnt offerings and sacrifices combined. No wonder Jesus told His listeners *to obey and do everything they were told to but at the same time not to copy their lifestyle (Matt. 23:1-2).* This teacher even congratulated Jesus that He was right in the answer given. After hearing him finish, Jesus also said something very remarkable. He said, ***"You are not far from the kingdom of God."*** Call it clash of the titans if you like. These two surely had done their homework well regarding the Scriptures. They applauded each other for being conversant with the Scriptures. Notice that Jesus did not tell this man to get born again, like He told Nicodemus, to enter into the kingdom of God but rather said *he was not far from it.*

Unlike Nicodemus, this teacher knew and understood the Scriptures from cover to cover. He was *"an expert in the law" (Matt. 22:34-35).* Jesus asked Nicodemus that, *"You are Israel's teacher, and do you not understand these things" (John 3:10)*? In other words, if he was a teacher of the word, then he had to know what was being discussed at the time. But the second teacher was fully trained and equipped for his job.

> *"Christians need no other reason to be avid readers of the Word of God. Realising that Scripture is 'God-breathed' is motivation enough . . . . When the mind and spirit of a biblical author interact in vibrant dialogue with the mind and spirit of the reader, the highest purpose of the inspired Word is fulfilled. We should soar every time we read the Word of God."—David L. McKenna*

Chapter Nineteen

JESUS CHRIST ON THE SABBATH

This is one of the topics that generate lots of debates over what day we are to worship God and what to do on this day when it is agreed upon. There are those who say if God is not worshipped on a particular day, then the whole issue of even serving Him becomes null and void. Such, for this reason, become judgmental and see all others who don't worship on a particular day as evil and lost. On the other hand, there are those who also conclude that the day one chooses to serve God does not matter but the motives surrounding these gatherings in serving Him is what matters most.

One thing we must always bear in mind is the fact that God is supreme when it comes to robbing our minds with His. It is written that: *"Can you fathom the mysteries of God? Can you probe the limits of the Almighty? 8 They are higher than the heavens—what can you do? They are deeper than the depths of the grave—what can you know? 9 Their measure is longer than the earth and wider than the sea" (Job 11:7-9).*

Aside God creating the world, everything in it, resting on the seventh day and hallowing it, thereby making it holy, there are other two main reasons why He instituted the Sabbath for mankind. Once you understand the purposes for which God institutes a law, a command or a decree in the Scriptures, it becomes a delight to observe it without reading any wrong religious meanings into it.

Just as all nations on earth have their national flags, which serve as signs for other nations to see and know where they are coming from, God also has His own way of marking His children for the world to see to identify them from others. During marriage ceremonies, for instance, a wedding ring is placed on each of the partners' fingers to serve as signs of their love for each other. No matter how deeply you claim to be in love with someone, the moment you see him or her wearing a wedding ring, you should know that he or she is no longer available to enter into any marital relationship again unless you are of course the type who sees nothing wrong with adultery. One of the reasons for which the Sabbath was introduced by God was to serve as a sign between Him and His children.

THE SABBATH IS A SIGN BETWEEN GOD AND HIS CHILDREN

> *Then the LORD said to Moses, 13 "Say to the Israelites, 'You must observe my Sabbaths.* ***This will be a sign between me and you for the generations to come,*** *so that you may know that I am the LORD, who makes you holy . . . 16* ***The Israelites are to observe the Sabbath, celebrating it for the generations to come as a lasting covenant.*** *17* ***It will be a sign between me and the Israelites forever,*** *for in six days the LORD made the heavens and the earth, and on the seventh day He abstained from work and rested.'" (Exod. 31:12-17)*

It is extremely important that you understand the fact that God does not make mistakes to be corrected later. There is nothing like an amendment to His Word. He ceases to be God if He should descend to that level of saying something today and later coming back to change His mind on it. As it is written: ***"He who is the Glory of Israel does not lie or change His mind; for He is not a man, that He should change His mind"*** *(1 Sam. 15:29). "But* ***the plans of the LORD stand firm forever, the purposes of His heart through all generations****" (Psalm 33:11).* ***"I will not violate my covenant or alter what my lips have uttered"*** *(Psalm 89:34).*

God, in His own wisdom chose the Sabbath among all that is found on this earth to be the sign that distinguishes His children from the rest of mankind. He said this was going to be a lasting covenant that was to last forever between Him and the Israelites. Unless, of course, there are no Israelites alive today, the sign still remains because it says it was going to be forever, and God does not change His mind. In several places, God said through the prophets: *"Also I gave them my Sabbaths* ***as a sign between us,*** *so they would know that I the LORD made them holy . . . Keep my Sabbaths holy,* ***that they may be a sign between us.*** *Then you will know that I am the LORD your God" (Ezek. 20:12, 20).* Please remember that Israel is only the firstborn nation to be joined by other nations later. Abraham was to be the father of many and not just one nation (Gen. 17:3-8). Israel was the first seed of nations planted.

THE SABBATH IS A DAY OF REST FOR GOD'S CHILDREN

The second purpose for establishing the Sabbath is that, it is written: *"There are six days when you may work, but the seventh day is* ***a Sabbath of rest****, a day of sacred assembly.* ***You are not to do any work****; wherever you live, it is a Sabbath to the LORD" (Lev. 23:3).* Again, we will go to the book of Job to remind ourselves with the question *"What profit is it to me, and what do I gain by not sinning . . . 6 If you sin, how does that affect Him? If your sins are many, what does that do to Him? 7 If you are righteous, what do you give to Him, or what does He receive from your hand" (Job 35:3, 6-7)?*

What does one give to God or take from Him by either observing or not observing the Sabbath? Nothing! Whether we observe the Sabbath or not, God will forever remain who He is. *"Your wickedness affects only a man like yourself and your righteousness only the sons of men" (Job 35:8).* God says: *"I gave them my decrees and made known to them my laws,* ***for the man who obeys them will live by them****" (Ezek. 20:11).* Apart from it serving as a sign, the Sabbath is also meant to serve as a resting mechanism for the children of God to have time to relax their muscles from work. It then serves as health inducing mechanism, and prevents stress.

> *So be careful to do what the LORD your God has commanded you; do not turn aside to the right or to the left. 33 Walk in all the way that the LORD your God has commanded you,* ***so that you may live and prosper and prolong your days in the land that you will possess.*** *(Deut. 5:32-33)*

At one time, God said through Moses that "*Take to heart all the words I have solemnly declared to you this day, so that you may command your children to obey carefully all the words of this law. 47* ***They are not just idle words for you—they are your life. By them you will live long in the land*** *you are crossing the Jordan to possess" (Deut. 32:46-47).* For instance, if you desire to be wealthy, you just have to obey carefully all the words about wealth creation in this law. It is written: *"But remember the LORD your God, for it is He who gives you the ability to produce wealth, and so confirms His covenant, which He swore to your forefathers, as it is today" (Deut. 8:18).* You don't pray and fast to be wealthy. You become wealthy by applying the principles in this law.

In the same way, if you intend to be healthy, you have to search the Scriptures to learn how it is done. It is written: *"If you listen carefully to the voice of the LORD your God and do what is right in His eyes (concerning what is done to achieve good health), if you pay attention to His commands and keep all His decrees (on health issues from His own Word),* ***I*** *(God)* ***will not bring on***

you any of the diseases I brought on the Egyptians, for I am the LORD, who heals you *(Exod. 15:26).* Why wait till you are attacked by a disease before praying to be delivered? Prevention, they say, is better than cure.

> ***This day I call heaven and earth as witnesses against you that I have set before you life and death, blessings and curses.*** *Now choose life, so that you and your children may live 20 and that you may love the LORD your God, listen to His voice, and hold fast to Him.* ***For the LORD is your life****, and He will give you many years in the land He swore to give to your fathers, Abraham, Isaac and Jacob. (Deut. 30:19-20)*

No-one has ever seen God before. So it is the application of His principles that brings life to an individual. Like Job, we should be constantly reminding ourselves that *"how can a mortal be righteous before God?"* It is hard to even answer God once out of a thousand questions. His wisdom is profound and His power vast. *"Can you fathom the mysteries of God or probe the limits of the Almighty?"* There is absolutely nothing religious about the Sabbath. The Sabbath, among other laws, is there simply for your identification with God and well-being. It enables you to rest and start work the following day full of energy and vitality. Jesus said, *"The Sabbath was made for man and not man for the Sabbath."* It was not even made for God, but man.

> *"The Bible is a window in this prison-world, through which we may look into eternity."—Timothy Dwight (1752-1817)*

"For the LORD is your life." We are told to choose life so that we and our children may live and prosper in the land. That life is simply to choose the way of God in the Scriptures. You don't go to heaven to hug or kiss God on His throne to show how much you love Him. ***"This is love for God: to obey His commands. And His commands are not burdensome"*** *(1 John 4:3).* Do not allow yourself to be brainwashed to only see the "religious" side of the commands in the Scriptures. Get closer to discover things for yourself before drawing that conclusion.

MISAPPROPRIATING THE SABBATH LAW

With this background, let's now come back to the LORD Jesus Christ and His dealings with the teachers of the law and Pharisees. The Pharisees had subjected the observance of the Sabbath to so much religion that it became a crime to even heal a person on this day. How sad! They forgot the principles behind the Sabbath and chose to observe it blindly. Jesus asked them at one time, *"Now if a child can be circumcised on the Sabbath so that the Law of Moses may not be broken,* ***why are you angry with me for healing the whole man on the Sabbath****? 24* ***Stop judging by mere appearances****, and make a right judgment" (John 7:23-24).*

If the Sabbath was made for man, and not the other way round, then it is incumbent on those who enforce its implementation to always remember that it is applied to bring life, peace and joy to man. For instance, we are commanded to rest on this day. But must a doctor refuse treatment to a dying patient because he is observing the Sabbath? No! The Sabbath was made for man. The same way, all the commands and laws in the Scriptures are meant for man and not man for the laws and commands. Understand this concept and you are free indeed.

> *Another time He (Jesus) went into the synagogue, and a man with a shrivelled hand was there. 2 Some of them were looking for a reason to accuse Jesus,* ***so they watched Him closely to see if He would heal him on the Sabbath****. 3 Jesus said to the man with the shrivelled hand, "Stand up in front of everyone."*
>
> *4 Then Jesus asked them,* ***"Which is lawful on the Sabbath: to do good or to do evil, to save life or to kill?"*** *But they remained silent. 5 He looked round at them* ***in anger and, deeply distressed at their stubborn hearts****, said to the man, "Stretch out your hand." He stretched it out, and his hand was completely restored. 6* ***Then the Pharisees went out and began to plot with the Herodians how they might kill Jesus****. (Mark 3:1-6).*

Jesus' problem with these teachers was not about whether the Sabbath was still in force or not. It had nothing to do with that. But the issue was about ***"Which is lawful on the Sabbath****: to do good or to do evil, to save life or to kill?"* At one time when He was walking with His disciples along a cornfield, they began to pick some corn to eat because they were hungry. That was not lawful but as citizens of the land, Jesus taught that one must not die of hunger in the midst of food simply because he is observing the Sabbath. Remember again that, the Sabbath was made for man.

Understanding the purposes for which each and every command was given in the Scriptures is the key, not just rigidly and blindly applying them. As I went to buy books from my favourite bookshop some months back, I overhead one pastor complaining bitterly about what another famous pastor had taught on obedience to the Old Testament laws on TV. To make his point, this pastor quoted from Leviticus where God said the priest should not climb on an altar to expose his nakedness. He then proceeded to ask those of us around that "what is wrong with building story-buildings today?" From his understanding, that law was barring people from constructing story buildings then and today. As they were discussing this among themselves I chose to remain silent.

I chose that path because it is written *"He who guards his lips guards his life, but he who speaks rashly will come to ruin" (Prov. 13:3). A patient man has great understanding, but a quick-tempered man displays folly. (Prov. 14:29). Even a fool is thought wise if he keeps silent, and discerning if he holds his tongue. (Prov. 17:28)*

But this was the quotation: *"And do not go* ***up*** *to my altar* ***on steps****, (why?)* ***lest your nakedness be exposed on it****" (Exod. 20:26).* By relating this law to story-buildings, I realised he had not read to understand that verse but had only read it with the intention of waiting for an opportunity like that to just argue with others. As a layman looking into the Scriptures, you should ascertain the purpose for which that law was given because it was given by God and does not need any interpretations before understanding it. God was simply telling the priests not to go up His altars on steps. Those days, they wore long robes. So He was telling them that they would expose their nakedness to those below them if they went up on steps, period. Now, in a society where most of us wear pants and trousers, must we fight over a quotation like that with a fellow Christian? The law was given to man, not man for the law.

BE FULLY CONVINCED IN YOUR MIND

As to which day is the Sabbath, Paul gave a sound instruction in the book of Romans, which you need to read and understand. Addressing the issue of eating only vegetables and the eating of *"everything,"* he wrote that: ***"One man considers one day more sacred than another; another man considers every day alike. Each man should be fully convinced in his own mind.*** *6* ***He who regards one day as special, does so to the LORD*** *. . . 10* ***You, then, why do you judge your brother****? Or why do you look down on your brother? For we will all stand before God's judgment seat" (Rom. 14:5-6, 10).*

Christ commanded us to go and make disciples of all nations and baptise those who believe. Suppose you go to a country like Saudi Arabia where they rest on Fridays, must you miss an opportunity to preach the gospel to them on Fridays and insist on a particular day to worship when they will be at work? The Sabbath was made for man. Paul taught us that *"Each man should **be fully convinced in his own mind**."* Until you teach them to become fully convinced of the purposes of the Sabbath and what it represents, you would be doing your listeners great disservice by imposing a particular day of Sabbath on them, which is different from what they had in their country, thereby hindering the preaching of the Word. That would be the practice of sheer legalistic religion on your part.

Jesus asked, *"If any of you has a sheep and it falls into a pit on the Sabbath, will you not take hold of it and lift it out? 12 **How much more valuable is a man than a sheep! Therefore it is lawful to do good on the Sabbath**" (Matt. 12:11-12).* Making good use of the opportunity to preach the gospel to someone in Saudi Arabia on Fridays till he becomes fully mature in the things of God, and turning him from the judgment to come is more valuable than losing him because he could not observe the Sabbath on a particular day. Yet the Sabbath still stands for ever.

> *"I know the Bible is inspired because it finds me at greater depths of my being than any other book."—Samuel Taylor Coleridge (1772-1834)*

Chapter Twenty

JESUS CHRIST ON FULFILLING THE LAW

Much has been said about what Jesus meant and taught on fulfilling the Law. As usual, we will not add to this by burdening our minds with our own interpretation. It is always easier and simpler to listen to what the Master Himself said. We've been warned that *"If anyone adds anything to them, God will add to him the plagues described in this book. And if anyone takes words away from this book of prophecy, God will take away from him his share in the tree of life and in the holy city, which are described in this book" (Rev. 22:18-19).* Most teachers seem to forget this warning when they begin to dish out their so-called interpretations of the Scriptures.

> *Do not think that I have come to abolish the Law or the Prophets;* ***I have not come to abolish them but to fulfil them.*** *18 I tell you the truth, until heaven and earth disappear,* ***not the smallest letter, not the least stroke of a pen, will by any means disappear from the Law until everything is accomplished."*** *(Matt. 5:17-18)*

If you are one of those who think the content of the Old Testament is outdated and is no longer relevant for our time, and you are advocating its abolition, Jesus is saying that it will take the disappearing of both heaven and earth for *"a stroke of a pen"* to be deleted from it, period. And for heaven and earth to disappear simply means the death of God's kingdom because heaven is His throne and earth is His footstool. Scientists keep informing us that the heavens and the earth have been in existence for billions of years. But they have not yet told us anywhere that both of them have disappeared at any time in the past. Not that I have heard of! You can either take Jesus at His word or tell Him to go to hell with His teachings.

> *Anyone who breaks one of the least of these commandments and teaches others to do the same will be called least in the kingdom of heaven,* ***but whoever practises <u>and</u> teaches these commands will be called great in the kingdom of heaven.*** *(Matt. 5:19)*

DO NOT BE DECIEVED

Speaking as an apostle of Christ, James wrote: "***Do not merely listen to the word, and so deceive yourselves. Do what it says.*** *23 Anyone who listens to the word but does not do what it says is like a man who looks at his face in a mirror 24 and, after looking at himself, goes away and immediately forgets what he looks like. 25* ***But the man who looks intently into the perfect law that gives freedom, and continues to do this, not forgetting what he has heard, but doing it—he will be blessed in what he does****" (James 1:22-25).* The blessing comes from doing, not just hearing, memorising and quoting Scriptures at will. That amounts to nothing. Like the old saying goes, "*The sweetness of the pudding lies in the eating.*"

"We know that we have come to know Him if we obey His commands. 4 ***The man who says, "I know Him," but does not do what He commands is a liar, and the truth is not in him.*** *But if anyone obeys His word, God's love is truly made complete in him.* ***This is how we know we are in Him:*** *6 whoever claims to live in Him must walk as Jesus did" (1 John 2:3-6).* Jesus walked in obedience to the commandments of His Father. And even if we choose not to obey the voice of the God of the Old Testament, we should obey the teaching of Christ, which is the same as that of His Father; or Paul's, which is the same as that of Christ.

THE GREATEST IN THE KINGDOM OF HEAVEN

According to Jesus, the easiest way to identify someone who is either great or least in the kingdom of heaven is to watch what he or she does with the commandments of God in the Scriptures. "***But whoever practises and teaches these commands will be called great in the kingdom of heaven.***" Today's man has been brainwashed to think that it is absolute nonsense to even think of obeying the commandments. The ironic part of this is the fact that Paul's letters, which are mostly read to arrive at this conclusion, are the same writings that make a Gentile believer understand the Scriptures more. Just relax and we will soon get there and make things easier for your understanding.

> *For I tell you that unless your righteousness surpasses that of the Pharisees and teachers of the law, you will certainly not enter the kingdom of heaven. (Matt. 5:20)*

The reason Jesus said the above statement had nothing whatsoever to do with the commandments of God in the Scriptures. Although the Pharisees and teachers of the law sit in Moses' seat, they themselves had become blind in their way of life, and Jesus was admonishing his listeners to rise above their standards by living a righteous life than they did. Now, to explain how He came not to abolish but to fulfil *"the Law or the Prophets,"* He started by quoting a few verses from the Law to teach us how He came to fulfil them.

JESUS' DEFINITION OF FULFILLING THE LAW

Now, to explain how He came not to abolish but to fulfil *"the Law and the Prophets,"* Jesus began by quoting a few verses from the Law to teach what He meant by fulfilling them.

HOW TO AVOID MURDER JESUS' WAY

He quoted *Exodus 20:13* where it is written: *"You shall not murder."* On the subject of not abolishing the law but fulfilling it, He taught: *"But I tell you that anyone who is angry with his brother will be subject to judgment. Again, anyone who says to his brother, 'Raca,' is answerable to the Sanhedrin.* ***But anyone who says, 'You fool!' will be in danger of the fire of hell****" (Matt. 5:21-22).* Instead of waiting till someone is murdered first, Jesus taught the principles on how to extinguish the fire of anger in a person, which would grow out of proportion to lead to the loss of an innocent soul. The punishment for murder in the Law is death. So in order to save the lives of two people at a time, He taught that even calling someone a fool was going to lead one to hell. This is because an insult can lead to a fight which can also lead to death.

> *When tempted, no-one should say, "God is tempting me." For God cannot be tempted with evil, nor does He tempt anyone; 14* ***but each one is tempted when, by his own evil desire, he is dragged away and enticed.*** *15* ***Then, after desire has conceived, it gives birth to sin; and sin, when it is full-grown, gives birth to death.***

In this case, Jesus was teaching us to avoid murder with the power of forgiveness. It is written that the LORD does not delight in the death of a sinner but for him to repent of his sins. Both the murdered victim and the murderer would lose their lives when an act like this is committed. So He was teaching a better way of handling insults and anger which are the major causes of murder in society. God does not gain or lose anything by the death of someone as punishment for being a murderer. But that does not also give the green-light to anyone to use that as an excuse to kill his fellow human being. He fulfilled that law. Paul wrote that:

> *Since there is only one God, who will justify the circumcised by faith and the uncircumcised through that same faith, 31* ***Do we, then, nullify the law by this faith? Not at all! Rather, we uphold the law.*** *(Rom. 3:30-31)*

HOW TO AVOID ADULTERY JESUS' WAY

Jesus again quoted from *Exodus 20:14* where it is written: *"You shall not commit adultery"* to teach on how He came not to abolish that law but to fulfil it. This is how He puts it: *"You have heard that it was said, 'Do not commit adultery.' 28* ***But I tell you that anyone who looks at a woman lustfully has already committed adultery with her in his heart.****"* There are those who will do whatever it takes to sleep with a woman, because they claim they lusted after her in their hearts and have to go ahead and sleep with her because of what Jesus said. It is written: *"My people are destroyed from lack of knowledge" (Hosea 4:6).* The first clue is to recall that Jesus was speaking in parables when He said that.

Solomon asked the question that: *"Can a man scoop fire into his lap without his clothes being burned? 28 Can a man walk on hot coals without his feet being scorched? 29* ***So is he who sleeps with another man's wife; no-one who torches her will go unpunished*** *. . . 32 But a man who commits adultery lacks judgment;* ***whoever does so destroys himself****" (Prov. 6:27-29, 32).* Aside the dangerous side effects of engaging in sex, which have been hidden from the eyes of men, adultery leads to much embarrassments and beatings when caught. And this can lead to death because the penalty for committing adultery in the Scriptures is death.

There's an adage in my area which translates literally that, *"A tree that would pierce your eyes must be uprooted from the roots and not just cut from the trunk."* Little drops of water make a mighty ocean. Often, one does not intentionally plan to commit adultery or to fornicate until he or she is already in the act, when it becomes impossible to opt out. Jesus was teaching that adultery begins with merely lusting after someone to desire him or her before travelling through the other stages into the actual act. In a sense, you are in danger of committing adultery the moment you find yourself lusting after someone. That is where you should extinguish that desire because it ends in sleeping with the person. You've already committed the act if you cannot control it from the lusting stage.

Kelvin Baerg once said that *"The things that are foremost in our minds determine our actions and decisions. We become like our dominant thoughts."* Van Crouch also said once that *"You will never change your actions until you change your mind."* What Jesus was teaching had to do with how one uses his mind to control such feelings of lust in man before he or she is caught in the web and finds himself or herself unable to retreat. He fulfilled that law too.

> *"I entered the world's great library doors; I crossed their acres of polished floors; I searched and searched their stacks and nooks. And settled at last on the Book of books"—Author unknown.*

AN EYE FOR AN EYE?

Again, Jesus quoted from *Leviticus 24:19-20* where it is written: *"If anyone injures his neighbour, whatever he has done must be done to him: 20 fracture for fracture, eye for eye, and tooth for tooth.* ***As he has injured the other, so he is to be injured."*** At least we know that some of the commands were given because of the hardness of the people's hearts, which were not given from the beginning of time. Centuries of slavery had turned our forefathers' hearts hard that laws like these had to be introduced to sustain them at that dispensation.

> *In the past God spoke to our forefathers through the prophets at many times and in various ways, 2* ***but in these last days He has spoken to us by His Son, whom He appointed heir of all things****, and through whom He made the universe. 3* ***The Son is the radiance of God's glory and the exact representation of His being, sustaining all things by His powerful word.*** *After He had provided purification for sins, He sat down at the right hand of the Majesty in heaven. 4 So He became as much superior to the angels as the Name He has inherited is superior to theirs. (Heb. 1:1-4)*

Jesus said, *"My teaching is not my own. It comes from Him who sent me. 17 If anyone chooses to do God's will, he will find out whether my teaching comes from God or whether I speak on my own" (John 6:16-17).* If the law of *"an eye for an eye"* was to be in force at all times, then, like Mahatma Ghandi said, the whole world would have gone blind by now. Jesus came to teach the truth on forgiveness of sins, love for our neigbours and how to handle them.

He said, *"You have heard that it was said, 'Eye for eye, and tooth for tooth.'* ***But I tell you, Do not resist an evil person. If someone strikes you on the right cheek, turn to him the other also.*** *40* ***And if someone wants to sue you and take your tunic, let him have your cloak as well****" (Matt. 5:38-40).* It is unfortunate that most Christians, like the secular world, do not see the wisdom in Jesus' words and rather follow what they do, trying to avenge all wrongs done against them. You see this phenomenon in their prayer sessions where they spend most of their time raining down curses on their enemies. I don't know if they read the same Bible I read.

All that Jesus was teaching was on forgiveness of sins. Whether it is an eye which is gouged out or a tooth that is plucked from our mouths, Jesus says that once we have life we must not strike back. This may sound stupid to some of us but Paul wrote: *"Do not deceive yourselves. If any one of you thinks he is wise* ***by the standards of this age, he should become a "fool" so that he may become wise.*** *19* ***For the wisdom of this world is foolishness in God's sight****. As it is written: "He catches the wise in their craftiness." 20 And again, "The LORD knows that the thoughts of the wise are futile" (1 Cor. 3:18-19).*

The wisdom in this teaching on forgiveness was clearly revealed to Paul when he wrote to the Romans that *"Bless those who persecute you;* ***bless and do not curse*** *. . . 16 Live in harmony with one another. Do not be proud, but be willing to associate with people of low position. Do not be conceited. 17* ***Do not repay anyone evil for evil.*** *Be careful to do what is right in the eyes of everybody. 18* ***If it is possible, as far as it depends on you, live at peace with everyone****. 19* ***Do not take revenge, my friends, but leave room for God's wrath,*** *for it is written:* ***"It is mine to avenge; I will repay,"*** *says the LORD. 20* ***On the contrary: "If your enemy is hungry, feed him; if he is thirsty, give him something to drink****. In doing this, you will heap burning coals on his head."* ***Do not be overcome by evil, but overcome evil with good****" (Rom. 12:14-21).*

The modern-day "Pharisees," who advocate that the Old Testament is done away with, are the same people who quote from the Psalms and other places in the Old Testament Scriptures to rain down curses on their enemies' heads until they themselves are bound in chains of anger and resentment, which are prisons on their own. Yet Paul, whom they hold in high esteem than Jesus, is now telling us to bless and not curse anyone. Instead of getting angry, resentful and cursing your enemies, David said: ***In your anger do not sin;*** *when you are on your beds,* ***search your hearts and be silent.*** *5 Offer right sacrifices* ***and trust in the LORD"*** *(Psalm 4:4-5).*

Most of today's prayer sessions are just premeditated evil thoughts and wishes against one's supposed enemies taken to God to be executed on one's behalf. But before you take such a prayer request to God again, read this: ***"He who is pregnant with evil and conceives trouble gives birth to disillusionment.*** *15* ***He who digs a hole and scoops it out falls into the pit he has made.*** *16* ***The trouble he causes recoils on himself; his violence comes down on his own head"*** *(Psalm 7:14-16).* Job added this that: ***"Resentment kills a fool,*** *and envy slays the simple" (Job 5:2).* Sit down and search deep into your soul to find out why you resent someone in the first place. You suffer more than the person you resent. Resentment is a seed you plant which grows to bear fruits of more resentment. Each man reaps what he sows.

David was a warrior and had birds of the same feathers on his side that could fight and kill hundreds of soldiers at a time. He was in the midst of real battlefield action and realised he could not win without the help of God, and resorted to prayers mostly. In a sense, he was not relying on his strength alone to wage his battles. The life he had at each moment was given him by God and that should be the mentality of us all. Upon all the prayers, he still had to fight.

God promised to take the children of Israel to a land flowing with milk and honey but they had to fight their way through to possess it. Jacob had to work for fourteen years to marry the wife he loved. Joseph had to endure pains to reach the throne of Egypt. Even Jesus had to work. He had a treasurer in the person of Judas Iscariot. A treasurer's work is to handle money, and we are not told in the Bible that Jesus was receiving money from His Father in heaven. He took the teaching seriously as work.

A lazy man who refuses to work will remain poor and beggarly no matter how much prayer, fasting and giving of tithes and offerings he does. *"If a man will not work, he shall not eat" (2 Thess. 3:10).* The one who does not watch the intake of what goes into his belly and does not exercise will fall sick again and again. What is the wisdom in waiting till you are ill before going for healing sessions? Is that what Jesus needs to show how powerful He is? Fasting and prayers do not raise good children; it takes proper training and discipline to raise them.

JESUS ON LOVE FOR ENEMIES

Again, to fulfil the Law and the Prophets, Jesus said, *"You have heard that it was said, 'Love your neighbour and hate your enemy.'* ***But I tell you: Love your enemies and pray for those who persecute you, 45 that you may be sons of your Father in heaven . . .*** *46 If you love those who love you, what reward will you get? Are not even the tax collectors doing that? 47 And if you greet only your brothers, what are you doing more than others?* ***Do not even pagans do that? 48 Be perfect, therefore, as your heavenly Father is perfect"*** *(Matt. 5:43-48).*

Do you notice that Jesus is linking our ability to love our enemies to being perfect just as our Father is perfect? Ever since I realised that I have to love all mankind no matter their religion or the colour of their skin, I became free. When I meet people on the streets, I tune my mind to see people created in God's image and likeness, and refuse to see whether they are Moslems, Buddhists or Atheists. I only see mankind and I show my love towards them. ***"If anyone says, 'I love God,' yet hates his brother, he is a liar. For anyone who does not love his brother, whom he has seen, cannot love God, whom he has not seen. And He has given us this command: Whoever loves God must also love his brother."*** But care must be taken in order not to be lured into following other gods.

Jesus went further to expound on the Law and the Prophets by teaching on the moral principles behind them. He gave us just a few that could be written down for us to study. He dealt with murder, adultery, divorce, oaths, *"an eye for an eye,"* love for enemies, giving to the needy, prayer, fasting, worrying about tomorrow, judging others, asking, seeking and knocking, storing treasures in heaven instead of where they would be eaten by moths, bearing good fruits and others. Just a few of them have been written down. *"Jesus did many other things as well. If every one of them were written down, I suppose that even the whole world would not have room for the books that would be written" (John 21:25).*

Indeed, Jesus Christ our LORD and Saviour did not come to abolish the Law and the prophets but to fulfil them. The Law He came to fulfil also had nothing to do with the law of sacrificing bulls and goats. David learned from long ago that the Law was established to last forever. What I think and know does not come to play here. But with my humble study into the Scriptures, I have also learned that the content of the Holy Scriptures handed down to us were established to last forever. It is a delight to read and apply them if one truly understands them.

CHAPTER TWENTY-ONE

CHRIST'S CHARGE AGAINST THE PHARISEES AND TEACHERS OF THE LAW

It is of utmost importance that we know and understand why Jesus kept insulting the Pharisees and teachers of the law by calling them fools, blind, vipers and wolves in sheep skin. Mostly, He had a problem with them for their fine way of setting aside the commands of God in order to observe their own traditions. They had succeeded in rendering the Word of God nullified and replaced them with their own hypocritical traditions which Christ called yeast. *Jesus began to speak first to His disciples, saying: "Be on your guard against* ***the yeast of the Pharisees, which is hypocrisy****" (Luke 12:2).* Yeast is added to dough to make bread. The dough represents the original word of God which was being mixed with yeast (the traditions of the elders taught by the Pharisees) to turn the Word of God into something else.

> *While all the people were listening, Jesus said to His disciples, 46 "Beware of the teachers of the law. They like to walk around in flowing robes and love to be greeted in the market-places and have the most important seats in the synagogues and the places of honour at banquets. 47 They devour widows' houses and for a show make lengthy prayers. Such men will be punished most severely. (Luke 20:45-47)*

You would realise that nothing He said had anything whatsoever to do with the Scriptures of Moses and the Prophets per se, but on how they had twisted the Word of God to serve their own selfish interests. They had profaned the seat of Moses by making it a tool for robbing the people. No wonder they could turn the temple of God into a market-place. They claimed to follow Moses but were not following the dictates of him. Jesus told them that *"****If you believed Moses, you would believe me****, for he wrote about me. 47*

But since you do not believe what he wrote, how are you going to believe what I say *" (John 5:46-47)? "Has not Moses given you the law?* ***Yet not one of you keeps the law.*** *Why are you trying to kill me" (John 7:19)?*

They thought they were implementing the teachings of Moses but were far from the truth. Instead of searching into the Scriptures to know who Christ was, they were blinded by religion, and insisted that because Jesus came from Galilee, He was disqualified from being the promised Messiah to redeem us from our sins. Nicodemus went into Christ's defence once, and when the Pharisees were discussing Christ, they asked him: *"Are you from Galilee, too? Look into it and* ***you will find that a prophet does not come out of Galilee*** *" (John 7:52).*

They succeeded in converting the kingdom of God into a religious institution where they claimed to be superior to their fellows in the things of God, which was not true. They were appointed to administer the Word of God but they rather made it difficult to reach its intended recipients. They were angry with Jesus for healing a whole man because they claimed He was not supposed to heal on the Sabbath. Moses did not preach wickedness or barbarism for the sake of religion. Moses even preached that a city should be provided where someone who kills someone accidentally could flee for refuge. He also preached about providing food for the poor but not the lazy man.

> *Then Moses set aside three cities east of the Jordan, 42* ***to which anyone who had killed a person could flee if he had unintentionally killed his neighbour without malice aforethought. He could flee into one of these cities and save his life.*** *(Deut. 4:41-42)*

There is nothing like the first five books of the Bible, namely Genesis, Exodus, Leviticus, Numbers and Deuteronomy. These are the foundational truths of the entire Bible. All the best advice on military defence, insurance, prevention of diseases, cleanliness, solutions to all the issues of life are clearly written on the pages of these five books. But the servants of those in high places will tell you of how these things have been done away with and nailed to a cross. How can a command that says you should not to sleep with your mother be nailed to a cross?

The Constitution of any nation gives every citizen of that nation the right to say things by setting the records straight even if it is the president of the land who is going astray. We see that in the life of John the Baptist when he said to King Herod, *"It is not lawful for you to have your brother's wife" (Mark 6:18).* John the Baptist was bold in declaring that because it is written:

"If a man marries his brother's wife, it is an act of impurity; he has dishonoured his brother. They will be childless" (Lev. 20:21). All these laws were still in effect in the days of both Jesus and John. So Jesus was laying the grounds for the words of Scripture to be taught as the way and manner it was intended by the Father from the beginning.

Chapter Twenty-Two

JESUS CHRIST WAS A JEW

Much of the confusion regarding the teachings of Jesus is Christians' attempt to disassociate Him from the fact that He was born a Jew and practised Judaism till His death and resurrection. But the truth remains that He was born to Jewish parents, circumcised on the eighth day like every other Jewish child, lived a Jew, practised Judaism to the core, attended Jewish feasts, taught in Jewish synagogues, wore Jewish clothes, ate Jewish food, read Jewish books—the topmost being the Scriptures—spoke Hebrew, listened to Jewish songs, died a Jew, buried a Jew and was resurrected a Jew. His friends and disciples were all Jews. He lived among Jews for several days after the resurrection before His ascension into heaven. As Paul later did, Jesus didn't go to Arabia before He started His ministry; He rather sat with the teachers of the law, listening and asking them questions. Even His embalmment had to be delayed because His disciples were observing the Sabbath.

> *The women who had come with Jesus from Galilee followed Joseph and saw the tomb and how His body was laid in it. Then they went home and prepared spices and perfumes.* ***But they rested on the Sabbath in obedience to the commandment.*** *(Luke 23:55-56)*

These were disciples who had been with the LORD Jesus all this while and if there was any change in the observance of the commands of God in the Scriptures, they would have been in a better position to learn and experience them firsthand. Jesus knew all along about His death. It was not something that happened to Him unawares. Being the wisest of all, He must have told his followers how He wanted to be buried.

Because they were observing the Sabbath, the women even missed the opportunity to embalm His body. On the first day when they went to do this, His body was nowhere to be found because He had risen from the dead. "*On the first day of the week,* ***very early in the morning, the women took the***

spices they had prepared *(to embalm Him)* ***and went to the tomb.*** *2 They found the stone rolled away from the tomb, 3* ***but when they entered, they did not find the body of the LORD Jesus"*** *(Luke 24:1-3).*

Because He was killed by Jews, most Christians try to separate Jesus from His root. But the truth is that majority of the Jews loved Him and even wanted to make Him their King. Jesus didn't shy away from the fact that He was a Jew. Talking to the Samaritan woman, He said, *"You Samaritans worship what you do not know;* ***we worship what we do know, for salvation is from the Jews"*** *(John 4:22).* Jesus was not a Ghanaian, neither was He from the U.S., Britain or Russia. He was, and will forever remain, a full-blooded Jew for all eternity.

THE REAL KILLERS OF CHRIST JESUS

This should take us to the actual killers of Christ and the reasons behind His death. It will interest you to know that Christ was killed solely for political reasons. The Jews were being colonised by the Romans in those days. The citizens of the land were thinking of making Him their king because of the miracles He was performing, which the leaders thought was going to provoke the Romans to wage war against them. Politically speaking, they thought their national interest was at stake so the Sanhedrin decided on killing Him to secure their positions. Jesus was so popular that there was a time they wanted to make Him King by force that He had to withdraw to a mountain by Himself *(John 6:15).*

> *Therefore, many of the Jews who had come to visit Mary, and had seen what Jesus did, put their faith in Him. 46 But some of them went to the Pharisees and told them what Jesus had done. 47* ***Then the chief priests and the Pharisees called a meeting of the Sanhedrin.*** *"What are we accomplishing?" they asked. "Here is this man performing many miraculous signs. 48* ***If we let Him go on like this, everyone will believe in Him, and then the Romans will come and take away both our place and our nation.****" 49 Then one of them, named Caiaphas, who was high priest that year, spoke up, "You know nothing at all! 50* ***You do not realise that it is better for you that one man die for the people than the whole nation perish . . .*** *53* ***So from that day on they plotted to take His life."*** *(John 11:45-50, 53)*

Jesus knew these men from inside out. He once told them: *"Woe to you Pharisees, because you love the most important seats in the synagogues and greetings in the market-places" (Luke 11:43).* They had turned the things of God into sheer politics, and were playing purely by the rules of the game. Once they were in power, they sought to use their positions as the religious leaders to serve the Romans for their selfish gains. They had sold their souls to the devil and were just using religion to cover their diabolical intents. This practice is even worse today than it used to be in the days of these Pharisees. They knew exactly who Jesus was, in relation to the call on His life, but could not approve of Him at the expense of their servitude to the Roman government.

Nichodemus spoke for the whole council when he said to Jesus that *"Rabbi,* ***we know you are a teacher who has come from God. For no-one could perform the miraculous signs you are doing if God were not with Him****" (John 3:2).* They knew and believed in His message but could not accept Him for fear of losing their positions. John records that: ***"Many even among the leaders believed in Him. But because of the Pharisees they would not confess their faith for fear they would be put out of the synagogue;*** *43 for they loved praise from men more than praise from God" (John 12:42-43).*

At His trial, Pilate and the rest of the judges said they found nothing wrong in Jesus that warranted the death penalty but the Sanhedrin insisted He be killed. That is politics for you. They just wanted the man out of the scene. Nothing more, nothing less! "***Though they found no proper ground for a death sentence, they asked Pilate to have Him executed****" (Acts 13:28).* The idea that Christ was killed by the Jews is simply erroneous and out of place. There was an agenda to have Him killed by the leaders at the time so as to prevent the Romans from taking their place. *"If we let Him go on like this, everyone will believe in Him,* ***and then the Romans will come and take away both our place and our nation*** . . . ***You do not realise that it is better for you that one man dies for the people than the whole nation perish.***"

Jesus was a full-blooded Jew who lived and died among Jews, and was raised back to life a Jew. After His resurrection from the dead, He lived among the Jews for some time before ascending to heaven. Of the twelve disciples that followed Him, there was not even a single Gentile among them. Remember that He was sent to His own but His own did not receive Him.

A short history into the lives of the Israelites will help us understand the Bible and how we the Gentiles fit in without trying to dissociate ourselves from the Jews. Contrary to what you believe, a Christian should be proud to be associated with the Jews. If not for anything, we should always remember that *"they have been entrusted with the very words of God" (Rom. 3:1-2).*

> ***If some of the branches have been broken off, and you, though a wild olive shoot, have been grafted in among the others and now share in the nourishing sap from the olive root,*** *18* ***do not boast over those branches. If you do, consider this: You do not support the root, but the root supports you.*** *19 You will say then, "Branches were broken off so that I could be grafted in." 20 Granted. But they were broken off because of unbelief, and you stand by faith.* ***Do not be arrogant, but be afraid.*** *21* ***For if God did not spare the natural branches, He will not spare you either.*** *(Rom. 11:17-21)*

Most Jewish communities have been wiped out especially in Europe and other parts of the world just because people have branded the Jews as evil for killing Christ Jesus. This has resulted in the rise in anti-Semitism all over the world till date among even Christians. The Jews, out of defending themselves and their rights to exist, are always misconstrued as being the aggressors in the Middle East especially. But the true Jew who is not blinded by either politics or religion is the most loving human being you can ever come across. Just study the Old Testament Scriptures and you will understand what I'm saying. It's your responsibility as a Christian to be good to the Jew because he is your brother. Jesus was a Jew who taught Jews to take the Gospel of the Kingdom of God to the rest of the Gentile nations.

In the introduction of the Complete Jewish Bible, under the sub-heading, "The New Testament is a Jewish Book," Mr. David H. Stern wrote:

> *"For the central figure of the New Testament, Yeshua the Messiah, was a Jew who was born into a Jewish family in Bethlehem, grew up among Jews in Nazareth, ministered to Jews in the Galilee, and died and rose from the grave in the Jewish capital, Jerusalem—all in the land of Israel, the land God gave the Jewish people. Moreover, Yeshua is still a Jew, since He is still alive; and nowhere does Scripture say or suggest that He has stopped being Jewish. His twelve closest followers were Jews. For years all His disciples were Jews, eventually numbering 'tens of thousands' in Jerusalem alone. The New Testament was written entirely by Jews (Luke being, in all likelihood, a proselyte to Judaism); and its message is directed 'to the Jew especially, but equally to the Gentile.'* ***It was Jews who brought the Gospel to non-Jews, not the other way round. Paul, the chief emissary to the Gentiles, was a lifelong observant Jew, as is abundantly clear from evidence in the book of Acts. Indeed the main issue in the early Messianic Community—that is, the 'Church'—was not whether a Jew could believe in Yeshua,***

> ***but whether a Gentile could become a Christian without converting to Judaism!*** *The Messiah's vicarious atonement is rooted in the Jewish sacrificial system. The Lord's Supper is rooted in the Jewish Passover. Immersion (baptism) is a Jewish practice. The New Covenant itself was promised by the Jewish prophet Jeremiah. The very concept of a Messiah is exclusively Jewish, and that Jewish Messiah taught that 'salvation is from the Jews."*

I will implore you at this juncture to reread the four Gospels of Matthew, Mark, Luke and John and end it with the book of Acts. Remember this is a book about understanding the Bible.

> *"Born in the East and clothed in Oriental form and imagery, the Bible walks the ways of all the world with familiar feet and enters land after land to find its own everywhere. It has learned to speak in hundreds of languages to the heart of man. Children listen to its stories with wonder and delight, and wise men ponder them as parables of life. The wicked and the proud tremble at its warnings, but to the wounded and penitent it has a mother's voice. It has woven itself into our dearest dreams; so that Love, Friendship, Sympathy, Devotion, Memory, Hope, put on the beautiful garments of its treasured speech. No man is poor or desolate who has this treasure for his own."—Henry Van Dyke*

CHAPTER TWENTY-THREE

A SHORT HISTORY OF MAN

Paul summarises the beginning for us when he said: *"The God who made the world and everything in it is the LORD of heaven and earth and does not live in temples built by hands. 25 And He is not served by human hands, as if He needed anything, because He Himself gives all men life and breath and everything else. 26* ***From one man He made every nation of men, that they should inhabit the whole earth; and He determined the times set for them and the exact places where they should live****. 27 God did this so that men would seek Him and perhaps reach out for Him and find Him, though He is not far from each one of us" (Acts 17:24-27).*

Before Adam was created *"the earth was formless and empty, darkness was over the surface of the deep, and the Spirit of God was hovering over the waters" (Gen. 1:2)*. Out of that darkness and emptiness, God created the light, *"an expanse between the waters to separate water from water,"* the land and seed-bearing plants down to the creation of man. Before the turn of the creation of Adam, God had already established a system of doing things that was to apply for all generations.

> *And God said, "****Let the land produce living creatures according to their kinds:*** *livestock, creatures that move along the ground, and wild animals,* ***each according to its kind." And it was so.*** *25* ***God made the wild animals according to their kinds, the livestock according to their kinds, and all the creatures that move along the ground according to their kinds****. And God saw that it was good. (Gen. 1:24-25)*

GOD'S PURPOSE FOR CREATING MAN

It was after these verses were given that God went further to say that, *"Let us make man in our image, in our likeness,* ***and let them rule over the***

fish of the sea and the birds of the air, over the livestock, over all the earth, and over all the creatures that move along the ground" *(Gen. 1:26).* It is very important that you understand the context in which this is being discussed. God had already designed that the land should produce livestock, creatures that move along the ground and wild animals, each according to their kind.

Secondly, since there was going to be the reproduction of these living creatures, according to their kind, they would have to be ruled by the force or the power that created them after they had multiplied greatly on the earth. *"So God created man in His own image, in the image of God He created him; male and female He created them" (Gen. 1:27).* Now, the purpose for which man was created was to ***"let them rule over*** *the fish of the sea and the birds of the air,* ***over the livestock, over all the earth,*** *and* ***over all the creatures that move along the ground"*** *(Gen. 1:26).* This is very important to note.

> *"When the Bible declares that we are made in the 'image and likeness' of the Creator, it is affirming that creativity is at our core just as it lies at the core of the Creator of all things."—Matthew Fox*

Since the land was to reproduce living creatures according to their kinds, then their *"ruler"* also had to reproduce according to his kind in order to be able to rule not just over the fish of the sea, the birds of the air and all the creatures that move along the ground which Adam and Eve occupied at that time but over all the earth, as that was their mandated territory.

To fill that gap, *"God blessed them and said to them,* ***"Be fruitful and increase in number; fill the earth and subdue it****. Rule over the fish of the sea and the birds of the air and over every living creature that moves on the ground" (Gen. 1:28).* So we see that the man's position was simply a delegated one to represent God in manning the affairs of this earth. In a sense, God was creating a mini-heaven on earth to be supervised by man on His behalf. Because of that, man was created in the exact image and likeness of God to be able to effectively carry out his duties and responsibilities on this earth.

Adam was so created in the image and likeness of God that when Luke was listing the genealogy of Christ Jesus, he referred to Adam as *"the son of God."* He wrote: *"Now Jesus Himself was about thirty years old when He began His ministry. He was the Son, so it was thought, of Joseph, the son of Heli . . . 38 the son of Enosh, the son of Seth,* ***the son of Adam, the son of God"*** *(Luke 3:23-38).*

As the first son of God on earth, created in His image and likeness, Adam was to directly take his orders from his Father, as pertaining to his daily assignments on earth, on how to take charge of it. But along the line, he failed and allowed himself to be influenced by another power that was distinct and separated from that of God his Father. He then lost his position as the ruler and became subjected to the forces of the day. Because of that he was placed under a curse by His Father as punishment for what he had done.

> *"Cursed is the ground because of you; through painful toil you will eat of it all the days of your life. 18 It will produce thorns and thistles for you, and you will eat the plants of the field. 19 By the sweat of your brow you will eat your food until you return to the ground, since from it you were taken; for dust you are and to dust you will return." (Gen. 3:17-19)*

"So the LORD God banished him from the Garden of Eden to work the ground from which he had been taken" (Gen. 3:23). The loss of Adam's position or dominion to rule over the earth did not prevent the living creatures created earlier from reproducing after their kind; they rather kept multiplying. Because the leader, who was supposed to have seen to the controlling, directing, communicating, organising and carrying out all that is expected of a good leader, was banished from his post, everything on the face of the earth became chaotic. The man lost his senses, and the rest of the living creatures followed suit.

God planted a mustard seed in Adam and Eve in the beginning with the idea that they would grow to multiply and cover the whole earth. With the exception of his fellow human, God gave man the ability to take charge over the affairs of this earth and rule on His behalf.

The command to be fruitful and increase in number has been wrongly limited to mean giving birth to babies till the whole earth is filled with them. But prior to the creation of man, the animals had been created and were not commanded to be fruitful and increase in number yet they reproduced, according to their kind. The command simply had to do with representing God on earth to manage and rule on His behalf. Note that man was not given the power to rule over his fellow human being.

> *When I consider your heavens, the work of your fingers, the moon and the stars, which you have set in place, 4* ***what is man that you are mindful of him, the son of man that you care for him?*** *5 You made him a little lower than the heavenly beings and crowned him with glory and honour. 6* ***You made him ruler over the works of your hands; you put everything under his feet:*** *7 all flocks and herds, and the beasts of the field, 8 the birds of the air, and the fish of the sea, all that swim the paths of the seas. (Psalm 8:3-8)*

John wrote that *"Dear friends, **now we are children of God**, and what we will be has not yet been made known. But we know that when He appears, we shall be like Him, for we shall see Him as He is. 3 Everyone who has this hope in him purifies himself, just as He is pure" (1 John 3:2-3).* Adam was created in the image and likeness of God. He created the earth to endure for all eternity, and created humans to live that long to ***"Be fruitful and increase in number; fill the earth and subdue it. Rule over the fish of the sea and the birds of the air and over every living creature that moves on the ground."***

Isaiah wrote: *"For this is what the LORD says—He who created the heavens, He is God; He who fashioned and made the earth, He founded it; **He did not create it to be empty, but formed it to be inhabited**—He says: 'I am the LORD, and there is no other'" (Isaiah 45:18). David also wrote that **"The highest heavens belong to the LORD, but the earth He has given to man"** (Psalm 115:16).* Solomon wrote that *"Generations come and generations go, **but the earth remains forever**" (Eccl. 1:4).* He also wrote that *"I know that everything God does will endure forever; nothing can be added to it and nothing taken from it. God does it so that men will revere Him" (Eccl. 3:14).*

ADAM BROKE COVENANT WITH GOD

"Like Adam, they have broken the covenant—they were unfaithful to me" (Hosea 6:7). Adam was in a covenant with God to represent Him in running the affairs of life on His behalf. This was God's plan for creating man and the earth. But unfortunately, things didn't turn out the exact way God designed them, as man could not live up to God's expectations of him. Man became utterly corrupt and wicked on the earth he was supposed to rule over. ***"But the plans of the LORD stand firm forever, the purposes of His heart through all generations"*** *(Psalm 33:11).* ***"I will not violate my covenant or alter what my lips have uttered"*** *(Psalm 89:34).* God had no choice than to see to it that whatever He had planned was accomplished to the letter. He will cease to be who He is if He cannot do this. So He thought of a plan "B." The loss of man's authority and power grew to the point where:

> *The LORD saw how great man's wickedness on the earth had become, and **that every inclination of the thoughts of his heart was only evil all the time**. 6 **The LORD was grieved that He had made man on the earth**, and His heart was filled with pain. 7 So the LORD said, "I will wipe mankind, whom I have created, from the face of the earth—men and animals, and creatures that*

> *move along the ground, and birds of the air—for I am grieved that I have made them." (Gen. 6:5-7)*

Notice that God said He was going to wipe both men and animals from the face of the earth in addition to all the creatures that move along the ground, even though the creatures had done nothing wrong—so to speak. The reason is simply that it was man's sole responsibility to run the affairs of this earth. Without a man at the helm of affairs, there can only be confusion. The power to effect change on earth has been given to man. *"The highest heavens belong to the LORD, **but the earth He has given to man**" (Psalm 115:16)*. If there are things going wrong on earth, a man should arise and search through the Constitution of the Father to carefully study what is supposed to be done and head straight into action by solving it.

Study the Bible from the very first page of Genesis down to the last page of Revelations, and you will realise that God only moves into action when there is a man available to be used. We fail to see the potential God has implanted in us and have been blinded to the original purpose for which we were created in the first place. God asked Moses once, ***"Why are you crying out to me? Tell the Israelites to move on"*** *(Exod. 14:15)*. No matter how great or small you are, just stick to the words of the Father and, like Gideon, He will turn you into a mighty warrior to change things on earth.

NOAH FAVOURED FOR BEING RIGHTEOUS

So until a man or a *"ruler"* was found, the earth had to be wiped off of all its content to prevent the chaotic scene that would result. *"But Noah found favour in the eyes of the LORD" (Gen. 6:8)*. There are some spiritual bulldozers around today who claim they can pray to receive favours from space to be given to other men on earth. I don't know how they do that; so I'll reserve my comment. But I do know how Noah received his favour from God and, as a result of that, was saved from being wiped off from the face of the earth along with the rest of the disobedient.

> *This is the account of Noah: **Noah was a righteous man, blameless among the people of his time**, and he walked with God (Gen. 6:9).*

Please note that Noah didn't have to travel to another continent to live his righteous and blameless life. He actually lived and walked with God *"among the people of his time"* who had become evil so much so that God was grieved He had even made man. That was all that God needed. He didn't need a church to start all over again if the roots had been corrupted. Remember He created Adam as a single individual and got Eve out of him down to us. It's therefore not necessarily about the numbers.

> *"Throughout the Bible, a mysterious energy of God pulsates, which, when planted within people, makes for formidable accomplishment."—Gordon MacDonald*

According to His laid-down principles, which could not be revoked even by Himself, God could not destroy Noah with the rest of the people once he was righteous and blameless. This is why He could not destroy Lot too in Sodom. It is written that: "*The soul who sins is the one who will die. The son will not share the guilt of the father, nor will the father share the guilt of the son.* ***The righteousness of the righteous man will be credited to him, and the wickedness of the wicked man will be charged against him*** *" (Ezek. 18:20).* ***For the wages of sin is death****, but the gift of God is eternal life in Christ Jesus our LORD. (Rom. 6:23)*

GOD'S COVENANT WITH NOAH

In executing this, God caused the land to be flooded with water for several months after commanding Noah and his descendants to build an ark to shelter them. After the land was dried up, God entered into a covenant with him. Note carefully the words of this covenant and compare them with what was said to Adam and Eve when they were created. God said:

> *"****Be fruitful and increase in number and fill the earth****. 2 The fear and dread of you will fall upon all the beasts of the earth and all the birds of the air, upon every creature that moves along the ground, and upon all the fish of the sea;* ***they are given into your hands*** *" (Gen. 9:1-2)*

This covenant is very similar to what was made with Adam and Eve before the fall. Through righteousness, God saw in Noah what He had lost in Adam. He then decided to use Noah to take man to his original purpose for being created. He renewed the same covenant He made with Adam with Noah "*to be fruitful, increase in number and fill the earth.*" But Noah's descendants after him could not continue in their father's footsteps; they went into sin, trying to make a name for themselves by building a tower to reach heaven. God had to intervene by confusing their language, making it impossible for them to communicate with each other. God had to find someone else to continue with the agenda of having a man created in His image and likeness to serve as His representative to rule on His behalf again.

This was necessary because God was not going to change His mind from what He had previously planned before creating man as a result of man's failure. That would have equally made Him a failure. Elbert Hubbard once said, *"There is no failure except in no longer trying."* Harry Wilson also once said, *"Men don't fail, they give up trying."* We also know that *God is not man, that He should lie,* ***nor a son of man, that He should change His mind. Does He speak and then not act? Does He promise and not fulfil*** *(Num. 23:19)?*

To remedy the situation of continuing with His plans, He had to look for someone like Noah to continue with His plan. He found that in Abram (later called Abraham).

ABRAHAM CHOSEN TO CONTINUE WITH THE COVENANT

> *The LORD had said to Abram, "Leave your country, your people and your father's household and go to the land I will show you. 2* ***I will make you into a great nation and I will bless you; I will make your name great, and you will be a blessing****. 3 I will bless those who bless you, and whoever curses you I will curse; and all people on earth will be blessed through you." (Gen.12:1-3)*

For whatever reason best known to Him, God had already planned in advance how He was going to make this great nation out of Abraham. The plan was to take his descendants to a foreign nation to have them serve as slaves in a particular land for a specific period of time before later giving them the power to plunder that nation of its possessions for His people.

> *As the sun was setting, Abram fell into a deep sleep, and a thick and dreadful darkness came over him. 13 Then the LORD said to him,* ***"Know for certain that your descendants will be strangers in a country not their own, and they will be enslaved and ill-treated four hundred years.*** *14 But I will punish the nation they serve as slaves, and afterwards they will come out with great possessions . . . 16* ***In the fourth generation your descendants will come back here,*** *for the sin of the Amorites has not yet reached its full measure." (Gen. 15:12-16)*

To further strengthen this covenant with Abraham, God later confirmed it with some strong words, but this time, not without a condition. God does not show favouritism. Adam died and forfeited his destiny for sinning against God though he was His son. God wiped the descendants of Noah from the face of the earth for turning their backs to Him. Even Satan (a.k.a. Lucifer), who was in heaven but chose to rebel against his Creator, paid the price of being banished from the presence of God. Our Creator does not and cannot tolerate sin and sinners in His presence. He had to make that point clear to Abraham from the very beginning of the covenant they were entering since He does not give free lunch to people. This was communicated to Abraham in these words:

> *When Abram was ninety-nine years old, the LORD appeared to him and said, "I am God Almighty;* ***walk before me and be blameless.*** *2 I will confirm my covenant between me and you, and will greatly increase your numbers." 3 Abram fell face down, and God said to him, "As for me, this is my covenant with you:* ***You will be the father of many nations.*** *5 No longer will you be called Abram; your name will be Abraham,* ***for I have made you a father of many nations.*** *6* ***I will make you very fruitful; I will make nations of you and kings will come from you****. 7 I will establish my covenant as an everlasting covenant between me and you and your descendants after you for the generations to come, to be your God and the God of your descendants after you. 8* ***The whole land of Canaan, where you are now an alien, I will give as an everlasting possession to you and your descendants after you; and I will be their God."*** *(Gen. 17:1-8)*

Abraham was destined to become the father of *many nations* starting from being a great nation in *Genesis 12:1-3,* as we read earlier. The firstborn "son" of those nations is the nation of Israel. It is written: "*Then say to Pharaoh, 'This is what the LORD says:* ***Israel is my firstborn son****, 23 and I told you,* ***'Let my son go, so that he may worship me'"*** *(Exod. 4:22-23).* The firstborn son was later to have many nations as brothers and sisters serving the same God and living on the same earth with the same precepts, laws, principles, decrees, statutes and commandments.

Just as God had planned how He was going to make a great nation out of Abraham by sending his descendants to a foreign land to serve as slaves before growing to become a great nation later, He had also established the idea of later grafting the Gentiles into the Jewish tree long before making this covenant with Abraham. This is because, originally, God only created man in His own image and likeness to be fruitful and rule over in His kingdom. His intent from the beginning was not to create nations separated from each other and speaking different languages and not able to understand each other. This was later revealed to Paul in the New Testament when he wrote:

> *In reading this, then, you will be able to understand my insight into the mystery of Christ, 5 which was not made known to men in other generations as it has now been revealed by the Spirit of God's holy apostles and prophets. 6* ***This mystery is that through the gospel the Gentiles are heirs together with Israel, members together of one body, and sharers together in the promise in Christ Jesus.*** *(Eph. 3:4-6)*

Now, this promise of making Abraham the father of many nations had to do with something in the future, which Abraham himself would not be around to witness as he was a mortal being compared to God who is immortal. God thought it wise to institute a sign which was to serve as a reminder to his descendants that He was actually going to do what He had promised Abraham their forefather. The sign of circumcising every male child in the society was chosen.

CIRCUMCISION TO SERVE AS SIGN OF THE COVENANT

> *Then God said to Abraham, "As for you, you must keep my covenant, you and your descendants after you for the generations to come. 10 This is my covenant with you and your descendants after you, the covenant you are to keep: Every male among you shall be circumcised. 11* ***You are to undergo circumcision, and it will be the sign of the covenant between me and you.*** *12 For the generations to come every male among you who is eight days old must be circumcised, including those born in your household or bought with money from a foreigner—those who are not your offspring. 13 Whether born in your household or bought with your money, they must be circumcised.* ***My covenant in your flesh is to be an everlasting covenant.*** *14 Any uncircumcised male, who has not been circumcised in the flesh, will be cut off from his people; he has broken my covenant." (Gen. 17:9-14)*

It is important that you take note of the fact that the actual covenant was that Abraham and his descendants were to walk before Him *"blameless,"* and God, on His part, was to make him grow to become a great nation on a piece of real estate for all generations. The covenant of circumcising the male whether native-born or alien was only to serve as *"the sign"* of the actual covenant. As an example of the actual covenant, when God called the Israelites out of Egypt, He said through Moses that:

> *Be sure to keep the commands of the LORD your God and the stipulations and decrees He has given you. 18* ***Do what is right and good in the LORD'S sight, so that it may go well with you and you may go in and take over the good land that the LORD promised on oath to your forefathers.*** *(Deut. 6:17-18)*

As you begin to read the Bible, especially the books of *1 Kings and 2 Kings* for yourself, you will realise from the history of God's people that they prospered immensely whenever they obeyed the voice of God but suffered from various plagues and hardships when they lived to please themselves. It will interest you to know from here the purpose for which the LORD had so much love for the Israelites, and continues to do so today.

> *"How great you are, O Sovereign LORD! There is no-one like you, and there is no God but you, as we have heard with our own ears. 23* ***And who is like your people Israel—the one nation on earth that God went out to redeem as a people for Himself, and to make a name for Himself,*** *and to perform great and awesome wonders by driving out nations and their gods from before your people, whom you redeemed from Egypt?* ***You have established your people Israel as your very own forever, and you, O LORD, have become their God."*** *(2 Samuel 7:22-24)*

GOD'S PURPOSE FOR CHOOSING ABRAHAM

Before going any further, we need to know God's purpose for which He called Abraham and chose to make him the father of many nations. He always gives His own reasons for doing everything: "*Then the LORD said, 'Shall I hide from Abraham what I am about to do? 18* ***Abraham will surely become a great and powerful nation,*** *and all nations on earth will be blessed through him. 19* ***For I have chosen him,*** *[why?]* ***so that he will direct his children and his household after him to keep the way of the LORD by doing what is right and just, so that the LORD will bring about for Abraham what He has promised him'"*** *(Gen. 18:17-19).*

"This great book, the Bible, this most precious volume is the heart of God made legible; it is the gold of God's love, beaten out into gold leaf, so that therewith our thoughts might be plated, and we also might have golden, good, and holy thoughts concerning Him"—John Bunyan. (1628-1688)

Abraham's mandate upon his life was to direct or teach his children after him to always choose to follow the ways of God by doing what is just and right at all times. He was mandated to do this because back then, the requirements of God, His commands, His decrees and laws were revealed to him although we have not been told they were specifically written on any tablets of stones like Moses had. It is the covenant God entered with Isaac, Abraham's son, that reveals this to us.

THE COVENANT CONTINUED IN ISAAC

God said to Isaac "*Stay in this land for a while, and I will be with you and will bless you. For to you and your descendants I will give all these lands* ***and will confirm the oath I swore to your father Abraham.*** *4 I will make your descendants as numerous as the stars in the sky and will give them all these lands,* ***and through your offspring all nations on earth will be blessed,*** *[why?]* ***because Abraham obeyed me and kept my requirements, my commands, my decrees and my laws.****" (Gen. 26:3-5)*

We should know by now the oath that was sworn to Abraham. The LORD Himself said that He would confirm the oath He swore to Abraham through His son because he fulfilled his part of the deal in obeying His requirements, commands, decrees and laws. Hidden in the above verses is the secret for when the firstborn son was to remain until the arrival of his brother nations. *"Through your offspring, all nations on earth will be blessed."* There was a particular offspring who was going to usher in the arrival of the other brother nations. We'll get to know later that that offspring is Jesus Christ.

THE SAME COVENANT CONTINUED IN JACOB

After the death of Isaac, God delivered the same message to his son Jacob in a dream:

> *He had a dream in which he saw a stairway resting on the earth, with its top reaching to heaven, and the angels of God were ascending and descending on it. 13 There above it stood the LORD, and He said: I am the LORD, the God of your father Abraham and the God of Isaac. I will give you and your descendants the land on which you are lying. 14 Your descendants will be like the dust of the earth, and you will spread out to the west and to the east, to the north and to the south.* ***All people on earth will be blessed through you and your offspring.*** *15 I am with you and will watch over you wherever you go, and I will bring you back to this land.* ***I will not leave you until I have done what I have promised you.****" (Gen. 28:12-15)*

After the confirmation of this oath to Jacob, the stage was set for God to give birth to the *"firstborn son"* of His nations. The principle behind the covenants with Adam, Noah, Abraham, Isaac and Jacob was for them to first grasp the requirements, commands, decrees and laws of God and later teach them to their children's children till the whole earth is covered in the knowledge of God. The Father had previously arranged that the children of Jacob became slaves in Egypt and have them serve for a period of not less than four centuries. When they grew in size to become a nation, He called a man by name Moses to lead them to the land He had promised Abraham, Isaac and Jacob to give birth to *"the firstborn son."*

MOSES, GOD'S REPRESENTATIVE TO THE "FIRSTBORN SON"

Moses led the people of Israel from Egypt through the desert to the crossing of the red sea. He became a representative between God and the nation of Israel and was responsible for settling disputes among the people all by himself. This became tiring and time consuming as he could do this for a whole day without rest. It was until Jethro, his father-in-law, came to witness this one day, and advised him on what to do that this was rectified. "*The LORD works righteousness and justice for all the oppressed. 7* ***He made known His ways to Moses, His deeds to the people of Israel"*** *(Psalm 103:6-7).*

> *The next day Moses took his seat to serve as judge for the people, and they stood round him from morning till evening. 14 When his father-in-law saw all that Moses was doing for the people, he said, "What is this you are doing for the people?* ***Why do you alone sit as judge while all these people stand round you from morning till evening?***

> *15 Moses answered him, "Because the people come to me to seek God's will. 16 Whenever they have a dispute, it is brought to me,* ***and I decide between the parties and inform them of God's decrees and laws."***
>
> *17 Moses' father-in-law replied, "What you are doing is not good. 18 You and these people who come to you will only wear yourselves out. The work is too heavy for you; you cannot handle it alone. 19 Listen now to me and I will give you some advice, and may God be with you.* ***You must be the people's representative before God and bring their disputes to Him*** *(God). 20* ***Teach them the decrees and laws, and show them the way to live, and the duties they are to perform.*** *21 But select capable men from all the people—men who fear God, trustworthy men who hate dishonest gain—and appoint them as officials over thousands, hundreds, fifties and tens. 22 Have them serve as judges for the people at all times, but have them bring every difficult case to you; the simple cases they can decide themselves. That will make your load lighter, because they will share it with you. 23 If you do this and God so commands, you will be able to stand the strain, and all these people will go home satisfied."*
>
> *24* ***Moses listened to his father-in-law and did everything he said.*** *25* ***He chose capable men from all Israel and made them leaders of the people, officials over thousands, hundreds, fifties and tens.*** *26 They served as judges for the people at all times. The difficult cases they brought to Moses, but the simple ones they decided themselves. (Exod. 18:13-26)*

Prior to the giving of the law and decrees to the people of Israel, Moses knew them, and as to how he knew them is a different topic I cannot touch on in this book. Until the arrival of Jethro, Moses was single-handedly settling disputes among the people and at the same time teaching them *the decrees and laws of God*. As the representative between God and the people, God delivered a message to be given to the people on one occasion:

> *Then Moses went up to God, and the LORD called to him from the mountain and said, "This is what you are to say to the house of Jacob and what you are to tell the people of Israel: 4 'You yourselves have seen what I did to Egypt, and how I carried you on eagle's wings and brought you to myself. 5* ***Now if you obey me fully and keep my covenant, then out of all nations you will be my treasured possession. Although the whole earth is mine,*** *6* ***you will be for me a kingdom of priests and a holy nation.'*** *These are the words you are to speak to the Israelites." (Exod. 19:3-6)*

Please bear in mind that it is a group of human beings that make up a nation and not just the land. So for a nation to be referred to as holy, the people living in it have to be holy themselves. Birds of a feather flock together. God Himself is holy and has commanded His children to be holy just as He is. This process was the same used by God in dealing with the Gentile believers as we read in one of Peter's letters: *"As obedient children, do not conform to the evil desires you had when you lived in ignorance. 15* ***But just as He who called you is holy, so be holy in all you do;*** *16* ***for it is written: 'Be holy, because I am holy'"*** *(1 Pet. 1:14-16).* Man has to be in the likeness of his Creator to live in His nation.

You shouldn't forget that when God covenanted with Abraham, He asked him to walk before Him blameless, which he did. There is no free lunch anywhere even with God. There is truly nothing like something for nothing as Napoleon Hill used to say. God is light and there is no darkness in Him. He does not show favouritism. When Lucifer rebelled against His rule in heaven, He banished him from there. When Adam and Eve sinned, He drove them out of Eden and when their descendants made Him regret creating them, He wiped them off the face of the earth but left Noah and his immediate family.

The same way, the members comprising this firstborn nation were not just going to be allowed to have everything on a silver platter just because they were the descendants of Abraham. No! Just like their great grand papa, they were also expected to walk before Him *"blameless"* and to see to it that they fully obeyed His voice at all times to qualify for citizenship of this holy nation. Once they had agreed to walk before the Lord, they were to see themselves as aliens on earth and live their lives with a different mindset, although they were still living among the pagan nations like Noah did. They were to leave behind their former ways.

The same thing was communicated to the Gentiles who had come to know God when Peter wrote that: *"Once you were not a people,* ***but now you are the people of God****; once you had not received mercy, but now you have received mercy. 11 Dear friends,* ***I urge you, as aliens and strangers in the world, to abstain from sinful desires, which war against your soul****. 12* ***Live such good lives among the pagans*** *that, though they accuse you of doing wrong, they may see your good deeds and glorify God on the day He visits you" (1 Pet. 2:10-12).*

Accepting the message to follow God is a way of life. It is not only a season of waiting to travel in some spaceship to a different continent to live the good life there in the future. You live that good life right here on earth in the midst of pagans and the rest of mankind like Lot did in Sodom but with a renewed mindset from what you previously had. Peter wrote about Lot that he was *"**a righteous man, who was distressed by the filthy lives of lawless men** 8 (for that righteous man, living among them day after day, was tormented in his righteous soul by the lawless deeds he saw and heard)" (2 Pet. 2:7-8).* You can still be righteous among evildoers on earth. It's a choice you make.

You must see yourself as an alien with a different passport in this world when you turn to the LORD. You no longer think or do things according to the pattern of this world again. You offer your body as a living sacrifice, holy and pleasing to God as that becomes your spiritual act of worship. You do not conform any longer to the pattern of this world. But rather, you get transformed by the renewing of your mind through the word you received to turn you back to God *(Rom. 12:1-2).* Moses communicated this to the people and they gave him their response to be delivered back to God.

> *So Moses went back and summoned the elders of the people and set before them all the words the LORD had commanded him to speak. 8 The people all responded together, "**We will do everything the LORD has said.**" So Moses brought their answer back to the LORD. (Exod. 19:7-8)*

HOW MOSES BECAME THE PERMANENT SPOKESPERSON FOR GOD

Before the nation of Israel was born, God spoke to Adam, Noah, Abraham, Isaac and Jacob. But prior to the birth of His first nation, Moses served as the communication link between Him and His people. God decided to speak to Moses in the presence of the people so that they would learn to put their trust in the words of Moses as the exact Words of the LORD.

> *The LORD said to Moses, "I am going to come to you in a dense cloud, **so that the people will hear me speaking with you and will always put their trust in you.**" Then Moses told the LORD what the people had said. (Exod. 19:9)*

The reason God wanted them to put their trust in Moses was the fact that when a prophet of the LORD is among the people, He revealed Himself to him in visions, and speaks to him in dreams. *"**But this is not true of my servant Moses; he is faithful in all my house.** 8 **With him I speak face to face, clearly and not in riddles;** he sees the form of God" (Num. 12:7-8).* All the teachings from Moses do not require any interpretations from anyone again because they were not presented in riddles or parables, unlike the other prophets who followed after him. Therefore, you can only seek to understand and teach what he preached because they were established to last forever. That's the difference.

Something remarkable happened after the people heard the voice of the LORD. They became very frightened when they heard Him speak for the first time and decided to choose their own mode of communicating with Him. Being in the presence of the Almighty and hearing Him speak was beyond their comprehension. They thought they would die if that continued.

> *When the people saw the thunder and lightning and heard the trumpet and saw the mountain in smoke,* ***they trembled with fear. They stayed at a distance and said to Moses, "Speak to us yourself and we will listen. But do not have God speak to us or we will die."*** *(Exo. 20:18-19)*

That wasn't God's way of talking to His children since the days of Adam, Noah, Abraham, Isaac, Jacob and Joseph. So Moses had to explain why God chose to speak to them in that frightening mode:

> *Moses said to the people,* ***"Do not be afraid, God has come to test you, so that the fear of God will be with you to keep you from sinning."*** *(Exod. 20:20)*

For this is what you asked of the LORD your God at Horeb on the day of the assembly when you said, "Let us not hear the voice of the LORD our God nor see this great fire any more, or we will die." 17 The LORD said to me: What they say is good. 18 ***I will raise up for them a prophet like you from among their brothers; I will put my words in his mouth, and he will tell them everything I command him.*** *19 If anyone does not listen to my words that the prophet speaks in my name, I myself will call him to account" (Duet. 18:16-19).*

THE PROPHET'S BOUNDARIES

God provided the answer to their request by not speaking directly to them again, from then onwards. Since Moses was a mortal being and was also going to die later like his ancestor Abraham, God decided to provide another prophet after him to be a representative between them like Moses did. That prophet, just like his predecessor must carry only the voice of God at all times and not add to or subtract from it. The people on their part were also to receive the words of the prophet as those from God Himself. But a boundary was established from the very onset for the prophet to operate within. The prophet could not just say anything at will and go scot-free:

> *"**But a prophet who presumes to speak in my name anything I have not commanded him to say, or a prophet who speaks in the name of other gods, must be put to death.**" (Deut. 18:20)*

To speak in the name of other gods is defined by God Himself here as to say or teach anything that He has not said. All principles or ideas that contradict the Word of God are ways of speaking in the name of other gods. No prophet is required to speak anything that has not been commanded by God and must under no circumstance speak in the name of other gods. This goes to those who teach the philosophies of this world and back them in a sugar-coated manner with Scriptural verses, and brand them in churches as inspired of God. This is a different topic altogether that has to be treated in details in another book.

HOW TO IDENTIFY GOD'S MESSAGE

> *You may say to yourselves, "**How can we know when a message has not been spoken by the LORD?**" (Deut. 18:21)*

Since God did not want to leave us wondering how to identify a true prophet from the fake one, He asked the very question I would have asked Him if I had the chance, and gave a straight-to-the-point answer.

> ***If what a prophet proclaims in the name of the LORD does not take place or come true, that is a message the LORD has not spoken. That prophet has spoken presumptuously**. Do not be afraid of him. (Deut. 18:22)*

There are several reasons why most of the modern-day Pharisees are doing everything in their power to discredit the Old Testament, and this verse is one of them. What do you think would happen if a "prophet" is looked at deep in the eye and told of how good a liar he is, and is actually beaten to death for speaking lies in the name of God? Most of them would disappear from the scene as the majority of their so-called prophesies don't come to pass. Take note that God did not say the failure of a prophecy was going to be as a result of someone's failure to bind the devil, not praying enough or fasting enough. It has nothing to do with any of those.

For instance, if a prophet boldly declares in the Name of God that a particular country is going to move from a third-world category to a first-world category in the next five years, and that does not happen, that is what the LORD has not spoken. In the same way, if he looks at a thirty-year old woman, tells her in the Name of God that she is going to be married the following year, and that does not happen, that too, is something the LORD has not spoken. The Law says you should not be afraid of such a "prophet." Kill him to deter others from speaking lies in the Name of God (Deut. 18:20). Paul wrote to Timothy: *Those who sin are to be rebuked publicly,* ***so that others may take warning*** *(1 Tim. 5:20).*

ONE GOD, ONE NATION, ONE CONSTITUTION

This is where it all started from. The Words of the Bible, especially those recorded in the Old Testament as well as that of the New Testament, were all dictated by the Most High God Himself *"through"* people. It is written: ***"Moses then wrote down everything the LORD had said"*** *(Exod. 24:4).* Being the first nation to be given birth to, they needed a new set of commands, rules, laws, decrees and statutes to serve as a Constitution for them. These were delivered to them *through* Moses. I am yet to see a nation that does not have a Constitution to govern itself, and has been able to develop. God has His own Constitution for His nations too written in the pages of the Bible. These were penned down by Moses but were God's own Words:

> *Then the LORD came down in a pillar of cloud . . . 6 and said, "Listen to my words: 'When a prophet of the LORD is among you. I reveal myself to him in visions, I speak to him in dreams. 7* ***But this is not true of my servant Moses; he is faithful in all my house.*** *8* ***With him I speak face to face, clearly and NOT in riddles;*** *he sees the form of GOD.'" (Num. 12:5-8)*

Though Moses was a prophet like any other prophet, his mode of communicating with God was distinct from the rest. The others, as we will get to know later, received their messages through dreams, visions and riddles. But God said, ***"This is not true with my servant Moses...*** With him I speak face to face, ***clearly and not in riddles."*** This particular Constitution was going to serve as the standard for all generations and even the nations that were going to be joined or grafted into the "firstborn son." So there was no need to deliver or present the Constitution in riddles, dreams or visions to warrant any interpretations to distort them in the future.

"The Bible, thoroughly known, is literature itself—the rarest and richest in all departments of thought and imagination which exists."—James Anthony Froude (1818-1894)

The Constitution may be written on a tablet of stone or on the hearts of men. But the underlying factor is that these words written down by Moses were meant to serve all generations and nations that were going to join Israel as one nation. There is only One True God who does not change His mind. And even if you are led by the Holy Spirit of God, this same Constitution applies. The Holy Spirit does not approve of stealing, murdering, lying, coveting, and sleeping with one's mother, quarrelling, engaging in orgies and the rest.

> *There is one body and* ***one Spirit—just as you were called to one hope when you were called****—5 one LORD, one faith, one baptism; 6* ***One God and Father of all, who is over all and through all in all.*** *(Eph. 4:4-6)*

The LORD did not call the Israelites out of Egypt because they were special than the rest of men. He had His plans in mind long before even Abraham was called. Israel was only the beginning of a bigger plan that involved the redemption of the whole earth back to Him. Israel, like every other nation, was chosen first on the basis of God's grace.

> *For you are a people holy to the LORD your God. The LORD your God has chosen you out of all the peoples on the face of the earth to be His people, His treasured possession. 7* ***The LORD did not set His affection on you and choose you because you were more numerous than other peoples****, for you were the fewest of all peoples. 8* ***But it was because the LORD loved you and kept the oath He swore to your forefathers that He brought you out with a mighty hand and redeemed you from the land of slavery, from the power of Pharaoh king of Egypt.*** *(Deut. 7:6-8)*

Again, we should remind ourselves that if it was not because of anything done by the people themselves, apart from the love God had towards them and His desire to fulfil the covenant made with Abraham, Isaac and Jacob, then Israel was the only firstborn son or nation to be followed by other nations through the offspring spoken about earlier since He does not show favouritism to one particular person or nation. The grace shown to the people of Israel would have to be as well extended to other nations for them to also have the opportunity to share in His blessings for all mankind

Now that we know how we are related to the Israelites in the sight of God, we should also understand the fact that whatever was written for them was written for us too. The Bible is simply the Book containing the dos and don'ts of life. It was the Pharisees and teachers of the Law who chose to make a religion out of it, and succeeded in making it complicated for people to understand.

Democracy is being praised today by even those in the middle-east as the best form of governance because it seems to give freedom to individuals to express themselves. But even in democracy, there are laws and decrees that have to be fully obeyed by the citizens of the land to live in peace. The one who obeys the laws in a democratic environment is righteous and therefore does not burden himself with what lawbreakers love to do.

In the same vein, the kingdom of God, which is far more superior compared to a democracy, has its own laws, decrees, commands, statutes and precepts written in the pages of the Bible. And this makes life smooth for every individual who obeys them fully. It is written: *And if we are careful to obey all this law before the LORD our God, as He has commanded us, that will be our righteousness (Deut. 6:25).*

GOD'S BLESSINGS OR CURSES ARE CONDITIONAL

> *This is what the LORD says—your Redeemer, the Holy One of Israel: "I am the LORD your God,* ***who teaches you what is best for you, who directs you in the way you should go.*** *18* ***If only you had paid attention to my commands, your peace would have been like a river, your righteousness like the waves of the sea.*** *19 Your descendants would have been like the sand, your children like its numberless grains; their name would never be cut off nor destroyed from before me." (Isaiah 48:17-19)*

There is a well-known verse in the Bible that has been elaborated by several authors in the past centuries. It reads, "*Do not be deceived: God cannot be mocked. A man reaps what he sows. 8 The one who sows to please his sinful nature, from that nature, will reap destruction; the one who sows to please the Spirit, from the Spirit, will reap eternal life" (Gal. 6:7-8).* We now know from the start that God does not change His mind. He has given mankind a set of Constitution to follow for blessings, and curses if we decide to refrain from them:

> *See, I am setting before you today* ***a blessing and a curse****—27* ***the blessing if you obey the commands of the LORD your God that I am giving you today;*** *28* ***the curse if you disobey the commands of the LORD your God and turn from the way that I command you today*** *by following other gods, which you have not known. (Deut. 11:26-28)*

James Allen explains the principles of law better in one of his works. I'll quote from him verbatim, and it is my prayer that you give careful thoughts as you read along. He wrote:

> *"Now while law punishes,* ***its primary office is to protect****. Even the laws which man makes are framed by him to protect himself from his own baser passions. The law of our country is instituted for the protection of life and property,* ***and it only comes into operation as a punishing factor when it is violated. Offenders against it probably think of it as cruel, and doubtless regard it with terror, but to them that obey, it is an abiding protector and friend, and can hold for them no terror*** *. . .*
>
> ***"Law cannot be partial****. It is an unvarying mode of action,* ***disobeying which, we are hurt; obeying, we are made happy. Neither protestation nor supplication can alter it, for if it could be altered or annulled the universe would collapse, and chaos would prevail."***

Most Christians today have been made to believe that the word, "law", should not even come into play in their worship of God. But how can you be in a team of human beings if there are no laws governing affairs? We are serving the God of law and order. The kingdom of God is not some form of democracy where anything that seems right in each man's eyes goes. This kingdom does not operate by using lawyers to twist and turn the Constitution in their favour each time to suit their lifestyles. Laws are there to protect us. God made us to function well under His laws in the Bible. Paul wrote:

> *Everyone must submit himself to the governing authorities, for there is no authority except that which God has established. The authorities that exist have been established by God. 2 Consequently, he who rebels against the authority is rebelling against what God has instituted, and those who do so will bring judgment on themselves. 3* ***For rulers*** *(including God)* ***hold no terror for those who do right, but for those who do wrong. Do you want to be free from fear of the one in authority*** *(God included)****? Then do what***

> ***is right and he will commend you.*** *4 For he is God's servant to do you good.* ***But if you do wrong, be afraid, for he does not bear the sword for nothing. He is God's servant, an agent of wrath to bring punishment on the wrongdoer.*** *5 Therefore, it is necessary to submit to the authorities, not only because of possible punishment but also because of conscience. (Rom. 13:1-5)*

Carefully studying the Words of the Scriptures and comparing them to what is actually happening these days, one would think that some of these modern-day Pharisees and *"super-apostles"* read novels, and not the Bible, to teach what they preach in the name of God. Whenever there are diseases, plagues, wars, disasters like earthquakes, floods, crimes, and any social vices in society, we are told to increase our prayer time, fast more, and bind the devil and his demons to stop them. When we want to prosper in our fields of endeavours too we are told to do the same. Yet God has laid down the reasons and causes of all disasters and even diseases and the keys to prosperity, in the Bible.

> *"As the sun illumines not only the heaven and the whole world, shining on both land and sea; but also sends his rays through windows and small chinks into the furthest recesses of a house; so the Word, poured out everywhere, beholds the smallest actions of human life."— Clement of Alexandria (C. 150-215)*

The ways of peace, prosperity, good life, health and all the desires of the human heart that do not oppose the ways of the Almighty have been clearly stated in the Scriptures for us to either choose to follow or not. As you read these verses below, I want you to carefully search for where the devil or even demons come in. It is written: *"I said you are 'gods'; you are all sons of the Most High." But you will die like mere men; you will fall like every other ruler (Psalm 82:6-7).* The power to choose life or death was given to man by God Himself. That power is restored to us with knowledge into His Word when one gets to know that he was created in the image and likeness of his Creator. As you read the next lines, I want you to note the conditions being mentioned by God to receive all that He has promised His children.

BLESSINGS FOR OBEDIENCE

> ***If you fully obey the LORD your God and carefully follow all His commands*** *that I give you today,* ***The LORD your God***

> ***will set you high above all the nations on earth.*** *2* ***All these blessings will come upon you and accompany you if you obey the LORD your God:*** *3 You will be blessed in the city and blessed in the country. 4 The fruit of your womb will be blessed, and the crops of your land and the young of your livestock—the calves of your herds and the lambs of your flocks. 5 Your basket and your kneading trough will be blessed. 6 You will be blessed when you come in and blessed when you go out.*
>
> *7 The LORD (not your own power) will grant that the enemies who rise up against you will be defeated before you. They will come at you from one direction but flee from you in seven. 8 The LORD (not your efforts) will send a blessing on your barns and on everything you put your hand to. The LORD your God (not your prayers) will bless you in the land He is giving you. 9 The LORD (not your pastor's hand) will establish you as His holy people, as He promised you on oath,* ***if you keep the commands of the LORD your God and walk in His ways.*** *10* ***Then all the peoples on earth will see that you are called by the name of the LORD, and they will fear you.*** *11 The LORD (not your scheming) will grant you abundant prosperity—in the fruit of your womb, the young of your livestock and the crops of your ground—in the land He swore to your forefathers to give you.*
>
> *12 The LORD (not your fasting) will open the heavens, the storehouse of His bounty, to send rain on your land in season and to bless all the work of your hands. You will lend to many nations but will borrow from none. 13 The LORD (not binding devils and demons) will make you the head, not the tail.* ***If you pay attention to the commands of the LORD your God that I give you this day and carefully follow them, you will always be at the top, never at the bottom.*** *14* ***Do not turn aside from any of the commands I give you today, to the right or to the left,*** *following other gods and serving them. (Deut. 28:1-14)*

These are some of the favourite verses repeatedly quoted by the prosperity preachers of today. There is absolutely nothing wrong with quoting these verses. As far as I'm concerned, they are not even quoting them that much. But the truth is that something has to be done on the part of the individual Christian to see the fulfilment of these promises in his life. That something is: ***"If you fully obey the LORD your God and carefully follow all His commands that I give you today****, The LORD your God will set you high above all the nations on earth."*

There is no way around it. Also note that we were not told by the Father that failure to pray, fast, bind and loose the devil or demons would prevent these blessings from reaching us. The one and only condition for all these blessings is: ***"If you fully obey the LORD your God and carefully follow all His commands that I give you today,"*** period. Principles, like the law of gravity, remain principles and never change, no matter where one goes. If you choose to live according to the principles of God, you become fruitful in all you do; and if you fail to live by them too, you pay the price for them. This will never change! It's as simple and straight forward.

CURSES FOR DISOBEDIENCE

Let's now turn to the other side of the coin to see the reverse side of these blessings. *15 However,* ***if you do not obey the LORD your God and do not carefully follow all His commands and decrees I am giving you today****, all these curses will come upon you and overtake you:*

> ***You will be cursed in the city and cursed in the country****. 17 Your basket and your kneading trough will be cursed. 18 The fruit of your womb will be cursed, and the crops of your land, and the calves of your herds and the lambs of your flocks. 19 You will be cursed when you come in and cursed when you go out.*
>
> *20* ***The LORD*** *(not Brother Lucifer)* ***will send on you curses, confusion and rebuke in everything you put your hand to, until you are destroyed and come to sudden ruin*** *(why?)* ***because of the evil you have done in forsaking Him****. 21* ***The LORD*** *(not demons)* ***will plague you with diseases until He has destroyed you from the land you are entering to possess****. 22* ***The LORD*** *(not Satan)* ***will strike you with wasting disease, with fever and inflammation, with scorching heat and drought, with blight and mildew, which will plague you*** *(till when?)* ***until you perish.*** *23 The sky over your head will be bronze, the ground beneath iron. 24 The LORD (not lack of prayer) will turn the rain of your country into dust and powder; it will come down from the skies (till when?) until you are destroyed.*
>
> *25* ***The LORD*** *(again, not Satan)* ***will cause you to be defeated before your enemies****. (How?) You will come at them from one direction but flee from them in seven, and you will become a thing of horror to all the kingdoms on earth. 26 Your carcasses will be food for all the birds of the air and the beasts of the earth, and there will be no-one to frighten them away. 27* ***The LORD*** *(not witches)* ***will afflict you with the boils of Egypt and with tumours, festering sores and the itch, from which you cannot be cured****.*

28 ***The LORD*** *(not fetish priests)* ***will afflict you with madness,
blindness and confusion of mind.*** *29 At midday you will grope
about like a blind man in the dark.* ***You will be unsuccessful in
everything you do; day after day you will be oppressed and
robbed,*** *with no-one to rescue you.*

*30 You will be pledged to be married to a woman, but another will
take her and ravish her. You will build a house, but you will not
live in it. You will plant a vineyard, but you will not even begin to
enjoy its fruit. 31 Your ox will be slaughtered before your eyes, but
you will eat none of it. Your donkey will be forcibly taken from you
and will not be returned. Your sheep will be given to your enemies,
and no-one will rescue them. 32* ***Your sons and daughters will
be given to another nation, and you will wear out your eyes
watching for them day after day, powerless to lift a hand.*** *33
A people that you do not know (like the Chinese investments in other
countries) will eat what your land and labour produce, and you will
have nothing but cruel oppression all your days. 34* ***The sights you
see will drive you mad.*** *35* ***The LORD*** *(not generational curses))*
***will afflict your knees and legs with painful boils that cannot
be cured,*** *spreading from the soles of your feet to the top of your
head.*

*36 The LORD (not politicians) will drive you and the king you set
over you to a nation unknown to you or your fathers. There you will
worship other gods (other leaders), gods of wood and stone (heartless
leaders who pose as investors and make slaves out of your nation).
37 You will become a thing of horror and an object of scorn and
ridicule to all the nations where the LORD (not the economy) will
drive you.*

*38 You will sow much seed in the field but you will harvest little,
because locusts will devour it. 39 You will plant vineyards and
cultivate them but you will not drink the wine or gather the grapes,
because worms will eat them. 40 You will have olive trees throughout
your country but you will not use the oil, because the olives will
drop off (Ghana for instance, has several mineral deposits but is
still borrowing from other countries). 41* ***You will have sons and
daughters but you will not keep them, because they will go
into captivity*** *(the youth leave the shores of their countries to seek
greener pastures and their families call that blessedness. If only they
were told the sort of work they do out there to make a living). 42
Swarms of locusts will take over all your trees and the crops of your
land.*

43 ***The alien who lives among you will rise above you higher***
and higher, but you will sink lower and lower. *44 He will lend*
to you, but you will not lend to him. He will be the head, but you
will be the tail. (Have you thought of why America should owe
China huge sums of money?)

45 ***All these curses will come upon you. They will pursue you***
and overtake you *(till when?)* ***until you are destroyed,*** *(why?)*
because you did not obey the LORD your God and observe
the commands and decrees He gave you *(not because the devil*
and his demons were more powerful, and you failed to pray and fast
hard and long). 46 ***They will be a sign and a wonder to you and***
your descendants forever. *47 Because you did not serve the LORD*
your God joyfully and gladly in the time of prosperity, 48 ***therefore***
in hunger and thirst, in nakedness and dire poverty, you will
serve the enemies the LORD sends against you. *He will put an*
iron yoke on your neck until He has destroyed you.

49 The LORD (not any country) will bring a nation against you from
far away, from the ends of the earth, like an eagle swooping down, a
nation whose language you will not understand, 50 a fierce-looking
nation without respect for the old or pity for the young. 51 They will
devour the young of your livestock and the crops of your land until
you are destroyed. They will leave you no grain, new wine or oil, nor
any calves of your herds or lambs of your flocks until you are ruined.
52 ***They will lay siege to all the cities throughout the land until***
the high fortified walls *(the economy?)* ***in which you trust fall***
down. *They will besiege all the cities throughout the land the LORD*
your God is giving you . . .

58 ***If you do not carefully follow all the words of this law,***
<u>which are written in this book</u>, and do not revere this glorious
and awesome name—the LORD your God— *59* ***the LORD*** *(not*
Satan) ***will send fearful plagues on you and your descendants,***
harsh and prolonged disasters, and severe and lingering
illnesses. *60 He will bring upon you all the diseases of Egypt that*
you dreaded, and they will cling to you. 61 ***The LORD*** *(Brother*
Lucifer does not work in the disease manufacturing industry) ***will***
also bring on you every kind of sickness and disaster not
recorded in this Book of the Law *(like Lupus?), (till when?)* ***until***
you are destroyed. *62 You who were as numerous as the stars in*
the sky will be left but few in number, because you did not obey the
LORD your God. 63 ***Just as it pleased the LORD to make you***
prosper and increase in number, so it will please Him *(God is*
a compassionate God but there are times He enjoys destroying you) ***to***

> ***ruin and destroy you. You will be uprooted from the land you are entering to possess.***
>
> *64 Then the LORD (not rebels) will scatter you among all nations, from one end of the earth to the other. There you will worship other gods—gods of wood and stone, which neither you nor your fathers have known. 65 Among those nations you will find no repose, no resting place for the sole of your foot. There the LORD will give you an anxious mind, eyes weary with longing, and a despairing heart. 66 You will live in constant suspense, filled with dread both night and day,* ***never sure of your life.*** *67 In the morning you will say, "If only it were evening!" and in the evening, "If only it were morning!"—because of the terror that will fill your hearts and the sights that your eyes will see. 68 The LORD will send you back in ships to Egypt on a journey I said you should never make again.* ***There you will offer yourselves for sale to your enemies as male and female slaves, but no-one will buy you.*** *(Deut. 28:15-68)*

Carefully note that all that were said pertained to the future when the people were to conquer and occupy a certain piece of real estate to serve as the first nation of the LORD on earth. Depending on what they chose, their destinies were going to be decided on whether they chose to observe the commands and decrees of God or not. God earlier spoke to the Israelites to conquer the land. The sister nations to be given birth to were all to live by the same principles, because we are all called to inherit the same hope. These are all principles. And principles do not respect colour, race or religion. A cheerful heart works like good medicine. This is a principle which applies in China, North Korea, Ghana, and everywhere.

DESTROYED FOR LACK OF GOD'S KNOWLEDGE

To quote Dr. Joseph Goebbels again, *"If you tell a lie big enough and keep repeating it, people will eventually come to believe it."* God has given man the ability and power to correct all the wrongs done on earth. But out of ignorance, which they call knowledge, men, mostly some religious folks, have chosen to lay the blame on the devil and Adam for being responsible for the mess on earth. It is appointed unto every man to die once and after that, the judgment. The devil has no power over any man. It is the man who chooses to relegate his power and authority to another power aside what God has given him.

"The Bible is the Book that holds hearts up to the light as if held against the sun."—William A. Quayle (1860-1925)

Men have succeeded in overhauling the Word of God that it now seems like the devil is more powerful than God. But this is the time to reveal the plain and simple Word of God to His children who are willing to listen. My assignment is to teach these things and my only tool is the Holy Bible which they have again succeeded in convincing people not to even believe. Until they have given you the approval of what they want you to think and believe from the Bible, what one says are never taken.

The devil does not run the show until man relegates that power to him. Ignorance is related to darkness, and darkness is equated to the devil. There are blunt lies told in the Name of God today. It is the LORD God Almighty who runs the show in the affairs of men. It is written: ***"The LORD brings death and makes alive; He brings down to the grave and raises up.*** *7* ***The LORD sends poverty and wealth; He humbles and He exalts.*** *8 He raises the poor from the dust and lifts the needy from the ash heap; He seats them with princes and has them inherit a throne of honour.* ***For the foundations of the earth are the LORD'S****; upon them He has set the world" (1 Sam. 2:6-8).*

The LORD God has established His principles that if you choose to walk according to His ways, you are blessed and if not you are cursed and suffer from all kinds of afflictions that come upon men. Some truths are very painful to swallow but it is written: ***"Who*** *(including the devil)* ***can speak and have it happen if the LORD has not decreed it?*** *38* ***Is not from the mouth of the Most High that both calamities and good things come? Why should any living man complain when punished for his sins?*** *40* ***Let us examine our ways and test them, and let us return to the LORD****" (Lam. 3:37-40).*

The universe was not created by the devil, but God through Jesus Christ did. And if the universe was created by God, then the laws and principles that govern it are also created and implemented by God, not the devil. The devil has no power over man. We are told to resist him and he will flee. If man was given the power to resist him, then it is man's own action or inaction to be led into any other sins by this same force we've been empowered to resist, and make him flee. King Nebuchadnezzar wrote a letter once to the *"nations and men of every language, who live in all the world,"* telling them about the greatness of God: *"How great are His signs, how mighty his wonders! His kingdom is an eternal kingdom; His dominion endures from generation to generation" (Dan. 4:1-3).* Man must know and acknowledge that *"**the Most High is sovereign over the kingdoms of men and gives them to anyone He wishes** (Dan4:25).*

GOD'S MODE OF CALLING BACK HIS CHILDREN TO RETURN

We often hear the sweet by-and-by side of the Most High God, and if you dare say something about His "bad" side, you are branded as false and heretic. But it is not every bad thing that should be attributed to the devil. God has His own ways of drawing His children's attention to Him when they go astray. It is written in the book of Amos:

> *I (God) gave you empty stomachs in every city and lack of bread in every town,* ***yet you have not returned to me,*** *" declares the LORD. 7 "I also withheld rain from you when the harvest was still three months away. I sent rain on one town, but withheld it from another. One field had rain; another had none and dried up. 8 People staggered from town to town for water but did not get enough to drink,* ***yet you have not returned to me,*** *" declared the LORD. 9 "Many times I struck your gardens and vineyards, I struck them with blight and mildew. Locusts devoured your fig and olive trees,* ***yet you have not returned to me,*** *" declares the LORD. 10 "I sent plagues among you as I did to Egypt.* ***I*** *(God)* ***killed your young men with the sword****, along with your captured horses. I filled your nostrils with the stench of your camps,* ***yet you have not returned to me,*** *" declares the LORD. 11* ***"I overthrew some of you as I overthrew Sodom and Gomorrah****. You were like a burning stick snatched from the fire, yet you have not returned to me. (Amos 4:6-11)*

The purpose for which these things were happening was for the people to reconsider their ways to know whether they were living according to the right path or not. It takes understanding into the Scriptures to know how God deals with men. God says the reason why His people are destroyed is due to their lack of knowledge and not because of the power of the devil or demons. The Scriptures are what you need to live in perfect peace on earth, not big grammar. What you need to know from this stage is that, like every good father, God disciplines His children in order to see them turn to His perfect ways. It is written: *"Blessed is the man whom God corrects; so do not despise the discipline of the Almighty. 18* ***For He wounds, but He also binds up; He injures, but His hands also heal****" (Job 5:17-18).*

Again it is written in the book of Psalms: ***"For God is the King of all the earth****; sing to Him a psalm of praise. 8* ***God reigns over the nations****; God is seated on His holy throne. 9 The nobles of the nations assemble as the people of* *the God of Abraham, **for the kings of the earth belong to God;** He is greatly exalted" (Psalm 47:7-9).* Moses wrote: *"Remember the days of old; consider the generations long past. Ask your father and he will tell you, your elders, and they will explain to you. 8* ***When the Most High gave the nations their inheritance, when He divided all mankind, He set up boundaries for the peoples, according to the number of the sons of Israel"*** *(Deut. 32:7-8).*

> *But ask the animals, and they will teach you, or the birds of the air, and they will tell you; 8 or speak to the earth, and it will teach you,* ***or let the fish of the sea inform you. 9 Which of these does not know that the hand of the LORD has done this?*** *10* ***In His hand is the life of every creature and the breath of all mankind.*** *(Job 12:7-10)*

This came from the mouth of the man God said was *"blameless and upright; he feared God and shunned evil" (Job 1:1).* After all his worldly possessions were taken away from him, Job said, *"naked I came from my mother's womb, and naked I shall depart.* ***The LORD gave and the LORD has taken away;*** *may the name of the LORD be praised" (Job. 1:21).* A blameless and upright man who feared the LORD and shunned evil knew that it is God who gives and takes away from man not the devil. This same man is telling us that even mosquitoes, cockroaches, snails, bats and bedbugs know that it is the hand of the LORD that does everything in the life of every creature.

It is written: *"No-one from the east or the west or from the desert can exalt a man. "**But it is God who judges; He brings one down, He exalts another**" (Psalm 75:6-7).* This business of magnifying the devil over and above what God can do in a man's life is done primarily to put fear in the hearts of people and thereby pushing them to run for shelter from these men who later take advantage of their ignorance of the affairs of this earth. *"For God did not give us a spirit of timidity, but a spirit of power, of love and of self-discipline" (2 Tim. 1:7).*

I can continue this but it would divert our attention from the purpose of this book. Solomon wrote that *"When a man's ways are pleasing to the LORD, He makes even his enemies live at peace with him" (Prov. 16:7).* Your job is to be at peace with God and He will handle the rest.

> *"Everything that we read in the sacred books shines and glitters even in the outer shell; but the marrow are sweeter. He who wants to eat the kernel must first crack the shell."—St. Jerome (C. 342-420)*

A MAN REAPS WHAT HE SOWS

Everything that happens to a man under the sun happens to him for a reason. *"Do not be deceived: God cannot be mocked.* ***A man reaps what he sows. "The one who sows to please his sinful nature, from that nature, will reap destruction; the one who sows to please the Spirit, from the Spirit, will reap eternal life"*** *(Gal. 6:7-8).* James Allen wrote that *"The law 'Whatsoever a man sows that shall he also reap' is inscribed in flaming letters upon the portal of Eternity,* ***and none can deny it, none can cheat it, none can escape it.*** *He who puts his hand in the fire must suffer the burning until such time as it has worked itself out,* ***and neither curses nor prayers can avail to alter it."***

A student, who will not stick to his books but rely on examination malpractices to pass his exams, will soon complete the university with flying colours but cannot perform on the real job at hand. A society that allows corruption to thrive will soon find itself bombarded with different militant groups because people feel they are being denied of justice. A child that is taught from infancy to lie in front of his parents will grow thinking it is normal to do that, and even reach the presidency telling lies. No matter how small a seed is, we are surely bound to reap its fruits once it is sown. It may take decades to reap its fruits but no matter how long it takes, the fruits must grow up to meet someone's generation.

Paul was addressing this topic when He wrote to the Romans: "***God will give to each person according to what he has done****. 7 To those who by persistence in doing good seek glory, honour and immortality, He will give eternal life. 8 But for those who are self-seeking and who reject the truth and follow evil, there will be wrath and anger. 9* ***There will be trouble and distress for every human being who does evil****: first for the Jew, then for the Gentile; 10* ***but glory, honour and peace for every-one who does good****: first for the Jew, then for the Gentile. 11* ***For God does not show favouritism"*** *(Rom. 2:6-11).* He wrote a similar thing to the Colossians: ***"Anyone who does wrong will be repaid for his wrong and there is no favouritism"*** *(Col. 3:25).*

Being a Jew or a Christian is not a tag you wear on your chest and then go on living anyhow you like. God will not show any favour to a Jew or a Christian who goes against what the Constitution says but still claims that he is a child of God. It doesn't work that way. ***"We know that God does not listen to sinners. He listens to the godly man who does His will"*** *(John 9:31).* There's no tribalism with God; neither is there racism with Him. His principles do not respect colour, political affiliation or any creed. Whoever dances to His tunes gets the prize; not those who hear the sound of the beat but refuse to dance to it.

He is the God of order and decency. There is no cheating in His presence. It is written: *"Let all things be done decently and in order" (1 Cor. 14:40).* I read somewhere that *"What we think or what we know or what we believe is, in the end, of little consequence.* ***The only consequence is what we do.****"* It is what you do with your life that counts to God, not what you think or know. As you sow, so shall you reap. As you do not sow, so shall you not reap. It's as simple as that.

I read in one of Dr. Myles Munroe's books that *"Doing the right thing at the right time in the right way keeps you from doing the wrong thing at the wrong time in the wrong way."* After all the preaching, prophesying, teaching, healing, giving, tithing, praying, fasting, speaking in different kinds of tongues, acquiring wisdom into all that the Scriptures teach, what counts at the end of the day is what you do with them, not what you preach or prophesy with your lips.

JESUS ON REAPING WHAT YOU SOW

What did Jesus say about this subject? *"No good tree bears bad fruit, nor does a bad tree bear good fruit. 44 Each tree is recognised by its own fruit. People do not pick figs from thorn-bushes, or grapes from briers. 45* ***The good man brings good things out of the good stored up in his heart, and the evil man brings evil things out of the evil stored up in his heart****. For out of the overflow of his heart his mouth speaks" (Luke 6:43-45).*

Please listen carefully to Jesus as He makes this very clear to all of us. Whether it was a parable or not, this is what He said at one time: *"Not everyone who says to me, 'LORD, LORD,' will enter the kingdom of heaven,* ***but only he who does the will of my Father*** *who is in heaven. 22* ***Many will say to me on that day, 'LORD, LORD, did we not prophesy in your name and in your name drive out demons and perform many miracles?'*** *23* ***Then I will tell them plainly, 'I never knew you. Away from me, you evildoers!'****" (Matt. 7:21-23).*

PURPOSES OF "BAD DREAMS" AND SEVERE PAINS

Even sicknesses and illnesses are not caused by the devil as we have been made to believe, for they happen for a reason. God has His own principles which when studied and applied or not will bring or prevent them from attacking us. Whether this is a riddle or a parable, read this and believe what God says instead of listening to the folks who have grown in knowledge than their Master who called them. The workers of iniquity who are bound on making the Words of God null and void will always interpret any so-called "bad dreams" as the work of the devil and ask people to come to them for counselling. But those "bad" dreams are actually warnings from God alerting His children to watch their lives.

> ***For God does speak—now one way, now another—though man may not perceive it.*** *15* ***In a dream,*** *in a vision of the night,* ***when deep sleep falls on men as they slumber in their beds,*** *16* ***He*** *(God)* ***may speak in their ears and terrify them with warnings,*** *17* ***to turn man from wrongdoing and keep him from pride,*** *18* ***to preserve his soul from the pit, his life from perishing by the sword.*** *19* ***Or a man may be chastened on a bed of pain with constant distress in his bones,*** *20* ***so that his very being finds food repulsive and his soul loathes the choicest meal.*** *21 His flesh wastes away to nothing, and his bones, once hidden, now stick out. 22 His soul draws near to the pit, and his life to the messengers of death.*
>
> *23* ***"Yet if there is an angel on his side as a mediator,*** *one out of a thousand,* ***to tell a man what is right for him,*** *24 to be gracious to him and say, 'Spare him from going down to the pit; I have found a ransom for him'—25* ***then his flesh is renewed like a child's; it is restored as in the days of his youth.*** *26* ***He prays to God and finds favour with Him,*** *he sees God's face and shouts for joy; he is restored by God to his righteous state. 27* ***Then he comes to men and says, 'I have sinned, and perverted what was right, but I did not get what I deserved . . .*** *29* ***"God does all these things to a man***—*twice, even three times—30* ***to turn back his soul from the pit, that the light of life may shine on him."*** *(Job 33:14-30)*

You can choose who to believe after reading these verses. The so-called bad dreams do not come from any demonic forces but from the Most High God who loves you, and does not want to see you perish in your sins. He is warning you through those dreams against something unpleasant that is about to happen to you if you do not correct your steps by stepping into the perfect path of God established for His children. The same way, when you are sick, check your life if you have been walking according to the pattern laid down by God or not.

> ***But if men are bound in chains, held fast by chords of affliction,*** *9* ***He*** *(God)* ***tells them what they have done—that they have sinned arrogantly.*** *10 He (God) makes them listen to correction and commands them to repent of their evil. 11* ***If they***

> ***obey and serve Him, they will spend the rest of their days in prosperity and their years in contentment.*** *12* ***But if they do not listen, they will perish by the sword and die without knowledge.*** *(Job 36:8-12)*

For instance, let's assume that someone sinned arrogantly and is bound in chains, held fast by the chords of affliction or illness, and God decides to reveal to him what he has done wrong. "***If there is an angel on his side as a mediator****, one out of a thousand, to tell a man what is right for him,"* he would introduce him to God's Word regarding how he has faulted in applying the principles of God and the remedy of getting himself out. The mediator may act as someone who knows the Word of God thoroughly or as a doctor and refer this man to the Scriptures concerning his eating habits as an example. He may introduce him to some Scriptural verses like:

> *The LORD said to Moses, 23 "Say to the Israelites:* ***Do not eat any of the fat of cattle, sheep or goats.*** *24 The fat of an animal found dead or torn by wild animals may be used for any other purpose,* ***but you must not eat it.*** *25 Anyone who eats the fat of an animal from which an offering by fire may be made to the LORD must be cut off from his people. 26* ***And wherever you live, you must not eat the blood of any bird or animal****. 27 If anyone eats blood, that person must be cut off from his people. (Lev. 7:22-27)*

One thing I would urge you to do as you read verses like these in the Bible is to try to prove them with common sense before brushing them aside and calling them Jewish rituals. One of the best and surest ways to prove these things is through Science. But for obvious reasons, Science may not tell you the truth. The man Moses, who received these things from God, was not a daft person dictating things he had not proven. He was a very learned man. It is written about him that *"****Moses was educated in all the wisdom of the Egyptians*** *and was powerful in speech and action" (Acts 7:22).* He was a man who backed his speech with actions.

I often joke with my atheist friends that even if there is no God as they claim, then the person or the group of people who wrote the Bible should be worshipped as God. With the help of Science, we are now witnessing the harmful effects of eating the fats of animals and eating raw meat. *"The life of a creature is in the blood" (Lev. 17:11).* When you go for medical check up, they take your blood sample to determine whether you are ill or not. They do that because your life is in your blood. That is possible because we run on blood, and that makes us creatures.

The same way, all animals run on blood, not diesel. We can also take the blood samples of animals to determine whether they are sick or not. But how many of us do that before slaughtering these animals to eat? Until you check their blood samples, you would never know if they are healthy or not. Their blood would easily tell us but because God knew in advance that man would not do that, He made it a law, completely forbidding the eating of blood by His children. Once again, God is not going to go blind or have a sore throat because someone ate the fat of an animal or ate the blood of an animal. That law was made for man.

> *"Leave not off reading the Bible till you find your hearts warmed . . . . Let it not only inform you, but inflame you."—Thomas Watson*

If they obey (after this has been made known to them, and it is true that they had previously been eating the fats and blood of animals and they stop that practice) *and serve Him, they will spend the rest of their days in prosperity and their years in contentment. 12 But if they do not listen, they will perish by the sword* ***and die without knowledge*** *(Job 36:11-12).* ***"Then his flesh is renewed like a child's; it is restored as in the days of his youth.*** *26* ***He prays to God and finds favour with Him****, he sees God's face and shouts for joy;* ***he is restored by God to his righteous state.*** *27* ***Then he comes to men and says, 'I have sinned, and perverted what was right, but I did not get what I deserved*** *. . . 29 "God does all these things to a man—twice, even three times—30* ***to turn back his soul from the pit, that the light of life may shine on him"*** *(Job 33:25-30).*

SOME GREAT MEN OF GOD WHO GOT ILL

Illnesses and sicknesses are used as tools or instruments by God to straighten men when they are going off track in life on His health principles. I'm going to list a few men in the Scriptures who were very strong in the LORD but still got ill.

> *Hezekiah trusted in the LORD, the God of Israel.* ***There was no-one like him among all the kings of Judah, either before him or after him****. 6* ***He held fast to the LORD and did not cease to follow Him: he kept the commands the LORD had given Moses.*** *7* ***And the LORD was with him; he was successful in whatever he undertook.*** *(2 Kings 18:5-7)*

Hezekiah was a descendant of David but it is said about him that *"there was no-one like him among all the kings of Judah, either before him or after him."* David was said to have had the spirit of an angel. Yet there was no king like Hezekiah. That notwithstanding, it is written: *"In those days Hezekiah became ill and was at the point of death" (2 Kings 20:1).* God added another fifteen years to his life after he had made some serious prayers reminding God of how faithful he had been as a king in serving God.

ELISHA DIED FROM AN ILLNESS HE SUFFERED

Now, Elisha studied under Elijah and inherited a double portion of his power. He was later described as *"a holy man of God" (2 Kings 4:9).* He raised a boy back to life after his death *(2 Kings 4:32-37).* He also healed a man called Naaman of leprosy *(2 Kings 5:11-15).* When the head of a borrowed iron-axe sank under water he made it float back to the surface for the owner to take *(2 Kings 6:1-7).* This prophet was even capable of telling people the very words they spoke in their own bedrooms *(2 Kings 6:12).* Elisha was simply powerful.

If Elisha possessed the double portion of Elijah's power, then he must have been very powerful, and this showed in his life as he was able to perform some great miracles. Yet it is written: ***"Now Elisha was suffering from the illness from which he died"*** *(2 Kings 13:14).* Was it as a result of the power of Satan that this illness resulted in his death? That could not be. God knows why.

DANIEL SUFFERED FROM AN ILLNESS FOR SEVERAL DAYS

It is written about Daniel and his friends that *"To these four young men God gave knowledge and understanding of all kinds of literature and learning. And Daniel could understand visions and dreams of all kinds" (Dan. 1:17).* Daniel was a man who had the Spirit of God operating through him. Yet he himself said: *"I, Daniel, was exhausted* ***and lay ill for several days.*** *Then I got up and went about the king's business. I was appalled by the vision; it was beyond understanding" (Dan. 8:27).* Was he too attacked by the devil and his demons?

PAUL HAD AN ILLNESS

How about Paul, the apostle? Jesus first struck him with blindness to bring him down to his knees to humble him. Later, although we were not told the kind of illness he suffered from, he wrote to the Galatians that *"As you know,* ***it was because of an illness that I first preached the gospel to you.*** *14* ***Even though my illness was a trial to you, you did not treat me with contempt or scorn****. Instead, you welcomed me as if I were an angel of God, as if I were Christ Jesus Himself" (Gal. 4:13-14).* This was the same man who sent just handkerchiefs which had touched his body as healing materials for others. Was he ill because he failed to fast and pray hard, and as a result the devil overpowered him? Don't forget the fact that this man's revelations were revealed to him by Jesus Christ. But in the case of Paul it is easy to know, or at least guess, how or why he became ill. He wrote this to the Corinthians that:

> *I have worked much harder, been in prison more frequently, been flogged more severely, and been exposed to death again and again. 24* ***Five times I received from the Jews the forty lashes minus one.*** *25* ***Three times I was beaten with rods, once I was stoned****, three times I was shipwrecked. I spent a night and a day in the open sea. 26 I have been constantly on the move. I have been in danger from rivers, in danger from bandits, in danger from my own countrymen, in danger from Gentiles; in danger in the city, in danger in the country, in danger at sea; and in danger from false brothers. 27 I have laboured and toiled and have often gone without sleep;* ***I have known hunger and thirst and have often gone without food;*** *I have been cold and naked. 28 Besides everything else, I face daily the pressure of my concern for all the churches. (2 Cor. 11:23-28)*

From Paul's history, it is no surprise that the man could fall ill at a time in his ministry. Paul had a brother in the faith that he called his fellow-soldier named Epaphroditus. This man almost died risking his life for the work of Christ. Yet it is written about him that: *"Indeed* ***he*** *(Epaphroditus)* ***was ill and almost died. But God had mercy on him****, and not on him only but also on me, to spare me sorrow upon sorrow" (Phil.2:25-30).* This man sacrificed his life for the sake of the gospel of Christ and was considered a soldier in the faith. Did he stop fasting and praying?

TIMOTHY HAD HIS "FREQUENT ILLNESSES"

Timothy studied under Paul for a very long time that Paul started entreating the other churches to listen to him because he knew he had learned much about the mysteries of God. But that did not stop Timothy from having his frequent illnesses. Paul himself wrote to him that *"Stop drinking only water, and use a little wine* ***because of your stomach and your frequent illnesses*** *" (1 Tim. 5:23).* Paul did not send one of his famous handkerchiefs this time but recommended the drinking of *"a little wine"* as the solution for his *"frequent illnesses."* A. W. Tozer once wrote that ***"The churches are cluttered with religious amateurs culturally unfit to minister at the altar, and the people suffer as a consequence . . . Much that is being done in Christ's name is false to Christ in that it is conceived by the flesh, incorporates fleshly methods, and seeks fleshly ends."***

It is written that *"The LORD'S curse is on the house of the wicked, but He blesses the home of the righteous" (Prov. 3:33). "Like a fluttering sparrow or a darting swallow,* ***an undeserved curse does not come to rest*** *" (Prov. 26:2).* Religion or not, a man reaps what he or she sows. This applies to the Jew, Christian, Moslem, Buddhists, Communists and Atheists in all parts of the world. This principle is taught in several pages of the New Testament.

Jesus said: *"For the Son of Man is going to come in His Father's glory, with His angels, and then* ***He will reward each person according to what he has done*** *" (Matt. 16:27).* We are not going to be rewarded according to what we have prayed, preached, prophesied, fasted or tithed about, but what we have done with our lives. He also said that *"Give and it will be given to you. A good measure, pressed down, shaken together and running over, will be poured into your lap.* ***For with the measure you use, it will be measured to you*** *" (Luke 6:38).* Paul wrote that "***For we must all appear before the judgment seat of Christ, that each one may receive what is due to him for the things done while in the body, whether good or bad*** *" (2 Cor. 5:10).*

> *As I have observed, those who plough evil and those who sow trouble reap it. (Job 4:8)*

It is absolutely true that we should pray without ceasing. But how to pray and what to pray about have been twisted to just put fear in man to make him constantly afraid of the power of the devil rather than trusting in God and His Word. Your problem is not any devil but knowledge into the Holy Scriptures of God. Instead of sitting down and assessing their lives when there is a problem, today's Christian will hardly accept responsibility for anything that goes wrong in his life; he will rather choose to blame it on forces outside his own shortfalls. They always have to find a devil somewhere to blame for the predicament in their lives, and start cursing whatever they do not understand.

Life is all about applying the laws and principles established by God. Man does not know exactly how the majority of them work. But we all know that they exist and were all created by the unseen God. For instance, if there is a sudden flood in an area, those who would survive would be those who know the laws or principles on swimming. You don't swim with fasting and prayers. At that time, if I know all the verses in the Bible and start to quote them from cover to cover in the Name of Jesus, that would not solve my problem of getting drowned. Only the language of swimming would be spoken and understood there. And if there are Moslems or Buddhists who know how to swim they would be saved, but the Jew and the Christian would be left behind.

In the same way, if I'm interested in getting wealthy, then I must take upon myself to make sure that after earning any amount of money, my expenses should always be less than my income so that I can invest the difference. Some of the richest men today are in China yet most of them have not even heard of the Name of Jesus Christ before. It's all about the application of laws created by God the Father. And principles do not respect religions. They only respect applications.

SLANDERING CELESTIAL BEINGS FOR EVERY WRONG

Out of ignorance into these things, man would blame everything on something outside of himself because he is afraid, and then refuse to take full responsibility of his life. Whatever happens that man does not understand has to be blamed on the devil and demons in dark places. This reminds me of what Peter wrote:

> *This is especially true of those who follow the corrupt desire of the sinful nature and despise authority.* ***Bold and arrogant, these men are not afraid to slander celestial beings;*** *11* ***yet even angels, although they are stronger and more powerful, do not bring slanderous accusations against such beings in the presence of the LORD****. 12* ***But these men blaspheme in matters they do not understand****. They are like brute beasts, creatures of instincts, born only to be caught and destroyed, and like beasts they too will perish. (2 Pet. 2:10-12)*

Slander is a falsely spoken statement intended to damage the good opinion people have of someone. It is nobody's business to kill the devil. The guy will actually be around even after the next one thousand year rule of Jesus Christ. So what's your beef? Have you read in any part of the Scriptures where the devil was being bound by Jesus or the apostles, Job and his friends, or any other man in the entire Scriptures? Job and his three friends were among the wisest people in the knowledge of God. Yet not even Job himself accused the devil of being responsible of his illness. Read the whole book of Job to learn this. He was demanding the reason for his illness from God, not the devil.

Religious folks always want people to see how powerful they are by claiming things that are not even part of the teachings of the Bible. It reminds me of my school days when a particular footballer, mostly a defender, will make himself dirtier than the rest of his team-mates to receive applause from the girls. Drawing near to God is what you should seek, and not how to bind a devil. God has His own way of dealing with whatever cannot be seen with the naked eyes.

> *In the very same way, **these dreamers pollute their own bodies, reject authority and slander celestial beings.** But even the archangel Michael, when he was disputing with the devil about the body of Moses, did not dare to bring a slanderous accusation against him (the devil), but said, "The LORD rebuke you!" 10 **Yet these men speak abusively against whatever they do not understand; and what things they do understand by instinct, like unreasoning animals—these are the very things that destroy them.** (Jude 8-10)*

As I keep saying, I only believe what the Scriptures say and not what men tell me to think and believe. The power and authority to bind and lose was first proclaimed to Peter but I'm yet to read where in Scripture he went about binding and loosing the devil. This was a man who lived and dined with Jesus Christ for a period of not less than three years. He didn't waste his energy on that because he knew where those beings were. He wrote: *"God did not spare angels when they sinned, **but sent them to hell, putting them into gloomy dungeons to be held for judgment** (2 Pet. 2:4).*

True Christianity is about the kingdom of heaven on earth which brings peace into the hearts of men. But gradually, it has evolved to this stage where, instead of becoming free in the LORD, Christians are taught to believe that if they do not perform some rituals, they would be attacked and killed by the devil, demons and witches. The apostles and early Christians became so free in their hearts that they were no longer even afraid of death. Worldly possessions became nothing to them as they shared all they had among themselves, and no one lacked anything. Christianity is about freedom and peace of mind. Paul did not care about whether he was dead or alive. It didn't matter to him anymore. *For God did not give us a spirit of timidity, but a spirit of power, of love and of self-discipline (2 Tim. 1:7).*

And who said that joining yourself to the Christian faith means you would not face problems again? My friend, you will be persecuted whether you like it or not. That does not mean that the LORD has deserted you. Death, to me, is nothing as I died over ten years ago when I chose to study the Bible instead of seeking for my own selfish ambitions. And I know what is ahead of me as I have chosen this path. I'm no longer bothered whether I'm alive or *"asleep"* in the LORD, I owe my life to Him.

Jesus said, *"Blessed are those who are persecuted because of righteousness, for theirs is the kingdom of heaven. 11 Blessed are you when people insult you, persecute you and falsely say all kinds of evil against you because of me. 12 Rejoice and be glad, because great is your reward in heaven, for in the same way they persecuted the prophets who were before you" (Matt. 5:10-12).* Even Jesus' own brothers were against Him. There were times He could not go into some areas until it was appropriate to do so. They tried stoning Him at times. We just read about Paul's experiences. None of it was the sweet by-and-by that we often hear today from the tycoon prosperity teachers.

THE HERITAGE OF GOD'S CHILDREN

> *"See, it is I who created the blacksmith who fans the coals into flame and forges a weapon fit for its work.* ***And it is I who have created the destroyer to work havoc;*** *17 no weapon forged against you will prevail, and you will refute every tongue that accuses you.* ***This is the heritage of the servants of the LORD,*** *and this is their vindication from me," declares the LORD. (Isa. 54:16-17)*

Most Christians know these two verses but do not actually believe what it says. My dictionary defines a *heritage* as "the history, traditions and qualities that a country or society has had for many years that are considered an important part of its character." God is saying that it is He who created the destroyer to work havoc. But that havoc does not extend to His children. Therefore, no weapon that is forged against His children can prevail, because the destroyer takes his orders from our own Father. This is the heritage of the children of God.

> ***If you make the Most High your dwelling****—even the LORD, who is my refuge—10* ***then no harm will befall you, no disaster will come near your tent.*** *11 For He will command His angels concerning you to guard you in all your ways; 12 they will lift you up in their hands, so that you will not strike your foot against a stone. 13 You will tread upon the lion and the cobra; you will*

> *trample the great lion and the serpent. 14 "**Because he loves me,**" says the LORD, "**I will rescue him; I will protect him,** for he acknowledges my Name. 15 **He will call upon me, and I will answer him; I will be with him in trouble, I will deliver him and honour him**. 16 With long life will I satisfy him and show him my salvation." (Psalm 91:9-16)*

Charles H. Mackintosh once wrote that *"Our only refuge, our only resource, our only strength, our only comfort, our only authority, is the precious Word of God.* ***Take away that, and we have absolutely nothing; give us that, and we want no more.****"* How wonderful it feels to know there are people who feel and think the same way you do!

> *"I am thus particularly earnest to display in this work the literary excellence of the Holy Bible, because I have reason to apprehend it is too frequently laid by, under a notion of its being a dull, dry and unentertaining system, whereas the fact is quite otherwise: it contains all that can be wished by the truest intellectual taste; it enters more sagaciously and more deeply into human nature; it develops character, delineates manner, charms the imagination and warms the heart more effectively than any other book extant; and if once a man would take it into his hand without that strange prejudicing idea of flatness, and be willing to be pleased, I am morally certain he would find all his favourite authors dwindle in the comparison, and conclude that he was reading not only the most religious book but the most entertaining book in the world."—Samuel Jackson Pratt (1749-1814)*

THE PEDIGREE OF MOSES

Let's now continue with the history of Israel from where we left off. But before I continue with this I want us to hear the pedigree of Moses in the sight of God, after his death. We need that in later chapters. This is what is written about him in the Bible:

> *Since then, no prophet has risen in Israel like Moses, whom the LORD knew face to face, 11 who did all those miraculous signs and wonders the LORD sent him to do in Egypt—to Pharaoh and to all his officials and to his whole land. 12* ***For no-one has ever shown the mighty power or performed the awesome deeds that Moses did in the sight of all Israel.*** *(Deut. 34:10-12)*

When it was time for the people of Israel to start possessing the land God promised them, listen to what God said to Joshua, who at the time had succeeded Moses:

> *After the death of Moses the servant of the LORD, the LORD said to Joshua son of Nun, Moses' assistant: 2 "Moses my servant is dead. Now then, you and all these people, get ready to cross the Jordan River into the land I am about to give to them—to the Israelites. 3* ***I will give you every place where you set your foot, as I promised Moses****. 4 Your territory will extend from the desert to Lebanon, and from the great river, the Euphrates—all the Hittite country—to the Great Sea on the west. No-one will be able to stand up against you all the days of your life. As I was with Moses, so will I be with you; I will never leave you nor forsake you."*
>
> *6 "Be strong and courageous,* ***because you will lead these people to inherit the land I swore to their forefathers to give them****. 7 Be strong and very courageous.* ***Be careful to obey all the law my servant Moses gave you; do not turn from it to the right or to the left, that you may be successful wherever you go.*** *8* ***Do not let this Book of the Law depart from your mouth; meditate on it day and night, so that you may be careful to do everything written in it. Then you will be prosperous and successful."*** *(Joshua 1:1-8)*

We now know that the land promised to Abraham was the same one promised to Isaac, Jacob and his descendants. The same land that Moses spoke about was the same land that Joshua and the Israelites were supposed to possess. Now, after all the admonishing from God and Moses, let's see if Joshua obeyed the voice of God, and did what he was told to do before his death.

> ***As the LORD commanded His servant Moses, so Moses commanded Joshua, and Joshua did it, he left nothing undone of all that the LORD commanded Moses.*** *(Joshua 11:15) Israel served the LORD throughout the lifetime of Joshua and of the elders who outlived him, and who had experienced everything the LORD had done for Israel. (Joshua 24:31)*

JOSHUA'S FINAL WORDS TO THE PEOPLE

Before joining his forefathers, we need to hear what sort of advice Joshua also gave his fellow countrymen that he was leaving behind. Let's see if it will be anything different from what Moses his predecessor told him when it was his time to take over.

> *After a long time had passed and the LORD had given Israel rest from all their enemies around them,* ***Joshua, by then old and well advanced in years,*** *2 summoned all Israel—their elders, leaders, judges and officials—and said to them: "I am old and well advanced in years. 3 You yourselves have seen everything the LORD your God has done to all these nations for your sake; it was the LORD your God who fought for you . . . 6 "Be very strong:* ***be careful to obey all that is written in the Book of the Law of Moses*** *(the first time it was called so),* ***without turning aside to the right or to the left****. 7 Do not associate with these nations that remain among you; do not invoke the names of their gods or swear by them. You must not serve them or bow down to them. 8* ***But you are to hold fast to the LORD your God, as you have until now.***
>
> *9 The LORD has driven out before you great and powerful nations; to this day no-one has been able to withstand you. 10 One of you routs a thousand, because the LORD your God fights for you, just as He promised. 11 So be very careful to love the LORD your God. 12 "****But if you turn away and ally yourselves with the survivors of these nations that remain among you and if you intermarry with them and associate with them,*** *13* ***then you may be sure that the LORD your God will no longer drive out these nations before you****. Instead, they will become snares and traps for you, whips on your backs and thorns in your eyes, until you perish from the good land, which the LORD your God has given you.*
>
> *14 Now I am about to go the way of all the earth. You know with all your heart and soul that not one of the good promises the LORD your God gave you has failed. Every promise has been fulfilled; not one has failed. 15* ***But just as every good promise of the LORD your God has come true, so the LORD*** *(not Satan)* ***will bring on you all the evil He has threatened, until He has destroyed you from this good land He has given you.*** *16* ***If you violate the covenant of the LORD your God, which He commanded you, and go and serve other gods and bow down to them, the LORD'S anger will burn against you, and you will quickly perish from the good land He has given you.*** *(Josh. 23:1-16)*

So long as there were leaders like Moses and Joshua to walk strictly by the principles of the covenant, God also fulfilled His part to the letter.

We will see what will happen after the death of these leaders and their descendants who took their places. The Bible summarises that for us in the book of Judges:

> ***After that whole generation had been gathered to their fathers, another generation grew up, who knew neither the LORD nor what He had done for Israel.*** *11 Then the Israelites did evil in the eyes of the LORD and served the Baals. 12 They forsook the LORD, the God of their fathers, who had brought them out of Egypt. They followed and worshipped various gods of the peoples around them. They provoked the LORD to anger 13 because they forsook Him and served Baal and the Ashtoreths. 14 In His anger against Israel the LORD (not the devil) handed them over to raiders who plundered them. He sold them to their enemies all around, whom they were no longer able to resist. 15 Whenever Israel went out to fight,* ***the hand of the LORD*** *(not the hand of the devil)* ***was against them to defeat them, just as He had sworn to them*** *(in Deut. 28:15-68). They were in great distress.*
>
> *16 Then the LORD raised up judges, who saved them out of the hands of these raiders. 17 Yet they would not listen to their judges but prostituted themselves to other gods and worshipped them.* ***Unlike their fathers, they quickly turned from the way in which their fathers had walked, the way of obedience to the LORD'S commands.*** *18 Whenever the LORD raised up a judge for them, He was with the judge and saved them out of the hands of their enemies as long as the judge lived;* ***for the LORD had compassion on them as they groaned under those who oppressed and afflicted them.*** *19* ***But when the judge died, the people returned to ways even more corrupt than those of their fathers, following other gods and serving and worshipping them. They refused to give up their evil practices and stubborn ways.***
>
> *20 Therefore the LORD was very angry with Israel and said, "Because this nation has violated the covenant that I laid down for their forefathers and has not listened to me, 21* ***I will no longer drive out before them any of the nations Joshua left when he died.*** *22* ***I will use them to test Israel and see whether they will keep the way of the LORD and walk in it as their forefathers did."*** *(Judges 2:10-22)*

There were even times that the Word of the LORD became rare that there were no visions from the LORD again because the people had neglected His ways. It is written in the book of Samuel that *"In those days the word of the LORD was rare; there were not many visions" (I Samuel 3:1).*

THE PEOPLE ASKED TO HAVE A KING LIKE ANY OTHER NATION

In the days of Samuel when the ark of the LORD was captured by the Philistines, he told them: *"If you are returning to the LORD with all your hearts, **then rid yourselves of the foreign gods and the Ashtoreths and commit yourselves to the LORD and serve Him only, and He will deliver you out of the hand of the Philistines.** 4 So the Israelites put away their Baals and Ashtoreths, and served the LORD only" (I Samuel 7:3-4).* The only way out of afflictions is to keep the way of the LORD in the Scriptures.

Going strictly according to the Words of the LORD, "*Samuel continued as judge over Israel all the days of his life" (I Samuel 7:15).*

> *When Samuel grew old, he appointed his sons as judges for Israel . . . 3 But his sons did not walk in his ways. **They turned aside after dishonest gain and accepted bribes and perverted justice.** 4 So all the elders of Israel gathered together and came to Samuel at Ramah. 5 They said to him, "You are old, **and your sons do not walk in your ways;** now appoint a king to lead us, **such as all the other nations have.***

Prior to this time, God had told His children on several occasions not to do as the nations around them did in the land. But they saw that other nations beside them had kings who ruled over them. That was an institution from the wisdom of this world, which God had not sanctioned in His principles. They asked to be ruled by this system of the world too:

> *But when they said, "**Give us a king to lead us,**" this displeased Samuel; so he prayed to the LORD. 7 And the LORD told him: "**Listen to all that the people are saying to you; it is not you they have rejected, but they have rejected me as their king . . .** 9 Now listen to them; **but warn them solemnly and let them know what the king who will reign over them will do.**"*
>
> *10 Samuel told all the words of the LORD to the people who were asking him for a king. 11 He said, "**This is what the king who will reign over you will do: He will take your sons and make them serve with his chariots and horses** (the ministry of defence?), **and they will run in front of his chariots.** 12 Some he will assign*

> *to be commanders (ministers?) of thousands and commanders of fifties (governors?), and others to plough his ground and reap his harvest (the bankers?), and still others to make weapons of war and equipment for his chariots (the military?). 13 He will take your daughters to be perfumers and cooks and bakers (public servants?). 14 He will take the best of your fields and vineyards and olive groves and give them to his attendants (have you thought of where the ministers' huge salaries come from?).*
>
> *15 He will take a tenth of your grain and of your vintage and give it to his officials and attendants (taxes?). 16 Your menservants and maidservants and the best of your cattle and donkeys he will take for his own use (so-called government properties?). 17 He will take a tenth of your flocks, and you yourselves will become his slaves (just a modernised form of slavery). 18* ***When that day comes, you will cry out for relief from the king you have chosen, and the LORD will not answer you in that day."*** (Is there a country on earth today practising democracy which has all its citizens smiling all the time, praising the policies of its government led by the president and his ministers?)
>
> *19 But the people refused to listen to Samuel. "No!" they said. "We want a king over us. 20* ***Then we shall be like all the other nations,*** *with a king to lead us and to go out before us and fight our battles." 21 When Samuel heard all that the people said, he repeated it before the LORD. 22 The LORD answered, "Listen to them and give them a king." (I Samuel 8:1-22)*

The concept of democracy is often credited to some group of people from Greece. But the details of it were borrowed from the very pages of the Bible. Everything you need to know about how a democracy operates is in the Bible. As to whether God was pleased or not with the people's request for a king, let's read what He said through the mouth of Samuel concerning this issue.

> *Now, here is the king you have chosen, the one you asked for; see, the LORD has set a king over you. 14* ***If you fear the LORD and serve and obey Him and do not rebel against His commands, and if both you and the king who reigns over you follow the LORD your God—good!*** *15* ***But if you do not obey the LORD, and if you rebel against His commands, his hand*** *(principles)* ***will be against you, as it was against your fathers.***

> *16 "Now then, stand still and see this great thing the LORD is about to do before your eyes! 17 Is it not wheat harvest now? I will call upon the LORD to send thunder and rain.* ***And you will realise what an evil thing you did in the eyes of the LORD when you asked for a king."*** *19 The people all said to Samuel, "Pray to the LORD your God for your servants so that we will not die,* ***for we have added to all our other sins the evil of asking for a king****."*
>
> *20 "Do not be afraid." Samuel replied.* ***"You have done all this evil; yet do not turn away from the LORD, but serve the LORD with all your heart.*** *21* ***Do not turn away after useless idols.*** *They can do no good, nor can they rescue you, because they are useless. 22 For the sake of His great name the LORD will not reject His people, because the LORD was pleased to make you His own. (I Samuel 12:13-22)*

It is clear that although the LORD did not approve of their asking for a king in place of Him, He admonished them to still live their lives according to the same laws, commands and decrees that were given through Moses. The LORD does not change His mind and until this time His principles remain the same at all times. So we can go further to see what happened from there. We can now move on further to see how the first king fared and what was used as the yardstick to judge his performance.

> *"One must look a long time at the great masterpieces of art to appreciate their beauty and understand their meaning, so one must look a long time at the great verses of the Bible to appreciate their beauty and understand their meaning."—Reuben Archer Torrey (1850-1928)*

STANDARD FOR JUDGING THE PERFORMANCE OF THE FIRST KING

At his own discretion, Saul, the first king took a decision and acted foolishly in the sight of God, because he failed to comply with what was commanded him by the LORD at a point in his leadership. He paid dearly for this.

> *"You acted foolishly," Samuel said.* ***"You have not kept the command the LORD your God gave you;*** *if you had, He would have established your kingdom over Israel for all time. 14 But now*

> *your kingdom will not endure; the LORD has sought out a man after His own heart and appointed him leader of His people,* ***because you have not kept the LORD'S command."*** *(I Samuel 13:13-14)*

God has a system of wiping out sinners from the face of the earth. *"The soul that sinneth, it shall die."* Saul was sent on a mission by God to destroy the Amalekites. This was clearly stipulated in the writings of Moses. But he chose to go according to his own opinions. After Saul had given his reasons for why he chose that path let's hear God's response to what he did:

> *But Samuel replied:* ***"Does the LORD delight in burnt offerings and sacrifices as much as in obeying the voice of the LORD? To obey is better than sacrifices and to heed is better than the fat of rams.*** *23 For rebellion is like the sin of divination, and arrogance (to the Word of God) like the evil of idolatry.* ***Because you have rejected the word of the LORD, He has rejected you as king."*** *(I Samuel 15:22-23)*

The command to completely destroy these groups of people including women and children was given in the days of Moses and was clearly written down in the Book of the Law as part of the Word of God. The Amalekites could well be described as professional sinners, for which reason God wanted them to be completely destroyed. As their king was about to be executed, this is what was said about him: *"As your sword has made women childless, so will your mother be childless among women" (I Samuel 15:33).*

These people were not being killed in the name of imposing a religious belief or a church down their throats like what is done today, no! These were people who had lived and polluted the systems of things in the sight of God, and were supposed to be wiped out from the face of the earth. If Adam and Eve were banished from Eden, Abel cursed because he sinned, the people of Noah's day wiped out from the face of the earth because they sinned, and Lucifer thrown out of heaven because he sinned with his angels, then whoever sinned should bear in mind that the LORD still remains the same and does not change His mind.

The sinner will die through any and every means, *"for the wages of sin is death,"* period! Mere disobedience to this command caused the throne of Saul to be forfeited. The same principle continues unabated, because *"He who is the Glory of Israel does not lie or change His mind; for He is not a man that He should change His mind" (I Samuel 15:29).*

> *"Bibles laid open, millions of surprises."—George Herbert (1593-1633)*

GOD'S COVENANT WITH DAVID

During the kingship days of David, he decided to build a house for the LORD but God, through Nathan the prophet communicated something to him:

> *Now then, tell my servant David, "This is what the LORD Almighty says: I took you from the pasture and from following the flock to be ruler over my people Israel. 9 I have been with you wherever you have gone, and I have cut off all your enemies from before you.* ***Now I will make your name great, like the names of the greatest men of the earth.*** *10* ***And I will provide a place for my people Israel and will plant them so that they can have a home of their own and no longer be disturbed.*** *Wicked people shall not oppress them any more, as they did at the beginning 11 and have done ever since the time I appointed leaders over my people Israel. I will also give you rest from all your enemies.*
>
> *"The LORD declares to you that the LORD Himself will establish a house for you: 12 When your days are over and you rest with your fathers, I will raise up your offspring to succeed you, who will come from your own body, and I will establish his kingdom. 13 He is the one who will build a house for my Name, and I will establish the throne of his kingdom forever. 14 I will be his father, and he shall be my son. When he does wrong, I will punish him with the rod of men, with flogging inflicted by men. 15 But my love will never be taken away from him, as I took it away from Saul, whom I removed from before you. 16* ***Your house and your kingdom shall endure forever before me; your throne shall be established forever."*** *(2 Samuel 7:8-16)*

Note here again that the issue of making David great, like what was promised Abraham, has been brought up by God. Just like his fathers before him, the duration of this greatness will last forever. *Psalm 119* tells us what he did to qualify for this promise to his descendants. But we can take a short look at what he did to have this blessing bestowed on him. This was a man whose life was worth ten thousand fighting men *(II Samuel 18:3).*

> *The LORD has dealt with me* ***according to my righteousness; according to the cleanness of my hands He has rewarded me.*** *22* ***For I have kept the ways of the LORD; I have not done evil by turning from my God.*** *23* ***All His laws are before me; I have not turned away from His decrees.*** *24* ***I have been blameless before Him and have kept myself from sin.*** *(II Samuel 22:21-24)*

DAVID'S FINAL WORDS TO HIS SON SOLOMON

David was so righteous to the core that God Himself witnessed concerning him that apart from the sin he committed, by sleeping with another man's wife and later killing the husband to cover the shame, there was nothing faulty in his life. Can you dare to believe that? I do! To know whether David kept the ways of the LORD till death, we need to hear what he told Solomon when he was about to go the way of his fathers for his son to succeed him:

> ***When the time drew near for David to die***, *he gave a charge to Solomon his son. 2 "I am about to go the way of all the earth," he said. "So be strong, show yourself a man, 3 and* ***observe what the LORD your God requires: Walk in His ways, and keep His decrees and commands, His laws and requirements, as written in the Law of Moses, so that you may prosper in all you do and wherever you go, 4 and that the LORD may keep His promise to me***: *'****IF*** *your descendants watch how they live, and if they walk faithfully before me with all their heart and soul, you will never fail to have a man on the throne of Israel" (I Kings 2:1-4)*

Nothing has changed so far. No matter what the promise entailed, there was always a condition attached based on the individual's choices. There was (and still is) no way that is going to change, because the LORD does not change His mind and does not lie either. It's still a matter of reaping what a man sows. If you sow laughter, you will reap more laughter. In the same way, if you sow anger and resentment, you will reap more of those. If you sow sluggishness and refuse to put your hands to the plough, you will reap poverty and shame. If you believe the quote, that "As a man thinketh so is he," and believe that you can become wealthy without scheming, you will reap that too.

GOD'S COVENANT WITH SOLOMON

When Solomon was told to *"Ask for whatever you want me to give you"* in a dream, he asked for *"a discerning heart to govern your people and to distinguish between right and wrong."* God on His part was pleased with what he asked and promised among other things that ***"If you walk in my ways and obey my statutes and commands as David your father did, I will give you a long life"*** *(I Kings 3:5-14).* We should know by now how David walked with God.

During the time of building the temple of the LORD, "*The word of the LORD came to Solomon: As for this temple you are building,* ***if you follow my decrees, carry out my regulations and keep all my commands and obey them, I will fulfil through you the promise I gave to David your father****. 13 And I will live among the Israelites and will not abandon my people Israel" (I Kings 6:11-13).*

At the completion of the temple, the LORD appeared to Solomon a second time to stress on the importance of walking before Him blamelessly without turning to the right or to the left:

> *As for you,* ***IF you walk before me in integrity of heart and uprightness****, as David your father did,* ***and do all I command, and observe all my decrees and laws****, 5 I will establish your royal throne over Israel for ever, as I promised David your father when I said, 'You shall never fail to have a man on the throne of Israel.*
>
> *6* ***But if you or your sons turn away from me and do not observe the commands and decrees I have given you and go off to serve other gods and worship them,*** *7* ***then I will cut off Israel from the land I have given them and will reject this temple I have consecrated for my Name.*** *Israel will then become a byword and an object of ridicule among all peoples. 8 And though this temple is now imposing, all who pass by will be appalled and will scoff and say, 'Why has the LORD (not Satan) done such a thing to this land and to this temple?' 9* ***People will answer, 'Because they have forsaken the LORD their God,*** *who brought their fathers out of Egypt, and have embraced other gods, worshipping and serving them—****that is why the LORD*** *(not evil spirits)* ***brought all this disaster on them.*** *(I Kings 9:4-9)*

King Solomon began his journey with the LORD well but could not complete it with Him. ***"As Solomon grew old, his wives turned his heart after other gods, and his heart was not fully devoted to the LORD his God, as the heart of David his father had been"*** *(I Kings 11:4).* We need to see from this scenario whether God accepted the change in Solomon's attitude from how he started it.

> ***The LORD became angry with Solomon because his heart had turned away from the LORD*** *. . . 10 Although He had forbidden Solomon to follow other gods,* ***Solomon did not follow the LORD'S command****. 11 So the LORD said to Solomon, "Since this is your attitude and you have not kept my covenant and my decrees, which I commanded you, I will most certainly tear the*

> *kingdom away from you and give it to one of your subordinates.*
> *12 Nevertheless, for the sake of David your father, I will not do it during your lifetime. I will tear it out of the hand of your son. 13 Yet I will not tear the whole kingdom from him, but will give him one tribe for the sake of David my servant and for the sake of Jerusalem, which I have chosen." (I Kings 11:9-13)*

The kingdom of Judah passed on to Solomon's son Rehoboam and the other ten tribes of Israel went to Jeroboam. The LORD said to Jeroboam through a prophet that *"I tore the kingdom away from the house of David and gave it to you, but you have not been like my servant David who kept my commands and followed me with all his heart,* ***doing only what was right in my eyes****. 9 You have done more evil than all who lived before you. You have made for yourself other gods, idols made of metal; you have provoked me to anger and thrust me behind your back. 10 And because of this, I am going to bring disaster on the house of Jeroboam . . . 15 And the LORD will strike Israel, so that it will be like a reed swaying in the water: He will uproot Israel from this good land that He gave to their forefathers and scatter them beyond the River, because they provoked the LORD to anger by making Asherah poles. 16 And He will give Israel up because of the sins Jeroboam has committed and has caused Israel to commit" (I Kings 14:8-10, 15-16).*

> *"The Bible is my church. It is always open, and there is my High Priest ever waiting to receive me."—Charlotte Elliott (1789-1871)*

Now, under the kingship of Rehoboam the son of Solomon in Judah,

> *Judah did evil in the eyes of the LORD. By the sins they committed they stirred up His jealous anger more than their fathers had done. 23 They also set up for themselves high places, sacred stones and Asherah poles on every high hill and under every spreading tree. 24* ***There were even male shrine prostitutes in the land: the people engaged in all the detestable practices of the nations the LORD had driven out before the Israelites.****" (1 Kings 14:22-24)*

If you are one of those who do not believe the Bible's stance that there is nothing new under the sun, read those verses again. The people engaged themselves in all detestable practices one could think of to the extent that there were even legal male prostitutes with licences to ply their trade where women could rather pay for their services. If you think gayness and lesbianism is the final slot, then you haven't seen anything yet. Go surfing on the internet to know how far we've come. The worst is yet to come if people are not restrained in doing whatever seems right in their eyes.

After the death of Rehoboam, Abijah his son succeeded him but continued in the footsteps of his father by sinning against God. *"He committed all the sins his father had done before him; his heart was not fully devoted to the LORD his God, as the heart of David his forefather had been. 4 Nevertheless, for David's sake the LORD his God gave him a lamp in Jerusalem by raising up a son to succeed him and by making Jerusalem strong" (1 Kings 15:3-4).*

This continued for ages that one king will rise and follow the statutes of God and the land will be blessed in the process, and another king will succeed him and follow his own heart by worshipping idols, leading to God's wrath on the land. In the end, the LORD sent them into exile because He could no longer stand them again. I could go on and list what all the kings did but I don't want to "bore" you with this. But I will plead with you to take it upon yourself to read the two books of *1 Kings and 2 Kings* to learn how they all fared and how God responded to them.

But sending them into exile was not the end of the story. He was only waiting for them to realise how filthy they had become in their sins to turn back to Him. He could not desert them forever because of the covenant He had with Abraham, Isaac, Jacob and David. It was simply impossible for God to totally annihilate the descendants of the patriarchs and not make His promises made to them come to pass. That was out of the equation.

David prayed that *"Those who devise wicked schemes are near, but they are far from your law. 151 Yet you are near, O LORD, and all your commands are true. 152 Long ago I learned from your statutes that you established them to last forever" (Psalm 119:150-152). "He is the LORD our God; His judgments are in all the earth. 8* ***He remembers His covenant forever, the words He commanded, for a thousand generations,*** *9* ***the covenant He made with Abraham, the oath He swore to Isaac.*** *10* ***He confirmed it to Jacob as a decree, to Israel as an everlasting covenant:*** *11 'To you I will give the land of Canaan as the portion you will inherit'" (Psalm 105:7-11).*

A generation in the Bible is at least forty years. So if the covenant made with Abraham and his descendants was to last for at least a thousand years, then that would total forty thousand years. And man is barely six thousand years old. The journey to know God has barely started. This covenant between God and His children was confirmed to Israel as an everlasting covenant, which will never be revoked.

> *The LORD swore an oath to David,* ***a sure oath that He will not revoke****: "One of your own descendants I will place on your*

> *throne—12* ***if your sons keep my covenant and the statutes I teach them, then their sons shall sit on your throne forever and ever."*** *13* ***For the LORD has chosen Zion, He has desired it for His dwelling:*** *14* ***"This is my resting place forever and ever; here I will sit enthroned, for I have desired it****—15 I will bless her with abundant provisions; her poor will I satisfy with food." (Psalm 132:11-15)*

After AD 70 when Israel was sent into exile, and there was no nation called like that on earth until 1948, the so-called theologians of the day introduced their own interpretations of the Scriptures with all sorts of teachings regarding the Israelites or Jews who were the descendants of Abraham. The famous replacement doctrine came into being where they replaced Israel with the Gentile nations who had the gospel of Christ because there was no nation to represent Israel to fulfil the promises in the Bible as they were scattered all over the earth.

Others developed hatred for the Jews because they accused them of killing Jesus Christ and started making life difficult for them all over Europe and the rest of the world. But the Jews will forever remain on this earth. All of them are yet to enter the promise land. But, even if they should go back there and continue in their sinful ways like their ancestors did, they would still be banished from the land until they repent again. I'll recommend you read Pastor John Hagee's book, *"In Defence of Israel,"* to have a detailed understanding of how the Israelites have fared over the years in exile.

> *This is what the LORD says, He who appoints the sun to shine by day, who decrees the moon and stars to shine by night, who stirs up the sea so that its waves roar—the LORD Almighty is His name: 36* ***"Only if these decrees vanish from my sight," declares the LORD, "will the descendants of Israel ever cease to be a nation before me."*** *(Jer. 31:35-36)*

Until the waves of the sea cease to roar or the sun stops shinning or the moon and stars stop carrying out their assignments, both physical and spiritual Israel will remain intact for all generations. All the noise being made to wipe it off the map of the world and push them into the sea has been made since the time of Moses but Israel still remains. Israel can only be destroyed from within by following after the sinful nature of their ancestors. No outside force can ever destroy Israel. It can only be destroyed from within! God only sends nations to attack and defeat them as punishment for their sins. *"Judah will be inhabited forever and Jerusalem through all generations"*

(Joel 3:20). A nation that desires to see long days should embrace the Jews, for they have the keys for longevity.

> *"It is a great thing, this reading of Scriptures! For it is not possible to ever exhaust the mind of the Scriptures. It is a well that has no bottom."—John Chrysostom (C. 347-407)*

Chapter Twenty-Four

A NEW COVENANT BETWEEN GOD AND ISRAEL

So far, we've learnt that when God called the Israelites out of Egypt, He intended for them to inherit the land He promised their ancestors forever if only they would live according to His statutes and commands given through Moses. They failed and were banished from the land and sent into exile. Did that mean God failed and the devil had triumphed over Him? Did He change His mind and went in for a plan "B"? The Bible answers this question through the sayings of the prophets who lived in the midst of all the wrongs the children of Israel had engaged themselves in. God Himself tells us to:

> *"Remember this, fix it in mind, take it to heart, you rebels. 9* ***Remember the former things, those of long ago****; I am God, and there is no other; I am God, and there is none like me. 10* ***I make known the end from the beginning, from ancient times, what is still to come. I say: My purpose will stand, and I will do all that I please.*** *11 From the east I summon a bird of prey; from a far-off land, a man to fulfill my purpose.* ***What I have said, that will I bring about; what I have planned, that will I do"*** *(Isa. 46:8-11).*

No matter how sinful the children of Israel had become, God had no choice but to find a way to fulfil His promises to the patriarchs. There was no excuse for Him to disappoint the patriarchs and He could not utterly destroy their descendants from the face of the earth too. That could not happen. Whatever happened, a remnant would still have to be left behind because of the patriarchs. It is written:

> *The LORD will have compassion on Jacob; once again He will choose Israel and will settle them in their own land.* ***Aliens will join them***

> ***and unite with the house of Jacob.*** *2 Nations will take them and bring them to their own place. And the house of Israel will possess the nations as menservants and maidservants in the LORD'S land. They will make captives of their captors and rule over their oppressors." (Isaiah 14:1-2)*

At first, Abraham was supposed to be the father of the nation of Israel. Later, he was told to become the father of many nations. God is saying through Isaiah in this prophesy that *"Aliens* (or Gentiles) *will join them (Israel) and unite with the house of Jacob."* This is where the Jews also made the mistake, as they became selfish and wanted to keep God to themselves. This was later to become a bone of contention between them and Paul. But God says: *"Surely, as I have planned, so it will be, and as I have purposed, so it will stand . . . 27 For the LORD Almighty has purposed, and who can thwart Him? His hand is stretched out, and who can turn it back?" (Isaiah 14:24, 27). In days to come Jacob will take root, Israel will bud and blossom* ***and fill all the world with fruit*** *(Isaiah 27:6).*

As people from the Gentile nations are introduced to the gospel of the Kingdom of God, the knowledge of God will be revealed to all men no matter what part of the world they recide and the one nation that started from Abraham will grow to cover many nations but under the same God.

> *"In the Old Testament the New is concealed, in the New Testament the Old is revealed."—St. Augustine of Hippo (354-430)*

Chapter Twenty-Five

THE REASONS BEHIND ISRAEL'S EXILES

"The grass withers and the flowers fall, but the word of our God stands forever" (Isaiah 40:8). So much of the causal agents of God's anger and the remedies are hidden in the first chapter of the book of Isaiah the prophet. Although everything seemed bleak at the time of the kings who lived after David, God gave the redemptive tools to take them back when He said, ***"Zion will be redeemed with justice, her penitent ones with righteousness"*** *(Isa. 1:27).* Why was Zion going to be redeemed by these two traits? Let's give the microphone to God and hear what He has to say to that:

> *See how the faithful city has become a harlot!* ***She once was full of justice; righteousness used to dwell in her—but now murderers! . . .*** *23 Your rulers are rebels, companions of thieves; they all love bribes and chase after gifts. They do not defend the cause of the fatherless; the widow's case does not come before them. Therefore the LORD, the LORD Almighty, the Mighty One of Israel, declares: Ah, I will get relief from my foes and avenge myself on my enemies. 25 I will turn my hand against you; I will thoroughly purge away your dross and remove all your impurities. 26 I will restore your judges as in days of old, your counsellors as at the beginning.* ***Afterwards you will be called the City of Righteousness, the Faithful City.*** *(Isa. 1:21-26)*

TRANSFORMING A SINFUL NATION TO A CITY OF RIGHTEOUSNESS

Please note very carefully the tools or the requirements being used by God to transform *"a sinful nation, a people loaded with guilt, a brood of evildoers, children given to corruption" (Isa. 1:4)* into *"the City of Righteousness, the Faithful City"* in *verse 26.* In my short years that I have lived, I have learned that so much of the future lies hidden in the study of the past or what is referred to as history. *"Study history, study history—in history lie all the secrets of statecraft."*—Winston Churchill

We are often told today that the way to righteousness on earth is through, among other things, prayer, fasting, giving cash to God's ministry (bribing Him?) and binding the devil. But God told our forefathers that *"When you spread out your hands in prayer, I will hide my eyes from you;* ***even if you offer many prayers, I will not listen*** *" (Isa. 1:15).*

Does that sound contradictory to what Paul said in the New Testament to pray without ceasing? No! The simple truth is that there are some dos and don'ts of prayer. From my personal observations, over 90% of the prayer sessions I've witnessed are done in vain—out of ignorance. You can't bribe God, faking piety and offering Him gifts to have answers to prayer. The reason God is not going to answer some prayers is that ***"Your hands are full of blood,"*** so He says:

> *Wash and make yourselves clean.* ***Take your evil deeds out of my sight! Stop doing wrong,*** *17* ***learn to do right! Seek justice, encourage the oppressed. Defend the cause of the fatherless, plead the case of the widow.*** *(Isa. 1:16-17)*

After meeting this requirement of making yourself clean by taking your evil deeds out of His sight, abstaining from wrongdoing, living a righteous life, seeking justice at all times, encouraging the oppressed in society and defending the cause of the poor and vulnerable in your locality, what happens next? It is then that God Himself invites you to:

> ***"Come now, let us reason together,"*** *says the LORD. "Though your (previous) sins are like scarlet, they shall be as white as snow; though they are red as crimson, they shall be like wool. 19* ***If you are willing and obedient, you will eat the best from the land;*** *20* ***but if you resist and rebel, you will be devoured by the sword.*** *" For the mouth of the LORD has spoken. (Isa. 1:18-20)*

"But if you resist and rebel, you will be devoured by the sword." You are not likely to hear stuffs like these nowadays, because of the wrong understanding of Scriptural verses, like *"If we claim to be without sin, we deceive ourselves and the truth is not in us" (1 John 1:8).* God never tolerated sin. He does not tolerate it today, and will never tolerate it in the future. *"He who is the Glory*

of Israel does not lie or change His mind; ***for He is not a man, that He should change His mind*** *" (1 Sam. 15:29).*

It is written about God: ***"You are not a God who takes pleasure in evil; with you the wicked cannot dwell.*** *5* ***The arrogant cannot stand in your presence; you hate all who do wrong.*** *6* ***You destroy those who tell lies; bloodthirsty and deceitful men the LORD abhors*** *" (Psalm 5:4-6).* Whether you are led by the Holy Spirit or not, if you take pleasure in doing evil, the LORD hates you, and will destroy you some time to come. You are fasting and praying in vain if you will not stop sinning. You simply cannot dwell in God's presence with stains on your hands.

To hate is to dislike something or somebody very much. To abhor is to detest or loathe something. It's a feeling of strong hatred, especially for moral reasons. To destroy is to damage something so badly that it no longer exists or works. Now, the Scriptures say that because the LORD does not take pleasure in evil, He hates and abhors those who engage in them and for that matter will destroy them in the end.

WARNING TO SINNERS AND ABUSERS OF SCRIPTURES

If you happen to be one of those Christians who pretend to be members of the faith, attend church services, make noise in peoples' hearing with self righteousness, and always quote from God's Scriptures to cover up your sins, read this:

> ***But to the wicked, God says: "What right have you to recite my laws or take my covenant on your lips?*** *17* ***You hate my instruction and cast my words behind you.*** *18 When you see a thief, you join with him; you throw in your lot with adulterers. 19 You use your mouth for evil and harness your tongue to deceit. 20 You speak continually against your brother and slander your own mother's son. 21* ***These things you have done and I kept silent; you thought I was altogether like you. But I will rebuke you and accuse you to your face.*** *22* ***consider this, you who forget God, or I will tear you to pieces, with none to rescue."*** *(Psalm 50:16-22)*

"Why do you boast of evil, *you mighty man? Why do you boast all day long,* ***you who are a disgrace in the eyes of God?*** *2 Your tongue plots destruction; it is like a sharpened razor, you who practise deceit. 3* ***You love evil rather than good, falsehood rather than speaking the truth.*** *4 You love every harmful word, O you deceitful tongue! 5* ***Surely God will bring you***

down to everlasting ruin*: He will snatch you up and tear you from your tent;* ***He will uproot you from the land of the living****. 6 The righteous will see and fear; they will laugh at him saying, 7 Here now is the man who did not make God his stronghold but trusted in his great wealth and grew strong by destroying others" (Psalm 52:1-7).*

"Cast your cares on the LORD and He will sustain you; He will never let the righteous fall. 23 ***But you, O God, will bring down the wicked into the pit of corruption; bloodthirsty and deceitful men will not live out half their days"*** *(Psalm 55:22-23).* ***"The senseless man does not know, fools do not understand,*** *7* ***that though the wicked spring up like grass and all evildoers flourish, they will be forever destroyed"*** *(Psalm 92:6-7). "If the righteous receive their due on earth, how much more the ungodly and the sinner!" (Prov. 11:31).*

"A man cannot be established through wickedness*, but the righteous cannot be uprooted" (Prov. 12:3).* ***"The house of the wicked will be destroyed****, but the tent of the upright will flourish" (Prov. 14:11).* ***"Evil men will bow down in the presence of the good, and the wicked at the gates of the righteous"*** *(Prov. 14:19). "Do not those who plot evil go astray? But those who plan what is good find love and faithfulness" (Prov. 14:22).* ***"He who conceals his sins does not prosper, but whoever confesses and renounces them finds mercy"*** *(Prov. 28:13).*

"Although a wicked man commits a hundred crimes and still lives a long time, I know that it will go better with God-fearing men, who are reverent before God*. 13 Yet* ***because the wicked do not fear God, it will not go well with them, and their days will not lengthen, like a shadow"*** *(Eccl. 8:12-13).*

"Do you not know that the wicked *(or the sinner)* ***will not inherit the kingdom of God? Do not be deceived****: Neither the sexually immoral nor idolaters nor adulterers nor male prostitutes nor homosexual offenders 10 nor thieves nor the greedy nor drunkards nor slanderers nor swindlers will inherit the kingdom of God. 11* ***And that is what some of you were*** *(in the past). But you were washed, you were sanctified, you were justified in the Name of the LORD Jesus Christ and by the Spirit of our God" (1 Cor. 6:9-11).* Being a Jew or Christian does not matter. Once you engage in these things, you are wicked in the sight of God and are hated. You are being deceived if you think otherwise.

After reading these verses, you should now know what to say to anyone who reads John's letter: *"If we claim to be without sin, we deceive ourselves and the truth is not in us" (1 John 1:9)* to mean that you must wake up each morning expecting to commit sins and confess them to Jesus for forgiveness in the evening. Just look deeply into the person's eyes and you will be able to discern where he is coming from and who he is working for. It's the same distortion of the Bible to support the idea that, "*It's dull being good all the time. So why not spice up life with a little mischief. . . We need lies for the world to function and to smooth the interaction between us. Lies are the lubricant that dampens the friction that total honesty brings.*"

God has had His simple way of dealing with sin and sinners from past and present generations. "*By warfare and exile you contend with her—with His fierce blast He drives her out, as on a day the east wind blows. 9* ***By this, then, is Jacob's guilt be atoned for, and this will be the full fruitage of the removal of his sin:*** *When he makes all the altar stones to be like chalk stones crushed to pieces, no Asherah poles or incense altars will be left standing. 11* ***For this is a people without understanding; so the Maker has no compassion on them, and their Creator shows them no favour****" (Isa. 27:8-9, 11).*

Righteousness and justice are the two most important requirements for the establishment of a kingdom that even when the Queen of Sheba visited King Solomon, she identified these two as the purposes for which God established Solomon's throne. She said, "*Praise be to the LORD your God, who has delighted in you and placed you on the throne of Israel.* ***Because of the LORD'S eternal love for Israel, He has made you king to maintain justice and righteousness*** *(1 Kings 10:9).*

> . *"The Bible grows more beautiful, as we grow in our understanding of it."—Johann Wolfgang Von Goethe (1749-1832)*

Chapter Twenty-Six

BIBLICAL DEFINITION OF RIGHTEOUSNESS

Solomon, the wisest man who ever lived before Christ wrote: "*Kings detest wrongdoing, **for a throne is established through righteousness**" (Prov. 16:12). **In the way of righteousness there is life, along that path is immortality** (Prov. 12:28). **Righteousness exalts a nation,** but **sin is a disgrace to any people** (Prov. 14:34). **The fruit of righteousness will be peace; the effect of righteousness will be quietness and confidence forever** (Isa. 32:17).*

Just what is righteousness anyway, and how can an individual or a nation attain it? There are several definitions given to this word that one cannot choose what to believe again. There is also a doctrine that portrays the belief that it is simply impossible for one to live a righteous life in our day. The preachers of that belief take Job chapter 25 out of context, and this forms their stance. But the truth is that God has His own definition of righteousness and He also tells us what one will do to attain it. It is written: *"Just as He who called you is holy, so be holy in all you do; 16 for it is written: 'Be holy, because I am holy'" (1 Pet. 1:15-16).* But the truth is that God has His own definition of righteousness and He also tells us what one will do to attain it.

CHARACTERISTICS OF THE RIGHTEOUS

The positive effects of righteousness on an individual or a nation cannot be over emphasised. Asking the questions of who may dwell in His sanctuary and live on His holy hill, God, through the mouth of David said:

> *LORD who may dwell in your sanctuary? Who may live on your holy hill? 2 He whose walk is blameless and who does what is righteous,*

> *who speaks the truth from his heart 3 and has no slander on his tongue, who does his neighbor no wrong and casts no slur on his fellow-man, 4 who despises a vile man but honors those who fear the LORD, who keeps His oath even when it hurts, 5 who lends his money without usury and does not accept a bribe against the innocent.* ***He who does these things will never be shaken*** *(Psalm 15:1-5).*

According to the Creator, anyone who has the right to dwell in His sanctuary (or Church) or live on His holy hill (city or nation?) is the one who does what is righteous, walks blamelessly, and speaks the truth from his heart. Such a person must not be found slandering his fellow man and also be a man who does his neighbor no wrong. He or she must keep his word even when it hurts, fear the LORD and despise all evils done on earth. Such a man must not lend money at usury and should not take any bribe to thwart a case against the innocent. Is this hard or difficult for a Christian to do?

This is clear and goes straight to the point but Ezekiel did a very wonderful work by putting down the various qualities of what makes a righteous man. The definition of a righteous man is categorically given in the Scriptures. So is that of a sinner. There are myriads of teachings on who a sinner is. But the sad news is that no two of these teachings from some of the modern-day *super-apostles* are the same though they come from the same spirit.

> ***"Suppose there is a righteous man who does what is just and right.*** *6 He does not eat at the mountain shrines or look to the idols of the house of Israel.* ***He does not defile his neighbour's wife or lie with a woman during her period.*** *7* ***He does not oppress anyone, but returns what he took in pledge for a loan.*** *He does not commit robbery, but gives his food to the hungry and provides clothing for the naked. 8* ***He does not lend at usury or take excessive interest. He withholds his hand from doing wrong and judges fairly between man and man.*** *9* ***He follows my decrees and faithfully keeps my laws. THAT MAN IS RIGHTEOUS;*** *he will surely live, declares the Sovereign LORD." (Ezek. 18:5-9)*

This is just plain and simple language which is straight to the point. The last time I asked a teacher of the Bible to give me the definition of a righteous man, I ended up feeling dizzy at the long elaborations given. One does not need the Hebrew words translated in the above verses to understand what is being communicated to us by the Creator. You are either a righteous person or you are not, according to the Creator's standard, period.

A righteous man does not sleep with his neighbor's wife or sleep with a woman in her menstrual cycle for his own health. He pays back whatever he owes others and abhors bribing or cheating in all its various forms like in examinations at school. Feeding and clothing the poor in society are two of his major priorities. He does not worship any idol that will require him to offer his own children as sacrifices for other gods.

To lend at usury is the practice of lending money to people at unfairly high rates of interest. A righteous man does not charge these high interest rates on loans given out to the needy in the land. How do you expect a poor man to repay a thirty per cent rate on a given loan and still have something to live on? The borrower must not become the slave of the lender just because he (the borrower) is poor. It is written that *"The borrower is servant to the lender."*

Do you now see why you are always told that it is impossible to live a righteous life? The reason is simply because those teaching this subject of righteousness find it hard to keep up with God's standards themselves that they feel they have to lower it to their own level. Some of them are on boards of banks and lend at usury to rob the poor. Others too can't stay away from peoples' wives so they can't preach righteousness to you. How can the blind lead the blind without the two of them falling into a ditch?

> *"It is the best gift God has given to men. All the good Saviour gave to the world was communicated through this book. But for it we could not know right from wrong. All things desirable for man's welfare, here and hereafter, are to be found portrayed in it."—Abraham Lincoln (1809-1865)*

We've all heard of fire consuming the godless who refuse to walk according to the ways of God. Isaiah revealed to us what to do to escape such a burning. He asked, "***Who of us can dwell with the consuming fire?*** *Who of us can dwell with everlasting burning? 15* ***He who walks righteously and speaks what is right, who rejects gain from extortion and keeps his hand from accepting bribes, who stops his ears against plots of murder and shuts his eyes against contemplating evil***—*16* ***this is the man who will dwell on the heights, whose refuge will be the mountain fortress. His bread will be supplied, and water will not fail him***" *(Isa. 33:14-16).*

Isn't that plain and simple language to understand? Do you still need prayer and fasting to understand this? All these things are in the Old Testament. Now, which part of this sounds or feels like a yoke of bondage and is dragging you into the bottom of the sea? Is it the part not to sleep with your neighbor's wife or the part to feed and clothe the poor and needy if you can afford it? Or is it about not lending at usury? My major concern for writing this book is to do my very best not to judge anyone. My number one priority is to provoke you into reading the Bible for yourself, and stop listening to what most of the *"super-apostles"* are saying, which are mostly contrary to what the Bible actually teaches.

Jeremiah wrote that: *"Let not the wise man boast of his wisdom or the strong man boast of his strength or the rich man boast of his riches, 24* ***but let him who boasts boast about this: that he understands and knows me, that I am the LORD, who exercises kindness, justice and righteousness on earth, for in these I delight,****" declares the LORD (Jer. 9:23-24).* What does the LORD delight in? From Genesis to Revelation, God remains the same and does not change. He delights in righteous living on the part of us who occupy the face of the earth.

> ***Submit to God and be at peace with Him; in this way prosperity will come to you.*** *22 Accept instruction from His mouth and lay up His words in your heart. 23* ***If you return to the Almighty, you will be restored: If you remove wickedness far from your tent*** *24 and assign your nuggets to the dust, your gold of Ophir to the rocks in the ravines, 25* ***then*** *the Almighty will be your gold, the choicest silver for you. 26 Surely then you will find delight in the Almighty and will lift up your face to God. 27 You will pray to Him, and He will hear you, and you will fulfill your vows. 28* ***What you decide on will be done, and light will shine on your ways.*** *29 When men are brought low and you say, 'Lift them up!' then He will save the downcast. 30* ***He will deliver even one who is not innocent,*** *who will be delivered* ***through the cleanness of your hands.*** *(Job 22:21-30)*

Nothing on earth, including *"grace"* can take the place of righteous living when it comes to the relationship between God and man. The very foundation of God's throne is established on righteousness, justice, love and faithfulness. Take away these and God does not exist. That is why Scripture says: *"Zion will be redeemed with justice (not binding demons), her penitent ones with righteousness (not fasting and prayer or tithing)" (Isa. 1:27).* ***Righteousness and justice are the foundation of your throne;*** *love and faithfulness go before you (Psalm 89:14).* Total righteousness (the application of God's principles) and justice on a particular land takes away any power from either the devil, demons or witches. *Clouds and thick darkness surround Him;* ***righteousness and justice are the foundation of His throne*** *(Psalm 97:2).*

TAKING A CUE FROM OUR RIGHTEOUS FATHERS

If you desire to build a throne of your own today, start laying the foundation of righteousness and see what tomorrow will bring. Anthony Robbins wrote, *"Success leaves clues."* Paul wrote to us that: *"These things happened to them as examples and were written down as warnings for us, on whom the fulfillment of the ages has come" (1 Cor. 10:11).* We can look into the lives of some of the successful men in the Scriptures to emulate their footsteps if we also want to be like them. One of such men is David.

> *If you do whatever I command you and walk in my ways and do what is right in my eyes by keeping my statutes and commands,* ***as David my servant did****, I will be with you. I will build you a dynasty as enduring as the one I built for David and will give Israel to you. (1 Sam. 11:38)*

The Queen of Sheba was inspired to say to Solomon that *"Praise be to the LORD your God, who has delighted in you and placed you on the throne of Israel. Because of the LORD'S eternal love for Israel,* ***He has made you king, to maintain justice and righteousness****" (1 Kings 10:9).* You see, the purpose for which the third king after Saul was enthroned was that he was placed there to maintain God's throne on earth just as it is done in heaven. Jesus also told us to pray "your kingdom come, ***your will be done on earth as it is in heaven***" (Matt. 6:10). All these were in the Bible before the birth of our LORD and Saviour Jesus Christ. The Pharisees and teachers of the law knew everything about these but were not following them, because of their selfish intentions.

Even Jesus Christ our LORD and Saviour was set above His companions because He loved righteousness. It was (and is still) the power of His kingdom. It is written: *"But about the Son He says, Your throne, O God, will last forever and ever, and* ***righteousness will be the sceptre of your kingdom. 9 You*** *(Jesus)* ***have loved righteousness and hated wickedness; therefore GOD*** *(the Father)****, YOUR GOD has set you*** *(Jesus)* ***above your companions by anointing you with the oil of joy****" (Heb. 1:8-9).*

> *"You do well not to let drop from your hands the polished mirror of the holy Gospel of your LORD, for it provides the likeness of everyone who looks into it . . . . There the kingdom of heaven is depicted, visible to those who have a luminous eye."—Ephraem the Syrian (c. 303-373)*

The Bible is a complete book! It is meant for the whole of mankind and not just Christians or Jews alone. It was Adam's responsibility to live to the expectations of God but he lost it along the line. It's our turn now, and it is our responsibilities to stop blaming him and do the right thing that is expected of us today. All that Jesus Christ was coming to do has been plainly written down in the pages of the Old Testament. There is not a single thing Jesus Christ did that is not penned down in the pages of the Old Testament Scriptures. Once again, the Sanhedrin had their hidden agenda regarding Christ.

A typical example of the loss of righteousness and justice on the land was their nullification of the word of God by setting them aside so they could observe their own traditions, which had become a *"yoke of bondage"* to the people. For instance, they refused the healing of a whole man on the Sabbath day although they themselves would deliver their sheep if it fell into a ditch. Jesus Christ made sure He gave it to them by insulting their hypocrisy.

JESUS TO ESTABLISH THE KINGDOM WITH JUSTICE AND RIGHTEOUSNESS

> *For to us a child is born, to us a son is given, and the government will be on His shoulders. And He will be called Wonderful Counselor, Mighty God, Everlasting Father, Prince of Peace. 7 Of the increase of His government and peace there will be no end.* ***He will reign on David's throne and over his kingdom, establishing and upholding it with justice and righteousness from that time on and forever****. The zeal of the LORD Almighty will accomplish this. (Isa. 9:6-7)*

David prayed: *"May my tongue sing of your word, for all your commands are righteous" (Psalm 119:172).* Jesus never hides the fact that He was sent by God the Father to do His will. In the above verses, we are told that He was to reign on David's throne and over his kingdom. Not only was He going to do that but also to establish and uphold it with some two things from that time on forever. Those two items are righteousness and justice. Jesus didn't come to issue out licenses for us to engage ourselves in sins and later ask Him to forgive us. He rather came to put an end to it. He came to free us from our sinful nature that was prone to sins.

When the angel who spoke with Mary gave her the promise of becoming the mother of the Saviour, this is what he said, *"You will be with child and give birth to a Son, and you are to give Him the name Jesus. 32 He will be great and will be called the Son of the Most High. The LORD God will give Him the throne of His father David, 33 and He will reign over the house of Jacob forever;* ***His kingdom will never end"*** *(Luke 1:31-33).*

Now if His kingdom will never end and He was to establish and uphold it with justice and righteousness from that time on, then where are we today? His kingdom started from at least the day He was resurrected from the dead. *"He will not judge by what He sees with His eyes, or decide by what He hears with His ears; 4* ***but with righteousness He will judge the needy, with justice He will give decisions for the poor of the earth . . . 5 Righteousness will be His belt*** *and faithfulness the sash round His waist" (Isa. 11:3-5).*

One of Jesus' names is *"Prince of Peace."* Isaiah wrote that: ***"The fruit of righteousness will be peace; the effect of righteousness will be quietness and confidence forever"*** *(Isa. 32:17).* That should tell us how Jesus Christ obtained the Name *"Prince of Peace"*—through righteousness, of course! Christ is going to judge us according to the righteous deeds we do and not on the noise we make on earth as being saved. Holding mega crusades in pagan countries which do not yield fruits of righteousness in the land is just a noisy mega crusade.

Zephaniah wrote that *"Seek the LORD, all you humble of the land, you who do what He commands.* ***Seek righteousness****, seek humility; perhaps you will be sheltered on the day of the LORD'S anger" (Zeph. 2:3).* Even if you think you are not righteous today, you should make it your topmost priority to seek it with all your spirit, soul and body and you will surely find it. Do not be deceived. If Moses of all prophets could not step foot on the promised land because of anger, what is so special about you that you think Jesus Christ, who has never sinned before, would like to associate Himself with you? True Judaism and True Christianity are not about the quantity or numbers. It's about quality and purity of life manifesting in righteousness, leading to holiness. If God were only interested in the numbers, He would take the gospel to China and India first.

Without righteousness, all the hypocrisy of such pious living by the religious folks is done in vain. It's in such moments that all the sacrifices and offerings used to bribe God, like tithes, offerings, fake tears, become unnecessary and abhorrent to His nostrils. Personally, I feel I know exactly what Jesus would say to some people if He were here in person. He would say that *"You hypocrites! Isaiah was right when he prophesied about you: 'These people honour me with their lips, but their hearts are far from me. 9 They worship me in vain; their teachings are but rules taught by men'" (Matt. 15:7-9).*

> *"The multitude of your sacrifices—what are they to me?" says the LORD. "I have more than enough of burnt offerings, of rams and the fat of fattened animals; I have no pleasure in the blood of bulls*

> *and lambs and goats. 12* ***When you come to appear before me, who has asked this of you, this trampling of my courts?*** *13* ***Stop bringing meaningless offerings!*** *Your incense is detestable to me. New Moons, Sabbaths and convocations—****I cannot bear your evil assemblies.*** *14 Your New Moon festivals and your appointed feasts my soul hates. They have become a burden to me; I am weary of bearing them.* ***When you spread out your hands in prayer, I will hide my eyes from you; even if you offer many prayers, I will not listen. Your hands are full of blood;*** *16* ***wash and make yourselves clean. Take your evil deeds out of my sight! Stop doing wrong,*** *17* ***learn to do right! Seek justice, encourage the oppressed. Defend the cause of the fatherless, plead the case of the widow.****" (Isa. 1:11-17)*

All these were basic truths in the Scriptures which had to be followed by the citizens of the land but the Pharisees and teachers of the law who were to do the teaching had become corrupt and had become blind, in the process. Everything became polluted, as there was no-one to teach the right way of God. The Almighty had to come in again to rectify the situation, like He did in the days of Adam, Noah and Lot in Sodom and Gomorrah.

> *"God chose to use human effort and inclination, and earthly disciplines of writing and recording, as He chooses to use all worthy human work. He took the biblical author's skills, sanctified them, and used them for this glory in the transmission of His Word to future generations, including us."—Isabel Sanders Throop*

CHAPTER TWENTY-SEVEN

THE LOSS!

Then Peter began to speak: "I now realise how true it is that God does not show favouritism 35 ***but accepts men from every nation who fear Him and do what is right****" (Acts 10:34-35).* God's main purpose for creating man was for him to be fruitful and increase in number from the mustard seed stage, fill the earth and subdue it, rule over the fish of the sea and the birds of the air, and over every living creature that moves on the ground. Like we learned earlier, God used the mustard seed principle in putting Adam and Eve in the garden to procreate in order to do this. They failed Him in this regard and subsequent generations also followed in the same path. But for the covenant He made with Abraham, man would have been completely destroyed from God's presence.

After calling the children of Israel out of Egypt, He reminded them that it was not because of their righteousness that made Him choose them from all the people of the earth. Because of the oath He made with Abraham, Isaac, Jacob and David, He had bound Himself; He cannot revoke what He had said, because He does not change His mind. We also know that Israel was just the firstborn son of the nations promised Abraham. Like Adam, Israel was the first of the mustard seed nations planted with the idea of growing to cover the face of the earth. So even though the mustard seed planted could not make good use of the nutrients by listening to the voice of the Master Gardener to germinate well, the Gardener still had to make sure that Abraham became the father of many nations as promised.

> *If his sons forsake my law and do not follow my statutes, 31 if they violate my decrees and fail to keep my commands, 32 I will punish their sin with the rod, their iniquity with flogging; 33* ***but I will not take my love from him, nor will I ever betray my faithfulness.*** *34* ***I will not violate my covenant or alter what my lips have uttered.*** *(Psalm 89:30-34)*

Because of such promises, like these in the Bible, God had to find a way to restore the Israelites who are the firstborn sons of God and direct descendants of the patriarchs first and later come to deal with the rest of the Gentile nations who were to join later. Both the Israelites and the rest of mankind had lost the straight path to God and had lost everything, in the process.

> ***We have already made the charge that Jews and Gentiles alike are all under sin.*** *10 As it is written: "There is no-one righteous, not even one; 11 there is no-one who understands, no-one who seeks God. 12* ***All have turned away****, they have together become worthless; there is no-one who does good, not even one. 13 Their throats are open graves; their tongues practise deceit. The poison of vipers is on their lips. 14 Their mouths are full of cursing and bitterness. 15 Their feet are swift to shed blood; 16 ruin and misery mark their ways, 17 and the way of peace (with God) they do not know. 18 There is no fear of God before their eyes. (Rom. 3:9-18)*

The *"firstborn son,"* in addition to the rest of the Gentile world turned their backs on the Creator. Although He does not tolerate sin, He still could not utterly destroy them because He was constrained by what He had covenanted with the patriarchs. He decided to mend this all by Himself and return those He had sent into exile. We should again remind ourselves here that everything He promised them was to last forever and there was no way He was going to dishonour this, with the excuse that the patriarchs' descendants were responsible for the failure; still the promises had to stand: *"The LORD will be King over the whole earth. On that day there will be One LORD, and His Name the Only Name" (Zech. 14:9).*

REALLY UNDERSTANDING THE NEW COVENANT

> *"The time is coming," declares the LORD, "when I will make a new covenant with the house of Israel and with the house of Judah. 32 It will not be like the covenant I made with their forefathers . . ."33 This is the covenant that I will make with the house of Israel after that time," declares the LORD.* ***"I will put my law in their minds and write it on their hearts.*** *I will be their God, and they will be my people. 34 No longer will a man teach his neighbour, or a man his brother, saying, 'Know the LORD,' because they will all know me, from the least of them to the greatest," declares the LORD. (Jer. 31:31-34)*

This was a prophecy to be fulfilled in the future while the children of Israel were in exile. But because *"Judah will be redeemed by righteousness and justice"* and nothing else, they had to know the laws of God to be able to redeem themselves. They failed woefully when it was written on tablets of stone, and at the same time they had to be taught by someone who, like the Pharisees and teachers of the law, distorted them to suit their own selfish desires, leading to the downfall of the whole nation. So God said this time, He would put the same Law the forefathers had on stone tablets into the hearts and minds of everyone so that no-one would need the services of another man to do the teaching for him to understand the Scriptures.

> *"By reading the Scriptures I am so renewed that all nature seems renewed around me and with me. The sky seems to be a pure, a cooler blue, the trees a deeper green, light is sharper on the outlines of the forest and the hills. The whole world is charged with the glory of God, and I feel fire and music . . . . under my feet."—Thomas Merton (1915-1968)*

It is very important that you understand the content of this new covenant. If you comprehend it from this very moment, then you will cross a major milestone in your knowledge into the Bible. This is where most people get it wrong by spiritualising the whole concept of the new covenant as if it were a replacement of the old. The whole thing about the two covenants was about a change in position; nothing else. The same Laws that were written on stone tablets have now been transferred into the hearts and minds of the people:

> *Therefore say: 'This is what the Sovereign LORD says: I will gather you from the nations and bring you back from the countries where you have been scattered,* ***and I will give you back the land of Israel again.****' 18 "They will return to it and remove all its vile images and detestable idols. 19* ***I will give them an undivided heart and put a new spirit in them;*** *I will remove from them their heart of stone and give them a heart of flesh. 20* ***Then they will follow my decrees and be careful to keep my laws.*** *They will be my people, and I will be their God. 21 But as for those whose hearts are devoted to their vile images and detestable idols, I will bring down on their own heads what they have done, declares the Sovereign LORD." (Ezek. 11:17-21)*

The firstborn son was exiled because of disobedience to the laws and commands of the Creator. Since they could not be left in exile to rot, the

LORD had to take them back. But this time, He was to do something to help them follow His statutes by figuratively removing their hearts of stone and replacing them with a heart of flesh which has His own Spirit residing in them. And His Spirit was to enable them to follow His decrees and be careful to keep His laws. Isn't that plain to understand?

It didn't end there. He added again that if those who returned are still found doing the same things that prompted the exile, He would bring down on their heads what they do. Nothing changes! *"God is not man that He should change His mind."* Principles never change! God does not tolerate sin in any form. Lucifer and his angels were in heaven when they sinned, and they were "exiled." The children of Abraham sinned and were exiled as well. The location does not say anything; if you sin, you will be exiled and destroyed, in the process, leaving just a remnant whether in heaven or on earth.

Jesus Christ, our LORD and Saviour knew exactly what He was teaching when He taught His disciples to pray *"your kingdom come, your will be done on earth as it is in heaven" (Matt. 6:9-10).* Even if you should visit the throne room of the Most High God in heaven and sin there, you will be exiled. Going to heaven does not stop you from sinning. Don't forget that Brother Lucifer and the rest of those uncountable angels were in heaven but planned and actually executed the highest coup attempt of all time. That took place upstairs in the highest heavens. So those of you who think going to heaven will keep you from sinning should think again. A monkey is always a monkey, whether in coat and tie or not.

PURPOSE OF THE NEW COVENANT

The main purpose of the new covenant was to make everyone have access to the Law of God, which would be transferred from tablets of stones to the hearts and minds of the people to make it easier for everyone to obey.

When calling the children of Israel out of Egypt, God reminded them that it was because of the oath He swore to their forefathers that He was compelled to do so. The same way, in returning them from exile, He said: *"It is not for your sake, O house of Israel, that I am going to do these things, but for the sake of my Holy Name, which you have profaned among the nations where you have gone" (Ezek. 36:22).* He is still running affairs today just to hold in check the covenant He made with the patriarchs.

> *"For I will take you out of the nations; I will gather you from all the countries and bring you back into your own land. 25 I will sprinkle clean water on you, and you will be clean; I will cleanse you from all your impurities and from all your idols. 26 I will give you a new*

> *heart and put a new spirit in you; I will remove from you your heart of stone and give you a heart of flesh. 27* ***And I will put my Spirit in you and move you to follow my decrees and be careful to follow my laws."*** *(Ezek. 36:24-27)*

You see, it's only after the hearts of stones have been replaced with the hearts of flesh that the promised Holy Spirit of God is given to us. *Peter replied, "**Repent and be baptised every one of you,** in the Name of Jesus Christ for the forgiveness of your sins. **And you will receive the gift of the Holy Spirit**" (Acts 2:38).* Now, see what the Spirit of God is moving you to do. The presence of His Spirit in your heart, representing your whole being is to move you to be able to carefully follow the decrees and laws of God in the Scriptures. The Holy Spirit of God does not stay in you and give you the green light to now rather sin at will and claim you are under grace and not Law. Who taught you that—Jesus or Paul?

> *"My servant David will be king over them, and they will all have one shepherd.* ***They will follow my laws and be careful to keep my decrees.*** *25 They will live in the land I gave to my servant Jacob, the land where your fathers lived.* ***They and their children and their children's children will live there forever, and David my servant will be their prince forever.*** *26 I will make a covenant of peace with them; it will be an everlasting covenant. I will establish them and increase their numbers, and I will put my sanctuary among them forever. 27 My dwelling place will be with them; I will be their God, and they will be my people. 28 Then the nations will know that I the LORD make Israel holy, when my sanctuary is among them forever." (Ezek. 37:24-28)*

In the future when David will be resurrected to be their prince forever, the children of Israel will still be required to follow the laws of God and follow His decrees unabated. David said he learned a long time ago that the laws of God were established to last forever. But most of us do not see the wisdom in the Law; we choose to see only the *"eye for eye"* and *"tooth for tooth"* part, and that has blinded the whole of mankind. The same laws we find outdated today were the lights to David's feet that seven times a day, he thanked God for them. He wrote: *"Blessed is the man you discipline, O LORD,* ***the man you teach from your law;*** *13* ***you grant him relief from days of trouble,*** *till a pit is dug for the wicked" (Psalm 94:12-13).*

"To all serving in my Forces by sea, or land, or in the air, and indeed to all my people engaged in the defence of the Realm, I commend the reading of this book. For centuries the Bible has been a wholesome and strengthening influence in our national life, and it behoves on us in these momentous days to turn with renewed faith to this Divine source of comfort and inspiration."—King George VI (1895-1952)

Chapter Twenty-Eight

WHY JESUS HAD TO DIE ON MAN'S BEHALF

Because He could not change His mind from what He had planned earlier, whatever God says and commands become a law to Him too and He cannot go against it. So even though He had decided to do all these things to the Israelites by bringing them back to their ancestral land, He could not just sit up one day and start to implement them on His own. He had to go strictly according to what His Word says.

> *As heat and drought snatch away the melted snow, so the grave snatches away those who have sinned. (Job 24:19)*

God has declared somewhere that *"I take no pleasure in the death of the wicked,* ***but rather that they turn from their ways and live****" (Ezek. 33:11).* Paul taught us that *"the wages of sin is death, but the gift of God is eternal life in Christ Jesus our LORD", (Rom. 6:23).* He also said that *"**The sting of death is sin**, and the power of sin is the law" (1 Cor. 15:56).* In other words, the sting of death is placed on you when you sin. We do know from the Scriptures also that it's not every sin that leads to death. But we're again told not to pray for such sins. David wrote that *"But you, O God, will bring down the wicked into the pit of corruption;* ***bloodthirsty and deceitful men will not live out half their days****" (Psalm 55:23).*

> *If a righteous man turns from his righteousness and does evil, he will die for it. 19 And if a wicked man turns away from his wickedness and does what is just and right, he will live by doing so. 20 Yet, O house of Israel, you say, 'The way of the LORD is not just.'* ***But I will judge each of you according to his own ways.*** *(Ezek. 33:18-20)*

As you reach verses like these in the Scriptures, you should keep reminding yourself of the fact that God cannot change His mind and do anything contrary to what He had said and have written down in the pages of the Scriptures. He says that "*if a righteous man turns from his righteous ways and does evil, **he will die for it,***" period! So, covenant with the patriarchs or not, once they had sinned they were to die for their sins. That is because: "***The soul who sins is the one who will die.*** *The son will not share the guilt of the father, nor will the father share the guilt of the son.* ***The righteousness of the righteous man will be credited to him, and the wickedness of the wicked will be charged against him***" *(Ezek. 18:20).*

"***You are not a God who takes pleasure in evil; with you the wicked cannot dwell.*** *5 The arrogant cannot stand in your presence;* ***you hate all who do wrong.*** *6 You destroy those who tell lies; bloodthirsty and deceitful men the LORD abhors" (Psalm 5:4-6).* I just love to let the Bible do the talking without adding my own interpretations. *"Do not fret because of evil men or be envious of those who do wrong; 2* ***for like the grass they will soon wither, like green plants they will soon die away****" (Psalm 37:1-2).* "*The senseless man does not know, fools do not understand, 7 that though the wicked spring up like grass and all evildoers flourish, they will be forever destroyed (Psalm 92:6-7).*

Once again, since the wickedness of the wicked man will be credited to him, and the children of the patriarchs who were supposed to be the firstborn son had committed wickedness in the sight of God, they had to die for their sins. But if they all died for their sins too, then, the promises made to the patriarchs would not materialise. God would have lied to the patriarchs for not being able to fulfil the details of the covenant made to them. *"Something"* or *"Someone"* had to die on the children's behalf to execute this promise.

JESUS DIED AS A RANSOM TO SET THE FIRSTBORN SON FREE

> ***For this reason*** *Christ is the mediator of a new covenant,* ***that those who are called may receive the promised eternal inheritance—now that He has died as a ransom to set them free from the sins committed under the first covenant*** *. . . 18 This is why even the first covenant was not put into effect without blood . . . 22 In fact, the law requires that nearly everything be cleansed with blood, and without the shedding of blood there is no forgiveness. (Heb. 9:15, 18, 22)*

If God wanted to forgive them their sins, although He had said somewhere that the soul that sins will surely die, then there had to be some shedding of blood to atone for those who sinned, because He had established that only through the shedding of blood are sins forgiven. As a result, Christ became a ransom to set them free from the sins committed under the first covenant to enable them receive the promised eternal inheritance made to their forefathers. *He was oppressed and afflicted, yet He did not open His mouth; He was led like a lamb to the slaughter, and as a sheep before her shearers is silent, so He did not open His mouth" (Isa. 53:7).* Isaiah wrote that:

> *Surely* ***He took up our infirmities and carried our sorrows,*** *yet we considered Him stricken by God, smitten by Him, and afflicted. 5* ***But He was pierced for our transgressions, He was crushed for our iniquities; the punishment that brought us peace was upon Him and by His wounds we are healed*** *(from our previous sins). 6 We all, like sheep, have gone astray, each of us has turned to his own way;* ***and the LORD has laid on Him the iniquity of us all.*** *(Isa. 53:4-6)*

It is after this forgiveness of sins has been accomplished that God says through David that: ***"Blessed is he whose transgressions are forgiven, whose sins are covered.*** *2* ***Blessed is the man whose sin the LORD does not count against him and in whose spirit there is no deceit"*** *(Psalm 32:1-2). "For as high as the heavens are above the earth, so great is His love for those who fear Him; 12* ***as far as the east is from the west, so far has He removed our*** *(previous)* ***transgressions from us"*** *(Psalm 103:11-12).*

> *Therefore, since Christ suffered in His body, arm yourselves also with the same attitude, because he who has suffered in his body is done with sin. 2* ***As a result, he does not live the rest of his earthly life for evil human desires, but rather for the will of God.*** *3* ***For you have spent enough time in the past doing what pagans choose to do—living in debauchery, lust, drunkenness, orgies, carousing and detestable idolatry.*** *4 They think it strange that you do not plunge (now) with them into the same flood of dissipation, and they heap abuse on you. (1 Pet. 4:1-4)*

Chapter Twenty-Nine

THE KINGDOM OF GOD RESTORED

Jesus said, *"The kingdom of heaven is like a mustard seed, which a man took and planted in his field. 32 Though it is the smallest of all your seeds, yet when it grows, it is the largest of garden plants and becomes a tree, so that the birds of the air come and perch in its branches" (Matt. 13:31-32).* We now know that before Adam was created, *"the earth was formless and empty, darkness was over the surface of the deep, and the Spirit of God was hovering over the waters."* After dealing with the darkness and emptiness, God created and formed His *"son"* in His own likeness and image to represent Him on earth.

Likewise, it came to a point in time when there was another form of darkness and emptiness on the face of the earth as ***"We have already made the charge that Jews and Gentiles alike are all under sin****. 10 As it is written: "There is no-one righteous,* ***not even one****; 11 there is no-one who understands, no-one who seeks God. 12 All have turned away,* ***they have together become worthless;*** *there is no-one who does good,* ***not even one****. 13 Their throats are open graves; their tongues practise deceit. The poison of vipers is on their lips. 14 Their mouths are full of cursing and bitterness. 15 Their feet are swift to shed blood; 16 ruin and misery mark their ways, 17* ***and the way of peace*** *(with God)* ***they do not know****. 18 There is no fear of God before their eyes (Rom. 3:9-18).*

Had it not been the covenants entered with the patriarchs, God would have just sought out someone righteous and then destroy the rest like what He did in the days of Noah. By this time, there was not even one person who was righteous, and the way of peace had been lost to them. *Noah was a righteous man, blameless among the people of his time, and he walked with God (Gen. 6:9).* By then, it had become impossible to apply that rule.

REINTRODUCTION OF THE MUSTARD SEED PRINCIPLE

The next option available was this: *"The kingdom of heaven is like a mustard seed, which a man took and planted in his field. 32 Though it is the smallest of all your seeds, yet when it grows, it is the largest of garden plants and becomes a tree, so that the birds of the air come and perch in its branches" (Matt. 13:31-32).* Adam, the first *"son of God"* on earth, was planted as a mustard seed to multiply and increase in all areas. But he failed and rather produced dead fruits, leading to the death of the whole plant. God then chose His only begotten Son who was from the very beginning and planted Him in the new darkness and emptiness again to influence the mindset of those who had become unrighteous. *"What shall I compare the kingdom of God to? 21* ***It is like yeast that a woman took and mixed into a large amount of flour until it worked all through the dough****" (Luke 13:20-21).*

Jesus kept reminding us of the fact that He was sent by the Father to accomplish a mission. Yes! He was planted on earth to fulfil the command given to Adam to: *"Be fruitful and increase in number; fill the earth and subdue it. Rule over the fish of the sea and the birds of the air and over every living creature that moves on the ground" (Gen. 1:28).* Adam could not do these things because he sinned and was deposed of his authority and power. Jesus came to teach us how to exercise that authority and power then take us back to our original positions as sons of God. *"He came to that which was His own, but His own did not receive Him. 12* ***Yet to all who received Him, to those who believed in His Name, He gave the right to become children of God****—13* ***children born not of natural descent, nor of human decision or a husband's will, but born of God****" (John 1:11-13).*

John wrote concerning Jesus Christ that *"The Word became flesh and made His dwelling among us. We have seen His glory, the glory of the One and Only, who came from the Father, full of grace and truth . . . 18 No-one has ever seen God,* ***but God the One and Only*** *(Jesus Christ)***, who is at the Father's side, has made Him*** *(God the Father)* ***known****" (John 1:14, 18).* Surely, it would take someone who has been with the Father to make Him known to us regarding our responsibilities on earth. Adam did not have that opportunity. Though he was created in the likeness and image of God, Adam was a man who did not have access to the throne of heaven to know how things were done there in order to implement them on earth, as we just read—*"no-one has ever seen God."*

Paul learnt this principle of planting a mustard seed from his Master when he wrote to the Corinthians that *"For we are God's fellow-workers; you are God's field, God's building" (1 Cor. 3:9).* Did you get that? The Corinthians were the field, and the apostles were God's fellow-workers who were representing Him to run the affairs of the earth. Now listen to Paul: *"I planted the seed (the Corinthians), Apollos watered it (the Corinthians), but God made it (the Corinthians) grow" (1 Cor. 3:7).* They had become team players with God the Father to take care of this world.

SALVATION DEFINED

Salvation has much to do with the mindset of an individual. If you can put aside the polished and big grammatical aspects of the subject of salvation, and truly see the purpose of creating man from the Creator's own point of view, you would be free indeed. The King James Version of the Bible says: *"For as he thinketh in his heart, so is he" (Prov. 23:7).* To receive and believe in Christ is to accept what He taught and act upon them or put them into practice for the rest of your life. You then stick to His teachings and build upon them. *"For no-one can lay any foundation other than the one already laid, which is Jesus Christ."* Paul wrote that *"Follow my example, as I follow the example of Christ" (1 Cor. 11:1).* Jesus is a pattern for us to observe and learn what we are meant to do.

> *"Without the Bible we would never have known the abolitionist movement, the prison reform movement, the anti-war movement, the labour movement, the civil rights movement, the movement of indigenous and dispossessed peoples for their human rights, the anti-apartheid movement in South Africa, the Solidarity movement in Poland, the free-speech and pro-democracy movement in such Far Eastern countries as South Korea, the Philippines, and even China. These movements of modern times have all employed the language of the Bible."—Thomas Cahill*

Jesus said that the kingdom of God is like yeast that a woman took and mixed into a large amount of flour until it worked all through the dough" (Luke 13:20-21). Compare that to what Paul said: *"You are no longer foreigners and aliens, but fellow-citizens with God's people and members of God's household, 20 built on the foundation of the apostles and prophets, with Christ Jesus Himself as the chief cornerstone. 21 In Him the whole building is joined together and rises to become a holy temple in the LORD. 22* ***And in Him you too are being built together to become a dwelling in which God lives by His Spirit****" (Eph. 2:19-22).*

"The Word became flesh and made His dwelling among us." As the original mustard seed planted, He was the only foundation laid waiting for its

building to be built upon. Paul is now telling us that we become members of God's household when we are saved. And then the whole building, starting from the foundation is joined together, and rises to become a holy temple in the LORD. In Christ, who is the foundation, we too are being built together to become a dwelling in which God's Spirit lives.

> *You were taught,* ***with regard to your former way of life, to put off your old self,*** *which is being corrupted by its deceitful desires; 23 to be made new in the attitude of your minds; 24* ***and to put on the new self, created to be like God in true righteousness and holiness.*** *(Eph. 4:22-24)*

When a person believes and receives Jesus Christ, He or she is given the right to become a *"son"* or *"daughter" of God*, thereby taking the individual back to his or her original purpose of being created in the first place. You are created to be like God in true holiness on this very earth. Paul wrote to Timothy: ***"What you heard from me, keep as the pattern of sound teaching****, with faith and love in Christ Jesus" (2 Tim. 1:13).* I don't know about you but I happen to believe in the writings of Paul.

When Jesus came to earth, He just took twelve disciples and taught them to become like Him in every way. As a matter of fact, He was not interested in how the crowd received Him that He only spoke to them in parables throughout His entire ministry. At a point in time, His disciples came to ask Him why He had to speak in parables to them and His reply was, *"The knowledge of the secrets of the kingdom of heaven has been given to you,* ***but not to them****" (Matt. 13:10-11).* It took Him three years to tune His disciples' mindset to be like His.

As He taught them, He would test them by sending them in groups of two, and give them *the authority to trample on snakes and scorpions and to overcome all the power of the enemy.* He would pour Himself into them by revealing the secrets of the Kingdom to them that He could at a point in time, tell them: ***"He who listens to you listens to me; he who rejects you rejects me; but he who rejects me rejects Him who sent me"*** *(Matt. 10:16).* All these things were being done to ensure that the fruits of the mustard seed planted in the *"field"* germinate to become a full grown tree in which birds of the air (Gentile nations) could perch in. The miracles being done were just some side attractions for the people to believe in Him.

Jesus said: *"The Father loves the Son and has placed everything in His hands" (John 3:35). "I and the Father are one" (John 10:30). "If you really knew me, you would know my Father as well. From now on, you do know Him and have seen Him" (John 14:7).* We do know that: *"God exalted Him to the highest place and gave Him the Name that is above every name."* He was exalted to the point of becoming one with His Father. It is no wonder He said to His disciples that seeing Him was equal to seeing the Father.

> *I tell you the truth, unless a grain of wheat falls to the ground and dies, it remains only a single seed.* ***But if it dies, it produces many seeds.*** *(John 12:24)*

Christ Jesus was referring to Himself when he said this. We have been told that our attitudes should be the same as that of Christ Jesus *"who, being in the very nature God, did not consider equality with God something to be grasped, 7 but made Himself nothing, taking the very nature of a servant, being made in human likeness. 8 And being found in appearance as a man, He humbled Himself and became obedient to death—even death on a cross" (Phil. 2:6-8).*

Although He was in the very nature of God, He took upon Himself the nature of a servant, and humbled Himself to the systems of the day by mingling with mere men just to be able to teach and train twelve disciples to become like Him and bear much fruit in the end. With the sins and death of the human race, He would have remained a single seed until He had taught others to become like Him. The magnitude of Christ's humility was simply death in itself. But He did that for the love of man.

JESUS REVEALS THE HIDDEN POTENTIAL IN MAN

To reveal their true hidden God-like potentials to them, Jesus told His disciples, among other things, that ***"I tell you the truth, anyone who has faith in me will do what I have been doing. He will do even greater things than these, because I am going to the Father"*** *(John 14:12).* Such things were being said to convert their mindsets which had been seared in sin to that of righteousness with what the Creator meant for them. He was fine-tuning their thinking faculties to take responsibility over the affairs of the earth that were lost in Adam.

> *I no longer call you servants, because a servant does not know his master's business. Instead, I have called you friends,* ***for everything that I learnt from my Father I have made known to you.*** *(John 15:15)*

When they had matured in the teachings of Christ, He no longer classified them as being mere citizens of this world, although they were still occupying it. He said: *"**They are not of the world, even as I am not of it** . . . 18 **As you sent me into the world, I have sent them into the world**" (John 17:16, 18).* He went further to pray thus: *"My prayer is not for them alone. I pray also for those who will believe in me **through their message**, 21 **that all of them may be one, Father, just as you are in me and I in you**. May they also be in us so that the world may believe that you have sent me. 22 **I have given them the glory that you gave me, that they may be one as we are one**: 23 **I in them and you in me.** May they be brought to complete unity to let the world know that you sent me and have loved them even as you have loved me" (John 17:20-23).*

> *"This book accounts for the supremacy of England."—Queen Victoria (1819-1901)*

As to how to attain this position of being one with Him, He said: *"I am the true vine, and my Father is the gardener . . . 4 Remain in me, and I will remain in you. **No branch can bear fruit by itself; it must remain in the vine. Neither can you bear fruit unless you remain in me**. 5 I am the vine; you are the branches. If a man remains in me and I in him, he will bear much fruit; **apart from me you can do nothing**" (John 15:1, 4-5). "**If you obey my commands, you will remain in my love, just as I have obeyed my Father's commands and remain in His love**" (John 15:10).*

It was after they had qualified to take over from Him on earth that Jesus commissioned them to *"go and make disciples of all nations"* by way of reproducing themselves in people like He did in them. The message of the gospel then was to take man to his original purposes of being created in the likeness and image of God. This is what Christ came to do. He didn't come to establish a church or found a healing, faith, evangelism, prosperity or a prophetic ministry.

Again, you would recall what we read in the Psalms where it says *"I said, 'You are "gods"; you are all sons of the Most High.' But you will die like mere men; you will fall like every other ruler." (Psalm 82:6-7).* God's true potential planted in us is to know within our hearts that we are His sons and daughters. That makes us little "gods" on earth. But because that knowledge has been lost to us, we know and understand nothing and have been walking about in darkness ever since. As a result of this ignorance of who we really are, the foundations of the earth have been shaking because our responsibilities to fill the earth, rule over the fish of the sea and the birds of the air and every living creature that moves on the grounds have been neglected.

Jesus came to use Himself as an example for us to see and emulate Him in order to reveal our true hidden potentials to us. *It was He who gave some to be apostles, some to be prophets, some to be evangelists, and some to be pastors and teachers [for what purpose?], 12* ***to prepare God's people for works of service*** *[to do what?],* ***so that the body of Christ may be built up*** *[till when?] 13* ***until we all reach unity in the faith and in the knowledge of the Son of God and become mature, attaining to the whole measure of the fullness of Christ*** *(Eph. 4:11-13).*

You were taught with regard to your former way of life, to put off your old self, which is being corrupted by its deceitful desires; 23 to be made new in the attitude of your minds; 24 and to ***put on the new self, created to be like God*** *in true righteousness and holiness (Eph. 4:22-24).* If you do not know your destination, how would you know if you arrived? It doesn't matter how ugly one is today. Once your true potential is revealed to you, it's up to you to make up your mind and start preparing for that journey.

It doesn't matter whether you are a murderer, malicious, evil, greedy, envious, gossip, slanderous, insolent, arrogant, boastful, disobedient, senseless, faithless, heartless, ruthless, gay, lesbian, gambler, liar, or a thief. You may have committed all the abominable sins that one can think of. But once your true self which was created to be like God is revealed to you, there's hope for you to be transformed. You are the reason why Jesus came to earth. *"It is not the healthy who need a doctor, but the sick. 33* ***I (Jesus) have not come to call the righteous, but sinners to repentance****" (Luke 5:31).* Read that over and over again until it settles deep into your heart.

At the start, you need to learn the elementary teachings about Christ through repentance from all those acts that lead to death which is just the foundation. You'll then have to be taught on faith in God and instruction about baptism, the resurrection of the dead and eternal judgment *(Heb. 6:1-3). In fact, though by this time you ought to be teachers, you need someone to teach you the elementary truths of God's word all over again. You need milk, not solid food! 13 Anyone who lives on milk, being still an infant, is not acquainted with the teaching about righteousness. 14 But solid food is for the mature, who by constant use have trained themselves to distinguish good from evil (Heb. 5:12-14).*

Peter was just a mere fisherman when he met Jesus but later became the rock upon which Christ was going to build His Church after spending a period of three years with Him. Gideon was the least in his family and his clan was the weakest in the whole of Manasseh. Yet he became a mighty warrior leading an army to war after his true potential was revealed to him.

You and I may be taking milk today because of some limitations on our lives. But sooner or later, if we will only believe that we can mature to be like

Christ, we will also start eating strong meat showing we've mature to that stage. You may be the poorest and ugliest person on earth today. But you do have the potential to grow and become like Christ. So does everyone else who will dare to believe and strive to make this journey. God loves everyone. He does not discriminate between people.

CHAPTER THIRTY

THE GOSPEL ACCORDING TO JESUS CHRIST

Jesus came to redeem the whole world back to God but had to start with the children of the promise: ***"For the Son of Man came to seek and to save what was lost"*** *(Luke 19:10)*. At one point He told a parable: *"I have other sheep that are not of this sheep pen.* ***I must bring them also. They too will listen to my voice, and there shall be one flock and one shepherd"*** *(John 10:16)*. As it is written, He came *"as a light for revelation to the Gentiles and for glory to the people of Israel" (Luke 2:32)*.

Since both Jews and Gentiles alike were under sin, and there was not even one righteous person seeking God, Jesus said: *"I tell you the truth, no-one (whether Jew or Gentile) can enter the kingdom of God unless he is born again" (John 3:3)*. Although he was living and walking around, man's spirit which was created in the likeness and image of God had died and rendered him dead-walking in that state. So Jesus came to die in place of that dead-but-walking flesh to replace the old sinful nature, whose spirit had already died, and give birth to the renewed one, which had His own genes or DNA through His teachings.

> *I tell you the truth, whoever hears my word and believes Him who sent me has eternal life and will not be condemned;* ***he has crossed over from death to life****. 25 I tell you the truth,* ***a time is coming and has now come when the dead*** *(a parable that is figuratively talking about the Gentiles)* ***will hear the voice of the Son of God and those who hear will live.*** *(John 5:24-25)*

We already know that *"the sting of death is sin" (1 Cor. 15:56)*. And we also know that *"the wages of sin is death" (Rom. 6:23)*. Again, we've been informed that Christ spoke in parables to the crowd *(Matt. 13:34-35)*. Therefore, what Christ was saying in the above verses was that, because of their sins, they had all died in their spirits, irrespective of being a Jew or not, because the sting of death had been placed on everyone for sinning. But the time was coming, starting from His day, when those same dead people, who would hear His message and believe through obedience, would live. *"For God so loved the world that He gave His one and only Son, that whoever believes in Him shall not perish but have eternal life. 17 For God did not send His Son into the world to condemn the world,* ***but to save the world through Him****" (John 3:16-17). "The work of God is this: to believe in the one He has sent" (John 6:29).*

Belief in Jesus Christ leads one to obeying His words which propels one to lead a righteous life, resulting in having eternal life. The title of Jesus' message in His entire ministry was about *"the gospel of the kingdom of God"*. This was the same message He taught His disciples to preach to the lost tribe of Israel, and later taken to the Gentiles. *"Jesus travelled about from one town and village to another, proclaiming the good news of the kingdom of God. The twelve were with Him" (Luke 8:1).*

Chapter Thirty-One

BEGINNING THE JOURNEY OF PREACHING THE KINGDOM OF GOD

The same message that Jesus preached was the same one that His disciples preached when He was on earth. It was the same one preached after He ascended to heaven. And it was the same message that Paul and the rest of the apostles took to the Gentile nations. Very soon, we will get to know that the same message is to be preached and taught until the second coming of Christ. *"When Jesus had called the Twelve together, He gave them power and authority to drive out all demons and to cure diseases, 2* ***and He sent them out to preach the kingdom of God and to heal the sick****" (Luke 9:1-2).*

JESUS PREVENTED THE TWELVE FROM REACHING OUT—TO GENTILES

I realise that this is a very sensitive subject that most Christians shy away from. But for us to clearly understand the New Testament Scriptures especially those parts written by Paul, we would have to address this first. It has to do with the fact that Jesus told His disciples point-blank without mincing words not to take the gospel of the kingdom of God to the Gentiles when He was on earth. He only commanded them to "*go and make disciples of all nations*" after He had finished training them, and they were then well versed into the Scriptures.

Among other things, there are two reasons why He did that. The first was the fact that His disciples were all Jews at the time and would find it hard associating with Gentiles. Jews were not supposed to mingle with Gentiles or Samaritans at the time. That is why the woman at the well was surprised to even hear Jesus ask her for a drink. The Samaritan woman said to Him, *"You are a Jew and I am a Samaritan woman.* ***How can you ask me for a drink?*** *(For Jews do not associate with Samaritans).* Even if the Gentiles were converted at the time, the Pharisees would have found a ground to accuse Him of defiling the temple or the synagogues He was entering. Paul experienced a similar thing in his time with the Pharisees.

The Jews were so particular about this topic of getting themselves defiled by the Gentiles that even when they had Jesus arrested, and insisted that He be killed the same day, they refused to enter the palace of the Roman governor in order not to defile themselves, because the palace belonged to the Romans who were Gentiles from Italy. That was because they were going to eat the Passover after leaving the premises *(John 18:28).*

The second reason is to read and understand what God did when He took the children of Israel from Egypt. He said something remarkable that can be our guide as to how to first understand what Jesus said without taking offence, and also learning how to take the gospel message to the masses.

> *I will send the hornet ahead of you to drive the Hivites, Canaanites and Hittites out of your way. 29 But I will not drive them out in a single year,* ***because the land would become desolate and the wild animals too numerous for you.*** *30 Little by little I will drive them out before you,* ***until you have increased enough to take possession of the land*** *(Exod. 23:28-30).*

It is written about Jesus that *"He grew in wisdom and stature, and in favour with God and men" (Luke 2:52).* Although He was in the very nature of God, He did not try to be Jack of all trades by biting more than He could chew. He humbled Himself to the authorities on earth. He even paid taxes to the authorities. At a point, He was struck in the face by an official who thought He had not answered a high priest properly. Though He was hurt and could have done something to him, He only said, *"If I said something wrong, testify to what is wrong. But if I spoke the truth,* ***why did you strike me?"*** *(John 18:23).*

Although He was in the very nature of God, He was alone on earth in what He knew and wanted to get implemented. So He had to take time to train others to think like Him who would be transformed by the renewing of their minds until He (the new mustard seed) had increased enough to take possession of the land. If He had wanted to take the whole land at a go, He would have encountered many problems than what He suffered. If even Jews who had the knowledge of God were finding it hard to accept His teachings, how much more a Gentile who thinks it is okay to have sex with an animal? He had to drive those thoughts out little by little.

> *These twelve Jesus sent out* ***with the following instructions: "Do not go among the Gentiles or enter any town of the Samaritans.*** *6* ***Go rather to the lost sheep of Israel.*** *7 As you go, preach this message: 'The kingdom of heaven is near.'" (Matt. 10:5-7)*

Jesus had spoken much in parables concerning the salvation of the Gentiles. It is obvious then to know from the above verses that there was a time allocated for that to be done. Jesus Himself said, *"I have other sheep that are not of this sheep pen.* ***I must bring them also. They too will listen to my voice, and there shall be one flock and one shepherd****" (John 10:16).* Why then did He state it in plain language to His disciples not to go to the Gentiles and Samaritans? It had to do with timing. *"There is a time for everything and a season for every activity under heaven . . . a time to plant (a mustard seed) and a time to uproot" (Eccl. 3:1-2).*

Jesus said, *"I was sent only to the lost sheep of Israel" (Matt. 15:24).* When He was pressed to heal the daughter of a Canaanite woman, a Gentile, who was demon-possessed, Jesus first declined and told her *"It is not right to take the children's bread and toss it to their dogs" (Matt. 15:26).* The same Jesus, when He was sending His twelve disciples out told them not to go to the Gentiles but to the lost sheep, who were the Israelites. They had still not grown to take possession of the whole land. They had to go little by little. *"A journey of a thousand miles begins with a step,"* says the Chinese proverb.

> *Then He opened their minds so they could understand the Scriptures. 46 He told them, "This is what is written: The Christ will suffer and rise from the dead on the third day, 47* ***and repentance and forgiveness of sins will be preached in His name to all nations, beginning at Jerusalem.****" (Luke 24:45-47)*

We now know what message was left with the disciples, who they were told to preach to, where to start the preaching, and when to take it to all the nations. It is very important to note that when Christ opened their minds to come to the understanding of the Scriptures, He told them that everything about His life, starting from His birth to death, and the taking of His message into all the corners of the world was already written in the Scriptures. That should tell us that Jesus did not preach anything that was contrary to the Scriptures. He Himself said, *"Do not think that I have come to abolish the Law or the Prophets;* ***I have not come to abolish them*** *but to fulfil them" (Matt. 5:17).*

DURATION OF THE DISCIPLES' APPRENTICESHIP

We need to know how long His disciples were under Him for the training they received from the LORD as that will help us make a few judgments as we go along. That can be easily deduced from the criteria the disciples used when they were looking for someone to replace Judas after he had committed suicide. After learning from the Scriptures that *"May another take his place of leadership,"* they immediately got to work without wasting much time.

> *Therefore it is necessary to choose one of the men who have been with us* ***the whole time the LORD Jesus went in and out among us,*** *22* ***beginning from John's baptism to the time when Jesus was taken up from us.*** *For one of these must become a witness with us of His resurrection. (Acts 1:21-22)*

Peter said the above statements on how to choose someone to replace Judas. It was the same Peter who was told by Christ that *"And I tell you that you are Peter, and on this rock I will build my church, and the gates of Hades will not overcome it. 19 I will give you the keys of the kingdom of heaven; whatever you bind on earth will be bound in heaven, and whatever you loose on earth will be loosed in heaven" (Matt. 16:18-19).* We can then know from here that Peter and the rest of the Twelve, at least, spent not less than three years under the LORD'S feet receiving their training.

Chapter Thirty-Two

CHRONOLOGICAL STAGES IN SPREADING THE KINGDOM MESSAGE

Before His ascension into heaven, Jesus had told His disciples to *"stay in the city until you have been clothed with power from on high" (Luke 24:49).* Now it so happened that this *clothing with power from on high* which was promised them came on the day of Pentecost, which is one of the major Jewish festivals that draw Jews from all corners of the world. *"All of them were filled with the Holy Spirit and began to speak in other tongues as the Spirit enabled them" (Acts 2:4).*

UNDERSTANDING THE BOOK OF ACTS IS KEY

It takes the understanding of the book of Acts to really understand the New Testament Scriptures. If you get it wrong in this book, it will be extremely difficult for you to get it right in the rest of the New Testament books, apart from the four gospels. So we will take a step by step account to it and get the whole picture without reading anything from outside.

> *Now there were staying in Jerusalem* ***God-fearing Jews from every nation under heaven****. 6 When they heard this sound, a crowd came together in bewilderment,* ***because each one heard them speaking in his own language****. 7 Utterly amazed, they asked:* ***"Are not these men who are speaking Galileans? 8 Then how is it that each of us hears them in his own native language?*** *9 Parthians, Medes and Elamites; residents of Mesopotamia, Judea and Cappadocia, Pontus and Asia, 10 Phrygia and Pamphylia, Egypt and the parts of Libya near Cyrene; visitors from Rome, 11 (both Jews and converts to*

> *Judaism); Cretans and Arabs—we hear them declaring the wonders of God in our own tongues! (Acts 2:5-11)*

The first time I heard it said that "*the best way to hide a thing from a black man is to write it in a book because he would never read it,*" I got angry and started reading anything I could get my hands on, like I said earlier. I should respect your intelligence as you read the verses we just read. I'm not addressing the subject of speaking in tongues here. But we need to get exactly how the spread of the message about the Kingdom of God was done. So let's re-read what really happened in these verses.

It says that "***When the day of Pentecost came, they were all together in one place.***" We shouldn't forget the fact that all these men at the time were either Jews or converts to Judaism who had believed in Jesus Christ as the promised Messiah of the world. The apostles' Master, Jesus Christ, lived and died a Jew and also celebrated the Passover with them. Observing the Sabbaths was His custom. So it should not surprise us that His disciples were all together on the day of Pentecost, which is one of the major festivals of the Jews. This is because Jesus Christ would have been in their midst and even organise such a gathering if He were not in heaven.

Now it so happened that the Holy Spirit promised them by Jesus Christ came on this day of Pentecost. When all of them were filled with the Holy Spirit, they "*began to speak in other tongues as the Spirit enabled them.*" We can easily know where the disciples were when this took place, from how and where Jesus delivered His message. It is written: "***Each day Jesus was teaching at the temple****, and each evening He went out to spend the night on the hill called the Mount of Olives, 38* ***and all the people came early in the morning to hear Him at the temple****" (Luke 21:37-38)*. If His office was based at the temple courts, then His disciples would have continued from there.

The next thing to prove this is the fact that after Peter had answered their curiosity as to what speaking in tongues meant, as many as three thousand men joined them in a single day. The only place to house "*God-fearing Jews from every nation under heaven*" at that time of the year was the temple courts where the Jews had come to observe the Pentecost and return to their various nations thereafter. "***Every day they*** *(Christ's followers)* ***continued to meet together in the temple courts****" (Acts 2:46)*.

Probably because of this major festival when Jews from all walks of life gather, "*There were staying in Jerusalem God-fearing Jews from every nation under heaven." When they heard this sound, a crowd came together in bewilderment,* ***because each one heard them speaking in his own language.***" Strange sights and sounds indeed! Utterly amazed, those who had come to Jerusalem to observe the festival asked: "***Are not all these men who are speaking Galileans?***"

SPEAKING IN TONGUES EXPLAINED

We can estimate that there were a little over a hundred and twenty of the disciples gathered when this happened *(Acts 1:15)*. These God-fearing Jews who heard the disciples speaking in other languages were so surprised to see this that they came together and wanted to find out what was going on. So, hearing them speak in tongues or other languages, they, first of all, investigated and got to know that the disciples were not some group of people who had descended from another planet but were actually Galileans like every other Israelite.

"***Then how is it that each of us hears them in his own native language?***" In order not to step on anybody's toes, we need to take a closer look at the word *"native"* in this verse to understand the subsequent verses that will follow. Firstly, the word *"native"* means *connected with the place where you were born and lived for the first years of your life.* Secondly, it also means *connected with the place where you have always lived or have lived for a long time.* This means the Jews who came to witness this phenomenon heard the Disciples of Jesus Christ actually speaking in the tongues or the native languages of other people as if they had lived in those areas all their lives. They were fluent in expressing themselves in their tongues or languages.

Because the writer of the book of Acts did not want to leave us confused, the names of such areas whose native languages or tongues were being spoken by the disciples after the outpouring of the Holy Spirit were given, some of which included Egypt, Pontus and Asia, Mede, Elamites, Phrygia, Pamphylia, part of Libya near Cyrene, Rome, Crete and Arabic. Paul wrote that "***Undoubtedly, there are all sorts of languages in the world, yet none of them is without meaning***" *(1 Cor. 14:10).* The Holy Spirit enabled some to speak in Arabic tongues or languages. Much as I know my younger sister to be smart, I would be surprised to hear her speaking in Arabic all of a sudden.

I hope this is so clear, plain and straight to the point that even a toddler should not have any problem understanding it. The Jews who had travelled to the various nations like Libya, Crete and Rome were back home in Jerusalem to celebrate the Pentecost festival, and heard their fellow country-men speaking in the native languages of these areas they had travelled to and were, in the process, shocked to the bone. As any normal human being would do, they needed explanations to the whole thing.

*"**We hear them declaring the wonders of God in our own tongues!**"* Did you get that? Not only did they hear them speaking in their own languages. They actually heard and understood everything that was said. They were *"**declaring the wonders of God**" "as the Spirit enabled them."* For instance, the man who had returned from Libya heard and understood everything that was said by one disciple declaring the wonders of God with the native tongue of Libya, which the Holy Spirit enabled him to speak. *"Amazed and perplexed, they asked one another, "**What does this mean**?" Some, however, made fun of them and said, "They have had too much wine."*

Because they were coming from the various areas listed above, they may have lost touch of all that had happened in Jerusalem concerning the Christ and His message. *"Are you only a visitor to Jerusalem and do not know the things that have happened there in these days?" (Luke 24:18).* They were not around to know who Jesus was and what He had taught His disciples, which was beginning to bear fruits at that time. Someone had to come to their aid by way of explaining things further for them to understand what was going on that they were missing. *Then Peter stood up with the Eleven, raised his voice and addressed the crowd: . . .* He explained everything to them using the Scriptures.

When the people (the God-fearing Jews who had returned from these areas) *heard this, they were cut to the heart and said to Peter and the other apostles, "**Brothers, what shall we do?**" Peter replied, "Repent and be baptised, every one of you, in the name of Jesus Christ for the forgiveness of your sins. And you will receive the gift of the Holy Spirit . . . With many other words he warned them; and he pleaded with them, "**Save yourselves from this corrupt generation**" (Acts 2:37-40).* Both the curious who wanted to know the meaning of this and those who made fun of the whole process got their share of the explanations and were told what to do.

In the end, *"those who accepted His message were baptised, and about three thousand were added to their number that day."* There was not a single Gentile among them because we read in verse five that those who heard them were *God-fearing Jews who had come from every nation under heaven.* And until that time, the disciples still thought it was against their Law for a Jew to be associated with a Gentile. Now it is obvious that the reason God chose the day of Pentecost to fill the disciples with the Holy Spirit the first time was to enable Him have access to these men who would come from those areas and return with the message in order to start planting the mustard seed principle in their individual conscience. God has a reason for everything He does. Speaking in tongues at that time was to serve a specific purpose. Being filled with the Holy Spirit is one thing and speaking in a tongue is another.

There are those who teach that one is not filled with the Holy Spirit until he or she speaks in *"tongues."* I will rather listen to Paul as he wrote: *"And in the church God has appointed first of all apostles, second prophets, third teachers, then workers of miracles, also those having gifts of healing, those able to help others, those with gifts of administration,* ***and those speaking in different kinds of tongues*** (I heard Coach José Maurinho speaks more than a dozen different languages). *29 Are all apostles? Are all prophets? Are all teachers? Do all work miracles? 30 Do all have gifts of healing?* ***Do all speak in tongues?*** *Do all interpret?* Can they answer Paul's question—*do all speak in tongues*—for us? I didn't ask that question. Paul did. Are all miracle workers or prophets?

The modern-day *"super-apostles"* who have turned themselves into Jacks of all trades and want to portray themselves as some super-humans, who are more spiritual and understand the writings of Paul than the man who himself wrote these letters, will want to do all these things combined to showcase their spiritual muscles. Helping others is one of the gifts of the Holy Spirit but rarely do I hear even pastors beating their chest in public claiming they only have the gift of giving or helping others. Being effective and efficient in the administrative aspects of a Church is also one of the gifts of the Holy Spirit. But *do all administer?* Paul wrote: *"When I was a child, I talked like a child, I reasoned like a child.* ***When I became a man, I put childish ways behind me****" (1 Cor. 13:11).*

THE APOSTLES PRACTISE CHRIST'S TEACHING ON TRUE LOVE

Once they accepted the gospel of Christ and were baptised, *"they devoted themselves to the apostles' teaching and to the fellowship, to the breaking of bread and to prayer. Everyone was filled with awe, and many wonders and miraculous signs were done by the apostles."*

> ***All the believers were together and had everything in common.*** *45* ***Selling their possessions and goods, they gave to anyone as he had need.*** *46 Every day they continued to meet* ***together in the temple courts.*** *They broke bread in their homes and ate together* ***with glad and sincere hearts,*** *47 praising God and enjoying the favour of all the people. And the LORD added to their number daily those who were being saved. (Acts 2:44-47)*

Jesus told His disciples that *"I no longer call you servants, because a servant does not know his master's business. Instead, I have called you friends,* ***for everything that I learned from my Father I have made known to***

you *" (John 15:15).* What were some of the things He learned from the Father and made known to His disciples? *"For God so loved the world that* ***He gave His one and only Son****, that whoever believes in Him shall not perish but have eternal life" (John 3:16).* He taught them to also love their brothers like themselves and share whatever they had among them. He then went on to tell them to have the God-kind of love, which is greater than man's own. He defined a greater love for them to know and learn exactly what He meant.

> *Greater love has no-one than this,* ***that he lay down his life for his friends****. 14* ***You are my friends if you do what I command.*** *(John 15:13-14)*

This is the kind of love Jesus was referring to when He told His disciples to love one another. *"My command is this:* ***Love each other as I have loved you****" (John 15:12).* In His prayer, Jesus told the Father concerning the disciples that *"As you have sent me into the world, I have sent them into the world"*. So the same love the Father had was transferred to Jesus and was later transferred from Jesus to His followers, who were all Jews at the time. Peter wrote that *"****Above all, love each other deeply****, because love covers over a multitude of sins" (1 Pet. 4:8).*

The disciples had also taken over from Jesus after His ascension into heaven and were practising exactly what their Master taught them. You see, a typical Jew knew from the Scriptures what true love meant even before Christ. Before His coming to the scene, Gentiles were seen and treated like second class citizens by the Jews but that was even against the Law in the Old Testament. It is written:

> ***When an alien*** *(a Gentile)* ***lives with you in your land, do not ill-treat him****. 34* ***The alien living with you must be treated as one of your native-born****.* ***Love him as yourself****, for you were aliens in Egypt. I am the LORD your God. (Lev. 19:33-34)*

I have nothing more to say concerning this except to remind you that this is not coming from the Constitution of the United States but rather from the so-called *"yoke of bondage"* manual, which is considered outdated by most of the Christian communities in the world today. It is also written in the same *"yoke of bondage"* that:

> ***If one of your countrymen becomes poor and is unable to support himself among you****, help him as you would an alien or a temporary resident,* ***so that he can continue to live among you****. 36* ***Do not take interest of any kind from him****, but fear your*

> *God,* ***so that your countryman may continue to live among you.*** *37* ***You must not lend him money at interest or sell him food at a profit.*** *(Lev. 25:35-37)*

My eyes are filled with tears as I type these lines. There has never been a caring leader, president or father like the God of the Jews or the Israelites. There are dozens of such verses in the Old Testament Scriptures but for reasons known to the Pharisees and teachers of the law including the modern ones, they have cunningly set them aside so that they can observe their own traditions of keeping people in the dark.

Because He had not come to abolish the Law but to fulfil it, Big Brother Jesus Christ taught His disciples to go back and practise these laws in their daily lives. And because of the training they received, "***All the believers were together and had everything in common.*** *45 Selling their possessions and goods, they gave to anyone as he had need 46 . . . They broke bread in their homes and ate together with glad and sincere hearts, 47 praising God and enjoying the favour of all the people. And the LORD added to their number daily those who were being saved" (Acts 2:44-47).*

All the believers were one in heart and mind. No-one claimed that any of his possessions was his own, but they shared everything they had *. . . 34* ***There were no needy persons among them.*** *For from time to time those who owned lands or houses sold them, brought the money from the sales 35 and put it at the apostles' feet,* ***and it was distributed to anyone as he had need*** *(Acts 4:32-35).* If they were asked by Jesus to give food and drinks to even their enemies, how much more their own brothers and sisters in the faith! These were still Jews applying the Scriptures in their daily lives. Tell a modern-day Pharisee to sell one of his cars and give the money to the poor. And if you are not lucky, he would rain down curses on you, and give you the best lectures on how the poor in society are lazy these days.

There are millions of people who are not attending church gatherings, not because they don't want to but because they don't have a shirt to wear or even a pair of sandals to put on. I have been there for several years before, and I know what I'm talking about. The disciples saw to the satisfaction of peoples' needs, not taking from them. Jesus saw to it that those who followed Him in His walk were fed. He saw to their welfare. Jesus was a caring leader. He made sure He practised what He preached.

The Pharisees and teachers of the law thought killing Jesus would bring His ministry to an end in order for them to continue with their lies—replacing the commands of God with their traditions. That didn't happen as the mustard seed planted in Christ started bearing fruits in the disciples, enabling them to have the power to continue with the project that was started by Jesus. That is what a real leader does. If a project dies because of the death of a leader, then there was no leader in the first place. A true leader reproduces himself in his mentees. *Jesus took unschooled ordinary men like Peter and John, and turned them into the courageous few who could argue their case with even the Sanhedrin (Acts 4:13).* There has never been a leader like Jesus in the history of man!

One day, Peter healed *a forty-year old man (Acts 4:22) who was crippled from birth (Acts 3:2-10).* This astonished all the people, and they came running to the disciples in a place called Solomon's Colonnade *(Acts 3:11).* Peter took advantage of the situation to preach the message of the kingdom of heaven to them and *"many who heard the message believed, and the number of men grew to about five thousand" (Acts 4:4).* Realising this was going to start the Jesus-kind-of fever or scenario again, the Sanhedrin decided to crush this "movement" by arresting and questioning the disciples. To make matters worse for them, Peter gave *"the Name of Jesus Christ of Nazareth" (Acts 4:10)* as the power behind the healing of this man.

Witnessing the whole thing regarding the healing of this man, and the subsequent reaction of the people joining the disciples in this way, the Pharisees and teachers of the law knew they could not deny what the disciples had done. The man healed had been there for a very long time that even the Sanhedrin knew him and could not deny the fact that he had actually been healed.

> *Then they called them in again and commanded them not to speak or teach at all in the name of Jesus. 19 But Peter and John replied, "Judge for yourselves whether it is right in God's sight to obey you rather than God. 20* ***For we cannot help speaking about what we have seen and heard."*** *21 After further threats they let them go. They could not decide how to punish them, because all the people were praising God for what had happened. (Acts 4:18-21)*

Leaving their presence, they reported all that had happened to the others and prayed to God to empower them, which He did and they spoke the word of God boldly from then on. But that was going to later invite the wrath of the priests as they saw the preaching of the gospel of Christ about the Kingdom of God as a threat to their existence. For them, the way of God was about business as usual.

THE APOSTLES' PLACE OF MEETING AFTER CHRIST'S ASCENSION

> *The apostles performed many miraculous signs and wonders among the people.* ***And all the believers used to meet together in Solomon's Colonnade.*** *13 No-one else dared join them, even though they were highly regarded by the people. 14 Nevertheless, more and more men and women believed in the LORD and were added to their number. 15 As a result, people brought the sick into the streets and laid them on beds and mats so that at least Peter's shadow might fall on some of them as he passed by. 16 Crowds gathered also from the towns around Jerusalem, bringing their sick and those tormented by evil spirits, and all of them were healed. (Acts 5:12)*

There are those who teach that because Jesus said *"For the law was given through Moses; grace and truth came through Jesus Christ" (John 1:17)* and also said, *"It is finished" (John 19:30)* on the cross before His death and rose from the dead on a certain day, they explain that to mean that everything in the Old Testament was brought to a halt starting a new wave of teaching based purely on grace. Granted! I'm not going to argue with that, for *"We accept man's testimony,* ***but God's testimony is greater because it is the testimony of God****, which He has given about His Son" (1 John 5:9).*

We just heard Peter say that *"For we cannot help speaking about what we have seen and heard" (Acts 4:20).* What the apostles preached and did was what they had seen with their own eyes and heard from Christ Himself. They walked with Him for at least three years and ate and slept with Him in the same apartments. They were with Him when He travelled through all the villages teaching in the temples and synagogues. They did not receive their teaching via dreams or the so-called one-man revelations which are mostly received under the shower. Neither did they attend schools to gain their understanding into the Scriptures. The Pharisees of old had schools too but could not understand the Scriptures that they were put in Moses' seat to teach.

These apostles maintained their place of worship, which was part of the temple of God called Solomon's Colonnade. They were there because they rather had become the true Jews that God had intended and were bearing much fruits in the process. They were not to leave the temple to anywhere. Jesus did not establish a church that was separated from the temple. At one time He told His disciples that ***"They will put you out of the synagogue; in fact, a time is coming when anyone who kills you will think he is offering a service to God"*** *(John 16:2).* You see, the true application of the Scriptures in the midst of these people was going to provoke the Pharisees to prevent them from entering the temple premises. Paul, before his conversion, was a typical example: *"Going from house to house, he dragged off men and women and put them in prison" (Acts 8:3).*

Actually, I don't know which book is being read by some of the modern day Pharisees to teach these things as I believe most of their teachings come from reading novels; not the Bible. And I also can't tell if it is the same Jesus I know that they are talking about. If Jesus changed anything, His disciples would have been in a better position to practise them and leave us with examples to emulate. They experienced the workings of the Holy Spirit firsthand. I don't know why people will always try to claim to be more powerful than Jesus and the apostles. Jesus said, *"I tell you the truth,* ***no servant is greater than his master, nor is a messenger greater than the one who sent him****" (John 13:16). "When pride comes, then comes disgrace, but with humility comes wisdom"* (Prov. 11:2).

THE APOSTLES PERSECUTED

> ***Then the high priest and all his associates****, who were members of the party of the Sadducees,* ***were filled with jealousy****. 18 They arrested the apostles and put them in public jail. (Acts 5:17-18)*

Jesus told His disciples that *"The teachers of the law and the Pharisees sit in Moses' seat. 3 So you must obey them and do everything they tell you. But do not do what they do" (Matt. 23:2-3).* What the apostles were doing after they had been taught by Christ was the responsibility of the teachers of the law and the Pharisees. Once the apostles were doing this and bearing much fruit, the land was being taken *"little by little."* The high priest and his associates became jealous and started persecuting the apostles. But that did not deter them. "*Day after day,* ***in the temple courts*** ***and from house to house****, they never stopped teaching and proclaiming the good news that Jesus is the Christ" (Acts 5:42).*

If one mustard seed planted in Jesus by God could result in producing twelve other mustard seeds, and each of the twelve was sent out to bear fruits just like the Father sent the first seed, then the twelve could also end up reproducing a hundred and fifty-six seeds in no time. One would chase a thousand, and two shall chase ten thousand. *"So the word of God spread. The number of disciples in Jerusalem increased rapidly* ***and a large number of priests became obedient to the faith****" (Acts 6:7).* Wow! Even priests under the former regime found it wise to join the disciples later. The real definition of Judaism had been made plain for them to understand and it was no longer hard for them to follow suit once they had insight into the practical aspects of the Scriptures.

Feeling threatened by the apostles' success story, *members of one of the synagogues named the Freedmen—Jews of Cyrene and Alexandria as well as the provinces of Cilicia and Asia—began to argue with one of the disciples named Stephen, but they could not stand up against his wisdom or the Spirit by whom he spoke (Acts 6:8-10).* So they secretly persuaded some men to serve as witnesses in laying false accusations on him. They killed him in the end.

> *On that day a great persecution broke out against the church at Jerusalem,* ***and all except the apostles were scattered throughout Judea and Samaria.*** *(Acts 8:1)*

Stephen was so powerful among the believers that his death caused panic among the believers and caused them to flee from Jerusalem. But the positive side of his death was the fact that "***Those who had been scattered preached the word wherever they went***" *(Acts 8:4).* In the process, although Jews did not associate with the people of Samaria *(John 4:9)*, ***Philip went down to a city in Samaria and proclaimed the Christ there***" *(Acts 8:5).* That was a plus as they learned to practise the pure love in the Scriptures to even love the aliens as themselves. They had learnt from Jesus to feed and clothe their enemies. There wasn't a better way to feed the Samaritans than to feed them with the Word of God.

Chapter Thirty-Three

TAKING THE GOSPEL TO THE GENTILES

God will always choose someone whose walk is blameless in His sight to be planted as a mustard seed in the soil of darkness with the aim of growing big to cover the whole land. When it was time to fully accept the Gentiles into the assembly of the believers in Christ to fulfil the promise made to Abraham, God chose a Roman soldier named Cornelius. *"**He and all his family were devout and God-fearing**; he gave generously to those in need and prayed to God regularly" (Acts 10:2). "**He is a righteous and God-fearing man, who is respected by all the Jewish people**" (Acts 10:22).* This man had a vision one afternoon where he was distinctly told to send for Peter to explain the message of the kingdom of heaven to him and his family *(Acts 10:3-8).*

About noon the following day, Peter also went to his roof to pray. He fell into a trance and had a vision of his own:

> *He saw heaven opened and something **like** a large sheet being let down to earth by its four corners. 12 **It contained all kinds of four footed animals, as well as reptiles of the earth and birds of the air**. 13 Then a voice told him, **"Get up, Peter. Kill and eat."** 14 **"Surely not, LORD!" Peter replied. "I have never eaten anything impure or unclean**." 15 The voice spoke to him a second time, **"Do not call anything impure that God has made clean."** 16 This happened three times, and immediately the sheet was taken back to heaven. (Acts 10:11-16)*

Before continuing with this, we need to be reminded again of who Peter was until this time of having this vision. For the start, he had been with Jesus for three years, studied under Him and, at this time, had become the leader of the church. Because he was chosen by Christ, he would have been in a better position to learn everything that pertains to godliness from the

Master. By this time he had literally become a miracle-working man just like his boss.

This same Peter was the one having some catnap whiles waiting for his food to be prepared and saw something like a large sheet with all kinds of reptiles, all kinds of four-footed animals and birds of the air on it being let down to earth in a trance. He didn't understand what that meant. To add to his confusion, a voice told him to kill all those animals on the sheet and eat. To someone born and bred a Jew, that was an abomination and was simply unheard of because:

> *The LORD said to Moses and Aaron, 2 "Say to the Israelites: Of all the animals that live on land,* ***these are the ones you may eat****: 3 You may eat any animal that has a split hoof completely divided and that chews the cud. 4* ***There are some that only chew the cud or only have a split hoof, but you must not eat them . . .***
>
> *20* ***All flying insects that walk on all fours are to be detestable to you . . .*** *41* ***Every creature that moves about on the ground is detestable; it is not to be eaten.*** *42* ***You are not to eat any creature that moves about on the ground, whether it moves on its belly or walks on all fours or on many feet; it is detestable . . .*** *Do not make yourselves unclean by any creature that moves about on the ground. (Lev. 11:1-4, 20, 41-44)*

To *detest a thing is to hate it very much*. Another word that comes to mind is to loathe something. Even though this was not happening in reality, in a trance, Peter was so shocked that a Jew of his calibre would be asked to eat all these creatures combined without making any distinctions as to which ones to eat and which ones not to eat. As a matter of fact, a Jew does not consider those creatures as food.

A pig for instance was not created to be eaten as food but as a mobile garbage can on feet which is responsible for clearing the land of various animal wastes. The vulture is the flying type which sees from far, and eats dead animal wastes left in the jungles of the forests to prevent the spread of diseases. Have you thought about why an eagle can see from a thousand mile distance?

Such flying creatures are there to locate wherever the carcass may be. There are those created in the seas and various water bodies to clean them of toxic wastes. These "garbage cans" would have to be mobile in order to get to these wastes. *"Can you fathom the mysteries of God? Can you probe the limits of the Almighty? (Job 11:7)*. Now, must you eat the "garbage can" with its content? Find time to give a serious thought to all the creatures that the Israelites were told not to eat and see if there is anything religious or ritualistic about them.

As expected of every Jew, Peter exclaimed in amazement that he had never eaten anything impure or unclean in his lifetime. Note here again that this was the same man who had been with Jesus in His entire ministry. So if Jesus had come to sanctify all creatures as food to be eaten and made them holy, then Peter and the rest of the apostles would have been eating such creatures long before us. But Peter, out of shock exclaimed he had never eaten anything like that though Christ had "sanctified" them. And Peter, unlike Paul, studied under Jesus in person. The plain and simple truth is that Jesus Christ did not sanction the eating of such creatures anywhere in the Bible. *Peter replied, "Surely not, LORD!* ***Nothing impure or unclean has ever entered my mouth****" (Acts 11:8).*

> *While Peter was wondering about* ***the meaning of the vision****, the men sent by Cornelius found out where Simon's house was, and stopped at the gate. (Acts 10:17)*

Being a man of the Scriptures, Peter knew instantly that this was a vision to him in parables from above, communicating something else, and should not just be taken literally. So, he started thinking about its meaning. *"When a prophet of the LORD is among you,* ***I reveal myself to him in visions, I speak to him in dreams****" (Num. 12:6).* He didn't reach the bottom of understanding the vision when the men sent by Cornelius came looking for him. After telling him their mission, Peter went with them the next day *(Acts 10:23).*

> *As Peter entered the house, Cornelius met him and fell at his feet in reverence . . . 27 talking with him, Peter went inside and found a large gathering of people. 28 He (Peter) said to them:* ***"You are well aware that it is against our law for a Jew to associate with a Gentile or visit him. But God has shown me*** (through the vision) ***that I should not call any man*** (especially Gentiles) ***impure or unclean."*** *(Acts 10:25-28)*

Peter was still a Jew after Christ had been with them and gone to heaven. It was here that God was fulfilling the promise Jesus made that He had another sheep pen outside the Israelites, and they would also need to hear His voice and repent. Jesus said He had other sheep which were not of the Israelites' pen and would have to save them too. He said this in parables, so the apostles could not grasp its full meaning. Even after the death and resurrection of Christ, it was still against the apostles' law for Jews to associate with Gentiles. You should now understand why Jesus told the Grecian woman that it was wrong for Him to take the children's bread and toss it to their dogs. The dogs referred figuratively to the Gentiles.

This vision was used by God to tell Peter, who was then the leader of the Church, that it was time to take the gospel to everyone including the *"dogs."* This vision had absolutely nothing whatsoever to do with being given the green-light or the permission to start eating every kind of creature one finds on the market or in the bush. You are entitled to eat all you want. But just don't misinterpret the Bible as a basis to do that. It is simply not in there. In the end, Peter was able to confess this that ***"I now realise how true it is that God does not show favouritism,*** *35* ***but accepts men*** *(both Jews and Gentiles)* ***from every nation who fear Him and do what is right"*** *(Acts 10:34-35).* Now, let me ask you this question, Modern Pharisee Reader: was this vision about eating bats, vultures and frogs?

"While Peter was still speaking these words, the Holy Spirit came on all who heard the message. 45 The circumcised believers who had come with Peter were astonished that the gift of the Holy Spirit had been poured out ***even on the Gentiles.*** *46* ***For they heard them speaking in tongues and praising God"*** *(Acts 10:44-46).* You see, even until this time the disciples including Peter of all people had no idea that the Gentiles too would receive salvation and be baptised with the Holy Spirit although Christ had said that on several occasions in His parables. Note here too that, when the Gentiles received the Holy Spirit and were speaking in tongues, the disciples understood everything they said because they heard them *"praising God."* How else could they tell they were praising God if they didn't understand the tongue being spoken? In my area, when someone who used to curse and speak all manner of abusive languages turns a new leaf and starts speaking decently, we say he or she is now speaking in a different tongue.

> *The apostles and the brothers throughout Judea heard that the Gentiles also had received the word of God. 2 So when Peter went up to Jerusalem,* ***the circumcised believers criticised him*** *3* ***and said, "You went into the house of uncircumcised men and ate with them."*** *(Acts 11:1-3)*

Peter began and explained everything to them precisely as it had happened (Acts 11:4). When they heard this, they had no further objections and praised God, saying, ***"So then, God has granted <u>even the Gentiles</u> repentance unto life"*** *(Acts 11:18).* As we go along, you will get to understand the grace that Paul was referring to in his teachings. In a typical Jew's mind in those days, a Gentile was just like any other creature that could only be bought as a slave. But these were traditions they inherited from their ancestors because God never said that a Gentile should be regarded in that sense.

Even back in the olden days when Solomon was dedicating the temple, he knew a Gentile could also come and pray towards heaven to have answers to his prayers just like a native Israelite born in the land. But religion blinds people to the simple truths of the Scriptures, and people try to apply their own rules to what God had in mind from the beginning. A portion of Solomon's prayer during the dedication of the temple of God reads:

> ***"As for the foreigner** (the Gentile) **who does not belong to your people Israel but has come from a distant land** because of your name—42 for men will hear of your great Name and your mighty hand and your outstretched arm—**when he** (the Gentile) **comes and prays towards this temple, 43 then hear from heaven, your dwelling place, and do whatever the foreigner** (the Gentile) **asks of you, so that all the peoples of the earth may know your Name and fear you, as do your own people Israel,** and may know that this house I have built bears your Name." (1 Kings 8:41-43)*

That is the prayer of a typical spiritual Jew with a circumcised heart. Allowing a Gentile into the temple courts was punishable by death in Jesus' day. Now that the temple is no longer in place, the area is open to tourists from all walks of life. But that temple will be rebuilt soon and we'll see if Gentiles will be allowed to enter there. The man who built the original temple never wrote anywhere that Gentiles should not be allowed into its premises. So what happened? Studying the Bible is like pure honey on my tongue. I have this sensation anytime I'm reading the Bible. It's a great feeling to read, study and understand something in the Bible for yourself.

Even the disciples who had been with Jesus Christ for three years were surprised that Gentiles could be saved, and receive the Holy Spirit. But all those teachings were inherited from their elders who had set aside the commands of God in order to observe their own traditions which were more important to them than the Word of God. It is written:

NO DENOMINATIONS IN THE KINGDOM OF GOD

> *This is what the LORD says: "Maintain justice and do what is right, for my salvation is close at hand and **my righteousness will soon be revealed** . . . 3 Let no foreigner (or Gentile) who has bound himself to the LORD say, 'The LORD will surely exclude me from His people.' And let not any eunuch complain, 'I am only a dry tree.'4*

> ***For this is what the LORD says: "To the eunuchs who keep my Sabbaths, who choose what pleases me and hold fast to my covenant—****5* ***to them I will give within my temple and its walls a memorial and a name better than sons and daughters; I will give them an everlasting name that will not be cut off.***
>
> *6* ***And foreigners*** *(or Gentiles)* ***who bind themselves to the LORD to serve Him, to love the Name of the LORD, and to worship Him, all who keep the Sabbath without desecrating it and who hold fast to my covenant—****7* ***these I will bring to my holy mountain and give them joy in my house of prayer. Their burnt offerings and sacrifices will be accepted on my altar; for my house will be called a house of prayer for all nations."*** *8 The Sovereign LORD declares—He who gathers the exiles of Israel:* ***"I will gather still others*** *to them* ***besides those already gathered."*** *(Isa. 56:1-8)*

Since they refuse to take the Word of God in its simplest and raw form, both Jewish and Gentile believers spiritualise these things and always try to postpone them into some future dispensation. But the future becomes today when the truths of the Scriptures are revealed to the people. We can wait till eternity to reach the future, and it will never come until we understand what is supposed to be done. There is nothing like separate denominations in the Kingdom of God. Denominations exist today simply because both Jews and Christians refuse to obey the plain and simple Word of God. There are some truths hidden in those eight verses we just read, which I cannot touch on now.

I deeply adore you the reader with everything in me and for that matter I'm according you with my utmost love and respect as I type these things. I love to make the Word of God come alive in your heart and mind to create a burning desire in you that you may search the Scriptures for yourself without even contacting me again to ask for further questions. That is my motivation, and the greatest gift you can give me is to write and tell me you cannot sleep until you have read at least a chapter in the Bible each day. I'll be waiting to hear from you. Let Bible study become a second nature to you. Let's continue.

> *This is what the LORD says: "As for all my wicked neighbours who seize the inheritance I gave to my people Israel, I will uproot them from their lands and I will uproot the house of Judah from among them. 15 But after I uproot them, I will again have compassion and will bring each of them back to his own inheritance and his own country. 16* ***And if they*** *(the Gentile nations)* ***learn well the ways***

> ***of my people** (the Israelites) **and swear by my Name, saying, 'As surely as the LORD lives'—even as they** (the Gentiles) **once taught my people** (the Israelites) **to swear by Baal—then they** (the Gentiles) **will be established among my people** (the Israelites). 17 But if any nation does not listen, I will completely uproot and destroy it," declares the LORD. (Jer. 12:14-17)*

It's true that God does not show favouritism. *"From one man He made every nation of men, that they should inhabit the whole earth; and He determined the times set for them and the exact places where they should live. 27 God did this so that men would seek Him and perhaps reach out for Him and find Him, though He is not far from each one of us" (Acts 17:26-27).* A country might refuse me VISA because I'm a Ghanaian but God looks down on us all and sees brothers and sisters from the same Father who do not recognise each other. If we can pursue justice and righteousness, then God loves all of us on earth as one people with a common destiny.

REASONS FOR EXCLUDING GENTILES FROM GOD'S ASSEMBLY

Please allow me to help you understand why the Jews disassociated themselves from the Gentiles completely. If you and I grasp how it happened, I believe the Jew will now fall in love with the Gentile and vice versa. It happened in the days of Nehemiah after he had rebuilt the temple of God. Because of the exile, the Israelites had forgotten the commandments of the LORD so the elders decided to gather them at one place and have the Scriptures read in their hearing so they could walk in them.

> *On that day the Book of Moses was read aloud in the hearing of the people and there **it was found written that no Ammonite or Moabite should ever be admitted into the assembly of God**, 2 because they had not met the Israelites with food and water but had hired Balaam to call a curse down on them. (Our God, however, turned the curse into a blessing.) 3 **When the people heard this law, they excluded from Israel all who were of foreign descent.** (Neh. 13:1-3)*

Friend, it is important for you to know that the Scriptures were not given in a day. At the time of reading this from the law, the people had not had the benefit of reading the book of Ezekiel, which was to come at a later time. It is true we have it written in the book of Moses never to allow any Moabite or

Ammonite into the Assembly of God because of the sins committed by their forefathers against God but it is also written in the book of Ezekiel that:

> *The soul who sins is the one who will die.* ***The son will not share the guilt of the father,*** *nor will the father share the guilt of the son. The righteousness of the righteous man will be credited to him,* ***and the wickedness of the wicked will be charged against him.*** *(Ezek. 18:20)*

> *26 If a righteous man turns from his righteousness and commits sin, he will die for it; because of the sin he has committed he will die. 27* ***But if a wicked man turns away from the wickedness he has committed and does what is just and right, he will save his life.*** *28* ***Because he considers all offences he has committed and turns away from them, he will surely live; he will not die.*** *(Ezek. 18:26-28)*

The Jews at the time did not have access to these Scriptures, and since it was going to be difficult for them to start screening every foreigner or Gentile to identify whether he or she was from these two countries, they made it simple. They just decided to simply bar every Gentile completely from coming into the Assembly of God. But I want to ask if they did not read the prayer of Solomon. They definitely had a point. But you cannot adjust the Word of God to make a thing simple for you.

The second reason why they did that was the Sabbath which was not being kept properly because the foreigners were not Jews and were only coming to Jerusalem mainly to trade in goods and services. It is written in the Law: *"Remember the Sabbath day by keeping it holy. 9 Six days you shall labour and do all your work, 10 but the seventh day is a Sabbath to the LORD your God.* ***On it you shall not do any work, neither you nor your son or daughter, nor your manservant or maidservant, nor your animals, nor the alien*** *(or the Gentile)* ***within your gates****" (Exod. 20:8-10).*

> *In those days I (Nehemiah) saw men in Judah treading winepresses on the Sabbath and bringing in grain and loading it on donkeys, together with wine, grapes, figs and all other kinds of loads. And they were bringing all this into Jerusalem. Therefore I warned them against selling food on that day. 16* ***Men from Tyre who lived in Jerusalem were bringing in fish and all kinds of merchandise and selling them in Jerusalem on the Sabbath to the people of Judah.*** *17 I rebuked the nobles of Judah and said to them, "What is this wicked thing you are doing—desecrating the Sabbath day? 18* ***Didn't your forefathers do the same things, so that our God***

> ***brought all this calamity upon us and upon this city?*** *Now you are stirring up more wrath against Israel by desecrating the Sabbath." (Neh. 13:15-18)*

The mustard seed principle applies in everything that starts small. Once the Gentiles were allowed to enter the city and permitted to run their businesses uninterruptedlyon the Sabbath, the Jews were also going to follow suit, especially the youth who mostly do not even understand the basis of the Sabbath. The moment people see others doing something that does not kill them they turn to abhor laws barring them from doing likewise, without taking the time to learn why the laws were introduced in the first place. This, I believe is the weakness in a democracy. Anything that seems right in the eyes of a particular person or group is allowed to go on without thinking of its future impact on society as a whole. It is said that *"No man is an island, entire of itself; every man is a piece of the continent, a part of the main"*—John Donne (1572-1631).

The third reason the Gentiles were barred from the assembly was to prevent the people of God from inter-marrying with the Gentiles, who were idol worshippers, so as not to repeat what happened to their forefathers. A typical instance was what happened to Solomon. Once you are married to someone, the two of you become one. Paul wrote: *"Do you not know that your bodies are members of Christ Himself? Shall I then take the members of Christ and unite them with a prostitute?* ***Never!*** *16* ***Do you not know that he who unites himself with a prostitute is one with her in body? For it is said, "The two will become one flesh"*** *(1 Cor. 6:15-16).* Read the next verses carefully.

> *Moreover,* ***in those days I saw men of Judah who had married women from Ashdod, Ammon and Moab.*** *24 Half of their children spoke the language of Ashdod or the language of one of the other people,* ***and did not know how to speak the language of Judah.*** *25 I rebuked them and called curses down on them. I beat some of the men and pulled out their hair. I made them take an oath in God's Name and said: "You are not to give your daughters in marriage to their sons, nor are you to take their daughters in marriage for your sons or for yourselves. 26* ***Was not because of marriages like these that Solomon king of Israel sinned? Among the many nations there was no king like him. He was loved by his God, and God made him king over all Israel, but even he was led into sin by foreign women.*** *27* ***Must we hear now that you too are doing all this terrible wickedness and are being unfaithful to our God by marrying foreign women?*** *(Neh. 13:23-27)*

God was not just preventing His people from marrying outside Israel. But He was rather preventing them from going astray by copying what these nations did. *"Let no foreigner who has bound himself to the LORD say, 'The LORD will surely exclude me from His people.' And let not the eunuch complain, 'I am only a dry tree.' 4 For this is what the LORD says: 'To the eunuchs who keep my Sabbaths, who chooses what pleases me and hold fast to my covenant—5 to them I will give within my temple and its walls a memorial and a name better than sons and daughters; I will give them an everlasting name that will not be cut off'" (Isa. 56:3-8).* ***"I now realise how true it is that God does not show favouritism, 35 but accepts men*** *(both Jews and Gentiles)* ***from every nation who fear Him and do what is right"*** *(Acts 10:34-35).*

The LORD God does not show favouritism. Even a Jew who does not obey His commandments is considered an enemy or a Gentile in His sight simply because He loves righteousness and justice. A real Jew is the one who is circumcised in the heart and not just in the flesh. It is written: ***"The LORD is righteous in all His ways and loving towards all He has made*** *(including Gentiles). 18 The LORD is near to all who call on Him,* ***to all who call on Him in truth****. He fulfils the desires of those who fear Him; He hears their cry and saves them. 20* ***The LORD watches over all who love Him, but all the wicked He destroys****" (Psalm 145:17-20).*

It is again written that "The days are coming," declares the LORD, "when ***I will punish all who are circumcised only in the flesh****—26 Egypt, Judah (Jews), Edom, Ammon, Moab and all who live in the desert in distant places. For all these nations (including Judah) are really uncircumcised,* ***and even the whole house of Israel is uncircumcised in the heart****" (Jer. 9:25-26).*

> *Was a man already circumcised when he was called? He should not become uncircumcised. Was a man uncircumcised when he was called? He should not be circumcised. 19* ***Circumcision is nothing, and uncircumcision is nothing. Keeping God's commands is what counts.*** *(1 Cor. 7:18-19)*

Whoever calls on the Name of the LORD shall be saved. We are all one people from the same Father. If you should marry someone for instance, the most important thing is that at the end of the day, the language of God, which is His Word, is taught to your spouse and children. But this should be discussed with the potential spouse to know which angle you are heading toward before entering into the marriage. Later, when this condition is breached, then the other partner can be accused of marital unfaithfulness.

HISTORY BEHIND AMMONITES AND MOABITES

Now let me briefly tell you why God wrote in the law to have the Ammonites and Moabites wiped from the face of the earth. The fact that they did not bring food and water to the Israelites but rather wanted to have them cursed was one of the reasons. The main reason was that these two nations were the descendants of the two daughters of Lot who slept with him after getting him drunk. God was not going to let that go unpunished to have others do same in future.

> *Lot and his two daughters left Zoar and settled in the mountains, for he was afraid to stay in Zoar. He and his two daughters lived in a cave. 31 One day the older daughter said to the younger, "Our father is old,* ***and there is no man around here to lie with us, as is the custom all over the earth.*** *32 Let's get our father to drink wine and then lie with him and preserve our family line through our father . . . 36 So both of Lot's daughters became pregnant by their father. 37 The older daughter had a son, and she named him Moab;* ***he is the father of the Moabites of today****. 38 The younger daughter also had a son, and she named him Ben-Ammi,* ***he is the father of the Ammonites of today.****" (Gen. 19:30-38)*

Please note that what prompted the older sister to come up with that idea was that she felt it was *"the custom all over the earth."* But all over in the pages of the Bible God kept telling His people never to do things the way they are done in other nations. *"You must not do as they do in Egypt,* ***where you used to live****, and you must not do in the land of Canaan where I am bringing you.* ***Do not follow their practices.*** *4* ***You must obey my laws and be careful to follow my decrees****. I am the LORD your God. 5* ***Keep my decrees and laws, for the man who obeys them will live by them****. I am the LORD (Lev. 18:3-5).*

So, what does God's Word say concerning what they did? It is written: ***"No-one is to approach any close relative to have sexual relations****. I am the LORD. 24* ***Do not defile yourselves in any of these ways, because this is how the nations that I am going to drive out before you became defiled*** *. . . 29 Everyone who does any of these detestable things—****such persons must be cut off from their people****" (Lev. 18:6, 24, 29).* Lot was a righteous man but his descendants became defiled so they had to be wiped off from the face of the earth.

A NEW CREATION IN CHRIST

These were the regulations on Gentiles left behind. But later God introduced a new order, which made it possible for the Moabites and Ammonites to be freed from this curse if only they chose to walk according to His Word. *"The soul who sins is the one who will die.* ***The son will not share the guilt of the father,*** *nor will the father share the guilt of the son. The righteousness of the righteous man will be credited to him,* ***and the wickedness of the wicked will be charged against him"*** *(Ezek. 18:20).* Christ came to redeem us from the curse of the law imposed as a result of the previous sins committed by our ancestors, nailed them to the cross to enable the Gentiles, including the descendants of Moab and Ben-Ammi have access to God.

> ***So from now on we regard no-one from a worldly point of view.*** *Though we once regarded Christ in this way, we do so no longer. 17* ***Therefore, if anyone is in Christ, he is a new creation: the old has gone, the new has come!*** *18 All this is from God, who reconciled us to Himself through Christ and gave us the ministry of reconciliation: 19 that* ***God was reconciling the world*** *(including the Moabites and Ammonites)* ***to Himself in Christ, not counting men's sins against them****. And He has committed to us the message of reconciliation. (2 Cor. 5:16-19)*

This should be okay for now as I believe I have made you understand why the Jews in the days of Jesus and the apostles were preventing association with Gentiles. It started back in the days when Nehemiah wanted to avoid being exiled again at all cost. Some hard decisions were expected of him as the leader at the time, and he did his very best to do that. It is time for those of us living today to know how best we can also live in peace with each other after that barrier has been removed through our knowledge into the Scriptures. Keeping the commandments of God is what counts. We can now continue from where we left off.

TAKING THE MESSAGE OUTSIDE JERUSALEM

> *Now those who had been scattered by the persecution in connection with Stephen travelled as far as Phoenicia, Cyprus and Antioch,* ***telling the message only to Jews.*** *20* ***Some of them****, however, men from Cyprus and Cyrene,* ***went to Antioch and began to speak to Greeks also****, telling them the good news about the LORD Jesus. 21 The LORD'S hand was with them, and a great number of people believed and turned to the LORD. (Acts 11:19-21)*

The believers who were scattered as a result of Stephen's death were not in Jerusalem to know it was alright to preach the gospel to Gentiles as well as Jews. So, as they travelled along, they were still telling the message of the Kingdom of heaven to Jews only. Some of them, however, who had probably converted to Judaism but were from Greece and Cyprus saw the wisdom in the message and started taking it to their country-men. I would have done same!

News of this reached the ears of the church at Jerusalem, and they sent Barnabas to Antioch (Acts 11:22). By this time, Paul, like the priests we read about in chapter six of Acts, had believed and become obedient to the faith. When he saw what was going on and realised he needed help, Barnabas went in search of Paul to help him take care of his territory. *Then Barnabas went to Tarsus to look for Saul (a.k.a. Paul), 26 and when he found him, he brought him to Antioch. So for a whole year Barnabas and Saul met with the church and taught great numbers of people.* ***The disciples were called Christians first at Antioch*** *(Acts 11:25-26).*

PAUL PREACHED THE SAME KINGDOM OF GOD MESSAGE

We should note from the outset of Paul's life and ministry the purpose for which he was called: ***"This man is my chosen instrument to carry my name before the Gentiles and their kings, and before the people of Israel"*** *(Acts 9:15).* Note that his assignment was in two folds. There are those who teach the message of the Kingdom of heaven as if Paul had a gospel that was different from what the other disciples like Peter taught. Due to this, they try to follow the footsteps of the Jews who, for several generations distanced themselves from the Gentiles by also distancing themselves from the Jews of today. Paul was to carry the same message to both Gentiles and Israelites.

> *Surely, you have heard about the administration of God's grace that was given to me for you, 3 that is,* ***the mystery made known to me by revelation****, as I have already written briefly. 4 In reading this, then, you will be able to understand my insight into the mystery of Christ, 5 which was not made known to men in other generations as it has now been revealed by the Spirit to God's holy apostles and prophets. 6* ***This mystery is that through the gospel the Gentiles are heirs together with Israel, members together of one body and sharers together in the promise in Christ Jesus.*** *(Eph. 3:2-6)*

In trying to disassociate themselves from the Jews today, Christians are committing the same discriminatory acts of the Jews by viewing Gentiles as slaves who could never be accepted into the Assembly of God. But it was categorically stated in the Scriptures that Abraham would be the father of many nations including the Jewish nation, which was only the firstborn son. The mystery of God since the beginning of time was that *"the Gentiles are heirs together with Israel, members together of one body"* and sharers together in the promise made to Abraham *through* Jesus Christ.

"In the church at Antioch there were prophets and teachers: . . . 2 while they were worshipping the LORD and fasting, the Holy Spirit said, 'Set apart for me Barnabas and Saul for the work to which I have called them.' 3 So after they had fasted and prayed they placed their hands on them and sent them off. 4 The two of them, sent on their way by the Holy Spirit, went down to Seleucia and sailed from there to Cyprus. 5 ***When they arrived at Salamis, they proclaimed the word of God in the Jewish synagogues****. John was with them as their helper" (Acts 13:1-5).*

PAUL'S STYLE OF DELIVERING THE KINGDOM MESSAGE

Just like his colleagues, Paul continued in the footsteps of His Master Jesus Christ by preaching in the Jewish synagogues. We can learn how they taught when they entered the synagogues by looking at one example. "***On the Sabbath they entered the synagogue and sat down.*** *15* ***After the reading from the Law and the Prophets****, the synagogue rulers sent word to them, saying "Brothers, if you have a message of encouragement for the people, please speak" (Acts 13:14-15).*

You see, the apostles didn't have a problem with the Jews not believing in Jesus Christ. But whenever they entered a town or city, they only went in search of a synagogue of the Jews and sat among them as listeners and waited for an opportunity to make contributions. When that was achieved, they used that as an opportunity to teach them from the Scriptures starting from Abraham down to their age, which always ended with Christ Jesus. They didn't go around holding crusades outside to force people to accept Christ.

> *As Paul and Barnabas were leaving the synagogue, the people invited them to speak further about these things on the next Sabbath. 43* ***When the congregation was dismissed, many of the Jews and devout converts to Judaism followed Paul and Barnabas,*** *who talked with them and urged them to continue in the grace of God. (Acts 13:42-43)*

It takes dialogue and tact to persuade another man to part ways with his convictions that have taken him his whole life to build to accept something taught in a day. You need to sit down with such people and understand their way of thinking before trying to convince them. You show them respect when you do this, and they reciprocate by listening to you. For instance, even as I'm writing this book, no-one knows that I even read the Bible. Friends know me for reading as a hobby but I don't let them know I even read the Bible. I always wait for an opportunity for a discussion on a subject to explain things to them from the Scriptures without quoting any Scriptures before them. At the end of the day, conveying the principle is what counts. You can preach thousands of sermons to people without mentioning the Name of God or Jesus Christ.

On the next Sabbath almost the whole city gathered to hear the word of the LORD (Acts 13:44). In his letter to the Ephesians, Paul wrote that *"Be completely humble and gentle; be patient,* ***bearing with one another in love****" (Eph. 4:2).* Love conquers all. Bearing with one another in love, he humbled himself to everyone and brought himself down to their level, sat and listened to them before making his contributions. On the basis of this, almost the whole city, young and old, rich and poor, Jews and Gentiles gathered the next Sabbath to hear him teach again. The sheep will always go where the grass is green.

PAUL CONCENTRATES ON GENTILES

> *When the Jews saw the crowds,* ***they were filled with jealousy and talked abusively against what Paul was saying****. Then Paul and Barnabas answered them boldly: "****We had to speak the word of God to you first. Since you reject it and do not consider yourselves worthy of eternal life, we now turn to the Gentiles.****" (Acts 13:46)*

This is where most Christians miss the point and come up with the doctrine of replacement that God has rejected the Jews and chosen the Gentiles instead. That's simply laughable and erroneous. Before Paul was converted, there were at least five thousand Jews who had believed and become obedient to the faith. There were even priests among them who had turned to the faith. There was not a single Gentile among the Twelve that followed Jesus for three years. Paul and Barnabas themselves were Jews.

This happened because Paul and Barnabas were teaching mainly outside Jerusalem, where there were Jews who had not even heard of the name of Christ before. Just as Peter experienced, it was difficult for such Jews to be told *"to kill and eat all kinds of creatures combined."* They were those that Paul was talking about that, since they rejected the message he was bringing them, he was taking it to the Gentiles who would listen. And the next thing is that it was not their refusal that prompted the taking of the message to the Gentiles. Paul's major purpose of being called was to do that from the beginning.

> *The word of the LORD spread through the whole region. 50 But the Jews (those who didn't believe the message) incited the God-fearing women of high standing and the leading men of the city. They stirred up persecution against Paul and Barnabas, and expelled them from their region. (Acts 13:49-50)*

The Jews were lording their powers over their followers by tying heavy loads on their shoulders but they themselves were not willing to lift a finger to move them. When Paul and Barnabas came to teach about brotherly love and kindness, the Jews realised that their source of income was going to be stopped. So they incited the prominent figures around, and had them expelled. This became the norm that they had to experience it on several occasions.

> *At Iconium Paul and Barnabas went* ***as usual into the Jewish synagogue****. There they spoke so effectively that* ***a great number of Jews and Gentiles believed****. 2* ***But the Jews who refused to believe*** *(note the difference between the Jews)* ***stirred up the Gentiles and poisoned their minds against the brothers.*** *(Acts 14:1-2)*

When it comes to business, the right way will always be contested, and people are willing to go any length as regards the path they have chosen for their lives, whether it is good or evil. Not everyone believes in the resurrection of the dead to be judged later according to what they've done while they were alive. Such people only believe in the here and now, and if you dare try to put any stumbling block on their sources of income, then they would make sure you are eradicated from the scene. That was what happened to Jesus Christ. When this group of Jews realised they could not stop Paul and Barnabas, they rather turned their attention to the Gentiles by polluting their minds with different teachings or doctrines. We can trace the source of that principle, from the Scriptures.

TRACING THE SOURCE OF FALSE DOCTRINES

> *They worshipped the LORD,* ***but they also appointed all sorts of their own people to officiate for them as priests in the shrines at the high places.*** *33* ***They worshipped the LORD, but they also served their own gods in accordance with the customs of the nations from which they have been brought.*** *34* ***To this day they persist in their former practices****. They neither worship the LORD nor adhere to the decrees and ordinances, the laws and commands that the LORD gave the descendants of Jacob, whom He named Israel. (2 Kings 32-34)*

As a result of this poisoning of their minds, *"the people of the city were divided; some sided with the Jews, others with the apostles" (Acts 14:4)*. The descendants of these men are still in our midst today through the application of that same principle. It is written: *"They would not listen, however, but persisted in their former practices. 41* ***Even while these people were worshipping the LORD, they were serving their idols. To this day their children and grandchildren continue to do as their fathers did****" (2 Kings 17:40-41)*. King Solomon was right in saying *"there is nothing new under the sun."*

THE KEY TO UNDERSTANDING THE NEW TESTAMENT

> *Some men came down from Judea to Antioch and were teaching the brothers:* ***"Unless you are circumcised, according to the custom taught by Moses, you cannot be saved."*** *2 This brought Paul and Barnabas into sharp dispute and debate with them.* ***So Paul and Barnabas were appointed, along with some other believers to go up to Jerusalem to see the apostles and elders about this question.*** *(Acts 15:1-2)*

If you understand what we are about to discuss here, you would be in a position to not only understand the Bible but also teach it as well. You are about to understand all the books of the New Testament with the exception of the four gospels, at least. So I need your utmost attention on this.

The Jews who refused to believe in the gospel decided to stir up the Gentiles against the apostles and also poison their minds against them. They did that by going behind Paul and Barnabas, teaching the Gentiles that unless they were circumcised in the flesh, they would not be saved. This seemed to have worked perfectly to their plans as both Paul and Barnabas, including others, had to be sent to Jerusalem, the headquarters, to seek instructions on how to counter that menace. The Galatian church bought into this lie, and was actually following those teachings. Paul wrote to them that *"even if we or an angel from heaven should preach a gospel other than the one we preached to you, let him be eternally condemned" (Gal. 1:8).*

But before we proceed on this, we should identify exactly what was being discussed. The question was about what the Gentile must do to be saved. They claimed he had to be physically circumcised in the flesh to be saved, and until that was done, there was no way he could be saved. My question then is, if salvation was going to be attained only through circumcision of the male organ, then how was the woman going to be saved? Salvation in itself is simply a gift from God. No-one works for it. Salvation is not bought with circumcision.

When God called the Israelites from Egypt, He told them that *"The LORD did not set His affection on you and choose you because you were more numerous than other peoples, for you were the fewest of all peoples" (Deut. 7:7). "Understand, then, that it is not because of your righteousness that the LORD your God is giving you this good land to possess, for you are a stiff-necked people" (Deut. 9:6).* Out of arrogance, the Jews had lost track of the fact that they in addition to the Gentiles had all sinned and fall short of the glory of God, and needed to repent just like everyone else. They were still with the mentality that mere circumcision in the flesh made one saved after reading Jeremiah 9:25-26.

Physical circumcision was the sign of the spiritual covenant between God and the descendants of the patriarchs. The actual covenant in itself is for the children to follow the LORD'S commands, laws, statutes, decrees and precepts for all generations. The circumcision in the flesh was the sign to tell or show God that they were going to live by His rules and regulations, which He established to last forever. Even, back in the Old Testament days, the Jews were aware of this fact. The New Testament Jews made this an issue because they wanted to take advantage of the Gentiles who were not conversant with the things of God to frustrate them in believing the gospel.

> *"The days are coming" declares the LORD,* ***"when I will punish all who are circumcised only in the flesh***—*26 Egypt, Judah, Edom, Ammon, Moab and all who live in the desert in distant places.* ***For all these nations are really uncircumcised, and even the whole house of Israel is uncircumcised in heart."*** *(Jer. 9:25-26)*

This should be plain to understand as it is straight to the point. Merely bearing the physical circumcision in your flesh is just like having access to the Words of God without putting them into practice. It's still zero over eight as my uncle used to say! Even though the Israelites were physically circumcised in the flesh, God says they were not really circumcised in their hearts, which made them equal to the Egyptians and Ammonites and the other Gentile nations.

With the wisdom he had, Paul was inspired to recommend that *"Each one should retain the place in life that the LORD assigned to him and to which God has called him. This is the rule I lay down in all the churches. 18 Was a man already circumcised when he was called? He should not become uncircumcised. Was a man uncircumcised when he was called? He should not be circumcised" (1 Cor. 7:17-18).* It is obvious Paul had read *Jeremiah 9:24-25,* and did not have problems teaching the truth of God from the Scriptures. Paul stated the reason why the Jews who belonged to the other group wanted the Gentiles to be circumcised, in these words:

THE JEWS' REASONS FOR INSISTING ON CIRCUMCISING THE GENTILE BELIEVERS

> *Those who want to make a good impression outwardly are trying to compel you to be circumcised.* ***The only reason they do this is to avoid being persecuted for the cross of Christ.*** *13* ***Not even those who are circumcised obey the law, yet they want you to be circumcised that they may boast about your flesh.*** *(Gal. 6:12-13)*

Immediately after Paul and his crew had arrived in Jerusalem and made their reports, ***then some of the believers who belonged to the party of the Pharisees stood up and said, "The Gentiles must be circumcised and required to obey the Law of Moses"*** *(Acts 15:5).* Now we know the source of the argument. The Pharisees had tried and failed in doing all they could to wipe out the name of Jesus from Jerusalem. There is a saying: "*if you can't beat them, join them.*" They joined the apostles but with their own agenda to mingle with them and be able to trace their roots, and know firsthand how they would be faring as they teach their message about the Kingdom of God.

"The apostles and elders met to consider this question. After much discussion, Peter got up and addressed them . . . ***We believe it is through the grace of our LORD Jesus that we*** *(the Jews)* ***are saved, just as they*** *(the Gentiles)* ***are****" (Acts 15:6, 11).* Once again, the LORD does not show favouritism. It is the same grace that was extended to save the Jews that was later extended to save the Gentiles too. God created men; not races of any particular groups of people. It is by grace that all men including Jews are saved, and not because

one is of special favour than the other. Now, Mr. Gentile Pharisee who claims that the Gentile is under grace, please be reminded that Abraham and his descendants were also saved by the same grace. Grace is not limited to Gentiles alone, making our worship of God different from the Jews. Jews and Gentiles are all under grace, and serve the same God.

James, who was one of the leaders who gathered to address this issue of circumcision before salvation for the Gentiles, made a suggestion that was later implemented by the elders. He said, *"It is my judgment, therefore, that* ***we should not make it difficult for the Gentiles who are turning to God.*** *20 Instead we should write to them, telling them to abstain from food polluted by idols, from sexual immorality, from the meat of strangled animals and from blood" (Acts 15:19-20).*

Logically speaking, it would be very unfortunate for someone to take the gospel to a place like China, Japan or North Korea, and immediately try to compel the people there to be circumcised, and insist that they should not eat frogs again before they could be saved. It was suggested at this gathering that, things were not made difficult for those who were turning to Christ. The idea behind that stance they took was that: ***"For Moses*** *(i.e. the Old Testament Scriptures)* ***has been preached in every city from the earliest times and is read in the synagogues on every Sabbath"*** *(Acts 15:21).*

It was agreed at this meeting that letters be written to the Gentiles wherever they were, and the basic truths of the Scriptures revealed to them. By all means, after they had believed the gospel, they would be going to the synagogues on every Sabbath, at least. And whenever they went there and the Scriptures were read, then they would be in a position to ask questions as to why they should or should not do this or that. You don't force your religious beliefs down the throats of others. I have read about crusades and campaigns in the name of God but all of them were carried out based on worldly ambitions. Jesus did not invade Jerusalem with an army of soldiers.

THE APOSTLES ADDRESS THE CIRCUMCISION BEFORE SALVATION ISSUE

The idea of writing letters to the Gentiles is the basis of Paul's letters to the various Gentile Churches in the New Testament. So basically, the issue of the Pharisaic Jews with the apostles was about what the Gentile must do to be saved and not whether one should obey or not obey the statutes of God in the Scriptures, like *"Thou shall not steal and murder"* as it is widely taught today. With that conclusion, the apostles wrote this letter to be distributed among the Gentile believers:

The apostles and elders, your brothers,

To the Gentile believers in Antioch, Syria and Cilicia:

Greetings.

We have heard that some went out from us ***without our authorization*** *and disturbed you,* ***troubling your minds by what they said****. 25 So we all agreed to choose some men and send them to you with our dear friends Barnabas and Paul—26 men who have risked their lives for the name of our LORD Jesus Christ. 27 Therefore we are sending Judas and Silas to confirm by word of mouth what we are writing. 28* ***It seemed good to the Holy Spirit and to us not to burden you with anything beyond the following requirements****: 29 You are to abstain from food sacrificed to idols,* ***from blood, from the meat of strangled animals and from sexual immorality. You will do well to avoid these things****. Farewell! (Acts 15:23-29)*

For the records, Paul was among the elders who took this decision, and it was mainly his responsibility to see to it that these things were taught to the Gentile believers who were being confused. A real Jew who has been circumcised in the heart does not need someone to tell him to abstain from blood. A real Jew also knows that *"he who sins sexually sins against his own body" (1 Cor. 6:18)* because sex involves the transfusion of blood, which results in the transfer of whatever diseases that are stored in the bloodstream of each partner to the other and therefore, he does not need to be told. The duty to take the gospel to the Gentile nations was squarely placed on Paul's shoulders by God.

Now you, if you call yourself a Jew: if you rely on the law and brag about your relationship to God; 18 ***If you know His will and approve of what is superior because you are instructed by the law****; 19* ***if you are convinced that you are a guide for the blind****, a light for those who are in the dark, 20 an instructor of the foolish, a teacher of infants,* ***because you have in the law the embodiment of knowledge and truth****—21* ***you, then, who teach others, do you not teach yourself****? (Rom. 2:17-21)*

If the Pharisees and teachers of the law who sit in Moses' seat were to teach the raw word of God in the Scriptures, they would have been the true teachers of the Word of God. This is because *"the embodiment of knowledge and truth"* are plainly covered in the pages of the Scriptures. Jesus said: *"Thy word is truth."* With all humility, I will say that this is my call to reveal these truths which have been knowingly or unknowingly kept secret from the masses just because of selfish ambitions of organisations and institutions masquerading as Christians. Jesus again promised us that *"There is nothing concealed that will not be disclosed, or hidden that will not be made known" (Matt. 10:26).*

Paul wrote: *"What advantage, then, is there in being a Jew, or what value is there in circumcision? 2 Much in every way!* ***First of all, they*** *(the Jews)* ***have been entrusted with the very words of God"*** *(Rom. 3:1-2).* ***He made known His ways to Moses, His deeds to the people of Israel*** *(Psalm 103:7).* If you possess the written form of your country's Constitution but refuse to obey it, that does not render it nullified. Paul wrote again that ***"In the past God spoke to our forefathers through the prophets at many times and in various ways"*** *(Heb. 1:1).* The Old Testament writings are still the Words of the Father and will forever remain so.

But we have some "experts" today who claim they have been to heaven and were told that it is now okay to eat the blood of creatures simply because they claim Christ has redeemed them from "*the curse of the law*" and has therefore made everything clean. Solomon said that, "*though it costs you all you have, get understand.*" If you have understanding, you would not allow blood into your system apart from that of your spouse through sex or when it has to be done to save a life. One major way to abstain from blood is to abstain from sex. In my personal view, half of the monies spent on banning cigarettes smoking should be spent on teaching the youth to stay away from sex. It is the major cause of more than half of the world's deadly diseases.

"The men were sent off and went down to Antioch, where they gathered the church together and delivered the letter. 31 ***The people read it and were glad for its encouraging message"*** *(Acts 15:30-31).* ***"As they travelled from town to town, they delivered the decisions reached by the apostles and elders in Jerusalem for the people to obey.*** *5 So the churches were strengthened in the faith and grew daily in number (Acts 16:4-5).*

Back in those days, the Gentile believers who received this letter telling them to abstain from sexual immorality, meat of strangled animals and blood were glad to hear that. The question is, are we any different from them? It is now assumed that a teenager, for instance, cannot abstain from sex and for that matter they are encouraged to only confess their sins to the LORD in prayers after the sinful act because they claim Jesus is at the right side of God interceding on their behalf. It's as if Jesus has nothing to do again, and His only responsibility is to wait for us to present our sins to Him to be relayed to the Father on our behalf for forgiveness.

PAUL HAD TIMOTHY CIRCUMCISED

We need to learn how not to make dogmas out of the Scriptures. We have learned that getting yourself circumcised or not does not count until one is fully obeying the words of God wholeheartedly. But let's see what Paul did with Timothy when he wanted to take him along in his ministry but realised he was going to encounter problems with the Jews:

> *He came to Derbe and then to Lystra, where a disciple named Timothy lived, whose mother was a Jewess and a believer, but whose father was a Greek. 2 The brothers at Lystra and Iconium spoke well of him. 3* ***Paul wanted to take him along on the journey so he circumcised him because of the Jews who lived in that area****, for they all knew that his father was a Greek. (Acts 16:1-3)*

Why would Paul of all people do a thing like that by personally circumcising or seeing to it that Timothy was circumcised before taking him along? He wrote to the Corinthian church that *"each one should retain the place in life that the LORD assigned him and to which God has called him. This is the rule I lay down in all the churches. 18 Was a man already circumcised when he was called? He should not become uncircumcised.* ***Was a man uncircumcised when he was called? He should not be circumcised****" (1 Cor. 6:17-18).* Why didn't he follow his own rule?

"Do you see a man skilled in his work? He will serve before kings; he will not serve before obscure men" (Prov. 22:29). Paul had had reports about Timothy on how good and capable he was. He realised he could mentor him to take after him. But there was a problem at hand because Timothy had a Grecian father although his mother was Jewess and a believer at the same time. The next, and the most serious, issue was the fact that there were Jews in the areas that Paul would be taking him. And if he was to take an uncircumcised Gentile to any of the Jewish synagogues or the temple in Jerusalem, he would be accused of defiling these places and possibly stoned to death.

To avoid confrontations with the Jews, he simply had Timothy circumcised. I often hear people say that Christianity is not a religion but a way of life. That is very true but the most important thing is to have the kingdom of God revealed to you and know the purpose for which you were created. *"Live in harmony with one another. Do not be proud, but be willing to associate with people of low positions. 17 Do not be conceited. Do not repay anyone evil for evil.* ***Be careful to do what is right in the eyes of everybody. 18 If it is possible, as far as it depends on you, live at peace with everyone*** *(Rom. 12:16-18).*

The Scriptures are meant for bringing peace to men; not imprisonment. The Sabbath was made for man, and not man for the Sabbath. Paul was a typical Jew to the core but never wanted to create stumbling blocks in delivering his message to the Gentiles, who had different cultures from that of the Jews. *"As his custom was, Paul went into the synagogue, and on three Sabbath days he reasoned with them from the Scriptures" (Acts 17:2).* He was a skilled man who knew what his assignment was. He became all things in order to win some at all costs.

A spiritual Jew who is circumcised in the heart is not different from a Gentile believer in Christ who practises the Word of God. We are all serving the same God of the patriarchs. Not even for a day did Paul disown the Jewish faith. Yes, he had enemies among them but he was among them at their synagogues every Sabbath. At one time when he was greatly distressed in Athens because the city was full of idols, ***"he reasoned in the synagogue with the Jews*** *and the God-fearing Greeks, as well as in the market-place day by day with those who happen to be there" (Acts 17:17).*

When he was in Corinth, he actually stayed and worked with a tentmaker like himself who was a Jew, named Aquila: *"Every Sabbath he reasoned in the synagogue, trying to persuade Jews and Greeks" (Acts 18:4).* Paul, like Peter, also first concentrated his teaching on the Jews more than the Gentiles. It was the refusal of some of the Jews to accept his teaching that finally led him to turn his attention fully to the Gentiles:

> *But when the Jews opposed Paul and became abusive, he shook out his clothes in protest and said to them, "Your blood be on your own heads! I am clear of my responsibility.* ***From now on I will go to the Gentiles."*** *(Acts 18:6)*

Because of their selfishness, they had become arrogant in their thinking that it was impossible for the Gentiles to be saved apart from being circumcised in the flesh. They became abusive towards Paul, and resorted to beating him on several occasions. He then decided to limit his teaching to the Gentiles alone.

> *I have worked much harder, been in prison more frequently, been flogged more severely, and been exposed to death again and again. 24* ***Five times I received from the Jews the forty lashes minus one.*** *25* ***Three times I was beaten with rods, once I was stoned,*** *three times I was shipwrecked. I spent a night and day in the open sea. 26 I have been constantly on the move. I have been in danger from rivers, in danger from bandits, in danger from my own countrymen, in danger from Gentiles; in danger in the city, in*

> *danger in the country, in danger at sea; and in danger from false brothers. (2 Cor. 11:23-26)*

It was as a result of beatings like these that made him concentrate his attention on the Gentiles instead. But that does not mean he stopped being a Jew as we will soon see. Even after saying he was no longer going to the Jews, he still went to them anyway. After leaving Corinth to Ephesus, *"**he himself** (not Timothy or Barnabas) **went into the synagogue and reasoned with the Jews.** 20 When they asked him to spend more time with them, he declined. 21 But as he left, **he promised, 'I will come back if it is God's will'**" (Acts 18:19-21).* This simply suggests that he had problems dealing with the Jews in Corinth, and decided to limit his message to the Gentiles in that city but not the entire Jews in other communities.

When in Ephesus this time, *"**Paul entered the synagogue and spoke boldly there for three months,** arguing persuasively about the kingdom of God" (Acts 19:8).* The first place to find a Gentile in those days was not in the Jewish synagogue. Calling the elders in Ephesus to bid them good-bye, Paul said: *"You know that I have not hesitated to preach anything that would be helpful to you but have taught you publicly and from house to house. 21 **I have declared to both Jews and Greeks that they must turn to God in repentance and have faith in our LORD Jesus**" (Acts 20:20-21).* It was the same mustard seed planted by Jesus that was bearing fruits in the ministries of Peter and Paul. There was no difference. Paul did not come to introduce a church that was separated from that of Christ's own. He didn't name his work as the ministry of grace. He preached the message of the Kingdom of God just as his Master.

PETER AND PAUL IN THE SAME MINISTRY OF GOD'S KINGDOM

On his return from the Gentile nations, He went back to Jerusalem to meet the elders. *"**Paul greeted them and reported in detail what God had done among the Gentiles through his ministry**" (Acts 21:19).* Because they were working in unison, he had to make a report to the headquarters, on his return. They were all serving the same God. The same assignment was being attended to by these two institutions.

> ***For God, who was at work in the ministry of Peter as an apostle to the Jews, was also at work in my ministry as an apostle to the Gentiles.** 9 James, Peter and John, **those reputed to be pillars, gave me and Barnabas the right hand of fellowship***

> *when they recognised the grace given to me.* ***They agreed that we should go to the Gentiles, and they to the Jews.*** *10 All they asked was that we should continue to remember the poor, the very thing I was eager to do. (Gal. 2:8-10)*

The true Judaism which Jesus knew, preached and lived was the same one that the apostles knew, practised and preached. We are to follow the footsteps of Christ and the apostles, not what the modern-day Pharisees and teachers of the law want us to believe.

> *When they heard this, they praised God. Then they said to Paul:* ***"You see, brother, how many thousands of Jews have believed, and all of them are zealous for the law!"*** *(Acts 21:20)*

I believe we've now reached the climax of understanding the New Testament Scriptures. After Paul's detailed report on what had been achieved in his ministry among the Gentiles, the Jewish disciples or apostles in Jerusalem on the same mission with him and serving the same Jesus were also reporting to Paul on how successful they had been among the Jews. Through their ministry, "***thousands of Jews had believed in the faith***." But as it were, "***they were now zealous for the law."*** And the reason they were zealous for the law was because the true meanings and basic truths hidden in them had been revealed to them, like Jesus did with the Twelve and, in the process, they found it a delight to observe them. You will recall that the Pharisees and teachers of the law had found a fine way of setting aside the commands of God in order for them to observe their own traditions.

> *Oh, how I love your law! I meditate on it all day long. 98* ***Your commands make me wiser than my enemies****, for they are ever with me. 99* ***I have more insight than all my teachers****, for I meditate on your statutes. 100* ***I have more understanding than the elders****, for I obey your precepts. 101 I have kept my feet from every evil path* ***so that I might obey your Word****. 102 I have not departed from your laws, for you yourself have taught me. 103 How sweet are your words to my taste, sweeter than honey to my mouth! 104* ***I gain understanding from your precepts****; therefore I hate every wrong path. 105* ***Your word is a lamp to my feet and a light for my path****. 106 I have taken an oath and confirmed it,* ***that I will follow your righteous laws . . .*** *111* ***Your statutes are my heritage for ever; they are the joy of my heart.*** *112* ***My heart is set on keeping your decrees to the very end.*** *(Psalm 119:97-112)*

PAUL LIKE JESUS, LIVED IN OBEDIENCE TO THE LAW

After these reports, there were rumours circulating among the Jews in Jerusalem *that Paul had been teaching all the Jews who live among the Gentiles to turn away from "Moses," . . . and telling them not to circumcise their children again or live according to their customs" (Acts 21:21).* They were saying this because they had misunderstood his teaching in places like Corinth where he said: *"Circumcision is nothing and uncircumcision is nothing. Keeping God's commands is what counts."* He never said anywhere that the Jews were to stop circumcising their children. That was said to the Gentiles who were being forced into having themselves circumcised before they could be saved. He said to the Gentiles that *"Each one should remain in the situation which he was in when God called him" (1 Cor. 7:20).* That was not intended at any Jew. He also said that keeping God's commandments is what counts.

God Himself instituted the covenant of circumcision to be the sign between Him and the children of the patriarchs for all generations. Therefore, no-one including Paul, has the right to teach its abolition. It's impossible for anyone to teach us that it has been done away with. But at the same time, it should not be used as a decoy to preach anything contrary to what God has said. God did not say it was going to serve as the yardstick for even the Israelites to be saved. He said it was the *"sign"* of the covenant. So observing the actual covenant was the issue, and not the sign of it. Let's stick to the Word.

> ***This is my covenant with you and your descendants after you,*** *the covenant you are to keep: Every male among you shall be circumcised. 11* ***You are to undergo circumcision, and it will be the sign of the covenant between me and you.*** *12 For the generations to come every male among you who is eight days old must be circumcised, including those born in your household or bought with money from a foreigner—those who are not your offspring. 13 Whether born in your household or bought with your money, they must be circumcised.* ***My covenant in your flesh is to be an everlasting covenant.*** *14 Any uncircumcised male, who has not been circumcised in the flesh, will be cut off from his people; he has broken my covenant. (Gen. 17:10-14)*

Note very carefully from the above verses that even from the days of Abraham, Gentiles were eligible to be circumcised and live peacefully among the Jews. Getting the Gentiles circumcised was not what Paul had a problem with. But in Abraham's day it was mostly Gentile slaves bought by the Israelites who were made to be circumcised. In that sense, although they were circumcised like the Jews, they were still regarded as second class citizens of the land. Paul wanted to get rid of that mentality from their conscience.

"You were bought at a price; do not become slaves of men" *(1 Cor. 7:23).* This is why he didn't want the Gentiles to be forced into this slavery mentality again. You remember he had Timothy circumcised when he thought it was necessary to enhance the gospel of Christ. So, for both a Jew or a Gentile to be circumcised or not is not a big deal in the sight of both God and Paul, as it is there to serve a purpose—*"the sign"* for something bigger. The real thing it represents is the big deal. Once God says it is to be an everlasting covenant, it has to be. But the most important thing about this is for us to understand what the sign represents.

To prove that Paul was not guilty of any of the accusations levelled against him, it was suggested that he joined some Jews in their purification rites, and pay their expenses, *"so that they can have their heads shaved.* ***Then everybody will know there is no truth in these reports about you, but that you yourself are living in obedience to the law"*** *(Acts 21:24).* Paul is one of the most fearless and unselfish figures I have ever read about in all of history, and he is one of my role models aside my mother, when it comes to sacrificing one's life for a cause. He would never agree to do anything if it was against his conscience. Before coming to Jerusalem, he said he knew that wherever he went, prison and hardship awaited him *(Acts 20:23).* So he would never do a thing like that out of fear or pleasing anyone.

But what did he do? *"The next day Paul took the men and purified himself along with them.* ***Then he went to the temple to declare when the days of purification would end and the offering would be made for each of them"*** *(Acts 21:26).* He did this to prove to the Jews in Jerusalem that he was still in obedience to the words of *"Moses"* and therefore, could not preach anything against it. Even doing this could not deter the Jews who did not belong to the faith to find a way to wrongfully accuse him of things he had not done.

> *When the seven days were nearly over, some Jews from the province of Asia saw Paul at the temple. They stirred up the whole crowd and seized him, 28 shouting, "Men of Israel, help us!* ***This is the man who teaches all men everywhere against our people and our law and this place. And besides, he has brought Greeks into the temple area and defiled this holy place"*** *. . . 30 The whole city was aroused, and the people came running from all directions. Seizing Paul, they dragged him from the temple, and immediately the gates were shut. (Acts 21:27-30)*

This is the problem Jesus would have confronted if He had tried to save Gentiles with the Jews in His day. He would not have been able to survive for even a month since He was right in their midst in Jerusalem. Had it not been the arrival of one Roman commander, Paul would have been stoned to death right there because they actually wanted to have him killed, like they did Christ. But I hope you can now easily deduce that none of the allegations levelled against him was based on facts and were therefore unfounded.

They had these qualms with Paul simply because of a communication gap between them. If they had had the time to sit Paul down and actually listened to him on personal basis without basing their arguments on just hearsay, they would have realised that Paul was teaching exactly what Jesus had introduced. Only that Paul's assignment was to extend to the Gentiles as well as Jews. He was a true Jew, just like any of them. Immediately after his arrest, Paul said, ***"I am a Jew, born in Tarsus of Cilicia**, a citizen of no ordinary city" (Acts 21:39).*

Later when one high priest ordered him to be struck on the mouth for saying something he thought was not right, Paul insulted him and called him *"whitewashed wall"* because he did not know at the time that he was the high priest. But when his attention was drawn to it, he apologised and said, *"Brothers, I did not realise that he was the high priest; **for it is written: 'Do not speak evil about the ruler of your people'**" (Acts 23:5).* Even there and then, he was showing them that he was still in obedience to the law: he quoted from *Exodus 22:28* and that was part of *"Moses."* The Bible can really be fun if you truly study it.

After they had given him the chance to explain himself, *"there was a great uproar, and some of the teachers of the law **who were Pharisees stood up and argued vigorously. "We find nothing wrong with this man,"** they said. "What if a spirit or an angel has spoken to him?" (Acts 23:9).* At just one sitting, there were some of the Jews who were trying to have him killed one moment and within that same moment some agreeing that Paul might have had an encounter with an angel or a spirit. Isn't that fascinating? It's not boring as you think.

You see, the only thing that distinguished Paul from the rest of the Jews was the fact that He belonged to the group of believers taught by Jesus, which they used to call the Way in those days. In his defence at Felix's presence, Paul said: *"I admit that I worship the God of our fathers as a follower of the Way, which they call a sect. **I believe everything that agrees with the Law and that is written in the Prophets,** 15 **and I have the same hope in God as these men, that there will be a resurrection of both the righteous and the wicked**" (Acts 24:14-15).* Paul believed in everything the Jews were teaching that agreed with God's Law, and not what the traditions of the elders taught. He also had the same hope as the Jews in his time. So where do you stand now Mr. or Miss Christian? Which of the laws do you have?

Part of the reasons he was in Jerusalem was to *"bring gifts to the poor and to present offerings" (Acts 24:17)*. He was ceremonially clean when they found him in the temple courts. *"I have done nothing wrong against the law of the Jews or against the temple or against Caesar," (Acts 25:8)* he said before Festus at one time. Paul gave us a clue as to the particular group of Jews who were actually harassing him. It was the group that belonged to the Sadducees because they did not believe in the resurrection of the dead. So if what Paul was teaching was correct that Christ Jesus had risen from the dead, and that His followers would also follow suit by being raised in a later date, then that would render the beliefs and religion of the Sadducees null and void. So they tried to have him killed at all costs. Politics and business as usual!

We know this from what Paul said to king Agrippa in his defence. He said: ***"It is because of my hope in what God has promised our fathers that I am on trial today.*** *7 This is the promise our twelve tribes are hoping to see fulfilled as they earnestly serve God day and night. O king, it is because of this hope that the Jews are accusing me. 8* ***Why should any of you consider it incredible that God raises the dead****" (Acts 26:6-8)?* Festus said concerning Paul that the whole Jewish community had petitioned him to let not Paul live any longer. But this was an exaggeration of the facts *(Acts 25:24)*. Thousands of Jews had believed by that time, and were zealous for the law. So it wasn't all the Jews who were saying that. He had his figures tampered with by someone.

In continuing, Paul said: *"I am saying nothing beyond what the prophets and Moses said would happen—23 that the Christ would suffer and,* ***as the first to rise from the dead,*** *would proclaim light to His own people and to the Gentiles" (Acts 26:22-23). At this point Festus interrupted Paul's defence. "You are out of your mind, Paul!" he shouted. "Your great learning is driving you insane" (Acts 26:24)*. I suspect Festus was somehow affiliated to this group who did not believe in the resurrection of the dead. I'm also glad to know from this verse that Paul was a very learned man. He didn't just come out of the blue claiming God has called him to the ministry without learning.

It is written that *"Moses was educated in all the wisdom of the Egyptians and was powerful in speech and action" (Acts 7:22). "Daniel and his three friends were ten times better than all the magicians and enchanters when it came to every matter of wisdom and understanding on anything they were asked" (Dan. 1:20)*. They were voracious readers, for they understood by books. Unlike our day, we are often told that God uses the foolish things of this world to shame the wise. That is true. Yet God never used a foolish man to accomplish any of His plans. Just how can the blind lead the blind without both of them falling into a ditch? Excuse me! Who among the Disciples of Christ was a fool? Judas Iscariot died for being a "fool."

Apart from doing his work as a missionary, Paul knew his rights as a citizen, and appealed to those in authority on the land when he had to do so. The man was simply learned and if anyone desires to follow in his footsteps, he also has to do justice to his learning.

Chapter Thirty-Four

ANSWERING THE HARD QUESTIONS FROM PAUL

> *Bear in mind that our LORD'S patience means salvation, just as our dear brother Paul also wrote to you with the wisdom that God gave him. 16* ***He writes the same way in all his letters, speaking in them of these matters. His letters contain some things that are hard to understand, which ignorant and unstable people distort, as they do the other Scriptures, to their own destruction.*** *17* ***Therefore, dear friends, since you already know this, be on your guard so that you may not be carried away by the error of lawless men and fall from your secure position.*** *(2 Pet. 3:15-17)*

It is written: *"For as he thinketh in his heart, so is he" (Prov. 23:7 KJV)*. Thoughts precede actions. The way you think about a particular subject reflects in how you receive it, and it later shows in what you do with it. I didn't have the privilege of attending school uninterruptedly. The most difficult subject for me was Mathematics. I never understood the reasons for mixing numbers with alphabets and never had the courage to tell anyone the reasons behind my inability to solve Maths problems. As a result, I became the daftest Maths student in every class I found myself in.

About four years after my SSS, I was watching a video CD by Bishop David Oyedepo. He was using the principles of solving Maths problems to clarify some points and kept repeating the fact that, Mathematics was the easiest subject on earth. He went further to say that if you want to solve problems in Maths, you just have to observe the examples given by the one teaching it. The following day, I asked my brother to teach me a topic in Maths, with the intention to apply what I heard from the Bishop.

My brother started teaching me something under linear equations. You might be tempted not to believe this. But even after my Senior Secondary School days, I could not solve even a simple linear equation. My only problem was the fact that I didn't understand how numbers could be mixed with alphabets, like I said. Now, with the Bishop's voice echoing at the back of my mind, I heard my brother say to me that, the x and y in the equations represented numbers. The second I heard him say those words, I had my *"miracle encounter with truth."* I wish I had heard that from the very beginning.

I remember I cried tears of joy in an examination hall after my remedial classes because, for the first time, I was making calculations to arrive at an answer to a Maths question. To me, that was a great miracle, because I used to just tick any of the objectives, and hardly did I ever have an appreciable mark. I was delivered through the preaching of Bishop Oyedepo that day. It is not every time that you need to have a twelve-year blood flow cease to experience God's miracle. Just having access to an information that helps you take another step ahead in life is a miracle in itself and should not be taken for granted.

So what I'm trying to say is that, if Peter's remark that, "Paul's letters are difficult to understand," keeps on ringing at the back of your mind, and you regard both of them, then, that is what you will always get. It will forever remain difficult for you to understand. Using the principle of *"a little here and a little there,"* you can choose to occupy yourself with that or believe what Paul wrote himself that ***"For we do not write to you anything you cannot read or understand"*** *(2 Cor. 1:13).* This is my mentality every time I read the Bible. There is nothing I cannot read and understand. The writer of those words intended for me to read and understand them.

One thing you must know from here is the fact that the attacks on Paul's ministry was not coming from just one source like maybe the Jews, for instance. This was a man who was being attacked from all angles that one could hardly stand. Read these verses again to know what he was dealing with:

> *I have worked much harder, been in prison more frequently, been flogged more severely, and been exposed to death again and again. 24* ***Five times I received from the Jews the forty lashes minus one.*** *25 Three times I was beaten with rods, once I was stoned, three times I was shipwrecked. I spent a night and day in the open sea. 26 I have been constantly on the move. I have been in danger from rivers,* ***in danger from bandits, in danger from my own countrymen, in danger from Gentiles;*** *in* ***danger in the city, in danger in the country,*** *in danger at sea;* ***and in danger from false brothers.*** *(2 Cor. 11:23-26)*

The Jews who did not belong to the faith were attacking and beating him. There were bandits on his neck, his own country men did not understand him and always sought to kill him, Gentiles also felt threatened that he was introducing a different God to their people putting his life always in danger in both the cities and in every country he entered. The last but not least of his problems was the facts that there were others who claimed to be in the same faith with him but were teaching false doctrines: doctrines which were different from what Jesus taught and left with the disciples. But mostly when people read the New Testament in particular and read Paul's letters warning us to be wary of these teachings, then straight away our attentions are drawn to the Jews alone.

After receiving the teachings that a Gentile, for instance, is not required to be forced into obeying the Law of Moses and circumcised before saved, these false teachers went out teaching the Gentiles not to obey the whole Law (Torah), which makes up the precepts that our forefathers like David learned long time ago to last forever. Peter was then writing to his students to be careful and not get carried away by celebrating the fact that they were not required to obey any laws when reading Paul's letters, which would result in following the footsteps of these men who had become lawless in the process. He continued: "***Therefore, dear friends, since you already know this, be on your guard so that you may not be carried away by the error of lawless men and fall from your secure position*** *(2 Pet. 3:17).*

PAUL BEFORE HIS CONVERSION

So far, we have learnt from the book of Acts that Paul was a full blooded Jew who practised Judaism, like his Master Jesus Christ. But we need to make some distinctions here so that we don't get excited and get things mixed up. Before his conversion and subsequent call-up by Christ, he was already a Jew then. He was a Jew still after his encounter with Christ Jesus. So we need to know the type of Jew he was and the type he became after the conversion.

> ***For you have heard of my previous way of life in Judaism****, how intensely I (Paul) persecuted the church of God and tried to destroy it. 14* ***I was advancing in Judaism beyond many Jews of my own age and was extremely zealous for the traditions of my fathers.*** *(Gal. 1:13-14)*

The word *zealous* is defined as showing great energy and enthusiasm for something, especially because you feel strongly about it. And to take something to the extreme is to take it to its highest degree or peak. To combine those two words to describe how Paul felt about the traditions of the elders is something not to be taken lightly. He was deeply in love with his convictions.

Aside being a Jew, Paul was extremely zealous for *"the traditions of his fathers"* that had been handed down from generations gone by. In other words, he was a typical example of the Pharisees Jesus had to deal with. They had found a fine way of setting aside the commandments of God in order to observe their own traditions. He was advancing in this to the extent that no-one his age could compete with him in that area. When he realised there was a threat to these traditions coming from the Disciples of Christ, he took it upon himself to completely destroy it.

Jesus told His disciples that *"They will put you out of the synagogues; in fact,* ***a time is coming when anyone who kills you will think he is offering a service to God****" (John 16:2).* Paul felt he had to fulfil that prophecy. He was full of passion for what he believed in. Had it not been for Christ's own intervention, he would have succeeded in this because he actually went from house to house searching for the disciples to kill or imprison. There was no one stopping him. *"But Saul (Paul) began to destroy the church. Going from house to house, he dragged off men and women and put them in prison" (Acts 8:3).* I just love this man.

> *Meanwhile, Saul was still breathing out murderous threats against the LORD'S disciples. He went to the high priest 2 and asked him for letters to the synagogues in Damascus,* ***so that if he found any there who belonged to the Way, whether men or women, he might take them as prisoners to Jerusalem.*** *(Acts 9:1-2)*

As of this time, the disciples were still gathering in the synagogues and the temple because they didn't have any religion outside the true Judaism Christ came to expound on. The distinguishing factor between them was that they belonged to the group who believed in the teachings of Jesus Christ, which the Sanhedrin referred to as the Way. He wanted to wipe this group from the temple and the synagogues entirely.

> *If anyone else thinks he has reasons to put confidence in the flesh, I have more: 5 circumcised on the eighth day, of the people of Israel, of the tribe of Benjamin, a Hebrew of Hebrews;* ***in regard to the law, a Pharisee;*** *6 as for zeal, persecuting the church;* ***as for legalistic righteousness, faultless.*** *(Phil. 3:4-6)*

At the tail end of his ministry when he was arrested in Jerusalem, Paul told the crowd that *"I am a Jew, born in Tarsus of Cilicia, but brought up in this city.* ***Under Gamaliel I was thoroughly trained in the law of our***

fathers and was just as zealous for God as any of you are today*"** *(Acts 22:3).* He declared at one time before the Sanhedrin that ***"I am a Pharisee, the son of a Pharisee" *(Acts 23:6).* So, Paul was only deeply connected to the traditions of the elders and not the real Judaism that Jesus Christ came to teach. Mostly, it was this legalistic observance of the traditions of the elders imposed on the Gentiles that he was teaching us not to obey, and not the actual Torah of God.

He wrote to the Colossians that "***See to it that no-one takes you captive through hollow and deceptive philosophy, which depends on human tradition and the basic principles of this world rather than on Christ*"** *(Col. 2:8).* He again wrote to the Philippians to *"watch out for those dogs, those men who do evil, those mutilators of the flesh" (Phil. 3:2).* Circumcision was the sign of the covenant but they wanted to force the Gentiles to be circumcised at all cost. He called them dogs and mutilators of the flesh.

> *Since you died with Christ to the basic principles of this world, why, as though you still belonged to it, do you submit to its rules: 21 "Do not handle; Do not taste; Do not touch?" 22* ***These are all destined to perish with use, because they are based on human commands and teachings.*** *23 Such regulations indeed have an appearance of wisdom, with their self-imposed worship, their false humility and their harsh treatment of the body, but they lack any value in restraining sensual indulgence. (Col. 2:20-23)*

We will now take one of his letters written to the Gentile believers to see how he taught on our relationship to the Jews. Misunderstanding these letters has been the cause of confusion in Christendom, and people have sort to explain the New Testament to suit them. But the Bible is a complete book, which starts from Genesis and ends at the last page of Revelations. I have chosen the book of Romans to do this. All the other books apart from the four gospels and Revelations share almost the same message.

> *"The Bible has furnished, and still furnishes, the basic, most fundamental building blocks of Western Civilization. Therefore, this is true: If you live in this Civilization and don't have a fair knowledge of the Bible, you are basically uneducated. You may know a lot of things, but you won't have the foggiest notion of where all these things came from, what they all mean, how they are interrelated, what to use them for, and generally what makes them tick."—Robert L. Short*

Chapter Thirty-Five

PAUL'S LETTER TO THE ROMANS

You would recall that in the book of Acts, we realised that some of the brothers who claimed to be in the faith were insisting that the Gentiles would have to be circumcised, and made to observe all the laws of Moses before they could be saved. As a result of that, Paul and Barnabas were sent to the elders in Jerusalem to address this issue. It was agreed upon that a letter be written and circulated to the Gentile believers telling them what needed to be done. The book of Romans was one of such letters dictated by Paul but actually written by Tertius *(Rom. 16:22).*

I'm sorry to announce to you that I haven't had any formal training in communication. But from my own experience, I have learnt that a letter comes in a complete whole. What I mean is that you can't just pick a line or a phrase, a sentence or even a paragraph from someone's letter of about five pages, for instance, then start interpreting it and claim you've covered everything in it without reading from the introduction, organisation and language used before even arriving at the conclusion of it. The possibility of misunderstanding and having a completely different message from that of the writer of such a letter is very high.

In order to avoid that, I have done my best to cover most parts of this letter to the Romans. But my appeal to you is that you set aside a personal time of your own to read this book for at least three times in a month to fully grasp the blessings in this letter. Do this with the rest of the New Testament Scriptures. Remember you can do all things through Christ who strengthens you *(Phil. 4:13).*

PAUL'S PURPOSE FOR WRITING THE BOOK OF ROMANS

For starters, we need to ask ourselves that "What was the purpose for writing this letter in the first place?" Reading the book of Acts gives us the answer: "*some men came down from Judea to Antioch and were teaching the brothers that* ***unless you are circumcised, according to the custom taught by Moses, you cannot be saved"*** *(Acts 15:1). "Then some of the believers who belonged to the party of the Pharisees stood up and said, '****The Gentiles must be circumcised and required to obey the law of Moses'*** *(Acts 15:5).* The recipients of this letter were also Gentile believers who are loved by God and called to be saints *(Rom. 1:7).* Paul was therefore writing this letter to clear their minds of this issue and also teach them what to do.

To debunk the idea that one is not saved until he is physically circumcised in the flesh, he wrote in this letter that ***"A man is not a Jew if he is only one outwardly, nor is circumcision merely outward and physical.*** *29* ***No, a man is a Jew if he is one inwardly; and circumcision is circumcision of the heart, by the Spirit, not by the written code.*** *Such a man's praise is not from men, but from God" (Rom. 2:28-29).* Before continuing, we need to know the *"written code"* being spoken of here so that we don't jump into any immature conclusions.

THE WRITTEN CODE EXPLAINED

> *Then God said to Abraham, "As for you, you must keep my covenant, you and your descendants after you for the generations to come. 10 This is my covenant with you and your descendants after you, the covenant you are to keep:* ***Every male among you shall be circumcised.*** *11* ***You are to undergo circumcision, and it will be the sign of the covenant between me and you.*** *12* ***For the generations to come every male among you who is eight days old must be circumcised, including those born in your household or bought with money from a foreigner—those who are not your offspring.*** *13* ***Whether born in your household or bought with your money, they must be circumcised. My covenant in your flesh is to be an everlasting covenant.*** *14 Any uncircumcised male, who has not been circumcised in the flesh, will be cut off from his people; he has broken my covenant" (Gen. 17:9-14).*

Because this was a law, every Jew or Israelite had to be circumcised on the eighth day after birth. It was a covenant which had to be obeyed by every male child born in the land. It then became a written code like owning a passport of the country of birth. Since it was required by law to do this, Paul was teaching that ***"A man is not a Jew if he is only one outwardly,*** *nor is circumcision merely outward and physical. 29* ***No, a man is a Jew if he is one inwardly;*** *and circumcision is circumcision of the heart, by the Spirit,*

***not by the written code**. Such a man's praise is not from men, but from God."*
Circumcised people still walk around and live contrary to God's principles.

We also learned earlier that Jews did not associate themselves with Gentiles. Had it not been Peter's experience with the Gentiles in Cornelius' house where he and other Jewish believers saw the Holy Spirit come on the Gentiles, just like they had, leading to the speaking in tongues, they would have had a hard time taking the gospel to the Gentiles even though Jesus Christ told them to go into all nations with the gospel. For fear of the Jews who did not belong to the faith, some of the believers from the group of the Pharisees insisted that the Gentiles had to be circumcised and obey the laws of Moses.

ABRAHAM: FATHER OF BOTH CIRCUMCISED AND UNCIRCUMCISED BELIEVERS

Paul gave the reason for this group of Jews' main motive behind the stance they took, when he wrote to the Galatians church that *"Those who want to make a good impression outwardly are trying to compel you to be circumcised. **The only reason they do this is to avoid being persecuted for the cross of Christ.** 13 **Not even those who are circumcised obey the law, yet they want you to be circumcised that they may boast about your flesh**" (Gal. 6:12-13).*

You see, because the written code says so, they were not doing the requirements of the law although they were physically circumcised in the flesh. They were trying to use the Gentiles as cover to avoid being accused of desecrating the temples and synagogues by having them just circumcised in the flesh and not in the heart, which was the more important thing. Paul gave the true purpose of this act of circumcision by stating that:

> *"**And he** (Abraham) **received the sign of circumcision, a seal of the righteousness that he had by faith while he was still uncircumcised. So then, he is the father of all who believe but have not been circumcised**, in order that righteousness might be credited to them. 12 And he is also the father of the circumcised who not only are circumcised but who also walk in the footsteps of the faith that our father Abraham had before he was circumcised." (Rom. 4:11-12)*

True circumcision in itself is the sign or the seal that is given after one is willing to live according to the principles of God. It is a matter of faith, leading to action in the heart of man. It is not just something done in the flesh as a ritual and then going out with one's chest out claiming one is righteous and therefore, saved. Salvation has to do with totally repenting from one's old ways and turning to that of God and His Christ. Abraham did not receive the promise because he was already circumcised or obeying written codes like Moses gave the children of Israel:

> ***It was not through law that Abraham and his offspring received the promise*** *that he would be heir of the world,* ***but through the righteousness that comes by faith.*** *14 For if those who live by the law are heirs, faith has no value and the promise is worthless, 15 because law brings wrath. And where there is no law there is no transgression. (Rom. 4:13-15)*

CIRCUMCISION WITHOUT OBEDIENCE IS BASELESS

Before the circumcision, Abraham first had faith in God and made it manifest in his actions. James wrote that *"Was not our ancestor Abraham considered righteous* ***for what he did*** *when he offered his son Isaac on the altar? 22* ***You see that his faith and his actions were working together, and his faith was made complete by what he did.*** *23 And the Scripture was fulfilled that says, "Abraham believed God, and it was credited to him as righteousness," and he was called God's friend" (James 2:21-23).* Repentance from old habits through faith in action goes before circumcision. Keeping God's commands is what counts; not just cutting the flesh.

> *Circumcision has value if you observe the law (Torah), but if you break the law (Torah),* ***you have become as though you had not been circumcised.*** *26* ***If those who are not circumcised keep the law's*** *(Torah's)* ***requirements, will they not be regarded as though they were circumcised?*** *27* ***The one who is not circumcised physically and yet obeys the law*** *(Torah)* ***will condemn you who, even though you have the written code and circumcision, are a law-breaker.*** *(Rom. 2:25-27)*

Circumcision in itself is just one of the laws or written codes in the Scriptures. But Paul is saying that it only has value if the one being circumcised is going to walk in the ways of God. That is why he said in his letter to the Galatians that, even those who were circumcised were not obeying the law. This corresponds with what he wrote to the Corinthian church that *"Circumcision is nothing and uncircumcision is nothing. Keeping God's commands is what counts" (1 Cor. 7:19).* Circumcision is meaningless if one will not keep the commands of God. This comes down to the fact that circumcision is the seal of righteousness. It's like a pledge that one will adhere to what God has said.

Circumcision in the flesh without repentance is only a ritual. Let's hear John the Baptist on this topic. The kingdom of God is not about a whole bunch of some religious practices imposed on people as they turn to God. It's about a complete U-Turn from the systems of this world to live by God's standards.

> *People went out to him from Jerusalem and all Judea and the whole region of the Jordan. 6 Confessing their sins, they were baptised by him in the Jordan river. 7 But when he saw many of the Pharisees and Sadducees coming to where he was baptising, he said to them: "You brood of vipers! Who warned you to flee from the coming wrath? 8* ***Produce fruit in keeping with repentance.*** *9* ***And do not think you can say to yourselves, 'We have Abraham as our father.' I tell you that out of these stones God can raise up children for Abraham.*** *10 The axe is already at the root of the trees,* ***and every tree that does not produce good fruit will be cut down*** *and thrown into the fire." (Matt. 3:5-10)*

God is not in short supply of people to inherit Abraham's blessing. The attitudes of most of today's Christians seem to portray the impression that Christ is in need of people to serve Him. Once they get themselves baptised, they turn to lead their lives in their former sins claiming Christ is at the right side of God interceding on their behalf. Until you repent of such behaviour, I've got news for you: ***"The axe is already at the root of the trees*** *(you and I),* ***and every tree that does not produce good fruit will be cut down*** *and thrown into the fire."*

THE NEED FOR REPENTANCE FROM OUR FORMER WAY OF LIFE

So, why is repentance an important aspect in salvation? Why can't we just confess with our mouths that Christ is LORD, get saved and then continue living just the way we used to, knowing that Christ is interceding for all our sins? We'll do well to state exactly why we need to repent of our sins the way Paul puts it himself without adding to them. It is because:

> ***The wrath of God is being revealed from heaven against all the godlessness and wickedness of men who suppress the truth by their wickedness,*** *19 since what may be known about God is*

> *plain to them. 20 For since the creation of the world God's invisible qualities—His eternal power and divine nature—have been clearly seen, being understood from what has been made,* ***so that men are without excuse*** *. . . 22 Although they claimed to be wise, they became fools 23 and exchanged the glory of the immortal God for images made to look like mortal man and birds and animals and reptiles.*
>
> *24 Therefore God gave them over in the sinful desires of their hearts to sexual impurity for the degrading of their bodies with one another. 25 They exchanged the truth of God for a lie, and worshipped and served created things rather than the Creator—who is forever praised. Amen. 26 Because of this, God gave them over to shameful lusts. Even their women exchanged natural relations for unnatural ones. 27 In the same way the men also abandoned natural relations with women and were inflamed with lust for one another. Men committed indecent acts with other men, and received in themselves the due penalty for their perversion.*
>
> *28 Furthermore, since they did not think it worthwhile to retain the knowledge of God,* ***He gave them over to a depraved mind, to do what ought not to be done****. 29 They have become filled with every kind of wickedness, evil, greed and depravity. They are full of envy, murder, strife, deceit and malice. They are gossips, 30 slanderers, God-haters, insolent, arrogant and boastful; they invent ways of doing evil: they disobey their parents; 31 they are senseless, faithless, heartless, ruthless. 32* ***Although they*** *(Jews and Christians?)* ***know God's righteous decree that those who do such things deserve death, they not only continue to do these very things but also approve of those who practise them.*** *(Rom. 1:18-32)*

Paul started this dialogue by stating that *"The wrath of God is being revealed from heaven* ***against all the godlessness and wickedness of men who suppress the truth by their wickedness."*** In other words, the reason for this wrath coming on mankind was because of the godlessness and wickedness on earth caused by the tenants living on earth. Although the Jews had the laws of God and were even circumcised, they too were not living by the requirements of the law. Therefore, no-one was going to be exempted from the judgment because he was circumcised in the flesh or have the written codes in his possession. How does God judge us?

> ***God "will give to each person according to what he has done."*** *7 To those who by persistence in doing good seek glory, honour and immortality, He will give eternal life. 8 But for those who are*

> *self-seeking and who reject the truth and follow evil, there will be wrath and anger. 9* ***There will be trouble and distress for every human being who does evil:*** *first for the Jew, then for the Gentile; 10* ***but glory, honour and peace for everyone who does good:*** *first for the Jew, then for the Gentile. 11* ***For God does not show favouritism.*** *(Rom. 2:6-11)*

Jesus said, *"If anyone loves me, he will obey my teaching . . . 24 He who does not love me will not obey my teaching. These words you hear are not my own; they belong to the Father who sent me" (John 14:23-24).* He also says that not all who call Him LORD will be saved but those who do the will of the Father (Mat. 7:21). The verdict is that God will give to each man according to what he or she has done. This is because God does not show favouritism in what He does. He loves all men. The Jews were not going to be exempted because they had the law. If they had the law but were living as though they didn't, then *"there* ***will be trouble and distress for every human being who does evil:*** *first for the Jew, then for the Gentile."* Why would God do that?

> ***For it is not those who hear the law*** *(Torah)* ***who are righteous in God's sight, but it is those who obey the law*** *(Torah)* ***who will be declared righteous.*** *14 (Indeed, when Gentiles, who do not have the law (Torah), do by nature things required by the law (Torah), they are a law (Torah) for themselves, even though they do not have the law (Torah), 15* ***since they show that the requirements of the law*** *(Torah)* ***are written on their hearts,*** *their consciences also bearing witness, and their thoughts now accusing, now even defending them." Rom. 2:13-15)*

It is only when one is living according to the standards or requirements of the law of God that one is declared righteous in His sight. You can't be righteous in the sight of God by just having the Bible, and regularly quote from it, if you don't actually live your life according to what is written in it that you've been quoting. In the same way, if someone who has never had access to the Bible's information is living his or her life according to the principles in it, God will declare him or her righteous although this person does not have access to the information in the Bible. This is because God does not show favouritism to anyone be it Jew or Gentile.

> *You (whether a Jew or a Christian who owns the Bible) who say that people should not commit adultery, do you commit adultery? You who abhor idols, do you rob temples? 23 You who brag about the law (like knowing the principles written in the Bible), do you dishonour God by breaking the law? 24 As it is written: "God's*

Name is blasphemed among the Gentiles (or unbelievers) because of you. (Rom. 2:22-24)

At the time of writing this letter, what Paul was saying in these three verses were directed at the Jews for saying the Gentiles could not be saved because they were not circumcised and did not have the law of Moses too. Yet although they had the two, they themselves were doing the same things that the Gentiles who didn't have the written codes and circumcision were doing. There was no difference between the two groups.

> ***We have already made the charge that Jews and Gentiles alike are all under sin.*** *10 As it is written:* ***"There is no-one righteous, not even one; there is no-one who understands, no-one who seeks God.*** *12* ***All have turned away, they have together become worthless; there is no-one who does good, not even one.*** *13 Their throats are open graves; their tongues practise deceit. The poison of vipers is on their lips. 14 Their mouths are full of cursing and bitterness. 15 Their feet are swift to shed blood; 16 ruin and misery mark their ways, 17 and the way of peace (with God) they do not know. 18 There is no fear of God before their eyes. (Rom. 3:9-18)*

"Now we know that whatever the law says, ***it says to those who are under the law,*** *so that every mouth may be silenced and the whole world held accountable to God. 20* ***Therefore no-one will be declared righteous in His sight by observing the law; rather through the law we become conscious of sin (Rom. 3:19-20).*** So far Paul is not saying anything different from what he had been saying all along. The law in itself did not make anyone righteous by the mere fact that one has access to them. But read carefully the last part of those verses. He says that, through the law, we become conscious of sin. This means the law clearly brings to our notice what sin is.

RIGHTEOUSNESS THROUGH FAITH IN CHRIST JESUS

> *But now a righteousness from God,* ***apart from law,*** *has been made known,* ***to which the Law and the Prophets testify.*** *22* ***This righteousness from God comes through faith in Jesus Christ to all who believe. There is no difference,*** *23 For all have sinned and fall short of the glory of God, 24 and are justified freely by His grace through the redemption that came by Christ Jesus. (Rom. 3:21-24)*

Under the Old covenant, one was expected to be circumcised in the flesh, and required to obey the Law of Moses. It is written: *"And if we are careful to obey all this law before the LORD our God,* ***as He has commanded us, that will be our righteousness****" (Deut. 6:25)*. At the end of the day, they failed with this approach so God introduced the one which was capable of reaching men everywhere on earth because the time for fulfilling the promise to Abraham was due. ***This righteousness comes through faith in Jesus Christ***. And Paul is saying there is no difference between the two, which is absolutely true, because it was through faith that Abraham received the promise, not through the observance of laws.

JUSTIFICATION BY FAITH APART FROM LAW

> *Where, then, is boasting? It is excluded. On what principle—on that of observing the law? No, but on that of faith. "28* ***For we maintain that a man is justified by faith apart from observing the law****. 29 Is God the God of Jews only? Is He not the God of Gentiles too? Yes, of Gentiles too, 30 since there is only one God, who will justify the circumcised by faith and the uncircumcised through that same faith. 31 Do we, then, nullify the law by this faith? Not at all! Rather, we uphold the law. (Rom. 3:27-31)*

A man has to have faith in God and make that faith count by what he does, which shows in his righteous living according to the Word of God. The mere fact of being circumcised and having the written codes in one's possession does not make any difference. So until the righteous requirements of the law are met in one's life through faith in God and His Christ, circumcision does mean nothing. God does not show favouritism. He is not going to destroy a Gentile who, even though he has no written codes in his possession, is living according to the righteous requirements of the law, and allow a Jew who has both the circumcision and the written codes but is living in sin to live, simply because he or she is a Jew. Nope!

> ***Therefore, the promise comes by faith, so that it may be by grace and may be guaranteed to all Abraham's offspring—not only to those who are of the law but also to those who are of the faith of Abraham****. He is the father of us all (both Jews and Gentiles). 17 As it is written: "I have made you a father of many nations." He is our father in the sight of God, in whom he believed—the God who gives life to the dead and calls things that are not as though they were . . . 23* ***The words "it was credited to him" were written not for him alone,*** *24* ***but also for us, to***

> ***whom God will credit righteousness***—*for us who believe in Him who raised Jesus our LORD from the dead. 25 He was delivered over to death for our sins and was raised to life for our justification (Rom. 4:16-17, 23-25).*

God's promise to Abraham was for him to become the father of many nations. And just as righteousness was credited to him through his faith in God before the law of circumcision, his children from these Gentile nations who were to join him in this promise were to follow suit and inherit the promise through faith in God simply because God had established that righteousness would be credited to those who believe in Him through the faith in Christ Jesus. This is achieved purely on the basis of God's grace and not by works of circumcision or observing the law before attaining it, because that was not what happened in Abraham's case.

> ***You see, at just the right time, when we were still powerless, Christ died for the ungodly.*** *7 Very rarely will anyone die for a righteous man, though for a good man someone might possibly dare to die. 8* ***But God demonstrates His own love for us in this; While we were still sinners, Christ died for us.*** *(Rom. 5:6-8)*

We discussed earlier how Christ Jesus took our punishment upon Himself, paid the price that we were supposed to pay, and died on our behalf. The wages of sin is death and every soul that sinned was supposed to receive the death penalty. But He paid that price for us and atoned for us with His own blood. Therefore, we were no longer required to be circumcised in the flesh and required to observe the Law of Moses for sinners before we could be saved.

> ***Since we have now been justified by His blood****, how much more shall we be saved from God's wrath through Him! 10 For if, when we were God's enemies,* ***we were reconciled to Him through the death of His Son,*** *how much more,* ***having been reconciled****, shall we be saved through His life! 11 Not only is this so, but we also rejoice in God through our LORD Jesus Christ,* ***through whom we have now received reconciliation.*** *(Rom. 5:9-11)*

The Gentile, through the blood of Christ, is justified by his faith in the LORD Jesus Christ. Just like the Jew, the Gentile is now reconciled back to God. But he did not receive this by being circumcised in the flesh or observing the Law of Moses. "*Consequently, just as the result of one trespass was condemnation for all men,* ***so also the result of one act of righteousness was justification that brings life for all men****. 19 For just as through the* *disobedience of the one man (Adam) the many were made sinners, so also through the obedience of the one man (Jesus) the many will be made righteous" (Rom. 5:18-19).*

DEAD TO SIN. ALIVE IN CHRIST WITH A NEW LIFESTYLE

> *What shall we say, then? Shall we go on sinning,* ***so that grace may increase?*** *2 By no means!* ***We died to sin; how can we live in it any longer? 3 Or don't you know that all of us who were baptised into Christ Jesus were baptised into His death?*** *4 We were therefore buried with Him through baptism into death in order that,* ***just as Christ was raised from the dead through the glory of the Father, we too may live a new life.*** *(Rom. 6:1-4)*

Writing on the same subject, Paul wrote to the Colossians that *"In Him you were also circumcised,* ***in the putting off of the sinful nature, not with a circumcision done by the hands of men but with the circumcision done by Christ,*** *12 having been buried with Him in baptism and raised with Him through your faith in the power of God, who raised Him from the dead" (Col. 2:11-12).* The reason the Gentile believer does not need to be circumcised and forced into observing the law of Moses is that his old sinful nature was buried with Christ when he was symbolically baptised and raised a new man who could no longer live in sin again.

> *If we have been united with Him like this in His death, we will certainly also be united with Him in His resurrection. 6* ***For we know that our old self was crucified with Him so that the body of sin might be done away with, that we should no longer be slaves to sin—*** *7* ***because anyone who has died has been freed from sin.*** *(Rom. 6:5-7)*

Just as circumcision was the seal of righteousness, baptism is symbolic on the part of the believer that his old sinful self, which only knew how to sin, has died and is buried under the water representing Christ's death, and is resurrected a new being or creation when he is brought back from under the water representing Christ's resurrection from the dead. The law of his sinful nature that made him a slave to sin is dead and is buried for good. *"Set your minds on things above, not on earthly things. 3* ***For you died, and your life is now hidden with Christ in God****" (Col. 3:2-3).*

> ***Now if we died with Christ,*** *we believe that we will also live with Him. 9* ***For we know that since Christ was raised from***

> ***the dead, He cannot die again; death no longer has mastery over Him.*** *10* ***The death He died, He died to sin once for all; but the life He lives, He lives to God.*** ***In the same way, count yourselves dead to sin but alive to God in Christ Jesus.*** *12* ***Therefore do not let sin reign in your mortal body so that you obey its evil desires.*** *13 Do not offer the parts of your body to sin, as instruments of wickedness,* ***but rather offer yourselves to God, as those who have been brought from death to life; and offer the parts of your body to Him as instruments of righteousness.*** *14* ***For sin shall not be your master,*** *because you are not under law, but under grace. (Rom. 6:8-14)*

Since Christ rose from the dead, He cannot die again. Christ did not commit any sin Himself. But He took our sinful nature upon Himself and died to redeem us from the curse of the law, which is death. He did that because of us. So if we should go back and sin again, then it is like saying that Christ should come and die again to redeem us the second time. Because of this, Paul is saying that we should count ourselves dead to sin but alive to God. And someone who is dead to sin in his conscience does not need a law to lead a righteous life. It's like saying he or she has been programmed to live in righteousness for the rest of his or her life.

He said the same thing in the book of Hebrews when he wrote that *"It is impossible for those who have been enlightened, who have tasted the heavenly gift, who have shared in the Holy Spirit, 5 who have tasted the goodness of the word of God and the powers of the coming age, 6* ***if they fall away, to be brought back to repentance, because to their loss they are crucifying the Son of God all over again and subjecting Him to public disgrace****" (Heb. 6:4-6).*

Peter also shared the same sentiment when he wrote that *"If they have escaped the corruption of the world by knowing our LORD and Saviour Jesus Christ* ***and are again entangled in it and overcome, they are worse off at the end than they were at the beginning.*** *21* ***It would have been better for them not to have known the way of righteousness,*** *than to have known it and then to turn their backs on the sacred command that was passed on to them. 22* ***Of them the proverbs are true: "A dog returns to its vomit,*** *a sow that is washed goes back to her wallowing in the mud" (2 Pet. 2:20-22).*

After salvation, we are supposed to keep it at the back of our minds that Christ is not going to come and die the second time for us, if we should go back and sin again. That would mean that we are signing our death warrants if we should continue in sin. A man with this mindset does not require a written code to let him abstain from sin. If he does, then he is like *"a dog returning to its vomit."* If you haven't seen a dog returning to its vomit before, please do to understand what Paul is teaching in these verses. I never want to see that again.

LIVING IN RIGHTEOUS SLAVERY LEADING TO HOLINESS

> *I put this in human terms because you are weak in your natural selves.* ***Just as you used to offer the parts of your body in slavery to impurity and to ever-increasing wickedness*** *(in the past),* ***so now offer them in slavery to righteousness leading to holiness.*** *20 When you were slaves to sin, you were free from the control of righteousness. 21 What benefit did you reap at that time from the things you are now ashamed of? Those things result in death! 22* ***But now that you have been set free from sin and have become slaves to God, the benefit you reap leads to holiness, and the result is eternal life.*** *23 For the wages of sin is death, but the gift of God is eternal life in Christ Jesus our LORD. (Rom. 6:19-23)*

The issue of why it sounds as if Paul is condemning obedience to the precepts of the Scriptures is addressed in the above verses. He is saying that just as someone who was not born again used to live in ever-increasing wickedness because he was a slave to his sinful nature, the same way, he should live his life in slavery to righteousness, which leads to holiness after he or she is saved. One of the definitions of a slave is *"a person who is so strongly influenced by something that they cannot live without it, or cannot make their own decisions."*

Someone who is born again has no choice but to live in righteousness for the rest of his or her remaining life on earth, because he or she is under slavery to righteousness. He died and was resurrected a new being with a different DNA which does not know how to sin. He or she is set free from his former slave-master under sin and is transferred to another *"Slave-Master,"* who is God. His former duty as a slave under the old regime was to sin unto death. But his new role under this new Slave-Master is to live a righteous life. He or she has no excuse. This righteous living makes the "slave" grow to become holy, like his Master, because they all eat the same food—righteousness.

He talked on the same line when he wrote to Timothy that: ***"Flee the evil desires of youth, and pursue righteousness, faith, love and peace, along with those who call on the LORD out of a pure heart.*** *23 Don't have anything to do with foolish and stupid arguments, because you know they produce quarrels. 24 And the LORD'S servant must not quarrel; instead, he must be kind to everyone, able to teach, not resentful. 25 Those who oppose him* *he must gently instruct, in the hope that God will grant them repentance leading them to a knowledge of the truth, 26 and that they will come to their senses and escape from the trap of the devil, who has taken them captive to do his will" (2 Tim. 2:22-26).*

He wrote to Titus telling him that *"For the grace of God that brings salvation has appeared to all men. 12* ***It teaches us to say "No" to ungodliness and worldly passions, and to live self-controlled, upright and godly lives in this present age*** *(Not wait till one is in heaven), 13 while we wait for the blessed hope—the glorious appearing of our great God and Saviour, Jesus Christ, 14* ***who gave Himself for us to redeem us from all wickedness and to purify for Himself a people that are His very own, eager to do what is good" (Titus 2:11-14).*** Your old sinful nature is dead after salvation. Take time to carefully study the Bible, after reading this book, to understand this teaching from the apostles of Christ Jesus.

John also preached on the same subject when he wrote that ***"No-one who lives in Him keeps on sinning. No-one who continues to sin has neither seen Him or known Him.*** *7 Dear children, do not let anyone lead you astray.* ***He who does what is right is righteous.*** *8* ***He who does what is sinful is of the devil,*** *because the devil has been sinning from the beginning. The reason the Son of God appeared was to destroy the devil's work. 9* ***No-one who is born of God will continue to sin, because God's seed remains in him; <u>he cannot go on sinning</u>, because he has been born of God"*** *(1 John 3:6-9).*

One is empowered through the knowledge acquired from the message of the gospel received, and is therefore sealed with the Holy Spirit of God to live a sin-free life. This is a choice made by the individual, because Jesus only forgave him or her of the old sins, and the individual is expected to continue living the righteous life from that point on. This is where you continue with the journey.

Peter wrote that *"Dear friends,* ***I urge you, as aliens and strangers in the world, to abstain from sinful desires, which war against your soul.*** *12* ***Live such good lives among the pagans*** *that, though they accuse you of doing wrong, they may see your good deeds and glorify God on the day He visits us" (1 Pet. 2:11-12).* This part is done by us. I hope you've not forgotten the axe John the Baptist spoke about. Nobody is going to live your righteous life for you.

IS THE LAW DEAD?

To drive this point home, Paul used one of the laws in the Scriptures as an example to make it easier to understand. But I think this has been one of the most misunderstood portions of the entire Bible for all time.

> *Do you not know, brothers—**for I am speaking to men who know the law** (Torah)—that the law has authority over a man only as long as he lives? 2 **For example**, by law a married woman is bound to her husband as long as he is alive, **but if her husband dies, she is released from the law of marriage**. 3 So then, if she marries another man while her husband is still alive, she is called an adulteress. **But if her husband dies, she is released from that law and is not an adulteress, even though she marries another man.***
>
> *4 **So, my brothers, you also died to the law through the body of Christ, that you might belong to another,** to Him who was raised from the dead, **in order that we might bear fruit to God.** 5 **For when we were controlled by the sinful nature, the sinful passions aroused by the law were at work in our bodies, so that we bore fruit for death.** 6 **But now, by dying to what once bound us, we have been released from the law so that we serve in the new way of the Spirit, and not in the old way of the written code.** (Rom. 7:1-6)*

The first thing to recall is the fact that Paul was using this as an "*example*" to make a point. Prior to chapter seven, he wrote: *Don't you know that when you offer yourselves to someone to obey him as slaves, you are slaves to the one whom you obey—**whether you are slaves to sin, which leads to death, or to obedience, which leads to righteousness?**" (Rom. 6:16).* So just as under the written code, a married woman is bound to her husband, and cannot marry another while her husband is still alive, the same way, our old sinful nature is bound in marriage to the sinful desires of the flesh while it remains in that unsaved state. But if the husband (in this case the sinful nature) dies, we are released from that law that binds us to obey only the sinful desires of the sinful nature in us, and marry another man of our choice with whom we fall in love (in this case righteousness) in the future.

Now listen very carefully. Paul is saying in verse four that, just as Christ came to die on our behalf, He took on Himself our old sinful nature which understood only the law of sin to the grave and resurrected with a completely different nature that understood the law or language of righteousness. After this is achieved, Paul wrote using past tenses in verse five that the law of the sinful nature bore fruit for death when we were controlled by it. It is the law of the sinful nature in the old man that we have been released from, and not the law that David learned about long ago, which was established to last forever. The written code on marriage which is part of Scripture used in these verses was used as an *"example."* The fact that Paul used it to explain a point means it is still in force. You still cannot marry if your husband is alive. That's what the written code says.

If we are to literally take Paul's words at face value, then what he said, *"we have been released from the law so that we serve in the new way of the Spirit, and not in the old way of the written code,"* should mean that someone can now marry another while the spouse is still alive and that would be okay with the Word of God. But that was not what Jesus taught on marriage. And that is not what Paul is teaching either. And if he teaches something that even contradicts his Master's teachings, he would have been a liar because no-one can build any other foundation apart from what Jesus has built.

> *What shall we say, then? Is the law sin? Certainly not! Indeed I would not have known what sin was except through the law.* ***For I would not have known what coveting really was if the law had not said, "Do not covet."*** *9 Once I was alive apart from law;* ***but when the commandment came, sin sprang to life and I died.*** *10 I found that the very commandment that was intended to bring life actually brought death. 11* ***For sin, seizing the opportunity afforded by the commandment, deceived me, and through the commandment put me to death.*** *12* ***So then, the law is holy, and the commandment is holy, righteous and good.*** *(Rom. 7:7, 9-12)*

The Law of Moses in itself is not the sin because the "resurrected" man is now living in righteousness. The main purpose of the law is bringing to the fore what constitutes sin and what does not. Paul says he found out that although the commandment was intended to bring life, it actually brought death to his former sinful man. How was that possible? His former sinful nature could not live in righteousness no matter how hard it tried. He could only sin because he was under slavery to the law of sin. And he realised that breaking the commandment attracted death penalty, because the wages of sin is death, according to the commandment. Therefore, his sinful nature deceived him and seized the opportunity afforded by the commandment, thereby putting him to death.

"The existence of the Bible, as a book for the people, is the greatest benefit which the human race has ever experienced. Every attempt to belittle it is a crime against humanity."—Immanuel Kant (1724-1804)

PROGRAMMED TO DO WHAT YOU DON'T WANT TO DO?

> ***We know that the law is spiritual; but I am unspiritual, sold as a slave to sin.*** *I do not understand what I do. For what I want to do I do not do, but what I hate I do. And if I do what I do not want to do, I agree that the law is good. As it is, it is no longer I myself who do it,* ***but it is sin living in me. I know that nothing good lives in me, that is, in my sinful nature.*** *For I have the desire to do what is good, but I cannot carry it out. For what I do is not the good I want to do; no, the evil I do not want to do—this I keep on doing.* ***Now if I do what I do not want to do, it is no longer I who do it, but it is sin living in me that does it.***
>
> *21 So I find this law at work: When I want to do good, evil is right there with me. 22 For in my inner being* ***I delight in God's law;*** *23* ***but I see another law*** *at work in the members of my body, waging war against the law of my mind and* ***making me a prisoner of the law of sin at work within my members.*** *24* ***What a wretched man I am! Who will rescue me from this body of death?*** *25* ***Thanks be to God—through Jesus Christ our LORD!*** *So then, I myself in my mind am a slave to God's law,* ***but in the sinful nature a slave to the law of sin.*** *(Rom. 7:14-25)*

These verses are some of the most misunderstood and misinterpreted verses in the entire Bible. I often hear from even the most respected teachers of our time alluding to these verses that although Paul was teaching about righteousness, he could not live a righteous life himself. How sad that they could misunderstand the writings of Paul to that extent! Others too use those verses as an excuse to indulge in various sinful desires of their hearts. They would often tell you in the face that if Paul could not lead a righteous life, what could they do themselves? H. L. Mencken puts it this way: *"The most costly of all follies is to believe passionately in the palpably not true."*

For starters, Paul was not the type of leader who did not practise what he preached. He lived what he taught. He wrote: ***"You are witnesses, and so is God, of how holy, righteous and blameless we were among you who***

***believed**. 11 For you know that we dealt with each of you as a father deals with his own children, 12 encouraging, comforting and urging you to **live lives worthy of God**, who calls you into His kingdom and glory (1 Thess. 2:10-12).*

> ***We put no stumbling-block in anyone's path, so that our ministry will not be discredited.** 4 **Rather, as servants of God, we commend ourselves in every way**: in great endurance; in troubles, 5 in beatings, imprisonments and riots; in hard work, sleepless nights and hunger; 6 **in purity**, understanding, patience and kindness; **in the Holy Spirit and in sincere love; 7 in truthful speech and in the power of God; with weapons of righteousness in the right hand and in the left**; 8 through glory and dishonour, bad report and good report; **genuine, yet regarded as impostors**; 9 known, yet regarded as unknown; dying, and yet we live on; beaten, and yet not killed; 10 sorrowful, yet always rejoicing; poor, yet making many rich; having nothing, and yet possessing everything. (2 Cor. 6:3-10)*

Paul lived a very righteous, blameless and holy life in his entire walk with God and men till his death. He simply sacrificed all he had to serve the LORD God with his whole heart *(Rom. 1:9)*. He did all that was expected of him and declared at the end of his ministry that he was innocent of the blood of all men *(Acts 20:26)*. He was ready not only to be bound but also to die for the Name of the LORD Jesus Christ who sent him *(Acts 21:12-14)*.

He wrote to the Corinthian church that they *"must not associate with anyone who calls himself a brother but is sexually immoral or greedy, an idolater or a slanderer, a drunkard or a swindler. **With such a man do not even eat**" (1 Cor. 5:11)*. He went further to ask them that ***"Do you not know that the wicked will not inherit the kingdom of God?** Do not be deceived: Neither the sexually immoral nor idolaters nor adulterers nor male prostitutes nor homosexual offenders 10 nor thieves nor the greedy nor drunkards nor slanderers nor swindlers will inherit the kingdom of God" (1 Cor. 6:9-10)*. He said that God's righteous decree against those who do such things is death *(Rom. 1:32)*.

Now, is it this same Paul who taught us that even drunkards and greedy persons are not going to have a place in the Kingdom of God the same man telling us that he could not do the very things he wanted to do? If that was the case, then male prostitutes would also give the excuse that they wanted to abstain but could not. The sexually immoral would say the same thing down to the swindlers, and every sinner would have an excuse for his or her sins and God should allow that without putting any axe to the tree. You might as well sleep with your mother and tell God you wanted to avoid it but could not.

Paul was speaking figuratively by using himself to represent the sinful nature in every man who has not yet been saved by the grace of Christ. He started by saying that ***"We know that the law is spiritual; but I am unspiritual, sold as a slave to sin.*** *15 I do not understand what I do.* What he means is that although he knew the value of the law (statutes of God) to be spiritual, yet his sinful nature could not permit him to live by them because that sinful nature was a slave to sin and could not obey another master. In verses *17-18,* he says that *"As it is, it is no longer I myself who do it,* ***but it is sin living in me.*** *18* ***I know that nothing good lives in me, that is, in my sinful nature.*** How could he say that he knew nothing good lived in him?

He wrote elsewhere that "*You were taught,* ***with regard to your former way of life, to put off your old self,*** *which is being corrupted by its deceitful desires; 23 to be made new in the attitude of your minds; 24* ***<u>and to put on the new self, created to be like God in true righteousness and holiness</u>****" (Eph. 4:22-24).* ***"If anyone is in Christ, he is a new creation: the old has gone, the new has come!"*** *(2 Cor. 5:17).* He also said that *"I have been crucified with Christ* ***and I no longer live, but Christ lives in me****. The life I live in the body, I live by faith in the Son of God, who loved me and gave Himself for me" (Gal. 2:20).* Peter also wrote that ***"His divine power has given us everything we need for life and godliness through our knowledge of Him who called us by His own glory and goodness"*** *(2 Pet. 1:3).* Because of these verses and several others that I cannot list here, Paul could not say what he said if he was talking about himself.

We just learnt from him that we are no longer under the law of sin to obey its desires, but listen to Paul again: *"Now if I do what I do not want to do,* ***it is no longer I who do it, but it is sin living in me that does it."*** *Again, he says "If anyone is in Christ, he is a new creation:* ***the old has gone, the new has come****" (2 Cor. 5:17).* There is no longer any sin living in the new creation again after Christ has died on our behalf nailing the punishment which is death to the cross. ***"Those who belong to Christ Jesus have crucified the sinful nature with its passions and desires"*** *(Gal. 5:24).*

After having this background, read the next verses carefully. ***"What a wretched man I am! Who will rescue me from this body of death?*** *25* ***Thanks be to God—through Jesus Christ our LORD****! So then, I myself in my mind am a slave to God's law,* ***but in the sinful nature a slave to the law of sin"*** *(Rom. 7:24-25).* In verse twenty-four, he asked of who was going to rescue him from that sinful nature preventing him from obeying the true Word of God. Finding the answer, he thanked God and said he could now do it through Jesus Christ his LORD. As of the time of writing these things, that had happened, and he had been set free from that law that made him sin even though he wanted to obey God's law.

> ***Therefore, there is now no condemnation for those who are in Christ Jesus,*** *2* ***because through Christ Jesus the law of the Spirit of life set me free from the law of sin and death.*** *3 For what the law was powerless to do* ***in that it was weakened by the sinful nature****, God did by sending His own Son in the likeness of sinful man to be a sin offering.* ***And so He condemned sin in sinful man,*** *4* ***in order that the righteous requirements of the law might be fully met in us, who do not live according to the sinful nature but according to the Spirit.*** *(Rom. 8:1-4)*

"You see, at just the right time, ***when we were still powerless, Christ died for the ungodly.*** *11 Not only is this so, but we also rejoice in God through our LORD Jesus Christ,* ***through whom we have now received reconciliation****" (Rom. 5:6, 11).* Christ's death at the right time on behalf of the sinner sets him free from the law of sin which made him follow only his sinful desires, resulting in death. The old self with its sinful nature is replaced with the law of the Spirit of Christ in order that the righteous requirements of the law of God might be fully met in us who do not live according to the sinful nature but according to the Spirit of God.

> *"So the Bible is primarily a book neither of science, nor of literature, nor of philosophy, but of salvation. In saying this we must give the word, 'salvation,' its broadest possible meaning. Salvation is far more than merely the forgiveness of sins. It includes the whole sweep of God's purpose to redeem and restore humankind, and indeed all creation. What we claim for the Bible is that it unfolds God's total plan."—John R. W. Stott*

Although the law of God was right, blameless and holy, it was still powerless in itself to save because of the fact that, no matter how hard an individual wanted to obey them, he fell short because the sinful nature in him was more powerful than his desires to walk according to the law. This rendered the law powerless in what it was meant to achieve. Even the circumcised Jews who were supposed to teach these things were found wanting. Yet, the more the individual sinned, the more he was going far away from God because the wages of sin is death. ***"Those controlled by the sinful nature cannot please God"*** *(Rom. 8:8).* I wish I would not add anything further again to the next verses from here onwards because they are self explanatory.

> ***You, however, are controlled not by the sinful nature but by the Spirit, if the Spirit of God lives in you****. And if anyone does not have the Spirit of Christ, he does not belong to Christ. 10* ***But if Christ is in you, your body is dead because of sin, your spirit is alive because of righteousness****. 11 And if the Spirit of Him who raised Jesus from the dead is living in you, He who raised Christ from the dead will also give life to your mortal bodies through His Spirit, who lives in you. (Rom. 8:9-11)*

The Spirit of God is holy. The Holy Spirit of God is poured into the heart of the man Jesus died for, and he is no longer controlled by the sinful nature again. The sign that one has the Spirit of Christ is his death to the sinful nature which shows in what he does with his life. This new self only bears fruits of righteousness because the old self died. It is in this stage that John said the new creation cannot sin again.

Solomon wrote: *"In the way of righteousness there is life; along that path is immortality" (Prov. 12:28).* Paul also wrote to the Romans that ***"Now that you have been set free from sin and have become slaves to God, the benefit you reap leads to holiness, and the result is eternal life****" (Rom. 6:22). "For those God foreknew He also predestined to be conformed to the likeness of His Son, that He might be the firstborn among many brothers" (Rom. 8:29).* ***"Both the One who makes men holy and those who are made holy are of the same family. So Jesus is not ashamed to call them brothers****" (Heb. 2:11).*

It is important to note here that the word *"righteousness"* in itself is not a religious word as people have made it. John wrote that *"Dear children, do not let anyone lead you astray.* ***He who does what is right is righteous, just as He is righteous****. 10 Anyone who does not do what is right is not a child of God" (1 John 3:7, 10).* David said: *"Seven times a day I praise you for your righteous laws. 165 Great peace have they who love your law and nothing can make them stumble. 172 . . . for all your commands are righteous (Ps. 119:10, 164-165, 172).*

> *"Because of lack of fortitude and faithfulness on the part of God's people, God's Word has many times been allowed to be bent, to conform to the surrounding, passing, changing culture of that moment rather than to stand as the inerrant Word of God judging the form of the world spirit and the surrounding culture of that moment."— Francis A, Schaeffer (1912-1984)*

THE SPIRIT-LED ARE SONS OF GOD

Righteousness is judged by the standards of God's law whether they are written on the tablets of stones or on our hearts and minds. And if we do the right things at all times according to the Word of God, we become holy in the process and holiness sets us on the path to eternal life. God is holy and when we become holy, we become like Christ Jesus who is our Big Brother. *"In the way of righteousness there is life; along that path is immortality."* Immortality starts from being righteous in the sight of God. When this is achieved, we become holy and godly. After this stage, we only "sleep" in the grave to wait for our LORD and Saviour's return even if we die.

> *Therefore, brothers, we have an obligation—**but it is not to the sinful nature**, to live according to it. 13 **For if you live according to the sinful nature, you will die; but if by the Spirit you put to death the misdeeds of the body, you will live,** 14 **because those who are led by the Spirit of God are sons of God**. 15 For you did not receive a spirit that makes you a slave again to fear, but you received the Spirit of sonship. And by Him we cry "Abba Father." (Rom. 8:12-15)*

Because Christians are no longer controlled by the sinful nature, what is expected of them is to no longer live according to our old sinful ways anymore. The reason is that, although we have been saved by the grace of God, we would die again if we are to go back and live our lives according to the old self, for the wages of sin is still death. The Spirit of God given us enables us to put to death all the misdeeds of the sinful nature. We become the true sons of God and are freed from the power of sin.

> *The Spirit Himself testifies with our spirit that we are God's children. 17 **Now if we are children, then we are heirs—heirs of God and co-heirs with Christ, if indeed we share in His sufferings in order that we may also share in His glory.** (Rom. 8:16-17)*

It is written in the book of Isaiah that *"Let no foreigner who has bound himself to the LORD say, 'The LORD will surely exclude me from His people.' And let not the eunuch complain, 'I am only a dry tree.' 4 For this is what the LORD says: 'To the eunuchs who keep my Sabbaths, who chooses what pleases me and hold fast to my covenant—5 to them I will give within my temple and its walls a memorial and a name better than sons and daughters; I will give them an everlasting name that will not be cut off.' 8 The Sovereign LORD declares—*

He who gathers the exiles of Israel: 'I will gather still others to them besides those already gathered'" (Isa. 56:3-5, 8).

It is our destiny to be given a name that is better than sons and daughters after we have been born again and become a new creation. What everlasting name is there to be given to us that is more than sons and daughters? We can only become like Christ to be given a name that is an everlasting one. So it says that if we are children of God, then we are heirs of God. And if heirs of God, then we are joint-heirs or co-heirs with Christ in His glory. But that is attained at a price. That price is that we must keep our sinful nature dead to the end, and make sure it is no longer having dominion over us. This is not attained by just declaring to the world with our mouths that we are joint-heir with Christ. We are expected to actually live it in your daily lives.

> *And we know that in all things God works for the good of those who love Him, who have been called according to His purpose. 29* ***For those God foreknew He also predestined to be conformed to the likeness of His Son, that He might be the firstborn among many brothers****. 30 And those He predestined, He also called: those He called, He also justified; those He justified, He also glorified. (Rom. 8:28-30)*

The culmination of the mustard seed planted in man is to see the redeemed man grow in knowledge of God to the stature of Jesus Christ, who is the first mustard seed planted on earth after the fall of man. John wrote that "*How great is the love the Father has lavished on us, that we should be called sons of God!* ***And that is what we are! The reason the world does not know us is that it did not know Him****. 2 Dear friends,* ***now we are children of God, and what we will be has not yet been made know. But we know that when He appears, we shall be like Him****, for we shall see Him as He is. 3* ***Everyone who has this hope purifies himself, just as He is pure****" (1 John 3:1-3).* We are destined to become like Jesus Christ in every way.

> *"The Bible is to us what the star was to the wise men; but if we spend all our time in gazing upon it, observing its motions, and admiring its splendour, without being led to Christ by it, the use of it will be lost to us."—Thomas Adams (1871-1940)*

TRANSFORMED THROUGH RENEWAL OF THE MIND

Because of the call upon our lives, we are expected to understand the sort of beings we become, which is far above the sinful nature and its resulting lifestyles. This understanding will enable us to pursue righteousness in all we do and lead us into complete holiness. At this stage, there is no need for the written codes before living a righteous life, because they are written on our hearts and minds.

> *Therefore,* ***I urge you****, brothers, in view of God's mercy,* ***to offer your bodies as living sacrifices, holy and pleasing to God—this is your spiritual act of worship****. 2* ***Do not conform any longer to the pattern of this world, but be transformed by the renewing of your mind****. Then you will be able to test and approve what God's will is—His good, pleasing and perfect will. (Rom. 12:1-2)*

Peter wrote that *"For this very reason,* ***make every effort to add to your faith*** *goodness; and to goodness, knowledge; 6 and to knowledge, self-control; and to self-control, perseverance; and to perseverance, godliness; 7 and to godliness, brotherly kindness; and to brotherly kindness, love. 8* ***For if you possess these qualities in increasing measure, they will keep you from being ineffective and unproductive in your knowledge of our LORD Jesus Christ****" (2 Pet. 1:8).*

But if anyone does not have them, he is short-sighted and blind, and has forgotten that he has been cleansed from his past sins*. 10 Therefore, my brothers,* ***be all the more eager to make your calling and election sure. For if you do these things, you will never fall,*** *11* ***and you will receive a rich welcome into the eternal kingdom of our LORD and Saviour Jesus Christ****" (2 Pet. 1:9-11).* You would do well to heed to this call.

In conclusion, I'll like to quote a few paragraphs verbatim from Tommy Tenney's book, *"The Way Of The Warrior,"* which I think summarises everything up to this stage. He wrote that:

> *"Within the samurai culture in Japan there existed a philosophy called bushido. This was known as 'The Way of the Warrior.' The teaching continued into the days of World War II when followers of the code became kamikaze pilots, willing to sacrifice their lives by flying their planes into American battleships.* ***They were willing to die for what they believed; it is a tragic commentary that most Christians cannot even live the things they hold dear****.*

> *"When someone became a samurai, he was agreeing to die at the behest of his earthly lord. In fact,* ***he began his service with the idea that he was already dead****. Does this sound like the Christian walk?* ***When we start on the path of salvation, we must be willing to die at the behest of God. In other words, when you became a Christian you gave up your rights, your privileges. As Jesus' servant, you are called to give your life to Christ****.*
>
> *"Once this is settled in your heart, you will not resist when God asks you to do something. Yet, many of us get into a quandary and start 'seeking God' more about things that rub against our flesh. If we have pledged to give our lives, then what is the problem when He asks us to give a little bit of money, go on a fast or whatever? We begin to question whether or not we can handle that kind of commitment.* ***The problem is that we did not understand what we were called to at the beginning—to lay down our lives and enter a war zone.***

This sums up what I want to convey to you, a Christian (or as you become a Christian), and begin to study the Bible for yourself. A Christian is dead to the systems of this world and is free from sins. This is not something you declare with your mouth only but actually something you do for your own good. Christ needs you to heal the world. Choose to be the mustard seed planted by God to heal the world today. You and I can contribute to the salvation of the earth. *"Sow for yourselves righteousness, reap the fruit of unfailing love, and break up your unploughed ground;* ***for it is time to seek the LORD, until He comes and showers righteousness on you****" (Hos. 10:12).*

> *"It is impossible to rightly govern the world without God and the Bible."—George Washington (1732-1799)*

NB: Most of the quotations on the Bible with reference to the authors and lifespan were taken from the "444 Surprising Quotes about the Bible" compiled by Isabella D. Bunn published by Bethany House Publishers.